ALSO BY SETH G. JONES

Waging Insurgent Warfare:
Lessons from the Vietcong to the Islamic State

Hunting in the Shadows: The Pursuit of al Qa'ida after 9/11

In the Graveyard of Empires: America's War in Afghanistan

A COVERT ACTION

A COVERT ACTION

REAGAN, THE CIA, AND THE COLD WAR STRUGGLE IN POLAND

Seth G. Jones

W. W. NORTON & COMPANY

INDEPENDENT PUBLISHERS SINCE 1923

NEW YORK • LONDON

For information about permission to reproduce selections from this book, write to Permissions, W. W. Norton & Company, Inc., 500 Fifth Avenue, New York, NY 10110

For information about special discounts for bulk purchases, please contact W. W. Norton Special Sales at specialsales@wwnorton.com or 800-233-4830

Manufacturing by LSC Communications Harrisonburg
Book design by Daniel Lagin
Production manager: Julia Druskin

Library of Congress Cataloging-in-Publication Data

Names: Jones, Seth G., 1972– author.
Title: A covert action : Reagan, the CIA, and the Cold War struggle in Poland / Seth G. Jones.
Description: First edition. | New York : W. W. Norton & Company, [2018] | Includes bibliographical references and index.
Identifiers: LCCN 2018012172 | ISBN 9780393247008 (hardcover)
Subjects: LCSH: Poland—History—1980–1989. | Espionage, American—Poland—History. | United States. Central Intelligence Agency—History.
Classification: LCC DK4442 .J66 2018 | DDC 327.1273043809/048—dc23
LC record available at https://lccn.loc.gov/2018012172

W. W. Norton & Company, Inc., 500 Fifth Avenue, New York, N.Y. 10110
www.wwnorton.com

W. W. Norton & Company Ltd., 15 Carlisle Street, London W1D 3BS

1 2 3 4 5 6 7 8 9 0

"The Lord will give strength unto his people."

—Psalms 29:11

*Inscribed on a monument at the Gdańsk Shipyard
in memory of those workers killed by Polish forces in
December 1970.*

Contents

Illustrations

A COVERT ACTION

PROLOGUE

In the slanting light of Maryland's Catoctin Mountain ridge, President Ronald Reagan stepped outside his cottage for a morning walk. It was December 12, 1981. The air was crisp and dry at Camp David. The temperature had dipped to freezing overnight, chilly for the former California governor.[1] A thin layer of frost clung gently to the windowpanes at the presidential retreat sixty miles northwest of Washington. Reagan relished his walks at Camp David. "It was great to be in a house with the knowledge you could just open a door and take a walk outdoors if you wanted," he recalled.[2] On some days, Reagan preferred to ride horses. A few months before, on a gusty October morning, he slipped out a back gate into the national forest and guided his horse to the stone ruin of Valley View Manor, a once gallant summer hotel.[3]

For Reagan, Camp David provided solace from the oppressive pace of work and visitors back in Washington. That is precisely what President Franklin D. Roosevelt had in mind when he converted a campground for government employees and their families into a presidential retreat in 1942. Roosevelt named Camp David "Shangri-La," the mythical utopia described by British author James Hilton in the 1933 novel *Lost Horizon*. The location was attractive for its seclusion. But Camp

David wasn't lavish. British prime minister Winston Churchill had allegedly quipped that Camp David was "in principle, a log cabin."[4]

Roosevelt had named the Aspen Lodge, where Reagan stayed, "The Bear's Den." It had a quaint kitchen and a comfortable living room with stuffed furniture, where Reagan liked to relax in an easy chair with his spit-polished shoes—or cowboy boots—perched atop a footstool. He and his wife, Nancy, would curl up there and watch movies: *The African Queen* starring Katharine Hepburn and Humphrey Bogart, *North by Northwest* with Cary Grant and Eva Marie Saint, and *Yankee Doodle Dandy* with the indomitable James Cagney. Aspen Lodge was situated atop a hill, and the living room's oversized windows offered a magnificent view of Catoctin Mountain Park and the valley below.[5]

Reagan briefly paused outside his door and soaked in the morning's tranquility. When he came to the White House in 1981, Reagan had embodied the raw optimism of Roosevelt and the small-town charm of Dwight Eisenhower—both of whom he admired.[6] After being struck by an assassin's bullet and losing over half his blood on March 30, 1981, Reagan's display of valor further endeared him to Americans.[7]

"Honey, I forgot to duck," he had whispered to Nancy, almost apologetically, shortly before he was wheeled into the operating room at George Washington University Hospital.[8]

After surviving the assassination attempt, Reagan faced a growing series of crises at home and abroad. Roughly 13,000 air-traffic controllers went on strike, threatening to shut down air travel in the United States. Overseas, Israeli forces launched periodic strikes into Lebanon as Reagan attempted to mediate an escalating crisis involving Israel, Syria, Lebanon, the Palestinian Liberation Organization, and Lebanese militias.

Back at Camp David, Reagan finished his walk and, feeling buoyant, returned to Aspen Lodge. At 12:10 p.m. that afternoon, he phoned the evangelist Billy Graham, a close friend, but couldn't get through. He spent the afternoon at his desk, reviewing paperwork.

It was peaceful at Camp David.

AN HOUR-AND-A-HALF DRIVE TO THE SOUTHEAST, CIA leadership was in a frenzy. At their headquarters in McLean, Virginia, CIA analysts had been monitoring events in Poland. They were scrambling to determine whether the Polish government, with Soviet support, was about to declare martial law. CIA director William "Bill" Casey realized that martial law, if enacted, meant that the Polish military would take charge of the country in an effort to crush Solidarity, Poland's flowering democratic movement. With new emergency powers, the government would likely send tanks into the streets, take over radio and television stations, and round up Solidarity members. A direct confrontation on the edge of Eastern Europe between the forces of democracy and totalitarianism would trigger one of the most serious crises of the Cold War.

The Soviets were putting tremendous pressure on Polish prime minister Wojciech Jaruzelski (pronounced VOY-chi-ekh Ya-ru-ZEL-ski) to act. The grassroots opposition movement led by Solidarity was potentially catastrophic for the Soviets. One CIA estimate said, "Poland presents the USSR with the most threatening and complex challenge to its vital interests to emerge in the postwar period."[9] The week before, a top secret CIA report had concluded that "the Polish government has completed its plans for imposing martial law and some recent activity is consistent with the final preparations that would precede the implementation of such plans."[10] The document also judged that the Soviet Union was making simultaneous preparations to deploy Red Army forces for a possible intervention in Poland, much like they had done in Czechoslovakia in August 1968 when Soviet forces quashed the political reform movement led by Alexander Dubček.

On the evening of December 12, word reached CIA headquarters that the Polish government had cut telephone communications between Poland and the West and closed the Polish border. The CIA sent out an alert to analysts assigned to the crisis, most of whom were comfortably at home on a Saturday night. Sensing the magnitude of the situation, CIA officials dashed back to headquarters and congregated in the Operations Center. CIA director Casey and his executive assistant attended the meeting, as did the director and deputy director of the Operations Center.

Casey took his seat at the table. With drooping jowls, stooped physique, and heavy rimmed glasses, Casey was easily the most powerful CIA director in a generation. He was an indefatigable opponent of Communism, determined to bloody Soviet noses around the globe. The group debated how to interpret the events and whether—and how—to report them to the White House. Some argued that it might be just another localized crackdown, several of which had occurred in recent days. Others guessed that it could be the beginning of a full government takeover. Shortly after midnight in Washington and 6:00 a.m. in Poland on December 13, one CIA analyst left to see whether there were intelligence updates that had come in by classified cables from the CIA station in Warsaw.

He soon returned and silenced the room: Jaruzelski had just announced martial law. Washington and Moscow were now on a collision course in Poland.[11]

———

ANXIETY BLANKETED WARSAW LIKE A THICK FOG, creeping into the city's neighborhoods, churches, and marketplaces. All week, Poland's state-controlled television had broadcast apocalyptic tales depicting Poland as a country on the verge of collapse, a propaganda blitz that disquieted even pro-government sycophants. One television commentator described a mood of "insurrection and tension."[12] Appearing on Polish television at 6:00 a.m. on December 13, against the backdrop of the red and white Polish flag emblazoned with a coat of arms, Jaruzelski addressed the nation. He appeared stiff and formal in front of the camera, wearing a pressed, olive green military uniform with eleven neat rows of ribbons on his chest. With his chin thrust upward from his hollow face and thinning hair, Jaruzelski parsed his words carefully.

"Our homeland is at the edge of an abyss," he said, his voice flat and his face nervously glancing down at his prepared notes. "The achievements of many generations and the Polish home that has been built up from the dust are about to turn into ruins. State structures are ceasing to function. Each day delivers new blows to the waning economy." Poland was sitting on the verge of Armageddon, he explained. "Strikes, strike alerts, protests have become standard. Even students are dragged into it. There are more and more examples of terror, threats, mob trials and direct coercion. Crimes, robberies and break-ins are spreading like a wave through the country." He then uttered the words that would earn him a villainous place in Polish history.

"I declare that today the Military Council of National Salvation has been formed. In accordance with the Constitution, the State Council has imposed martial law all over the country," he said.[13] Jaruzelski concluded his speech by reciting the opening lines of the Polish national anthem:

Poland has not yet perished,
So long as we still live.

The television image of Jaruzelski declaring martial law would be burned in the memories of Poles. The decision unleashed a series of dramatic events—from the arrests and beatings of Solidarity members to massive street protests and riots—that significantly reshaped Poland's history. The declaration of martial law was not entirely surprising. It had been widely rumored that Polish and Soviet officials had been planning martial law. A secret document later revealed that the Polish Ministry of Internal Affairs had been considering such an approach for several months. Though the document outlined alternative strategies to suppress Solidarity, the objective was straightforward: "to discipline society and reinforce the execution of power."[14] The classified document also foresaw the countervailing actions Solidarity supporters might take, like mass strikes, sabotage operations, and street demonstrations.

Polish officials had decided to act by early December. In secret

negotiations with the Soviets, General Florian Siwicki, chief of the Polish
General Staff, told his Soviet counterparts: "The enemy has said his final
word. The sides have clearly staked out their positions." In classic, over-
blown Marxist prose, Siwicki continued, "now what is needed is a resolute struggle against the counterrevolution."[15] Polish officials referred
to Solidarity as the "counterrevolutionaries" who were bent on sowing
destruction and disorder. For many Poles, martial law was an affront to
their freedom, but they had little recourse.

Bowing to Soviet pressure, the Polish government sent soldiers
into the streets in the early morning hours of December 13. Neighbors
were aroused by the dreadful sound of crowbars smashing windows and
doors, as Polish forces began arresting members of Solidarity and carrying them off to internment camps. All gatherings, processions, and
demonstrations—except for religious services—were now banned in
Poland. All trade unions and student organizations were suspended. All
mail and telephone communications were censored. The government
imposed a curfew and everyone over the age of thirteen had to carry an
identity card. Poland was now sealed off from the outside world.

———

MARTIAL LAW WAS THE BEGINNING of a long, tortuous journey for Lech
Wałęsa* (pronounced Lekh Va-WEN-sa), Solidarity's leader, who was
arrested along with scores of others. Born in 1943, Lech Wałęsa was an
improbable figure to lead Eastern Europe's most audacious dissident
movement. He was a shipyard worker who was proudly—if not
disdainfully—anti-intellectual, claiming that he had never read a serious
book in his life. But he had a gift for public speaking. When he expounded
the struggles of the dockworkers and union laborers, electrified crowds

———

* This book uses the Polish system of spelling, which employs the following
diacritics: ą, ć, č, ę, ł, ń, ó, ś, ź, ż. *Exception:* When a source of quoted material employs
no diacritics, the book follows the usage of the source.

thronged to hear him, flashing their traditional Solidarity "V" sign for victory. He could also move effortlessly between roles. "Walesa is not one, but 10 men: Solidarity leader, electrician, father, husband, actor, negotiator, and more," remarked Adam Michnik, a Polish writer and Solidarity activist. "He's a worker, with intellectuals around him. He's very nationalistic, without being chauvinistic; very Catholic, without being clerical. A kind of Polish synthesis."[16]

For Wałęsa, Solidarity was as much an ideological struggle about freedom and democracy as about supporting workers' rights and economic change. Founded in September 1980 when delegates from thirty-six regional trade unions met in Gdańsk and united under the name "*Solidarność*, the group had become a legitimate opposition movement by 1981. Its membership had swelled to ten million, a stunning achievement for an organization established only a few months earlier. With the imposition of martial law, Solidarity was now in a struggle for its survival. Students and academics rose to the challenge. Sit-in strikes began in most universities. Protestors described martial law by invoking George Orwell's novel *Nineteen Eighty-Four* and "Newspeak," the fictional language created by Orwell's totalitarian state of Oceania to squelch freedom of thought. The Strike Committee at the Polish Academy of Sciences in Kraków noted:

> [F]or the third time during the 20th century Poland is in captivity. The last two times were under a foreign occupier but now we are faced with a self-occupation. Let us not be deceived. It is not important what language the occupier speaks, German, Russian, or Newspeak! What is important is how the occupier behaves. In the middle of Europe, in the late 20th century, 35 million people have been stripped of their fundamental civil rights.[17]

In Warsaw, television cameras captured images of the bright blue, armored Star vehicles from the dreaded ZOMO (*Zmotoryzowane Odwody Milicji Obywatelskiej,* Motorized Reserves of the Citizens'

Militia), halting in front of the Polish Academy of Sciences. Security officials marched inside the academy, hustled some of its distinguished members into the snow, and stuffed them inside the vehicles. Labor unions
across the country responded with unblinking resistance. In Gdańsk, the
gates of the Lenin Shipyard were decked with flowers, as hymn-singing
crowds gathered before them. "Members of Solidarity, Compatriots!" the
Solidarity branch at Ursus appealed in a statement rushed to the media.
"The purpose of this attack is to liquidate our union . . . our answer must
be—in accordance with the statutes—an immediate general strike in the
whole country."[18]

BACK AT CAMP DAVID, Reagan was apoplectic. The week before, CIA
officials had briefed him that martial law was possible, but unlikely. They
had been wrong. Reagan viewed Solidarity as one of Eastern Europe's
most promising democratic movements, and was indignant that the
Soviets were trying to eliminate it. After a flurry of phone calls—from
Secretary of State Alexander Haig, Vice President George H. W. Bush,
and CIA Director Bill Casey—Reagan dashed back to Washington in the
early afternoon of Sunday, December 13. At 3:00 p.m., he met with his
national security team at the White House.

"Something must be done," he said emphatically. "We need to hit
them hard and save Solidarity."[19]

The stakes were high. The imposition of martial law in Poland was,
by far, the most significant crisis of Reagan's fledgling presidency. As
Secretary of State Al Haig wrote to Reagan in almost Machiavellian
terms, the crisis in Poland had massive implications for the U.S.-Soviet
struggle: "The importance of Poland's peaceful revolution is hard to
exaggerate. It weakens the Soviet Union and strengthens us on many
fronts."[20] It was also a watershed for Reagan himself. U.S. government
officials had already discussed allowing the CIA to provide covert assistance to Solidarity. But there was little consensus since some officials

in the State Department and White House were alarmed that U.S. aid to an opposition group behind the Iron Curtain was unnecessarily provocative. The situation was different now. In late December 1981, after a National Security Council meeting to debate U.S. policy options, Reagan wrote in his diary:

> I took a stand that this may be the last chance in our lifetime to see a change in the Soviet Empire's colonial policy re Eastern Europe. We should take a stand & tell them unless & until martial law is lifted in Poland, the prisoners were released and negotiations resumed between Walesa & the Polish govt. We would quarantine the Soviets & Poland with no trade, or communications across their borders.[21]

Reagan viewed the Polish struggle in black and white. The Soviet government was evil—irreconcilably evil—and the United States needed an offensive strategy that went behind the Iron Curtain. "Containment," the buzzword of the Cold War, was too static. It was time to adopt a more audacious strategy—"rollback." A free and democratic Poland could unhinge the Soviet grip on Eastern Europe, Reagan believed. Other states might follow. Later, he would say of the moment, "we were witnessing the first fraying of the Iron Curtain, a disenchantment with Soviet Communism in Poland, not realizing then that it was a harbinger of great and historic events to come in Eastern Europe." He then added, "I wanted to be sure we did nothing to impede this process and *everything we could to spur it along.* This was what we had been waiting for since World War II. What was happening in Poland might spread like a contagion throughout Eastern Europe."[22]

Reagan acted deliberately. Over the next several months, he approved several National Security Decision Directives (NSDDs) that authorized the United States to undermine Soviet control in Eastern Europe. One of the climactic decisions was to sign a presidential finding on November 4, 1982, which approved a CIA covert action program to provide money and other nonlethal assistance to Solidarity. The program was named "QRHELPFUL." It was one of the CIA's most significant gambles of the Cold War, since it required the CIA to recruit assets, establish a covert network, and aid a resistance movement behind the Iron Curtain.[23] As everyone involved realized, the program risked a confrontation with Moscow.

———

THIS IS THE STORY OF THE CIA'S EFFORT to strike at the heart of the Soviet Union in Eastern Europe, as seen through some of its most important characters: Reagan, Solidarity leader Lech Wałęsa, Polish leader Wojciech Jaruzelski, and CIA officials like Bill Casey and Richard "Dick" Malzahn. For thirty-five years, the United States had conceded Eastern Europe to the Soviet sphere of influence. But Reagan wanted a clean break. With his support, the CIA built a program that took the Cold War to the Soviet Union's backyard. QRHELPFUL was one of the United States' most successful covert action programs, yet also one of its least known and appreciated.

While Solidarity and the Polish people ultimately won their own freedom, CIA aid ensured that neither Jaruzelski nor the Soviet KGB (*Komitet Gosudarstvennoy Bezopasnosti*, Committee for State Security) could eviscerate the Polish opposition movement. The CIA provided money and resources to organize demonstrations, print opposition material, and conduct radio and video transmissions that boosted opposition support and morale while simultaneously eroding Soviet authority. QRHELPFUL was also cost-effective; the total bill amounted to less than $20 million (or roughly $40 million in today's dollars). What made QRHELPFUL particularly effective, however, was that it aided a grassroots organization that was *already* legitimate among Poles.

Within the United States, Reagan's decision to aid Solidarity was a political win-win. Liberals supported Solidarity because they were horrified by Warsaw and Moscow's suppression of a democratic opposition movement—one that was grounded in Poland's shipyards and mines, which appealed to left-leaning labor groups like the American Federation of Labor and Congress of Industrial Organizations (AFL-CIO). Conservatives were incensed at the Communist Soviet Union's aid in suppressing Solidarity. The long, grinding patience of Reagan and the CIA helped Solidarity survive even the bleakest days of persecution. And when Solidarity's opportunity finally came, as the Soviet Union neared an economic and military precipice, the Polish people embraced democracy.

Poland was, of course, not the only military or ideological battlefield between the United States and the Soviet Union. Another was Afghanistan. While the CIA provided money for equipment like fax machines and printing presses in Poland, the CIA's covert action program in Afghanistan, which had begun under President Jimmy Carter, combined both propaganda *and* weapons. The results became controversial and the U.S. success was double-edged. The Soviet Union bled itself nearly to death in the land known today as "the graveyard of empires." But awash in arms, some of which came from the CIA, Afghanistan deteriorated into a civil war in the 1990s. Several years later, the Taliban took advantage of the anarchy, established control, and granted safe haven to al-Qa'ida. Then came September 11, 2001.

There has been little written publicly about the CIA's covert action program in Poland.[24] Most Reagan biographers and American historians assume Reagan's actions ended with economic sanctions. One of the best recent biographies of Reagan, H. W. Brands's *Reagan: The Life*, discussed the Reagan administration's policy decisions after martial law. "In the end," Brands wrote, "[Reagan's] substantive response to the martial law declaration didn't go beyond the [sanctions] measures he described in the Christmas speech."[25] Those measures included the suspension of agricultural shipments, termination of U.S. credit insurance through the Export-Import Bank, and cancellation of landing privileges for Polish planes at American airports. The esteemed Polish historian Andrzej Paczkowski noted that the real facts behind outside assistance to

Solidarity "are still surrounded (unaccountably) by an aura of secrecy."[26] Much of that mystery can now be revealed.

A *Covert Action* relies on numerous documents that have been declassified over the past two decades from U.S. archives (including those available at the Ronald Reagan Presidential Library, National Security Archive, Woodrow Wilson International Center for Scholars, and Hoover Institution), Polish archives, Soviet archives, and Churchill Archives Centre (which house the Mitrokhin Archive). This evidence includes U.S., Soviet, and Polish transcripts; intelligence assessments; firsthand accounts; and secret records of meetings and conversations. The CIA Records Search Tool (CREST) at the National Security Archive, for example, includes situation reports, national intelligence daily briefs, information cables, special analyses, intelligence memoranda, and national intelligence estimates. Vast quantities of material pertaining to martial law were also made available at the *Instytut Pamięci Narodowej* (Institute of National Remembrance) in Warsaw. Finally, the European Solidarity Centre in Gdańsk made available a substantial amount of primary source information, including nearly 1,800 archival objects, documents, manuscripts, photographs, and video footage.

While not all documents from this era have been declassified, even from U.S. archives, they provide a much more detailed and comprehensive picture of what happened during key periods covered in this book: Polish and Soviet deliberations about martial law, CIA and other U.S. intelligence analysis, CIA covert action programs like Radio Free Europe / Radio Liberty and the "book program," Carter and Reagan administration discussions about Poland, and the struggles within Solidarity. In addition, a number of participants in these momentous events have now spoken publicly about them.

The story of QRHELPFUL is rich with symbolism. "Democracy triumphed in the cold war," Reagan wrote in the final chapter of his memoirs, "because it was a battle of values—between one system that gave preeminence to the state and another that gave preeminence to the individual and freedom."[27] Poland is perhaps the archetypal example of this ideological struggle. The 1989 Round Table Talks and the victory of Solidarity helped trigger the collapse of the Iron Curtain. One of Reagan's most significant advantages was his focus not only on containing but actually defeating the Soviet Union, and his understanding that defeating the Soviet Union meant defeating Communism. He recognized that the Cold War was more than a military struggle. *It was a war of ideas.* And Poland was one of the most important battlefields. QRHELPFUL sprang directly from this philosophy. It is a powerful reminder of the utility, necessity, and potential of political and information campaigns—particularly when they can aid populations already struggling for freedom.

The true patriots in Poland—and the ones who deserved the magnitude of the credit for the collapse of Communism—were the men and women of Solidarity, who paid a heavy price opposing the Jaruzelski regime. And Lech Wałęsa was their leader.

PART I

Chapter I

THE PEOPLE'S MAN

n the summer of 1980, the year before martial law, Lech Wałęsa was flat broke. The Lenin Shipyard in Gdańsk had fired him a few years prior for his political activism. He found periodic work as an electrician but was repeatedly charged with "hooliganism," a not-so-charitable label for opponents of the Polish Communist regime.[1] Wałęsa now spent his days peddling underground trade union literature.[2] His toolbox bulged with copies of newspapers and magazines like *Robotnik Wybrzeża* (*Coastal Worker*), which he clandestinely distributed to shipyards, factories, and churches throughout the city. The *Coastal Worker* was the official organ of the free trade unions and contained glib, crudely written articles that exposed corruption and injustice in the workplace. But its pages spoke the truth, at least as far as workers were concerned. And the workers loved Wałęsa. Here was their dream leader: daring, rebellious, and blue collar.

Wałęsa stood an unassuming five feet, six inches. He had a conspicuous double chin, beer hall mustache, portly cheeks, and heavy paunch. His working-class syntax was coarse, his sentences often ungrammatical, and his voice hoarse and raspy from years of heavy smoking. But he was a charismatic leader—a man of the people—with an innate ability to reduce complex issues to simple words that most Poles could understand. He would sweep into a room and whip a crowd into a frenzy, carefully fingering a cigarette.[3]

Wałęsa was spearheading an information campaign, determined to counter the Communist Party line Polish workers were fed by the government. Many Poles were starving for information, and they wanted uncensored newspapers and journals. Wałęsa gave it to them. He and his coworkers did most everything from scratch. "As underground publishers, we had to do the developing, prepare the ink and the frames for the silkscreen prints, write the copy—all that though there were only a few of us," one of his colleagues recalled.[4] But his dissident activity also raised the ire of the Polish regime, which had its secret police monitor his movements and listen to his conversations. "The walls in my apartment had ears," he confided.[5] The police dogged him when he left his two-room apartment, located in the Stogi quarter of Gdańsk. The buildings on Wrzosy Street, where the Wałęsa family lived in 1980, had tiny makeshift plots with coarse, sandy soil, making it difficult to grow anything.[6] His home wasn't posh, but it was tolerable for Wałęsa and a growing family that included his wife Danuta and children Bogdan, Sławek, Przemek, Magda, and Ania. Most of their daily activity took place in the larger room, where there was a couch, a small bed, a table, and a sewing machine.

But Wałęsa didn't complain. He hadn't grown up in wealth, and he didn't much care for it anyway.

———

WAŁĘSA WAS BORN IN THE HAMLET of Popowo, Poland, ninety miles northwest of Warsaw, on September 29, 1943. The Wałęsa family lived in a cramped house—or "shanty," as Wałęsa called it—on a four-acre farm, situated at the edge of marshland. The area "seemed a perfectly foolish place to build, unless purely as a temporary step, while waiting to embark on some new stage in one's life," Wałęsa remembered.[7] He held little nostalgia for his childhood home. A well-worn path led away from the house toward the local highway, where a solitary wooden cross marked a bend in the road. In the summer, Wałęsa, his sister Izabela, and brothers Edward and Stanisław liked to shuffle barefoot along the path and squeeze the soft dirt and sand through their toes. The family kept a cow for milk, and Wałęsa and his siblings gathered fresh mushrooms and apples in the forest.

Wałęsa's father, Bolesław, was a stout Pole with prominent cheekbones, a pronounced chin, thin mustache, and an even-keeled disposition. He was arrested by the Nazis during World War II and forced to work at labor camps near Lipno and Młyniec, Poland. Weakened by the macabre conditions at the camps, where prisoners were crowded into unheated winter quarters, Bolesław died in 1945, barely two months after returning home. Wałęsa, who was almost nineteen months old at the time, never knew his father.[8] A year later, Wałęsa's mother married Bolesław's brother, Stanisław, whose mercurial personality—good natured one moment and explosive the next—made him grueling to live with. Stanisław wasn't interested in politics, but he did enjoy listening to shortwave radio stations like Radio Free Europe.[9]

Although Wałęsa had few amicable memories of his stepfather, his mother, Feliksa, was his moral and spiritual anchor. She was an avid reader, with a passion for history and current affairs. In the evenings, Wałęsa and his siblings huddled around her by candlelight as she read aloud such classics as *The Sibylline Oracles*, prophecies written by Jewish and Christian writers; Henryk Sienkiewicz's *The Teutonic Knights*; and Józef Kraszewski's *An Ancient Tale*. "She had an attractive voice, gentle and soothing," Wałęsa recalled, "and we took great pleasure in these moments."[10] She used these stories to reinforce lessons of integrity and justice. Feliksa was also a devout Catholic and instilled in the young Wałęsa a deep respect for the church.[11]

Wałęsa's Catholic roots formed an essential part of his identity during the turbulent postwar period. Many Poles, including Polish Catholics, felt betrayed by the West for handing over Poland to the Soviet Union at the Yalta Conference. Not only did Yalta signify a sellout by Washington and London so soon after Poland's liberation from Nazi rule, but the West abandoned Poland to—of all countries—the godless Soviet Union.

———

FOR DECADES, YALTA HAD BEEN A MECCA for rich Russians, who were drawn to its temperate climate, emerald-blue waters, and vistas of the exposed limestone of the Crimean Mountains. Perched near the southern tip of the Crimean Peninsula on the Black Sea, Yalta boasted lush vineyards and orchards. Anton Chekhov wrote his final play, *The Cherry Orchard*, at Yalta, inspired by the red cherry trees outside his white dacha. In October 1854, during the Crimean War, nearby Balaclava had witnessed the slaughter of the British light cavalry at the hands of Russian artillery—the subject of Alfred, Lord Tennyson's epic poem, "The Charge of the Light Brigade."[12]

In February 1945, nearly a century after the carnage, the British and Russians were allies against Nazi Germany. Yalta, which had been occupied by Germany for much of the war, was now the most important city in the world, if only for a few days. The three stoic leaders—President Franklin D. Roosevelt of the United States, Prime Minister Winston Churchill of Great Britain, and Premier Joseph Stalin of the Soviet Union—gathered in dramatic fashion to discuss the continuing war in the Pacific theater, the final defeat of Nazi Germany, and the future division of Europe.[13]

Poland was at the top of the agenda at Yalta. Its strategic position, squeezed between East and West, led historian Norman Davies to label Poland "God's playground."[14] Coming into Yalta, Stalin desperately wanted a Poland run by pro-Soviet Communists. With his iron-gray mustache and white hair, Stalin was a ferocious negotiator. For centuries, invading armies had marched through Poland on their way to the Soviet Union, as Hitler's Wehrmacht had just done in World War II. The Soviets had paid a grisly price. More than 20 million people—a shocking

14 percent of the entire Soviet population—died due to combat fatalities, war-related diseases, murder, and starvation. They viewed Poland as an indispensable buffer against outside aggressors, especially in the event that Germany recovered and threatened Russia again. It would be critical, in that scenario, that the Red Army enjoy free passage through Poland. For Stalin, a truly independent Poland could not guarantee these rights.[15]

At Yalta, the chief point of contention about Poland was the makeup of the postwar Polish government. When Soviet armies advanced through Poland in late 1944, the Soviets had empowered a group of pro-Communist Poles in the city of Lublin—ninety miles southeast of Warsaw—as the provisional national government. The Lublin government was created in Moscow and imposed by Soviet authorities. The British and the Americans, however, still carried on wartime relations with the Polish government-in-exile in London. As Roosevelt had explained in a letter to Stalin, the United States would not recognize the Lublin government.[16]

Over the course of their meetings at Yalta, Washington and London ultimately agreed on a compromise: the Lublin government would be broadened to include representatives of other Polish political groups. The United States and Britain would then recognize Poland as a provisional government of national unity, and there would be free elections to choose a successor.[17] Roosevelt had made a critical concession, which he likely understood at the time, by agreeing to give more power to the Lublin Poles. In return, Roosevelt secured Stalin's support on several issues, including Soviet military participation in the Pacific theater and agreement on a voting formula at the United Nations that gave veto power to permanent members of the Security Council. In broad terms, Roosevelt's concession was prompted by a desire to cooperate with the Kremlin, a recognition of Soviet preponderance in Eastern Europe, and a desire to ensure active American participation in world affairs.[18] Still, Roosevelt did not fully realize at the time—nor can he necessarily be blamed for failing to comprehend—that the global competition with the Soviets was just beginning.

Stalin, it turns out, had no intention of taking the Yalta text as bind-
ing. Democratic elections were never held in Poland. The Soviets had
agreed to elections in Eastern Europe, but they were held without allied
supervision and under the aegis of provisional governments that were
largely the creation of the Soviet Union.[19] The Soviets established Communist governments in Eastern Europe and suppressed non-Communist
political parties.[20] In the "election" finally held in Poland in 1947, millions
of voters were disenfranchised, thousands of peasants and 142 candidates
were arrested, and the vote count was rigged. The election was neither
free nor unfettered. Foremen marched their factory workers to the polls
and told them to vote for the government. The British and American governments protested the blatant disregard for the provisions of Yalta. But
the Soviet government rejected the protests on the grounds that Western
sources of information in Poland were unreliable.[21]

Stalin achieved his goal of installing a friendly government susceptible to Soviet influence. The Cold War was just beginning.

FOR THE NEXT THIRTY-FIVE YEARS, Yalta remained the status quo in
Eastern Europe. For Lech Wałęsa, this was a heavy burden. "Having
been from the start a party to the struggle against Nazism, surely Poland
was entitled to recover her national independence at the end of the war. Is
it surprising therefore that the Yalta agreement should have aroused, and
should still arouse, a deep bitterness in the Poles?" he asked.[22]

During Wałęsa's childhood, Polish society experienced a profound
transformation. Stalin understood that the Poles would be difficult to
govern. He famously remarked that introducing Communism in Poland
was like putting a saddle on a cow.[23] In Poland, Communist leaders
resorted to brutal repression to maintain power.

The country's first postwar Communist leader, Władysław
Gomułka, recognized the tactical need to mold the saddle to the cow—
to take a slower "Polish road" to Soviet socialism. Gomułka did not, for

example, mandate forced collectivization of agriculture. He was eventually replaced by a Stalinist stooge, Bolesław Bierut, and the Soviets quashed internal resistance in Poland. The few Poles that opposed Stalinism and remained in Poland were discredited, imprisoned, or killed. Some fled the country. As the historian Norman Davies wrote: "In its essentials, the political history of postwar Poland is extremely simple. It tells how the USSR handed power to its chosen protégés, and how it has kept them in place ever since."[24] The Communist Party solidified its monopoly of power. The party and state were intertwined in the leader, Bierut, who straddled the twin posts of first secretary-general of Poland's Communist Party (the Polish United Workers Party) and president of Poland.

In agriculture, Bierut approved forced collectivization. The state took away land from peasants and corralled it into State Agricultural Enterprises and voluntary cooperatives. Collective farms increased from 12,513 in 1950 to 28,955 in 1955. The *metalozercy* ("metal-eaters"), who believed that steel was the necessary foundation for industrialization, pressed for virtually unlimited production of iron and steel in the revised Six-Year Plan for 1950–1955. In 1950, the state confiscated all Catholic Church property, with the exception of church buildings and churchyards. The police arrested priests in large numbers and harassed others. In 1953, Cardinal Stefan Wyszyński was arrested, imprisoned, and later placed under house arrest. The cult of Stalin pervaded Polish society as statues of the Soviet leader appeared in public places. Poland's leading industrial city, Katowice, was renamed "Stalinograd." Buildings were dedicated "to the name of J. V. Stalin." In art, socialist realism, which glorified Communist notions like the emancipation of the proletariat, gained approval. In the sciences, the prestige of Soviet biologist and agronomist Trofim Lysenko superseded Isaac Newton and Albert Einstein.[25]

Despite these changes, there were still embers of dissent among some Poles. The Catholic Church wasn't entirely suppressed, and church leaders encouraged political freedom from the rearguard. Marxism-Leninism had attracted only a few esteemed Polish supporters. In fact,

Polish Communist ideologues could only look back to a tiny cadre of recognized intellectual pioneers like the Polish philosopher Stanisław Brzozowski. A few others, such as the philosopher Leszek Kołakowski, made a serious attempt to marry Marxism with Poland's intellectual heritage, though Kołakowski later became a strident opponent of Marxism. Among the most important anti-Communist works was Czesław Miłosz's *The Captive Mind*, a searing critique of those who collaborated with the Stalinist regime in Poland. Banned throughout the Soviet Union, it was by far the most insightful and enduring account of the attraction of some Poles to Stalinism and, more generally, an indictment of the servile intellectual.

"His chief characteristic," Miłosz wrote, referring to the abject Communist intellectual, "is his fear of thinking for himself."[26]

———

IN 1967, A HAPPY-GO-LUCKY WAŁĘSA moved to the northern port city of Gdańsk, situated on Poland's Baltic coast. He had graduated from vocational school in nearby Chalin, worked for several years as a car mechanic in Łochocin at the *Państwowy Ośrodek Maszynowy* (State Machine Depot), and then completed a two-year obligatory stint in the Polish military. Wałęsa hoped Gdańsk would offer an exhilarating start to a new and more prosperous life. "There was the sea," he recalled, somewhat dreamily, and a school trip years earlier "had left me with the memory of something vast, stretching out endlessly—possibly freedom." It would be risky, he calculated, but he was single and carefree. "I let myself drift toward the Baltic region, by the sea where I would find—or lose—myself at last."[27]

Gdańsk (Danzig in German) had long been a strategically important city between Germany and Russia, and a vital industrial hub in Eastern Europe. In 1938, Adolf Hitler demanded annexation of the city, which was overwhelmingly populated by ethnic Germans. It had been a "free city" under the protection of the League of Nations since World War I, with special administrative ties to Poland. On August 29, 1939, Germany demanded that a Polish representative come to Berlin within twenty-four hours to receive German terms of surrender. The Poles refused. In the predawn hours of September 1, 1939, the Nazi battleship *SMS Schleswig-Holstein*, which was anchored in Gdańsk harbor, opened fire from its 15-inch guns. German panzers then rolled across the Polish frontier and World War II was under way.[28] After the war, Roosevelt, Churchill, and Stalin agreed to return Gdańsk to Poland following the Yalta Conference.

Gdańsk had a rich tradition of philosophers and writers. Polish author Paweł Huelle anointed it the city "by the cold sea."[29] The Baltic port was the birthplace of Günter Grass, the Nobel Prize–winning author perhaps best known for magic realism novels like *The Tin Drum*, and Arthur Schopenhauer, the writer whose works of "philosophical pessimism" like *The World as Will and Representation* lashed out against Hegelian idealism. By the time Wałęsa arrived in the city, Gdańsk epitomized Soviet-style industrialization in Poland. The *Nowy Port* (New Port) boasted a slew of over-sized shipyards, metallurgical and chemical plants, timber mills, and food-processing facilities.

The hulking Lenin Shipyard in Wałęsa's Gdańsk was the port's lifeblood. It was the largest such facility on the Baltic Coast, and it hummed with activity as massive cranes loomed overhead. Welding torches glowed against the hulls of half-built ships.[30] To house the throngs of workers, the city constructed grandiose, whitewashed apartment blocks made of concrete. One set of clunky apartment complexes, among the longest in Europe at over a half mile long, was built to look like waves from the nearby Baltic Sea. While Gdańsk had a blue-collar authenticity, it also had an exquisite architectural tradition. Baroque and gothic churches dotted the city's landscape, and vast granaries along the banks of the Vistula served as reminders of a bygone era. The city's elegant central quarter, which included *Główne Miasto* (Main Town) and *Stare Miasto* (Old Town), sat on a tributary of the Vistula and was lined with chic cafés and cobblestone lanes.

Wałęsa's decision to move to Gdańsk would be life-changing for him, with momentous repercussions for Poland and the entire Soviet bloc. Over the next decade, Gdańsk nurtured an eclectic mix of labor union activists, artists, Polish intellectuals, and Catholic Church officials who formed the hub of anti-regime opposition.

———

BUT WAŁĘSA WAS NOT YET INTERESTED in Cold War rivalries. He was a twenty-three-year-old in 1967, more interested in chasing girls than changing the world. In a series of photographs taken at the time, Wałęsa posed with friends in a pair of trousers which narrowed at the base, and wore a light-colored shirt and a silk scarf knotted around his neck. "In almost all the shots I'm pulling one or another of the girls toward me," he recalled, somewhat amused. "The girls meanwhile are visibly trying to disengage themselves from my possessive grasp, coy and consenting at the same time."[31] Behind this air of self-deprecation, however, lay raw self-confidence.

Shortly after arriving in Gdańsk, Wałęsa ran into a former colleague from vocational school who worked at the shipyard. He encouraged Wałęsa to apply for work there. Wałęsa hurried to the shipyard's employment office, filled out the forms, and was soon hired as employee number 61 878. The Lenin Shipyard in Gdańsk was already one of Poland's great socialist enterprises. The workforce, more than 15,000 strong, was a mixture of young peasant sons and older men, many "resettled" from the pre-war eastern provinces that had been incorporated into the Soviet Union as a result of Yalta.[32]

Wałęsa began work as a naval electrician in shop M-4 in the Mosinski crew, laying cables as thick as his forearms on large boats. His first job was to "do the ends," dividing the cables into sections and then separating and stripping the wires. The best workers in the shipyard—the elite—were placed in machine shop M-5, and they oversaw final assembly of the engines. Shop M-4, where Wałęsa ended up, involved general engineering and included skilled workers like lathe or milling machine

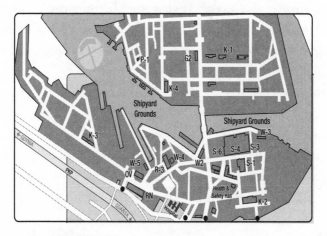

Gdańsk Lenin Shipyard

Legend: ● = Entrance gates; RN = Design and construction office; K-1 = Hull treatment and coloring department; K-2–K-4 = Hull assembly department; OV = Transport department; P-1 = Ship equipment testing department; R-3 = Machine and toll repair department; S-1 = Casting department; S-3 = Boiler and forging department; S-4 = Mechanical treatment department; S-6 = Gear production department; W-2–W-5 = Ship equipment department

operators. The outcasts of the shipyard worked in the hull.[33] Wałęsa started at 6:00 a.m. every morning in less-than-ideal conditions. "When I arrived our shipyard looked like a factory filled with men in filthy rags, unable to wash themselves or urinate in toilets," Wałęsa recalled. "To get down to the ground floor where toilets were located took at least half an hour, so we just went anywhere."[34] Only one in every seven workers made it through the first year of employment, since most detested the unpleasant conditions and low pay.[35]

Wałęsa first rented a small room from a genteel couple, Mr. and Mrs. Krol, at 28 Kartuska Street in Gdańsk, where he crammed in with three others. Wałęsa and his roommates were on the ground floor of a dilapidated building not far from the shipyard. Their room had one table surrounded by four beds, and the windows looked out on a busy road. It was not luxurious living, but the owners created a family-like atmosphere. Wałęsa helped the Krols with housework, mopped the floor on Saturdays, brushed fresh coats of white paint on the walls, and repaired the light fixtures. He also served as a chaperone for the family's oldest daughter when she went to dances. Among Wałęsa's most poignant memories with Mr. Krol was listening to Radio Free Europe, which elicited memories of Wałęsa's time with his stepfather.[36]

After several unremarkable relationships with local girls, Wałęsa finally met his match in 1968. "When a bright face with hazel eyes and long hair in a plait looked at me from a flower kiosk, I remembered that provocative but gently girlish gesture for a long time."[37] He returned a few days later and mustered up the energy to ask out the girl, named Danuta. She was eighteen and was quickly smitten as well:

> I liked him. He came to change some money and was in a big hurry. It all began when he borrowed a book from me and gave it back after a couple of days. I don't remember the title. I was about to leave and he asked if he could walk me home. First we would go to the movies every day, for maybe a month, then we got bored with that. I went with him to speedway matches a couple of times. We arrived at the following daily schedule: he would go to work at the Shipyard at six, after work he would come to me, we would talk for a few minutes, then he would go to his flat in Kartuska Street, went to sleep, come for me before six, waited for me to close the flower shop and then we would go for a walk.[38]

They were married on November 8, 1969. Wałęsa and Danuta began their new life in a rented room on Marchlewski Street, where they stayed only four months. They then moved into the attic of a private house in Suchanino, where they had a single room and a dark kitchen. "But at least we had it all to ourselves," recalled Wałęsa.[39] After a year they moved again, this time to a workers' hotel on Klonowicz Street. But the accommodations were insufferable because of the constant fighting and drunken rowdiness of several of the tenants. They finally settled in a two-room apartment in the Stogi area of Gdańsk, not far from the shipyard.[40]

———

By 1970, THE POLISH GOVERNMENT had attempted a handful of economic reforms, each of which had been frustrated by bureaucratic inertia. Władysław Gomułka, who had returned as Polish leader in 1956, was devoted to a Soviet-style economy, with centralized state planning and a series of five-year economic packages. But the Polish economy was in freefall, living standards were austere, and consumer goods were scarce.

One of the few remaining popular benefits of Poland's economy was the Gomułka regime's guarantee of low staple food prices, some of which had been frozen for a decade. Though there were shortages of basic commodities by 1970, they were relatively cheap. Almost unthinkably, the government decided to increase staple food prices by up to 36 percent because of the dire state of the economy. And they chose to do this on December 13, 1970, less than two weeks before Christmas.[41] In Gdańsk, thousands of shipyard workers marched on the Communist Party's regional headquarters, demanding that the price increases be withdrawn. Within a few days, the government faced strikes and protests across much of the country. Bloodshed came in the Baltic port cities of Gdańsk and Gdynia, where Gomułka ordered police and soldiers to neutralize what he now called "counter-revolutionary" forces.[42] The first confrontation with the security forces took place outside the Lenin Shipyard gate in Gdańsk. The workers had intended to march to the town hall with the centuries-old demands of Polish insurrectionaries: bread and freedom. Singing the Communist anthem, "The Internationale," they were greeted by a fusillade of bullets.[43]

"On returning to the workshop," recalled Wałęsa, who was a member of the strike committee at the time, "I heard a burst of gunfire. The crowd froze."[44] The situation began to spiral as Polish forces fired on terrified workers. Overall, forty-two people were killed and over a thousand were wounded. Wałęsa and other workers reacted with grief—and vitriol. They raised a flag with black ribbons and draped the murdered workers' helmets in black crepe and attached them to the shipyard gate. They daubed the blood of the victims onto bed sheets to form four red crosses, which they hung from a window of the shipyard hospital.[45] In a frenzy of passion, some began singing the Polish national anthem, putting dramatic emphasis on the last line of the opening stanza:

> *Poland has not yet perished,*
> *So long as we still live.*
> *What the alien force has taken from us,*
> *We shall retrieve with a sword.*[46]

Some used loudspeakers and shouted "Murderers! Murderers!" at security forces outside the gates. Armored cars, tanks, and army cordons took up positions around the Lenin Shipyard. A few workers began to construct improvised explosive devices using ingredients like acetylene, while others built makeshift mortars out of pipes. In the end, though, "there were very few of us who really wanted to battle the troops," said Wałęsa, "despite the foolhardy taunts of excited workers."[47]

Radio Free Europe broadcast details of the riots. Enraged Polish government officials lobbied the U.S. government to stop the "use of vituperative language."[48] A top secret KGB report suggested that it was a priority to expose stations like Radio Free Europe "as centers of ideological subversion, whose activities against the USSR and other socialist countries are funded and directed by the Central Intelligence Agency of the USA."[49] Still, the tragic events forced Gomułka's resignation as Poland's leader. He was replaced by Edward Gierek, a tall, burly Pole with a weakness for gaudy ties.[50]

Poland had now entered uncharted waters. Workers began to organize themselves outside the aegis of the Communist Party and formulated political and economic demands. More than thirty factories in the tough northwestern port of Szczecin set up a network of strike committees, which effectively controlled everyday life of the city. Their demands included the withdrawal of the price rises and a recognition that the strike committees were genuine representatives of the workforce. In late January, Gierek appeared at the gates of the occupied Warski Shipyard in Szczecin and began an unprecedented nine-hour confrontation, adopting a tone of frankness and humility.[51] He announced: "When it was proposed that I take over the leadership of the party, at first I thought I would refuse ... I am only a worker like you."[52]

Somehow Gierek's efforts succeeded. The workers shouted *"Pomożemy! Pomożemy!"* ("We will help you!") and eventually went back to work. There was a similar confrontation in the Lenin Shipyard and another triumph for Gierek as workers backed down—at least temporarily.[53]

———

BUT AN OPPOSITION MOVEMENT had begun to flower. Wałęsa's world had turned upside down. Because of his participation in the strike, he was now labeled a subversive and had to deal with constant harassment by Polish security forces.

"You have children, don't you Mr. Wałęsa?" the police would ask him at regular intervals after arresting him.

"Yes, of course," he answered.

"Do you want them to grow up without a father?" the police asked. "We know how tough things must be for you—you've got lots of kids, a small apartment, low wages. That's why you're taking these risks and letting yourself be exploited by radical militants. Borusewicz, Kuroń, Michnik—these guys are professionals paid by the CIA. If we put them in jail, there'll always be someone to post bail for them. Besides, they're the elite, and we can always control the elite. You we'll just have to crush. But maybe we can come to an understanding; we certainly have the means. You'd be able to buy a big house, and we could get you a high-paying job. Let bygones be bygones. What do you say?"

"No," said Wałęsa.

"What? No?" the police would respond. "Come, now—think of your future. In a few years, your children will be asking you why you didn't get them a better start in life. They'll accuse you of spoiling your life and theirs."[54]

The constant arrests and harassment took a toll on Wałęsa and his family, particularly his wife, Danuta. "In the early 1970s I tried shielding her from my political activities—partly because she was so caught up with our growing family and our domestic life, and perhaps also because discussing my plans openly doesn't come easy to me," said Wałęsa. "But I learned early on from experience that she was a lot calmer if I warned her for instance, 'Today they might lock me up for forty-eight hours.' The unexpected tends to trigger overreaction."[55]

———

TENSIONS IN POLAND CONTINUED TO RISE. In June 1976, the government once again introduced food price rises of 60 percent on average—and 69 percent on meat. Workers across the country went on strike again.[56] Polish security forces occupied the Baltic shipyards, and the strikers responded by electing a committee and drawing up lists of demands.[57] There was a palpable energy among Poland's workers.

Wałęsa became increasingly involved in organizing workers following his dismissal from the Gdańsk Lenin Shipyard in 1976 for criticizing the regime's trade unions. He was an electrifying speaker, firing up crowds with his booming voice. He organized unofficial rallies outside Gate Number Two of the Gdańsk Shipyard to demand that the authorities keep their promise to erect a memorial to the dead. Wałęsa also became active in the Free Trade Unions of the Coast and the Workers' Defense Committee (*Komitet Obrony Robotników*, or KOR), an opposition group founded by Antoni Macierewicz, Jacek Kuroń, and others in 1976. He distributed copies of opposition newsletters like the *Coastal Worker* and, in 1979, briefly went back to work at the Elektromontaż factory in Gdańsk. Wałęsa was now a hardened opposition member and a vibrant supporter of free trade unions in Poland.

In December 1979, the Gdańsk Shipyard management attempted to sabotage the commemoration of the 1970 massacre by sending workers home early, ostensibly as an "energy-saving measure." But some 5,000 turned up to listen to Wałęsa's call for the establishment of a free trade union, independent of Communist Party control. At the end of his speech, Wałęsa urged the crowd to return to the same spot the following year, bearing a large stone. "We'll build a mound with those stones, we'll cement them over, and that will be our monument. We'll erect it ourselves."[58] The essence of Wałęsa's call for greater freedom was captured in a song that was popular among some of the Polish workers:

> *There are no free trade unionists today.*
> *Wherever you turn, only private interest, money.*
> *What has become of concern for the workers?*
> *It has flown off to a far and distant land.*
> *All that's left is careerism and status.*
> *Worker be quiet! Shut your mouth!*
> *You must work, even for breaking your back*
> *You're paid in trouble and sorrow*
> *It you want to be free*
> *Join our ranks*
> *With the free union, with the free union*
> *With the free union, we'll live together.*[59]

———

BY THE SUMMER OF 1980, as confrontation loomed between the labor unions and the Polish government, Wałęsa was catapulted to the forefront of the opposition movement. He was now on a collision course with the Polish government's defense minister, Communist Party leader, and Soviet ally—Wojciech Jaruzelski.

Chapter 2

THE GENERAL

Hanging on the wall of Wojciech Jaruzelski's office in 1980, tucked away in Poland's Ministry of Defense, was an oversized map of Europe. Jaruzelski studied it religiously. The map divided Europe into two acrimonious Cold War camps. To the west was the NATO alliance, led by the United States. For Jaruzelski, the United States was not the sacrosanct "city on a hill" or beacon of democracy that Ronald Reagan described during the U.S. presidential campaign that year, but a powerful state riven by "colonial wars, racism, mafia, and economic disparities."[1] To the east were the Warsaw Pact nations, led by the Soviet Union. Jaruzelski had grown up in an era when most Poles loathed Moscow. Jaruzelski should have reviled them as well. During World War II, the Soviets deported Jaruzelski, his mother, and his younger sister, and sent his father to a labor camp.

But Jaruzelski was a cold-blooded realist. Poland lay in Moscow's—not Washington's—orbit, thanks to Yalta. Even in the summer of 1980, with growing opposition to the Polish government from shipyard workers and miners, Jaruzelski's allegiance to Moscow was unflinching. The Cold War map hanging in his office helped anchor him. "I knew many Soviet marshals and generals," Jaruzelski recalled. "Some were my friends. They also could read maps. I knew, full well that there was a limit beyond which the Polish 'schism' and the 'Polish heretic road' could not and would not be tolerated."[2] Jaruzelski did not support Moscow out of loyalty or affection, but out of survival.

As Poland's leader in 1980, Jaruzelski was the opposite of Wałęsa. Where Wałęsa could be volcanic, Jaruzelski was calm. Where Wałęsa was charismatic, Jaruzelski was drab. Jaruzelski carefully controlled his emotions and appeared unnaturally relaxed.[3] He was neither a populist nor a demagogue, but lived modestly and rarely travelled abroad.[4] Most Poles knew the dour general from his ramrod posture and trademark tinted glasses, which he wore not for style but because of snow blindness he had suffered during wartime imprisonment in a Soviet labor camp.[5]

Jaruzelski's life was full of contradictions. An ardent Communist, he grew up the child of a wealthy landowning family. An atheist, he had been educated by Catholic priests.[6] He sympathized with Karl Marx's essay "The Eighteenth Brumaire of Louis Napoleon," particularly Marx's conclusion that "people create their history by themselves but do not create it freely, nor in circumstances they themselves have chosen, but in those in which they directly find themselves, which were given them and inherited by them."[7] It didn't matter whether he supported the Cold War divisions or even Yalta, Jaruzelski surmised. These events were beyond his control. What mattered, instead, was how he dealt with the Cold War system that existed.

———

JARUZELSKI WAS BORN ON JULY 6, 1923, in the small town of Kurów, which lay seventy-five miles southeast of Poland's capital, Warsaw. When Jaruzelski was young, his family moved to the estate owned by his mother's parents in the village of Trzeciny, located in the farmlands northeast of Warsaw. His family belonged to a class of feudal landowners known as the *szlachta*, which included the privileged gentry of pre-Communist

Poland. His father, Władysław, fled the Russian army draft and eventually enlisted in the Polish army. Jaruzelski's initial image of the vaunted Red Army had been of a horde of conquering barbarians: "What struck me first was how many of them there were," he wrote later. "I had the impression that there were thousands upon thousands of them, with their long gray overcoats and great piles of rifles. I had the sense of a force that was terrible, strange, hostile."[8]

Much like Wałęsa, Jaruzelski was closest to his mother, Wanda, a fiercely independent Pole who had brought up her children—Jaruzelski and his sister Teresa—in a staunchly Catholic household.[9] By the soft light of oil lamps, Wanda read Jaruzelski and Teresa stories about swashbuckling Polish heroes struggling against their Russian foes. She also sent them off to church every Sunday to learn about God. The family had a pew of their own, elevated above those of common folk. Jaruzelski would not become religious in later years, finding sustenance in the teachings of Marx and Lenin instead. But his upbringing helps explain his bitter acknowledgment, however vexing at times, that the Catholic Church could not easily be excluded from public life in Poland.

At the age of ten, Jaruzelski's parents sent him to a Jesuit boarding school outside Warsaw, the School of the Marianist Brothers. Many of the students, though not Jaruzelski, hoped to become priests. Jaruzelski consumed the conservative views of his teachers, sang hymns that praised Poland's military dictator Józef Piłsudski, and studied the military campaigns of Spanish general Francisco Franco.[10] Jaruzelski passed his final exams in June 1939 and hopped on a train back to his home in Trzeciny. His world was about to collapse.

Less than three months later, on September 1, 1939, Hitler invaded Poland. For over a week, Jaruzelski watched a parade of retreating soldiers trudge by his house. The family then quickly packed and left in four horse-drawn carriages, accompanied by a handful of servants.[11] "We were persuaded the war would be short, and we took little baggage," Jaruzelski remembered. "We buried on the grounds the silver, porcelain, and crystal dishes."[12] Jaruzelski and his family joined thousands of others that fled east, and they found work as farm laborers in Lithuania.[13] As wealthy landowners, they were considered "socially dangerous elements" by the Russians.[14] A few months later, after Lithuania and the other Baltic states were seized by Soviet forces, Jaruzelski and his family were captured by the Red Army. The family was split up, with Wojciech, his mother, and his younger sister sent to a remote Siberian village near the Mongolian border. His father was deported to a labor camp in another part of Siberia.

The month-long train trip to Siberia—a journey twice the width of the United States—gave him a sense of the vastness of Poland's eastern neighbor. The young Jaruzelski cut wood and carried hulking 200-pound sacks. His family was eventually reunited in the Siberian city of Biysk, but his father died of dysentery in 1942.

In 1943, Jaruzelski made one of the most important decisions of his life: he joined the army.

———

JARUZELSKI ENLISTED IN THE FIRST POLISH ARMY and was sent to the Soviet Officer Training School at Ryazan, 120 miles southeast of Moscow. He was in the second class, headquartered in a massive, white-columned building on Lenin Square.[15] Jaruzelski loved Ryazan. "I was born again; I chose definitively the route of my existence," he recalled. "I believe I have kept a certain rigidity, a special posture, that was inculcated in me, without doubt, on Lenin Square in Ryazan."[16]

Amid the chaos of Europe in the 1940s, the army provided Jaruzelski with a sense of order and purpose. A Polish army allied with the Soviet Union was an irresistible attraction for the young Jaruzelski. In late 1943, he graduated from Ryazan and accepted his first command: the Eighth Company's Third Platoon. Jaruzelski quickly realized, with horror, that his soldiers were women. Too embarrassed to even give commands because he had expected to lead men, he asked for a new assignment. The army gave him the First Platoon in the First Polish Army under General

Zygmunt Berling, which fought alongside the Red Army in the liberation of Warsaw, the Oder and Elbe campaigns, and the Soviet conquest of Berlin.[17] One of his first billets was in Smolensk, in the house of a storekeeper who spent most of his time making *samogon*—home-brew vodka. Among the many lifelong lessons the Soviet Union taught Jaruzelski was an abhorrence of liquor. Soviet soldiers drank heroically, and Jaruzelski saw alcohol ravage them. He was so put off by the excessive drinking that he became a teetotaler for the rest of his life, though he occasionally sipped wine during toasts. Later in his military career, Jaruzelski even issued controversial directives that prohibited the sale or consumption of alcoholic beverages on military bases, including in officers' clubs, and outlawed parties during working hours.[18] It didn't make him popular among Polish soldiers, many of whom considered drinking vodka to be a national pastime.

In May 1945, Jaruzelski and his forces reached the Elbe. American troops had appeared around the same time on the opposite bank of the river, and, as he later recalled, "we greeted one another with very great warmth."[19] It was in the ranks of the Polish army that the young officer saw the way German forces had ruined his country. Rebuking the Nazi ideology, the young Jaruzelski turned to Communism.[20] World War II bonded him to Soviet troops. "Those of us who found ourselves in the army fighting side by side with the Russian soldiers developed an element of closeness. You can only achieve it in the trenches, fighting together."[21] The Soviets also provided something more tangible to Poland. "The USSR had genuine participation in our liberation" from Nazi Germany, Jaruzelski concluded, "and we remained in our border thanks to Stalin. The USSR provided security for Poland."[22]

But Jaruzelski was also a realist. He understood that Moscow's desire to bring Poland into its orbit was based on self-interest, as Stalin had lectured British prime minister Winston Churchill at Yalta. "The Prime Minister has said that for Great Britain the question of Poland is a question of honor. For Russia it is not only a question of honor but also of *security*," Stalin had remarked. Stalin continued:

It is sufficient that during the last thirty years our German enemy has passed through this corridor twice. This is because Poland was weak. It is in the Russian interest, as well as that of Poland, that Poland be strong and powerful and in a position in her own and in our interests to shut the corridor by her own forces. The corridor cannot be mechanically shut from outside by Russia. It could be shut from inside only by Poland. It is necessary that Poland be free, independent and powerful. It is not only a question of honor *but of life and death* for the Soviet state.[23]

This was the same Stalin, Jaruzelski recognized, who had massacred thousands of Poles in the Katyn Forest in Russia five years before.[24] "They fought for a free Poland, and they were slaughtered as innocents," Jaruzelski later remarked. "Far from their homes and their native land, they remained faithful to Poland and their soldiers' honor until the last moment. To the Polish officer, and the victim of Stalinist crimes, is due eternal honor," he said.[25] It was a blatant contradiction. As the Cold War began, Poland—and Jaruzelski—were now bound tightly to the very regime that had killed thousands of Polish soldiers without mercy.

———

IN 1945, BRITISH PRIME MINISTER Winston Churchill became increasingly concerned about Stalin's broader intentions in Eastern Europe, which would pull Poland deep inside the Soviet sphere of influence. In May, he sent a note to British foreign secretary Anthony Eden. "The proposed withdrawal of the United States Army to the occupational lines which were arranged with the Russians and Americans in Quebec, and which were marked in yellow on the maps we studied there, would mean the tide of Russian domination sweeping forward 120 miles on a front of 300 or 400 miles," Churchill wrote. "This would be an event which, if it occurred, would be one of the most melancholy in history. After it was over and the territory occupied by the Russians, Poland would be completely engulfed and buried deep in Russian occupied lands."[26]

Cold War Europe by the Early 1980s

It would spell the death of a free Poland, Churchill lamented. "The Russian demands on Germany for reparations alone will be such as to enable her to prolong the occupation almost indefinitely, at any rate for many years during which time Poland will sink with many other states into the vast zone of Russian-controlled Europe, not necessarily economically Sovietised but police-governed."[27]

A year after Yalta, a despondent Winston Churchill traveled to the small town of Fulton, Missouri, and delivered one of the defining speeches of the Cold War. "From Stettin in the Baltic to Trieste in the Adriatic, an iron curtain has descended across the Continent," he remarked. Churchill continued by warning that the Soviets had suppressed freedom and liberty in solidifying Soviet hegemony. "Warsaw, Berlin, Prague, Vienna, Budapest, Belgrade, Bucharest and Sofia, all these famous cities and the populations around them lie in what I must call the Soviet sphere, and all are subject in one form or another, not only to Soviet influence but to a very high and, in many cases, increasing measure of control from Moscow." Churchill was particularly concerned about Poland:

> The Russian-dominated Polish Government has been encouraged to make enormous and wrongful inroads upon Germany, and mass expulsions of millions of Germans on a scale grievous and undreamed of are now taking place. The Communist parties, which were very small in all these Eastern States of Europe, have been raised to pre-eminence and power far beyond their numbers and are seeking everywhere to obtain totalitarian control. Police governments are prevailing in nearly every case, and so far... there is no true democracy.[28]

———

WITH THE COLD WAR TAKING SHAPE IN 1947, Jaruzelski made another momentous decision: he joined the Communist Party. In his letter of application, dated June 24, 1947, Jaruzelski wrote: "I share totally the ideology and basic principles of the Party. I wish to work in the ranks of the Polish People's Republic for the good of the country and the society."[29] He was likely attracted to Communism's promise of providing social justice. From early childhood, Jaruzelski had been conscious of the huge social gap between his family and their peasants. "We need more justice in Poland," Jaruzelski once reflected.[30] He also believed that the West inflated its accomplishments. "There were many things in the West that we did not want to have here. You had colonialism at its full bloom then. You know that racism was also then far from being controlled. In all kinds of social movements in Western European countries, Communists had great influence. Such were the times."[31]

But his decision to embrace Communism was more than just ideological. It was eminently practical, just like his decision to join the army.
His country's future, he believed, rested on a firm and stable relationship
with its eastern neighbor. There was little choice but to take sides and
support Communism.[32] "We were the children of Yalta," said Jaruzelski. "Such were our realities. There were two ways to handle such realities: to go underground and fight with the partisans, prolonging the civil
war and bringing enormous losses to a country which had so often carried the burden of insurrections ending in defeat. Or one could operate
within the system, try to improve it, to expand the area of sovereignty as
much as possible."[33]

Jaruzelski had decided not just to survive in this system—but to
thrive in it.

———

JOSEPH STALIN HELD NO ILLUSIONS about the expansion of American
power and the coming clash of ideologies. He had remarked to a group
of visiting American labor leaders: "In [the] course of further development of [the] international revolution there will emerge two centers of
world significance: a socialist center, drawing to itself the countries
which tend toward socialism, and a capitalist center, drawing to itself
the countries that incline toward capitalism. Battle between these two
centers for command of [the] world economy will decide [the] fate of
capitalism and of communism in [the] entire world."[34] In the latter half
of the 1940s under Soviet rule, Eastern Europe became an armed camp.
Frontiers were closed. Security was returned to wartime footing. Eastern European economies were converted to military priorities. Military conscription, which had been carefully avoided since World War
II, was reintroduced.

In an evocative, if uninformed, communiqué to his bosses in
Moscow, Soviet ambassador to the United States Nikolai Novikov
expressed his growing fear that U.S. foreign policy was "characterized

in the postwar period by a desire for world domination." America's rise, he argued, occurred at the very moment that Britain abdicated its global empire, shedding colonies from Palestine to India. "The numerous statements by American government, political, and military leaders about the Soviet Union and its foreign policy in an exceptionally hostile spirit are quite typical of the current attitude of American ruling circles toward the USSR," Novikov continued. He concluded by accusing the United States of not simply being interested in ideological or economic domination, but military supremacy. "It ought to be fully realized that American preparations for a future war are being conducted with the idea of war against the Soviet Union, which in the eyes of American imperialists is the chief obstacle in the American path to world domination."[35] The United States was laying the groundwork for world domination, Novikov believed, through the establishment of naval and air bases, the procurement of new weapons, and the creation of a large land army.

The Soviet Union—including Soviet intelligence—now regarded the United States as its main adversary, and the KGB sought to influence events through a variety of means, from media manipulation to targeted assassination.[36] The KGB and the foreign military intelligence directorate of the Soviet Army General Staff, or GRU (Glavnoje Razvedyvatel'noje Upravlenije), recruited several Americans in the early years of the Cold War like Robert Thompson of the U.S. Air Force, Otto Verber of the U.S. Army, and Jack Dunlap of the National Security Agency. Over the course of the Cold War, the Soviets recruited more significant spies like the CIA's Aldrich Ames and FBI's Robert Hanssen.[37] Perhaps most importantly, the Soviets deployed the Red Army to expand power in Eastern Europe. The Soviet Union formally incorporated Estonia, Latvia, and Lithuania, along with part of eastern Poland, sections of East Prussia, Bessarabia, northern Bukovina, the eastern province of Subcarpathian Ruthenia in Czechoslovakia, and some territory on Finland's eastern border. The Red Army had seized most of these areas during World War II. As Soviet Foreign Minister Vjacheslav Molotov explained, the Soviets went "on the offensive" during the early postwar period to "extend the frontier of our Fatherland to the maximum."[38] They stationed Red Army forces across Eastern Europe, turning Bulgaria, Hungary, Poland, Romania, and eventually Czechoslovakia into satellite states.[39] In 1948, the Soviets blockaded Berlin from the United States, British, and French occupation zones, further dramatizing the conflict and formally dividing Germany.

The United States, on the other hand, drastically reduced its military footprint in Europe, handing Moscow an opportunity for expansion. In May 1945, there had been over three million U.S. troops in Europe.[40] But the United States quickly demobilized forces as government officials and members of Congress came under intense pressure from servicemen, their families, and a strong isolationist lobby to discharge soldiers rapidly. The United States cut its forces to 278,042 soldiers by 1946 and 79,495 by 1950.[41]

———

As COLD WAR TENSIONS continued to escalate, Jaruzelski's military career blossomed. The army promoted him to a colonel in 1954 and then to a brigadier general in 1956 at thirty-three years old—the youngest general in the army. Jaruzelski surged past officers that were much older and had credentials from Communist Party schools in Moscow. Around this time, he met his future wife, Barbara, a slim blonde that he described as "seductive."[42] But Jaruzelski would never be a family man. He was a creature of the army and reveled in its predictability and discipline. Over time, Jaruzelski and his wife spent their vacations separately, though they never divorced.[43] He spent most of his time working, beginning his day by swimming or playing volleyball. He arrived at his office by 9:00 a.m. like clockwork, took a two-hour lunch at home, and frequently worked until after midnight. He had no hobbies, except reading, which was entirely serious. According to one account, "close aides do not recall seeing him with a novel."[44] His lifestyle was modest to the extreme. He had a small house in Warsaw, but no country home like other general officers. He was a "towering personality," one of his colleagues described him, with an "exceptional attention to work coupled with an unusual intellectual receptivity" and "a continual hunger for knowledge."[45]

Perhaps more importantly, Jaruzelski had become a steeled Communist Party man. In Jaruzelski's letter of recommendation for his generalship, General Stanislav Poplavsky lauded Jaruzelski's political prowess. "Jaruzelski, in twelve years of service to the Polish People's Army, proved to be a devoted and hardworking officer, fully dedicated to the construction of socialism," he wrote. "He works systematically on perfecting his military and political knowledge. He is politically formed, active in Party and political activities, and influences his peers in a positive way."[46]

Jaruzelski also shed whatever attachment to Catholicism he embraced as a child. His long, painful time of forced labor during World War II—when no god had saved his family from suffering—had eroded his faith. "In Siberia my physical bonds with the Church were broken," he explained.[47] Jaruzelski was not a closet Catholic, biding his time under the shadow of Soviet Communism. He was a committed Marxist and a militant atheist. Over time, Jaruzelski accused the Catholic Church of serving as a bulwark for Poland's growing opposition movement, full of radicals and anti-regime opponents.[48] Jaruzelski even conducted witch-hunts within the military—not just targeting soldiers, but occasionally their wives and children as well—for Catholic practices like participating in catechism classes and holding funerals attended by priests. Some soldiers were transferred to lower service posts for their actions; a few were tossed out of the Polish military altogether. These and other steps were conducted as part of a sweeping effort, in Jaruzelski's eyes, of "immunization of the military against influences of the clergy."[49]

———

JARUZELSKI BECAME THE ARMY'S political commissar in 1960, deputy minister of defense in 1962, and chief of the General Staff in 1965. And then, at the age of forty-five, he became defense minister of the most important Soviet satellite in 1968. By this time, Jaruzelski had begun to show signs of age. He had thinning hair and an impenetrable face that showed little emotion.[50] He rarely cracked a smile. He was also self-assured, even obstinate. Jaruzelski worked hard and was well-organized, and expected the same of his staff. "He was feared nearly by all," recalled one of his subordinates. "The main reason for their fear was that he was very demanding and as a rule he had his own point of view on nearly everything, a view different from others. He who differed with him had to take leave from his post since there was no other choice."[51]

Jaruzelski was immediately tested as defense minister. On August 20, 1968, the Red Army invaded Czechoslovakia "like gentlemen," remarked Jaruzelski, with support from Bulgarian, Hungarian, and Polish forces. "We took care not to create harm."[52] Jaruzelski clearly hadn't bothered to ask the population of Czechoslovakia whether they agreed; 108 were brutally killed and another 500 wounded during the effort to crush Alexander Dubček's Prague Spring liberalization movement. There was sporadic nonviolent resistance, but it was suppressed. In the end, Jaruzelski had little compunction about ordering Polish troops to join the Soviet-led invasion.

Two years later, Dubček's liberalization had spread to Poland during the 1970 strikes in Gdańsk and Gdynia, in which Wałęsa had participated. Jaruzelski had ordered the deployment of Polish military forces across the country and placed them on high alert. Polish leader Władysław Gomułka called a meeting of top Communist Party and government officials, including Jaruzelski. Gomułka explained that he was authorizing the police and army to use weapons if necessary. Ten people were present, including Jaruzelski. No one protested. "These were not workers," Jaruzelski remarked. "These were people shooting at our militia soldiers."[53]

Jaruzelski emerged from the 1970 riots battle-tested and, at least to his staff, he had demonstrated calm under pressure. He was not prone to impulsive decisions and rarely became excited. He often retreated to his study during particularly tense moments to coolly evaluate his options and sift through their implications. "He never acted spontaneously and all his important pronouncements were, as a rule, composed, and thought through in advance, in the solitude of his study," recalled one of his subordinates. "At times, they were even rehearsed using a recorder, before they were officially pronounced."[54] Indeed, Jaruzelski was much more comfortable in the confines of his office, alone, than he was in public. He was nervous—sometimes even visibly shaking—before major speeches.

In the aftermath of the 1970 killing of Polish civilians, Gomułka resigned as Poland's leader and Edward Gierek took over. Jaruzelski vowed never again to shed the blood of Poles, if at all possible.[55] Yet he also felt Poland was now entering a dangerous period. The enemy was not just lurking outside Polish borders, but included subversive activists *inside* the country. Countering the danger required significant changes within the military. Jaruzelski began to transform the Polish army from an externally oriented combat army into an internal security force, closely linked to the Communist Party and pro-government civilian organizations like youth groups.[56]

———

By the late 1970s, Gierek's economic, social, and political programs hurtled Poland toward the abyss. When workers went on strike following an increase in food prices in 1976, the government responded with restraint. They arrested striking workers, but without resorting to violence. "Polish soldiers will not fire on Polish workers," Jaruzelski promised.[57] Yet battle lines were drawn. In September 1976, dissident intellectuals established the Workers' Defense Committee, or KOR, after several thousand strikers were attacked and jailed by authorities. KOR supported families of imprisoned workers, offered legal and medical aid, and disseminated news through an underground network. With Polish society fracturing and Moscow growing uneasy about anti-Soviet activism, Jaruzelski was increasingly torn: "I found myself, to use a descriptive phrase, between the 'anvil' of internal conflicts and the 'hammer' of external danger."[58]

Jaruzelski's Poland was not a full dictatorship. Intellectuals participated in opposition activity, and Poland developed an opposition counterculture without parallel in the Soviet bloc. This movement included at least two high-quality literary magazines and ten uncensored journals. Polish security agencies continued to operate with restraint under Jaruzelski's watchful eye. "We know all the addresses, we could destroy everything in one night," a police officer remarked, "but the high-ups won't allow us to."[59] The "high-ups," notably Polish leader Edward Gierek and Defense Minister Jaruzelski, believed that the flowering intellectual opposition was not a serious political threat. Besides, they hoped that tolerance might win the government a broader measure of cooperation from the intelligentsia. KOR activists were abused, harassed, sacked from their jobs, and detained for questioning—yet they were not generally held for longer than forty-eight hours.

As international news outlets covered Poland's growing opposition movement, more people took notice. One was Bill Casey, soon to become CIA director. If there was any Soviet satellite that was showing signs of cracking, Casey thought, it was now Poland.

Chapter 3

THE SPYMASTER

The year 1980 offered a tantalizing opportunity for Bill Casey. After serving in the Office of Strategic Studies (OSS), the predecessor of the CIA, during World War II, Casey wanted to get back into government. The Queens-born lawyer was a Republican and a fiery anti-Communist. He had been chairman of the Securities and Exchange Commission, under secretary of state for economic affairs, and chairman of the Export-Import Bank of the United States—any of which would have been capstones for most Washington careers. But not for Casey. He eyed a cabinet-level appointment. In early 1980, Reagan telephoned Casey, who was at his weekend house in Palm Beach, Florida, and asked if Casey would be willing to take over as campaign manager for Reagan's 1980 presidential bid.

"Bill, I'm thinking of some changes in my organization," Reagan started in. "You don't have to give me an answer now. But I want you to think about taking over."[1]

Casey was intrigued at the prospect of becoming Reagan's campaign manager, but not entirely sold. Reagan had been governor of California, but he was still a novice on the national political stage. Casey picked up the phone and called his friend Paul Laxalt, the charismatic Republican senator from Nevada: "I don't know these people, the Reagans. What are they like?" Casey inquired.

"Nancy is the strong one," Laxalt responded. "One smart tough lady. But they're neophytes on the national scene. You won't have to worry about one thing, though. Ron will take direction."[2]

On February 16, 1980, Casey hopped on an Eastern Air Lines Shuttle from New York to Boston. He went to a Holiday Inn near the airport and met Reagan. Casey said he would take over as campaign manager if—and only if—Reagan gave him full authority. Reagan agreed. Casey was back. Now all they had to do was win the election.

Casey was tall, stoop-shouldered, and partially bald with wisps of white hair on his head. He had a plump frame with large, full lips and fleshy chin that belied a crafty mind. He was energetic, thorough, and ambitious—qualities that served him well as a lawyer and investor. He was also a voracious reader. "You can tell a lot about a man from his books," he once remarked. "A hell of a lot more than you can tell from his bank account."[3] In the library at his Victorian house in Roslyn Harbor, Long Island, the shelves were stuffed with books on the American Revolutionary War, World War II, Christian missions to the third world, and ancient history.

Whatever intellect Casey possessed, however, he lacked charisma and clarity of speech. Casey mumbled. "It's real hard to hear him," one of his colleagues confided. "When you're riding in the car with him, and the radio's on, and he's mumbling, it drives you crazy."[4] Casey swallowed the final words of every sentence as new words began spilling to begin the next one, unable to keep up with a mind that was moving at lightning speed. His thick New York accent didn't help. "Years" sounded like "yihz," "saw" was "sore," "Florida" was "Flahrida," and "war" was "waw."[5] When Casey became CIA director, the joke around Washington was that Reagan picked him to save money; Casey wouldn't require a scrambler when talking on an unclassified telephone. Casey, of course, would have none of the criticism. "From personal experience," he shot back, "I can tell you that mumbling is more in the mind of the listener than in the mouth of the speaker."[6]

———

WILLIAM JOSEPH CASEY was born on March 13, 1913, in Elmhurst, Queens. He was named after his father. The Caseys were hardworking Irish immigrants who had fled to the United States during the Irish potato famine in the mid-nineteenth century. As a child, Casey was sinewy, with large, protruding ears and deep-set eyes. He wasn't an athlete by any stretch of the imagination, though he tried to compensate with the tenacity of a bulldog. As Ray Murphy, a close friend, remembered: "There was a gang of us got caught up in boxing one summer. Roy Tuck's yard was about the size of a ring. So we'd put on the gloves and go at it there—a bell, a timer, the works. Old Casey sure as hell didn't look like a boxer—all skin and bones. But the way he flailed away with those long arms, we called him 'Cyclone.'"

"One of the guys, Pete Drew, never took it easy on anybody, even a friend. Drew and Casey were in the ring one day and Drew threw a haymaker at Casey's chin. It missed and caught poor Casey right in the throat. His face turned every color of the rainbow. He went down on his knees. He was gasping, his eyes popping, blood running out of the corner of his mouth. He couldn't make a sound. We thought he was a goner. Damned if he wasn't back the next day, his neck all black and blue, ready to put on the gloves again."[7]

Casey's doggedness was shaped by two ideologies that profoundly influenced his childhood. One was Catholicism, which shaped his education, morals, and salvation. The other was liberalism. During the Great Depression, the Democratic Party had helped lift Casey's family from cash-strapped immigrants to middle-class New Yorkers. Casey sympathized with the plight of those less fortunate, but he also developed a strong work ethic. He held his first job at age nine, helping out at a nearby nursery. He picked vegetables at farms in the area and caddied during the summer at the Salisbury Club. After graduating from Baldwin High School on Long Island, Casey attended Fordham University in the Bronx, a Jesuit college one borough away. He was the first Casey to go to college. Fordham shaped his faith and confidence. As his wife Sofia later observed, "Bill got his self-assurance from the Jesuits. They let him know who he was. And they made him comfortable with who he was."[8] While Casey would never lose faith in Catholicism, he eventually abandoned the Democratic Party.

After Fordham, Casey moved to Washington, DC, and attended the School of Social Service at The Catholic University of America, brimming with idealism and inspired by Franklin D. Roosevelt's New Deal. But that didn't last long. Casey left Catholic University in 1935, convinced that social work was for women, and went off to St. John's University Law School. By the end of the decade, Casey had joined the Republican Party. Daniel Patrick Moynihan, the New York senator and erudite sociologist, wrote of the transformation, "As people in this country move from the working class to the middle class, they begin to feel more comfortable in the party of the middle class. This was particularly true of American Catholics in the twenties and thirties." This socioeconomic transition was integral for Casey, Moynihan concluded. "Casey is a product of that history. There is nothing aberrational about his politics. Casey's emergence as a conservative Republican was a perfectly natural political progression."[9]

After law school, Casey worked as an analyst in Washington for the Research Institute of America, a private company that produced slick newsletters with a focus on business and economics. His boss, Leo Cherne, recalled: "Bill had a roving, curious mind—possibly the most widely read person I've ever known. . . . But he was an embarrassment in a restaurant. There he'd be, expressing brilliant thoughts through a mouthful of food. He personified a Yiddish expression of my youth—a *graubyon*, a coarse young fellow."[10]

Casey—ever in search of an adventure—then joined the newly formed OSS, which had been established in 1942 as a U.S. wartime intelligence agency.

———

THE OSS SHARED JURISDICTION over foreign intelligence activities with the FBI and worked with the U.S. Army and Navy, which conducted intelligence operations in their areas of responsibility. The OSS was not always well-liked. Some OSS skeptics snickered at the service for hiring a contingent of East Coast elites to conduct secretive missions, sneering that the acronym stood for "Oh So Social" or "Oh Shush Shush."[11] While serving in the OSS, Casey cut his teeth on clandestine operations. He helped recruit agents from among businessmen in neutral countries like Sweden, who could move easily in and out of Germany. Inspired by his time at the Research Institute of America, Casey also helped establish a newsletter published by sympathetic Europeans, but secretly underwritten by the OSS. In June 1944, nineteen days after D-Day, Casey came ashore on the beaches of Normandy to evaluate how OSS teams that had infiltrated France were supporting the invasion. Casey later confessed that his arrival in Normandy was "the most exciting moment of my life."[12] In December 1944, Casey's formal title was chief of the OSS secretariat in the European theater of operations, an impressive promotion and a testament to William Donovan's faith in the thirty-one-year-old Casey.

William "Wild Bill" Donovan was the audacious head of the OSS. Casey remembered him for his "cherubic smile and twinkling blue eyes."[13] Donovan was a confidant—and classmate at Columbia Law School—of President Franklin D. Roosevelt. The *New Yorker* much later described Donovan as "a bold, charismatic, prescient, sometimes ridiculous, and potentially dangerous man" who was willing to take extraordinary risks.[14] Yet Casey was star-struck by Donovan and found him ruthlessly efficient. "His watchword," Casey recalled, "was 'the perfect is the enemy of the good' and he used it as he moved about improvising and implementing operations which in any other part of the American war machine would have required months for study, debate and clearance."[15] Casey hung a black-and-white photograph of Donovan on the wall of his office, a testament to his reverence. Both Casey and Donovan were Irish

Catholics, Wall Street lawyers, and insatiable readers with bullish per-
sonalities. Donovan gave Casey a poem that the younger man cherished
for the rest of his life. Written by Arthur Hugh Clough, the poem began:

> *Say not the struggle naught availeth*
> *the labor and the wounds are vain,*
> *the enemy faints not, nor faileth*
> *and as things have been they must remain*[16]

Casey's most intriguing task working for Donovan at the OSS was
smuggling agents behind German lines, a project codenamed "Faust."[17]
The OSS had dropped more than a hundred teams into France in
advance of D-Day. Those agents landed in friendly territory and were
often warmly welcomed by French peasants eager to drive out the Nazis.
But agents sent into Germany would be parachuting into the Nazi heartland. No resistance fighters would welcome them on the ground and no
safe houses would be waiting. If caught by the Gestapo, they would be
killed.[18] Recalling this work years later, Casey said, "all we could do was
pop a guy into Germany with a radio and hope to hear from him."[19]
Casey's OSS work was his advanced education in geopolitics, and he
came away convinced that covert war was essential and could be highly
effective. The OSS use of "deception, clandestine intelligence and covert
action," Casey later wrote, shortened the war and saved lives.[20] He also
concluded that authoritarian regimes like Nazi Germany and the Soviet
Union were susceptible to clandestine action because their oppressive
political systems created unhappiness among their populations. Reflect-
ing on his OSS experience, Casey believed that "every totalitarianism
creates its own internal vulnerability and that the will and imagination to assist dissident action can reduce, and may even deter and avoid,
slaughter and destruction."[21]

During the war, Casey relied on Polish, French, Belgian, Dutch, and
Czech secret agents to infiltrate Germany. Polish émigrés played a key
role in these operations. Casey formed sixteen teams of highly motivated

Poles who had witnessed Nazi barbarism in their homeland.[22] They were committed to their work, at least until the Yalta agreement handed Poland to Stalin. Then, overnight, Casey recalled, "the morale drained right out of our Poles. I could see it happening before my eyes. After [Yalta], they just went through the motions. They weren't worth a damn. I never forgot what caving in to the Russians did to those people."[23]

By the end of World War II, Casey had grave concerns about the Soviets. "We made seventy-four requests to the Russians for intelligence. They granted twenty-one. We granted twenty-three of twenty-four of their requests. Those are allies?"[24] What Casey had seen in Europe had confirmed his loathing of Communism. The Soviet Union had liberated Eastern Europe from the Nazis, then never let go.

———

IN 1947, THE COLD WAR ACHIEVED what Wild Bill Donovan had tried—and failed—to do: establish a central intelligence agency for the United States. As World War II wound down, Donovan hoped to turn the OSS into a permanent spy agency. But there was a growing push to demobilize wartime bodies. President Harry S. Truman agreed to disband the OSS in September 1945. But its death was short-lived. With a rising Soviet threat, Truman soon recognized the need for an intelligence organization, even in peacetime. Truman listened to advice from Donovan and Admiral William D. Leahy, chief of staff to the president, who helped hammer out details of the new agency. In 1947, Congress passed the National Security Act, and the Central Intelligence Agency was born.[25]

With an aggressive Soviet intelligence and propaganda campaign in Western Europe, Truman and several of his top officials realized that they needed to give the CIA the authority and capability to conduct covert action. "We were alarmed particularly over the situation in France and Italy," recalled State Department diplomat George Kennan. "We felt that the Communists were using the very extensive funds that they had in hand to gain control of key elements of life in France and Italy—particularly the publishing companies, the press, the labor unions, student organizations, women's organizations, and all sorts of organizations of that sort—to gain control of them and use them as front organizations."[26] These concerns led Truman administration officials to strengthen Western European democratic institutions and provide financial aid to political parties that challenged Communists in Western Europe. Truman often handed these assignments to the CIA, which covertly funded political parties in such countries as Italy, France, and West Germany.[27]

The White House provided policy guidance and authorization for the CIA to conduct covert action in documents like National Security Council (NSC) Directive 4-A in December 1947 and NSC Directive 10/2 in June 1949.[28] Collectively, these and other documents authorized the newly created CIA to conduct operations like propaganda, economic warfare, sabotage, and subversion against hostile foreign governments, particularly the Soviet Union and its satellites. "Covert," as spelled out in NSC 10/2, meant actions "which are so planned and executed that any U.S. Government responsibility for them is not evident to unauthorized persons and that if uncovered the U.S. Government can plausibly disclaim any responsibility for them."[29]

The U.S. hand would be hidden. The CIA conducted covert action programs in Western Europe, providing aid to Italy's Christian Democrats in their quest to win a parliamentary majority against a left-wing coalition that included the Italian Communist Party.[30] And the CIA attempted—and failed—to mobilize some émigré populations in Eastern Europe into guerrilla movements.[31] For Truman administration officials, the primary motivation for covert action was a growing concern about Soviet expansionism. As NSC 4-A concluded: "The USSR is conducting an intensive propaganda campaign directed primarily against the U.S. and is employing coordinated psychological, political and economic measures designed to undermine non-Communist elements in all countries."[32]

As the newly formed CIA began to explore covert activities in

Europe, Poland was among the most important targets. CIA officers began to focus on recruiting Polish émigrés.

———

THE NORTHWESTERN PARISIAN SUBURB of Maisons-Laffitte was an improbable location for one of the CIA's earliest Cold War covert-action programs. Maisons-Laffitte stands between the royal forest of Saint-Germain-en-Laye, adorned with majestic oak and beech trees, and the Seine River, the lifeblood of northern France. Originally known as Maisons-sur-Seine, the area was renamed in 1882 in honor of the wealthy French banker and politician Jacques Laffitte. Beginning in the late nineteenth century, Maisons-Laffitte began attracting affluent visitors to its vaunted thoroughbred racetrack.

It was here in Maisons-Laffitte that Jerzy Giedroyc, a poised, unassuming Polish emigré, settled in 1947 to print Polish dissident publications like *Kultura* (*Culture*).[33] Giedroyc's office occupied a rundown mock-Tudor villa at the end of a leafy lane. Over the next several decades, the villa would serve as a hub for anti-Communist propaganda, transforming Giedroyc into an enemy of Polish and Soviet intelligence agencies. Visitors smuggled in manuscripts and microfilms, and carted away books and magazines. These publications found their way into Poland and other countries in the Soviet bloc, hidden in almost every conceivable location: the soiled laundry of intellectuals' suitcases, the sports bags of visiting athletics teams, the luggage of Catholic priests, the costume crates of the Bolshoi Ballet, and even the personal luggage of Marshal Josep Tito of Yugoslavia.[34]

Giedroyc was born in Minsk on July 27, 1906, into a family descended from Polish-Lithuanian nobility. The family moved to Warsaw after World War I, and Giedroyc eventually studied law at Warsaw University. A year after graduating, he founded a magazine called *Bunt Mlodych* (Rebellion of Youth) in 1929, a raw, left-leaning, anti-Communist publication. During World War II, Giedroyc went to Romania and eventually to Rome, where he founded a publishing house, the Institut Littéraire. In June 1947 while in Rome, Giedroyc launched *Kultura*, which emerged as one of the leading Polish-émigré political and literary magazines during the Cold War. The Polish government-in-exile in London, which had been sidelined at Yalta, provided some seed money. A few months later, Giedroyc moved his operation from Rome to Maisons-Laffitte. *Kultura* quickly earned a reputation as an engaging journal with a political twist. It was patently anti-Soviet and published works by Polish authors that were banned or censored in Poland. Its pages boasted the works of Nobel laureates like Czesław Miłosz, author of *The Captive Mind*, and Wisława Szymborska. In its pages, *Kultura* created an "imagined community" of dissident writers and readers.[35] Thanks in large part to Giedroyc and his small band of Polish émigrés, Maisons-Laffitte became an international hub for Polish opposition and, even more importantly, an epicenter for anti-Communist ideology.

Despite his elegant surroundings, however, life in Maisons-Laffite was vexing for Giedroyc. Each day he fought a battle against bankruptcy. Giedroyc didn't always help his own cause. He was fiercely independent and frequently annoyed his contributors by publishing material from writers of opposing literary critiques. By March 1949, Giedroyc had grown tired, exasperated, and broke, as he explained in a letter to his friend Melchior Wańkowicz. "At stake is the future of *Kultura*," Giedroyc wrote. "As you can easily guess, this publication has a negative cash flow in spite of the slow but steady increase in the number of subscribers. I hoped that our reserves would last until the fall, but a catastrophic drop in the stock market in France makes me solvent for the next few months only."[36] Giedroyc conceded that he needed roughly $14,000 to stay afloat for another two years.

While most of his fundraising efforts had been fruitless, he had an epiphany. "In present circumstances, I think that the only way to get this kind of money is to make an appeal in the United States, even though I realize how difficult and nearly hopeless this might be."[37] In July, Giedroyc sent another letter to Wańkowicz complaining that while his situation was going from bad to worse, Józef Czapski, Giedroyc's coedi-tor and a former Polish Army officer and noted artist, better known as Jozio, would be making the first of two fundraising trips to North Amer-ica. As Giedroyc explained to Wańkowicz, "Jozio leaves in early Novem-ber. He will begin his tour in Canada where he was invited to give several lectures in French. This will not cover the cost of the air ticket, but it will take care of his living expenses in Canada, and whatever is left over will enable him to start off in the United States. We have grand hopes for the U.S., and I, in particular, place high hopes in the entire trip."[38]

Czapski's first trip was largely a flop. It was not the "golden fleece" that Giedroyc had hoped.[39] "Nothing new here," Giedroyc reported in the spring of 1950, "Józio is mad at me, I am mad at him, and we both dream of the dollar manna which somehow does not materialize."[40] By the summer, however, Giedroyc had cheered up. As he explained in another letter to Wańkowicz, "I have decided to go with him [to the United States] next time, which means in the winter. I hope for politi-cal and financial results."[41] It was a prophetic note. On his next trip to the United States, two officers from the Office of Policy Coordination (OPC), which had recently been created as a covert action arm of the CIA, contacted them.[42] They offered to provide Giedroyc and Wańkowicz an annual subsidy of nearly $10,000 beginning in the spring of 1950. In return, Giedroyc and Czapski would have to raise the distribution of *Kultura* in the West and smuggle a growing number of copies into Poland. Giedroyc and Czapski agreed.[43]

———

GIEDROYC WAS A VALUABLE CATCH for the OPC, barely two years old at the time. President Truman had established the office to plan and con-duct covert operations to counter Communist activities by providing assistance to émigré groups, distributing propaganda, and conducting subversive actions against hostile states—particularly the Soviet Union. The OPC was initially an independent organization that took guidance

from the Department of State in peacetime and from the Department of
Defense in wartime, but it was located at the CIA. At the time, the CIA
was headquartered in Washington's Foggy Bottom neighborhood, near
the modern-day State Department. Most of the CIA's buildings were
located on the hill above 23rd and E Streets, NW. In 1952, the OPC was
formally folded into the CIA.[44]

Support to *Kultura* was one of the CIA's early political covert action
operations, and it was given the cryptonym QRBERETTA. Over the
next several decades, CIA contributions to *Kultura* continued to rise.
Giedroyc established infiltration routes—or "ratlines"—into Poland
using tourists and businessmen to deliver the magazine. He also mailed
copies to selected addresses inside the country. Over the next several
decades, Giedroyc published hundreds of books and had them distributed into Poland.[45] The CIA's effort to fund *Kultura* was relatively modest, with annual contributions between $20,000 and $60,000 through
the mid-1960s and then rising to over $100,000 per year.[46] But these con-
tributions were sufficient to help keep the magazine in print.[47]

The Cold War may have been "cold" in the narrow sense that there
was no direct military conflict between the United States and Soviet
Union. But a dramatic—and largely covert—ideological struggle for the
hearts and minds of Eastern Europeans had begun.

———

WHILE CIA OFFICERS LEARNED the intricacies of covert action in Eastern Europe, Bill Casey was focused on striking it rich. At the Research
Institute of America, Casey compiled and analyzed legal and economic
data, turning out works like "Tax Sheltered Investments" in 1952 and
"Accounting Desk Book" in 1956. He went on to amass further wealth as
an investor. From 1957 to 1971, he was a partner in the New York law firm
Hall, Casey, Dickler & Howley. Casey then served stints at the Securities
and Exchange Commission, State Department, and Export-Import
Bank. Although he was recognized for his intellectual and analytical

skills, Casey earned a reputation for being disorganized. He misplaced papers and mumbled incomprehensible orders to his secretary, Connie Kirk. On one occasion, he misplaced his wallet at lunch.

The driver told Kirk what had happened. "Hey, I hear you lost your wallet," Kirk said to Casey, sympathetically.

"Who said that?" Casey snapped back. "Who told you that?"

On another occasion, when Kirk asked Casey to repeat himself while he was dictating, Casey shouted, "You know your trouble? You've got a hearing problem."

"He couldn't admit to any faults." Kirk shrugged. "You had to pretend he never made a mistake."[48]

For Kirk and others who worked with Casey, there was one other issue that remained consistent: Casey's virulent anti-Communism. From his OSS perch in Europe during the waning months of World War II, Casey became increasingly alarmed at Soviet attempts to expand their power and establish what he considered a godless ideology on defeated populations. Communism quickly replaced Nazism as the world's great evil, he concluded.[49] In a letter to a veteran of the French Resistance of World War II, Casey spelled out his desire to see the Soviets weakened across the globe: "I'm for throwing Castro out of Cuba and out of South America. I'm for encouraging Russia and China to feud with each other. I'm for putting on the pressure so we can open up Eastern Europe."[50]

By the late 1970s, Casey had amassed an impressive fortune and had become a significant Republican donor. In May 1979, Reagan's campaign brought him to New York, where he was supposed to speak to a Republican party dinner. Dr. William Walsh, a well-connected conservative, knew both Reagan and Casey. Walsh thought the two men should meet, and he set up a breakfast at the Colony Hill Hotel on Long Island, where Reagan was staying. As they talked, Casey ventured a rare compliment, "Carter would never have won if he'd gone up against you instead of Jerry Ford in '76."[51]

Four months went by. After Labor Day, someone from Reagan's staff called Casey. Would he help introduce the governor to potential donors in New York? "Let me put something together," Casey responded. He arranged a Sunday brunch with two dozen of the richest, most powerful Republicans in New York at the Hotel Pierre. The person most impressed with the fund-raiser was Nancy Reagan.[52]

Chapter 4
COVERT ACTORS

By the time Casey agreed to become Reagan's campaign manager in February 1980, a growing contingent of CIA officials believed that Reagan might actually win the election. For Richard "Dick" Malzahn, who was stationed at CIA headquarters and involved in covert action operations against the Soviets, Reagan's tough anti-Soviet position was welcome news. More broadly, Malzahn and many of his cohort felt foreign policy had suffered under President Jimmy Carter. The United States had suffered a string of foreign policy disasters like the capture of fifty-two U.S. hostages in Iran and the fall of the U.S.-supported Reza Shah Pahlavi regime to Shi'a fundamentalists. To men like Malzahn, who sought a more muscular, unapologetic American foreign policy, Reagan would be a fresh start.

Richard Malzahn was born into a Wisconsin household in 1934 to Lester and Dorothy Malzahn. The family lived in a brick house built in the mid-1920s on Milwaukee's East Side, near what is now the University of Wisconsin–Milwaukee campus and less than a mile from Lake Michigan. Malzahn thrived in Milwaukee. At Riverside High School he was an academic standout. Much like Bill Casey, Malzahn was more brains than brawn. He was the lead in the 1952 Junior/Senior play and headed one of the two debate clubs at the school in his last two years. But Malzahn lasted just two years on the high school football team, and the only position he could land on the basketball court was team manager. After graduating in 1952, he went to Yale on a scholarship, majoring in an honors program in history. Like Casey, Malzahn was also a member of the debate club in college, though he was more articulate than Casey. Where Casey mumbled, Malzahn was well-spoken—even loquacious. He lived in Davenport College, one of Yale's twelve residential colleges.[1] Davenport had a reputation as a party house—the house "dances, mixes, drinks and plays with equal intensity," bragged its first master, Emerson Tuttle—making it an ironic choice for the straight-laced Malzahn.[2]

It was at Yale that Malzahn became interested in the CIA—or, more accurately, that the CIA discovered Malzahn. In the early Cold War years, the CIA occasionally identified possible employees through "spotters," academics and others who provided names of prospective recruits.[3] Ivy League schools had a handful of them. At Yale, one was R. Berry Farrell, a Canadian with a Ph.D. from Harvard. Malzahn's roommate, John Chere, a close friend who had attended the same high school in Wisconsin, took Professor Farrell's class on international relations. Presumably tipped off by Farrell, the CIA contacted Cheres. Malzahn was also intrigued. He filled out a CIA application, took a written exam, and heard nothing until the summer of 1956, when the CIA offered him a job. In June, Malzahn and Cheres reported for work at the then-CIA headquarters at 2430 E Street, NW, in Washington.

The CIA was not Malzahn's first choice. He had wanted to attend graduate school and become a history professor, but his dreams were quickly dashed. He had applied for graduate programs at several Ivy League schools and was accepted at Harvard, Yale, and Columbia. But he couldn't cobble together enough money, and these schools didn't offer him a scholarship. Even after joining the CIA, Malzahn continued to work on a manuscript on political warfare that he had started at Yale as his senior thesis, titled *Mud, Blood and Men: A Study of War Policy and Military Strategy in Britain, 1914–1918*. He began the manuscript by quoting the military theorist Karl von Clausewitz: "We see that war is not merely a political act but a real *political instrument*, a continuation of political intercourse, a carrying out of the same by other means."[4] Malzahn then turned to the problems that Britain and its leaders, such as prime ministers Herbert Asquith and Lloyd George, faced in fighting a global war during World War I. Malzahn concluded that British leaders repeatedly failed to find a balance between the political and military art of war. "If a basic difference develops between the military and civil leaders of the state, this break must be corrected," Malzahn wrote. "Its continuance will lead to a divergence of war policy and military strategy which may well be fatal."[5] Malzahn's work on the manuscript shaped his views that political and covert action—not just guns and ammunition—were important elements of modern warfare.

While conducting research on the manuscript at the Imperial War Museum in England, Malzahn reached out to the legendary British military theorist B. H. Liddell Hart. In a handwritten letter, Malzahn politely requested a meeting: "I would like to discuss a few points that I am confused on with you, as well as hoping you might be able to suggest some sources of information to me that I am not aware of."[6] After they met, Malzahn asked Liddell Hart to review drafts of the manuscript, eventually striking up a correspondence. It became obvious that research and writing were not Malzahn's fortes. Liddell Hart wrote in one letter to Malzahn that "the errors . . . would take me many days to dictate explanatory notes on all of them, and I have got so much urgent work on hand that there is no chance of doing so."[7]

Malzahn never published the manuscript. He came in second in a contest to publish it at Yale University Press, and Macmillan wasn't interested in publishing it either. But Malzahn's focus on the political dimension of warfare, which was just as relevant for cold wars as for hot ones, would help prepare him for America's global struggle against the Soviet Union.

With his academic future now foreclosed, Malzahn's CIA career took off. He married a fellow CIA employee, Mildred Margretha McCormick, in 1959. In 1960, the CIA assigned him to The Hague. During the Vietnam War, he was sent to Saigon, where he worked to penetrate the Viet Cong. In 1972, the CIA moved him to Germany, where he cut his teeth on Soviet—including KGB—covert activity. He worked under chief of station Bill Graver in the Bonn station. In those years, the KGB was active in publicly releasing the names of CIA officers working under State Department cover. Malzahn was "outed" in a left-wing German publication, *Informations-Dienst*, almost certainly with help from the KGB.[8] But, undeterred, he remained in Germany.

During Malzahn's time at the Bonn station, the CIA stumbled upon one of its most important and productive sources of the Cold War. The man was a Pole, no less.

———

IN AUGUST 1972, AN EMPLOYEE at the U.S. embassy in Bonn was sorting through the morning mail when a letter caught his eye.[9] It was postmarked August 11, three days earlier, from Wilhelmshaven, a port on Germany's North Sea coast. The front of the envelope was addressed to "U.S.A. Ambassy Bonn" using a blue felt-tip pen. The letter, which was written in broken English, read:

DEAR SER,

I'M SORRY FOR MY ENGLISH.

I AM AN FORIGEN MAF FROM COMMUNISTISHCE KANTRY. I WANT TO MET (SECRETLY) WITH U.S. ARMY OFFICER (Lt. Colonel, Colonel) 17 OR 18, 19.08 IN AMSTERDAM OR 21, 22 IN OSTENDA. I HAVE NO MANY TIME. I AM WITH MY CAMRADE END THEY KAN'T KNOW.

IN AMSTERDAM I TELEPHONING TO U.S. AMBASY (MILLITARY ATACHE).

P.V.

P.S. THAT OFFICER MUST SPEAK RUSSIAN OR POLISH[10]

The letter was quickly passed to the CIA station chief, John P. Dimmer, Jr., a red-haired, slightly built down easter from Portland, Maine. Dimmer had no idea what "P.V.", the initials used to sign the document, meant. But he sent a cable to CIA headquarters—which had moved from Navy Hill in Washington, DC to McLean, VA a decade before—recommending that Bonn station try to make contact with him. Back in McLean, David Blee, the chief of the Soviet Division, weighed possible options and asked CIA officials at Bonn station to move expeditiously and meet with the letter's author. Dimmer asked Walter Lang, a forty-five-year-old CIA case officer serving under U.S. Army cover, to arrange a meeting with P.V. if he called the embassy.[11] On Thursday, August 17, P.V. kept his promise and called the embassy at 4:30 p.m. Lang took the call and arranged to meet that night at the central railroad station in The Hague between nine and ten o'clock. Lang said his partner, Henry Morton, another CIA case officer, would have a copy of *Time* magazine stashed under his arm.[12] P.V. arrived around 10:10 p.m., and Lang and Morton escorted him to a room in the nearby Central Hotel, where they began one of the most important CIA recruitment efforts of the Cold War.[13]

"My name," the mysterious letter writer said, "is Ryszard Kukliński." He was born in Warsaw on June 13, 1930, and was a lieutenant colonel on the Polish General Staff. Morton displayed his military identification and introduced himself as "Pulkownik Henryk," or "Colonel Henry." Lang described Kukliński as a well-placed and formidable officer: "He is a small man with tousled blond hair, penetrating blue eyes and the gestures and mannerisms of a man within whom an unbounded supply of energy is tightly bottled up. He smiles briefly from time to time, but humor seems to play only a small part of his general behavior pattern." Lang also praised Kukliński's clear vision: "He wanted us to know exactly what he wanted to do, and exactly what he could provide."[14]

———

RYSZARD KUKLIŃSKI WAS BORN to a working-class family. After World War II, Kukliński joined the Polish People's Army. He had a successful career and even helped with preparations for the Warsaw Pact invasion of Czechoslovakia in 1968. After the massacre of Polish workers in Gdańsk by Polish security forces in December 1970, however, Kukliński began to question the legitimacy of Communist rule and the USSR's control over Poland.[15]

Kukliński explained to Lang and Morton that he was captain of the *Legia*, a fifty-foot Polish government yacht with a crew of nine sailors. Kukliński was on a "sight-seeing trip" that was a cover for a Polish Army intelligence mission to spy on Western ports and naval installations. Their mission was to conduct reconnaissance and surveillance of the West European coastlines, rivers, ports, bridges, channels, and canals that they knew only from maps. Kukliński then outlined his motivation for reaching out to the United States. The Polish Army had not chosen to be part of the Soviet sphere of influence. He said Poland's interests were more closely aligned with the West than with Moscow, and he wanted Poland to be free of Soviet hegemony. He did not view the United States as an adversary and believed that the Polish and American armies should open a line of communication for their mutual security. Kukliński said he had reached this conclusion while serving as an officer on the General Staff, where he had access to Polish and Warsaw Pact secrets. For almost nine years, he had been involved in helping plan a "hot war" with the West. But everything he had seen confirmed his belief that Poland was on the wrong side.[16]

Morton asked him what materials he had access to as part of his job. Kukliński replied that he had in-depth knowledge of, and access to, Soviet war plans for Western Europe. These plans included the order of battle for Polish and Warsaw Pact forces in the event of war. Kukliński had extensive knowledge of the latest military exercises, since he had written many of the plans. He could provide reports on Soviet rockets, bombs, and tanks. He had access to classified documents that detailed the mobilization, deployment, and stationing of Warsaw Pact troops. He could also provide copies of the top secret Soviet journal *Voyennaya mysl'* (*Military Thought*). Overall, Kukliński assessed that NATO had a significant blind spot in its knowledge of Soviet war strategies, and he wanted to help close that gap to prevent war.[17]

Kukliński suggested that he and several colleagues could conduct subversive actions in the event of an unprovoked and surprise Soviet attack on the West. But Morton responded that the best way for Kukliński to achieve his goals was by operating alone and keeping the United States informed about their mutual enemy, the Soviet Union. "I will tell you all I know," Kukliński said. "You can copy all of my documents . . . When I help you, I am helping my country."[18] In the cable back to CIA headquarters, Lang described Kukliński as earnest, determined, and intelligent. "It seems we are indeed dealing with a man of far above [average] intelligence and talents," he wrote. He guessed that Kuklinksi was about five feet, nine inches tall, and 150 pounds "of solid bone and muscle." Lang then added: "Although I am his size and have at least a 10-pound advantage on him, I have the feeling I would not like to box, wrestle, or go at him in any way physically. He is one tough hombre." As Lang explained, Kukliński appeared sincere in his desire to prevent an East-West war and was acutely aware of the risks entailed: "I had the feeling he was scarcely nervous at all. Nervous or not, he certainly knows what his association with us means in real terms and it takes a brave man, knowing this, to take the step he took . . . He was there for business and was all business. I'm glad he's on our side." The cable ended with the team's observation that Kukliński was having a "catharsis" and was "torn with conflicts between his success in the world and Western idealism."[19]

As Lang and Morton wrapped up their meeting with Kukliński at the Central Hotel, Lang had one more burning question.

"What does P.V. mean," he inquired.

"I am the Polish Viking," Kukliński responded with a smile, thrusting his right index finger toward the ceiling.[20]

The CIA would eventually give Kukliński the name GULL, a nod to his passion for the sea. Over the next decade, Kukliński became a wildly productive source, averaging six exchanges per year and providing over 40,000 pages of Polish, Soviet, and Warsaw Pact documents to the CIA.[21] The classified documents described Soviet plans to attack NATO, the location of Soviet command-and-control bunkers, and Soviet techniques to foil spy satellite detection. As Bill Casey later remarked: "In the last forty years, no one has done more damage to communism than that Pole."[22]

———

BY 1980, CASEY AND MALZAHN had still never met—and they wouldn't until early 1981. But both had a passion for covert action, which would fundamentally reshape CIA activity in the 1980s. The only missing piece was the election of Ronald Reagan.

Over the spring and summer of 1980, Casey, who was by then Reagan's campaign manager, went everywhere with the candidate. Casey was initially stunned. As the historian Joseph Persico wrote, he "saw Reagan initiate nothing, give no orders, decide virtually nothing." Shortly after Casey took over as campaign director, Reagan remarked: "You're the expert, Bill. Just point me in the right direction and I'll go."[23]

Chapter 5

DUTCH

From his perch atop the podium at the Republican National Convention in Detroit, Ronald Reagan looked out at the audience and flashed his trademark grin. It was July 17, 1980. Bill Casey had helped focus Reagan's fumbling campaign. Before Casey, manager John Sears had repeatedly butted heads with Reagan's advisors like Ed Meese and Michael Deaver. Casey now watched Reagan work the crowd, who would barely let him speak.

"With a deep awareness of the responsibility conferred by your trust, I accept your nomination for the presidency of the United States," Reagan started in, as the frenzied crowd waved American flags, blared foghorns, and hopped out of their seats.

Over the course of his speech, Reagan chastised President Jimmy Carter's "mediocre leadership" in which America "drifts from one crisis to the next, eroding our national will and purpose." He lamented a "disintegrating economy" and an "energy policy based on the sharing of scarcity." Above all, he eviscerated Carter for a "sorry chapter" in U.S. national security. "America's defense strength is at its lowest ebb in a generation, while the Soviet Union is vastly outspending us in both strategic and conventional arms," Reagan thundered. "Our European allies, looking nervously at the growing menace from the East, turn to us for leadership and fail to find it."[1] Reagan served the audience a red-blooded Republican message: he advocated a strong defense, lower taxes, and leaner government.

Reagan stood six feet, one inch, with blue eyes, neatly parted dense hair, and wide shoulders set back. Even in private, he exuded the charisma of a Hollywood celebrity, though he hadn't acted in a movie since the 1964 crime film *The Killers*, in which he played the mob boss Jack Browning. Reagan had a shy tilt of the head and a puckish, lopsided grin that was disarming even for his political opponents. He was hard of hearing in his right ear from an ill-timed pistol shot near his head during a shootout scene, most likely while making the 1939 film *Code of the Secret Service*.[2] Reagan was now less than four months away from becoming the most powerful man in the world, the captain of a ship still caught in the tempest of the Cold War. Was he up to the task? Few would have guessed that the C student at Eureka College and former actor would ever have gone this far.

———

BORN IN TAMPICO, ILLINOIS, on February 6, 1911, Ronald Wilson Reagan was simply "Dutch" to his father, Jack, who thought he looked like a "fat little Dutchman." Much like Bill Casey, Reagan came from a family of Irish Catholics. But unlike Casey, Reagan never took to Catholicism. He followed in his mother Nelle's footsteps, who felt more comfortable worshiping under a Presbyterian roof. After graduating from Eureka College, Reagan held several jobs as a radio announcer. In April 1937, he traveled to California to cover spring training for the Chicago Cubs. With the help of a friend, Joy Hodges, Reagan finagled his way into meeting a talent agent, Bill Meiklejohn. Reagan took a screen test for Warner Bros. and did well. After returning to his home in Des Moines, he received a telegram from Meiklejohn on April 20, which said:

WARNER OFFERS CONTRACT SEVEN YEARS STOP
ONE YEAR OPTION STOP STARTING $200 A WEEK STOP
WHAT SHALL I DO.

Reagan wasted no time in responding:

SIGN BEFORE THEY CHANGE THEIR MINDS.[3]

While Reagan mostly acted in "B" movies, one of his few break-
throughs was *Knute Rockne, All American* (1940), the story of Notre
Dame's legendary football coach. The actor Pat O'Brien played Rockne,
and Reagan secured the role of terminally ill George "the Gipper" Gipp.
On his deathbed, Gipp told Rockne in a scene that Reagan would replay
for the rest of his life: "Someday, when things are tough, maybe you can
ask the boys to go in there and win just once for the Gipper."[4]

By 1947, age thirty-six, Reagan had started to develop political acu-
men and, importantly, a growing abhorrence of Communism.[5] Much like
Bill Casey in his early years, Reagan was a committed New Dealer and
had joined the Hollywood Democratic Committee, an organization that
supported the policies and the reelection of Franklin D. Roosevelt. But
the committee also had several alleged Communists in its midst, Reagan believed. Reagan became a member of the Screen Actors Guild, an
American labor union that represented film and television performers,
and became its president in 1947. Looking around the world, Reagan
became increasingly concerned about the tendency of Communist soci-
eties to squelch basic freedoms.[6] A few years later, he penned an article
for the magazine *Fortnight*, arguing that the "real fight with this new
totalitarianism belongs to the forces of liberal democracy, just as did the
battle with Hitler's totalitarianism."[7]

———

THURSDAY, OCTOBER 23, 1947, was an unusually balmy fall day in Washington. Outside, the temperature swelled to nearly ninety degrees by the

early afternoon. Inside the Old House Office Building on Capitol Hill, the political thermometer was even hotter as visitors crowded into a cramped room for hearings before the House Un-American Activities Committee. Originally established in 1938 to identify American citizens with Nazi ties, the committee focused after World War II on investigating disloyalty and subversive activities by those Americans suspected of having ties with the Communist Party. A coterie of Hollywood's most glamorous stars would be testifying today.

The flashbulbs exploded from excited cameramen as Ronald Reagan's lanky figure rose and wound its way through the maze of chairs, tables, and press. Reagan wore a khaki suit, neatly pressed white dress shirt, and blue knit tie, with his hair tidily combed. He was tall, with broad shoulders and lanky swimmer's arms that hung down below his torso. Reagan approached the front, halted, and held his right hand up as he took the oath. He appeared relaxed and self-assured, grinning affably.[8] Reagan was a "friendly" witness, along with several other Hollywood actors, because of his strong anti-Communist views.

Robert Stripling, chief investigator for the committee, turned to Reagan and began the questioning. "As a member of the board of directors, as president of the Screen Actors Guild, and as an active member, have you at any time observed or noted within the organization a clique of either Communists or Fascists who were attempting to exert influence or pressure on the guild?" Stripling asked.

"There has been a small group within the Screen Actors Guild which has consistently opposed the policy of the guild board and officers of the guild, as evidenced by the vote on various issues," Reagan politely responded. "That small clique referred to has been suspected of more or less following the tactics that we associated with the Communist Party."

"Would you refer to them as a disruptive influence within the guild?" Stripling interjected.

Reagan paused for a moment and then answered. "I would say that at times they have attempted to be a disruptive influence."

Stripling persisted, digging for more specifics. "You have no knowl-edge yourself as to whether or not any of them are members of the Communist Party?" he inquired.

"No, sir," Reagan replied, almost innocently. "I have no investigative force, or anything, and I do not know."

Stripling then moved dangerously into hearsay, asking Reagan to speculate. "Has it ever been reported to you that certain members of the guild were Communists?" he inquired.

"Yes, sir," said Reagan, choosing his words carefully. "I have heard different discussions and some of them tagged as Communists."

Stripling found an opening. "Would you say that this clique has attempted to dominate the guild?"

Reagan hesitated. "Well, sir, by attempting to put over their own par-ticular views on various issues . . ." he began.

"Mr. Reagan," Stripling interrupted, getting to the committee's broader concerns, "there has been testimony to the effect here that numer-ous Communist front organizations have been set up in Hollywood. Have you ever been solicited to join any of those organizations or any organiza-tion which you consider to be a Communist front organization?"

Reagan nodded that he had. "Well, sir," he answered, "I have received literature from an organization called the Committee for a Far-Eastern Democratic Policy. I don't know whether it is Communist or not. I only know that I didn't like their views and as a result I didn't want to have anything to do with them."

"Would you say from your observation that this is typical of the tactics or strategy of the Communists, to solicit and use the names of prominent people to either raise money or gain support," Stripling then queried.

"I think it is in keeping with their tactics, yes, sir," said Reagan.

"Do you think there is anything democratic about those tactics?" Stripling persisted.

"I do not, sir," answered Reagan.

Stripling now turned to recommendations. "Mr. Reagan," he asked, "what is your feeling about what steps should be taken to rid the motion-picture industry of any Communist influences?"

In answering, Reagan emphasized the principles of a democratic society and the importance of free speech. "Well, sir," he said assuredly, "ninety-nine percent of us are pretty well aware of what is going on, and I think, within the bounds of our democratic rights and never once stepping over the rights given us by democracy, we have done a pretty good job in our business of keeping those people's activities curtailed. After all, we must recognize them at present as a political party. On that basis we have exposed their lies when we came across them, we have opposed their propaganda, and I can certainly testify that in the case of the Screen Actors Guild we have been eminently successful in preventing them from, with their usual tactics, trying to run a majority of an organization with a well-organized minority. In opposing those people, the best thing to do is make democracy work."

Reagan ended his testimony by urging caution. He suggested that the U.S. government not adopt anti-democratic practices in its efforts to root out Soviet and Communist groups in the United States—an observation that anticipated Joseph McCarthy's anti-Communist witch hunts, which would begin two and a half years later. "Sir, I detest, I abhor their philosophy, but I detest more than that their tactics, which are those of the fifth column, and are dishonest, but at the same time I never as a citizen want to see our country become urged, by either fear or resentment of this group that we ever compromise with any of our democratic principles through that fear or resentment. I still think that democracy can do it."[9]

———

IN ADDITION TO HIS WILLINGNESS to testify before the House Un-American Activities Committee, Reagan also became an FBI informant. Under the source codename T-10, he provided confidential information about the role and identity of alleged Communists active in Hollywood, fingering several Screen Actors Guild members whom he suspected of being Communists.[10] Reagan held a strong aversion to Communism and the Soviet Union, as he wrote in an article in January 1951 that explained who was a "Red":

> Suppose we quit using the word Communist and Communism ... Substitute "pro-Russian" for the word Communist and watch the confusion disappear ... Democracy does guarantee the right of every man to think as he pleases, to speak freely and to advocate his beliefs. Democracy also provides defense against those who would deliver our nation into the hands of a foreign despot. Call them pro-Russian and take away the screen. If we must fight, make the enemy be properly uniformed.[11]

This was a challenging time for Reagan. His movie career was declining. His first wife, actress Jane Wyman, divorced him. Actress Patricia Neal bumped into a sullen Reagan at a Hollywood party. "His wife, Jane Wyman, had just announced their separation," Neal remarked. "And it was sad because he did not want a divorce. I remember he went outside. An older woman went with him. He cried."[12] Around this time, Reagan encountered Nancy Davis. He was not smitten with Nancy at first, and he continued to date other women. Perhaps unsurprisingly, Nancy found him somewhat detached. "Although he loves people, he often seems remote, and he doesn't let anybody get too close," she said. "He lets me come closer than anyone else, but there are times when even I feel that barrier."[13] Reagan soon warmed up to Nancy, and they began dating. On March 4, 1952, they were married at The Little Brown Church in the San Fernando Valley.

In 1954, General Electric hired Reagan to host an American anthology series titled *General Electric Theater*, which was broadcast on CBS radio and television. General Electric wanted someone with broad appeal who could act as a television host and company spokesman. The work rejuvenated Reagan. He visited hundreds of General Electric plants,

Rotary clubs, and Moose lodges, honing his public-speaking skills. In addition to signing "the fattest TV deal ever signed," according to movie columnist Hedda Hopper, Reagan also discovered something else: he enjoyed speaking to large audiences.[14]

———

As Reagan stumped for General Electric on television, radio, and in person, the U.S. government ramped up its own efforts, led by the CIA, to beam radio programs into Eastern Europe. A few years before, a group of prominent American businessmen, lawyers, and philanthropists—including Allen Dulles, who later became director of central intelligence—had launched the National Committee for Free Europe in New York City. Only a handful of people knew that the Free Europe Committee, as it was eventually called, was actually the public face of a political warfare program undertaken by the CIA. That operation, which soon gave rise to Radio Free Europe (RFE), would become another successful covert action campaign during the Cold War after QRBERETTA and the CIA's support to *Kultura*.[15]

RFE was designed to leverage émigré communities from Soviet-controlled areas of Eastern Europe to help undermine Soviet power and promote U.S. national interests. As CIA and State Department officials acknowledged, the use of radio programming was "essentially an instrument of psychological warfare" with several purposes: (1) keep alive "the hope of liberation in the satellite states"; (2) undermine efforts by Eastern European regimes "in their efforts to achieve full control of production and economic integration with the USSR"; (3) cause "doubts and fears among the quislings of the satellites" and encourage "high level defections"; and (4) encourage "an atmosphere favorable to the growth of resistance movements, for ultimate exploitation in war, or, at a propitious moment, in peace time."[16] These aims dovetailed with the establishment of the Office of Policy Coordination and its core goals:

The ultimate objective of U.S. policy toward the satellite states of eastern Europe is to weaken the grip of the Soviet Union upon them with the eventual aim of eliminating preponderant Soviet power there and enabling these nations to exist as free members of the European community . . . The western powers should maintain a strong propaganda offensive against the Communist regimes of eastern Europe, through radio broadcasts and all other available means, in order to maintain the morale of the people and to hinder efforts to establish full Soviet control in these nations, although western propaganda should not promise imminent liberation or encourage active revolt.[17]

There were obvious advantages in utilizing Polish and other émigrés. They came from countries the United States wanted to target, spoke local languages and dialects, understood local matters, possessed networks of family and friends back in Eastern Europe, and already harbored grievances toward their respective regimes. As the CIA soon discovered, however, there were plenty of downsides. Some individuals were far removed from local debates, others lacked substantial connections and influence, and many couldn't get along with each other. Frank Altschul, an investment banker who served on the Free Europe Committee's first board of directors, complained to Director of Central Intelligence Dulles that the committee was sometimes weakened by bureaucratic conflict and marginalized exile leaders.[18]

Editorial policy guidelines for Polish broadcasts during this period emphasized exposing the Bierut regime's "national front" as a Communist tool, reporting peasant resistance to collectivization, and denouncing regime officials.[19] In the words of Frank Wisner, director of the Office of Policy Coordination, the aim was to "compete within each country as an indigenous national station."[20] Regular programs included ten-minute newscasts at the top of every hour, political satire, talks by prominent Poles in exile, readings of books banned in Poland, and broader developments in the Communist world.[21] In the inaugural radio commentary to Polish listeners in May 1952, Jan Nowak-Jezioranski remarked:

> The struggle is being waged not in the forests, streets, or in the underground but in Polish souls—within the four walls of a Polish home. It is this struggle we wish to join here on the airwaves of Radio Free Europe ... We will tell you the truth ... which the Soviet regime wants to hide from you in order to kill the remnants of hope in your minds ... We will battle Russification ... We will counter the attempts to falsify our history and traditions. The day will come when the dawn of freedom will light up the Warsaw sky. It will be a day of triumph, your triumph.[22]

The CIA—and the U.S. government more broadly—wanted to avoid giving false hopes to Poles. One CIA memo indicated that the Soviets were serious about controlling Poland and other Eastern European states. "It would seem contrary to our best interests," the memo concluded, "to undertake any action which might be construed as sponsoring active opposition to the Soviets within any part of the Soviet Bloc."[23] Frank Altschul articulated a common sentiment that encouraging Poles to overthrow their regime would provoke a bloodbath in a country where the United States had no intention of directly intervening. "Our view in Radio Free Europe," Altschul wrote, "has been that in the present phase of the cold war to incite uprising in the prisoner states would be equivalent to inviting the mass suicide of our best friends in these countries."[24] Radio broadcasts supported passive resistance to the Soviet Union and the Soviet-backed government in Warsaw, but not active, violent resistance.

Still, CIA programs played a useful role in Eastern Europe. As Director Dulles argued, CIA propaganda efforts likely had "little practical effect in the Soviet heartland" and were more "valuable if directed at the periphery and Satellite areas."[25] In response, Soviet and Eastern

European intelligence agencies attempted to jam radio signals.[26] Soviet media outlets denounced individuals like Jerzy Giedroyc as imperialist stooges and CIA spies.[27] Radio Free Europe was a particular thorn in the side of Eastern European governments. The head of East Germany's foreign intelligence service, Markus Wolf, remarked that Radio Free Europe and similar programs "provided excellent counterpropaganda" and "were fast on their feet when any sign of instability arose in the Eastern bloc."[28] A classified Polish government document warned that the CIA was using radio stations and other forms of propaganda to elicit "provocative calls on Polish workers to lower their work efficiency" and to "cause activation of all sorts of hostile elements."[29] RFE programs broadcast revelations of terror by the Polish Communist Party thanks to Józef Światło, a senior Polish secret police official who defected to the West in 1953.[30]

It was only a matter of time before Poles lost their patience with their Soviet-backed regime. Adam Ważyk's "Poemat dla dorosłych" ("Poem for Adults") was viewed by some as a harbinger of things to come as Poles became disillusioned under the Soviet shadow:

> They ran to us shouting
> "Under Socialism
> A cut finger does not hurt."
> But they felt pain.
> They lost faith.
> . . .
>
> We should make demands on this earth,
> Which we didn't win in a game of chance,
> Which cost the lives of millions,
> Demands for the plain truth, for the harvest of freedom,
> For fiery, good sense,
> For fiery good sense.
> We should make demands daily.
> We should make demands of the Party.[31]

———

BY THE LATE 1960S, AS THE CIA BEAMED radio programs into Poland, Ronald Reagan had settled into his job as governor of California. He had switched from the Democratic to the Republican Party a few years earlier. "I didn't leave the Democratic Party" he famously quipped. "The party left me."[32] Reagan was elected following a bitter campaign against Governor Pat Brown, the Democratic incumbent. Brown had written a twenty-nine-page vitriolic attack titled "Ronald Reagan, Extremist Collaborator."[33] Abandoning decency, Brown had even remarked to a group of children in a thirty-minute campaign film: "You know I'm running against an actor. Remember this: you know who shot Abraham Lincoln, don't ya?"[34] Reagan refused to take the bait. He had changed considerably over time, both physically and emotionally. He had begun to age. Laugh lines created long seams in his face, which curved around his mouth. A set of shorter lines emanated from under his eye sockets and stretched down toward his cheekbones.[35] Reagan viewed the world in absolutist terms. "He is a guy who sees everything as all good or bad, no gray scale at all," remarked Robert "Macho Bob" Moretti, speaker of the California State Assembly.[36]

Reagan's extraordinary leap to political stardom drew national attention. In an exposé titled "A Guide to Reagan Country," the influential political scientist James Q. Wilson wrote that "Reagan Country," as he termed it, was neither small town nor urban. Instead, it consisted of suburban, homogenous, mostly Protestant communities of detached houses and lawns linked, often over great distances, by cars that seemed to put no price on gas. "I grew up in Reagan country—not Hollywood, but the lower-middle-class suburbs of Los Angeles," Wilson wrote.[37] Reagan's charisma and populism were attractive to many Californians. But whether they translated to Americans more broadly would soon be tested.

Reagan surrounded himself with a band of competent advisors, several of whom would play key roles during his presidency. William

"Bill" Clark, Jr., a rancher who had impressed Reagan as a county-level campaign organizer, was his chief of staff and later a justice of the state supreme court. Clark was a seemly, shy Californian, but tough as a piece of rawhide. He shared with Reagan a belief in the virtues of small government, military might, and anti-Communist resolve, along with a passion for horseback riding. Caspar W. Weinberger of San Francisco, better known as "Cap," was perhaps even tougher. Reagan's finance director, the former California assemblyman and chairman of the California Republican party, was eminently self-assured and a tenacious debater.[38] Finally, Edwin "Ed" Meese, III, a military intelligence officer and lawyer, served as Reagan's legal affairs secretary and later as his executive assistant and chief of staff.

Reagan focused mostly on domestic issues as governor—from confronting rioters at the University of California, Berkeley, to balancing the state budget and battling to curtail welfare spending. But he kept an eye on international matters. He remained deeply distrustful of the Soviet Union and its global expansion. A few years before his inauguration as governor, Reagan had given a speech in support of Barry Goldwater's presidential run. In the speech, which was aired on national television, Reagan invoked the souls of Poles and other populations under Soviet domination. "Is there not something of hypocrisy," he asked, with his voice rising in tone and self-assurance, "in assailing our allies for so-called vestiges of colonialism while we engage in a conspiracy of silence about the peoples enslaved by the Soviet colonies in the satellite nations?"[39]

After serving his two terms as governor, Reagan continued his crusade against the Soviet Union. In one radio address, he invoked the domino theory, which asserted that the fall of any country to the Soviet Union would risk the fate of an entire region. "Those who ridicule the domino theory believed it when Hitler was picking off small nations in Europe thirty-seven years ago," he remarked. "They just don't believe it applies when the enemy is Communist and the countries losing their freedom are Asian." Reagan believed that appeasement was not a worthy option.

"The term domino theory very simply describes what happens to our allies if we back down and let one ally be taken over by the communists because we don't want to be bothered."[40]

As Reagan surveyed the world, he saw Washington appeasing Moscow. He viewed Poland as a good example of falling dominos in Eastern Europe and lamented that "the young people of Poland had been born and raised and spent their entire lives under communist atheism."[41]

———

BY THE LATE 1970S, AS REAGAN WEIGHED running for president in the 1980 election, U.S. government officials led by President Carter's Polish-born national security adviser, Zbigniew Brzezinski, pushed for a more assertive policy in Eastern Europe.[42] This approach did not involve providing weapons to opposition groups, as the CIA would do in Afghanistan after the Soviet invasion in 1979. Instead, Brzezinski supported greater funding for Radio Free Europe and Radio Liberty, acknowledging: "I felt strongly that the Radio offered us the best means for influencing the internal political transformation of Communist systems and that more use should be made of this vital instrument."[43] Brzezinski had successfully helped fight off efforts by Senator William Fulbright to slash funding for Radio Free Europe and Radio Liberty, and he believed that Radio Free Europe's Polish Service was among the most important sources of information for Poles.[44]

Brzezinski and Carter also supported continuing CIA efforts to smuggle publications about democracy and regional cultures to the Soviet Union and Eastern Europe.[45] The "book program," as it was called, was a CIA covert action effort that began in 1956 and helped circulate nearly ten million émigré books, journals, and newspapers in Russian and Eastern European languages behind the Iron Curtain.[46] Among the many anti-Communist works distributed by the CIA and its assets was Czesław Miłosz's *The Captive Mind*.[47]

Brzezinski's objectives were modest. CIA and other U.S. government programs could be used to modify regime behavior and encourage political transformation in Poland and Eastern Europe, he believed,
but they should not be used to foment insurrection or regime change.[48]
With White House support, the CIA continued to wage an ideological
war against the Soviet Union and its satellite countries, however limited.
Both Soviet and Polish officials closely monitored these efforts.[49]

As one Soviet document concluded, CIA and other U.S. government
information programs were designed to conduct a "global psychological
war against the USSR and socialist countries" and to target the ideology
of Communism.[50] KGB reports increasingly voiced alarm at CIA propaganda efforts.[51] The KGB was also concerned about the growing opposition movement in Poland. On a trip to Poland in August 1979, General
Oleg Kalugin, the KGB's chief of counterintelligence, came away with
a sinking feeling that "there was a real problem" and that trade union
unrest represented "the beginning of the end" for the Soviets in Poland.[52]
One secret document from the Polish Ministry of Internal Affairs
(*Ministerstwo Spraw Wewnętrznych*, or MSW) suggested more aggressive and effective steps to jam Radio Free Europe and identify its personnel and plans. The document also encouraged Polish security officials to
continue "surveillance on the activities of the Roman Catholic clergy"
because of the church's sympathy for opposition groups.[53]

Soviet attempts to undermine Polish opposition were confounded
by a new actor in the struggle for freedom. Cardinal Karol Wojtyła, archbishop of Kraków, who was born in the Polish town of Wadowice, was
elected pope and took the name John Paul II. He was the first non-Italian
pope in 450 years, and he visited Poland in June 1979.[54] The arrival of
John Paul II was momentous and precipitated an alliance between Polish
workers, the intelligentsia, and the Catholic Church.

Lech Wałęsa was thrilled by the selection of a Polish pope and hoped
that Wojtyła's elevation might provide a boost to Poland's oppressed
workers. Bill Casey, a devout Catholic, viewed the pope as a potential

ally against the Soviet Union. So did Reagan. But a Polish pope could not have come at a worse time for Wojciech Jaruzelski, whose leadership was called into greater question by the rising influence of the pontiff. The country's troubles were increasing daily.

By 1980, the British historian Timothy Garton Ash observed that Polish leaders "were like the pilots of an airliner which has gone into a nosedive."[55]

PART II

Chapter 6

THE GDAŃSK AGREEMENT

In July 1980, the same month that Ronald Reagan addressed the Republican National Committee, the Polish government announced with little warning that it had raised the price of food and other consumer goods. Meat prices ballooned by as much as 60 to 90 percent. The price rises occurred in the midst of an already fragile political situation. The Polish economy was in a free fall, with declining growth rates, falling living standards, rising inflation, and shortages of consumer goods. Polish workers were also better organized through such groups as the Workers' Defense Committee, or KOR. It was an explosive combination. In early July, strikes erupted across Poland as anger swelled against the Gierek regime. Poles fumed about the income disparities between government officials and the public. Communist Party elites had access to stores where food was plentiful, and factory managers frequently received special allotments of meat and other groceries to share with family and friends.[1]

CIA analysts who were closely following these developments prepared a classified memorandum on July 20, warning that the labor disputes could lead to a Polish military response. The memorandum said that prior agreements between labor unions and the government had

become unglued and warned that if "the Polish leadership proved incapable of restoring order in a situation that had deteriorated into violent
confrontation, we believe the Soviets would, as a last resort, intervene."[2]
The stakes were high. Polish security agencies were also paranoid about
CIA activity in Poland, accusing the CIA of conducting "ideological sabotage" through Radio Free Europe.[3] As one sensitive Polish government
document explained, the CIA's objective was "attacking the internal situation in our country . . . with the goal of undermining Polish society."[4]
The KGB was equally concerned, noting in one top secret memo that the
CIA and other NATO intelligence agencies were waging a broad ideological war against the Soviet Union, including in such Eastern European
countries as Poland.[5]

There was, of course, some truth to Moscow and Warsaw's fears.
Reagan, who was in the final sprint of his presidential campaign on a
strong anti-Soviet platform, viewed the rise of Poland's labor opposition
as a fleeting opportunity to support a legitimate democratic movement
and undermine Soviet control in Eastern Europe. This put Poland in a
precarious position, torn between Wojciech Jaruzelski's government and
the Solidarity-led opposition movement; between the Soviet Union and
the United States; and between fiercely national Polish officials and Soviet
leaders alarmed that their stranglehold on Eastern Europe was slipping.

Unsurprisingly, Gdańsk—the hotbed of Polish opposition—was the
site of this dramatic struggle.

———

JUST BEFORE DAWN ON AUGUST 14, 1980, Lech Wałęsa—squat, square-
shouldered, and sporting a large mustache and a furrowed brow—stepped
out of his two-bedroom apartment in the Stogi quarter of Gdańsk. As
Wałęsa made his way to the Gdańsk Shipyard in the darkness, his shad-
owy silhouette moved across the street. He heard the wail of sirens in the
distance, an indication that a workers' strike had started. Glancing
around, he spotted an unmarked police car surely following him.

He hopped on a streetcar for the thirty-five-minute trek to the Lenin Shipyard. A million questions raced through his head. What if the strike was just what the police wanted? How were the police planning to respond? Would they gun down the strikers, as they did in December 1970?[6] Earlier that morning, activists had distributed leaflets and special copies of the *Coastal Worker* on streetcars and other strategic locations across the city. The trigger for the strikes was the sacking of Anna Walentynowicz (pronounced AN-a val-en-teen-OH-vitch) from the shipyard. Warmly referred to as "Pani Ania," or Mrs. Ania, she was a stout, soft-spoken, self-effacing woman in her early fifties who had worked for thirty years in the Lenin Shipyard as a welder and then a crane operator. Like many in the workers' movement, Walentynowicz held meetings in her house, where individuals discussed political issues and shared copies of opposition publications like the *Coastal Worker* and books like Aleksandr Solzhenitsyn's *Gulag Archipelago*.

In early August, only three months before Walentynowicz's retirement, the shipyard fired her after police accused her of stealing. Her alleged "crime" had been collecting candle stubs from a nearby graveyard to melt down and refashion into new candles for the anniversary of the December 1970 killing of Polish workers. But it was Walentynowicz's participation in the opposition movement that put her on the police radar. After the shipyard fired her, the response in Gdańsk was volcanic. "It was the drop that caused the cup of bitterness to overflow," Walentynowicz recalled.[7] For Gdańsk workers like Wałęsa, it was time to fight back, even though the timing was somewhat inauspicious. "I was haunted . . . by the feeling that August had come too soon, that we needed a year or two more of hard work to prepare" for organized resistance, said Wałęsa.[8]

But time was now something in short supply.

———

By 6:00 a.m., laborers from the K-1 and K-3 sections of the Lenin Shipyard stopped work and demanded the reinstatement of Walentynowicz and a 1,000-złoty pay increase (roughly $30).[9] They set off from the locker rooms on a march, bearing aloft makeshift banners and shouting to their colleagues to join them. Workers placed aside their blowtorches and scrambled down from half-finished ships. When the group of workers, which soon ballooned to over a hundred, reached the main gate, some wanted to spill out onto the streets as they had in 1970. "You know what happened in front of this gate in 1970!" several young leaders warned.[10] They barely managed to curb the surge forward by suggesting a moment of silence in memory of those killed in December 1970, and then sang the national anthem in unison. Alarmed at the deteriorating situation, Klemens Gniech, the director of the shipyard, climbed onto an excavator and promised negotiations—but only if the strikers first returned to work. The crowd of shipyard workers started to waver.[11]

Right then, Wałęsa hopped on the excavator behind Gniech. He tapped the director on the shoulder. "Remember me?" he said. "I worked here for ten years, and I still feel I'm a shipyard worker. I have the confidence of the workers here. It's four years since I lost my job."[12] The spirited electrician was an immensely charismatic figure—and the crowd roared its support for Wałęsa. Gniech backed down. Under Wałęsa's leadership, the workers formed a strike committee with delegates from the shipyard. Negotiations commenced in the Health and Safety Hall, where Wałęsa squared off against Gniech across a long table in the neon-lit hall. The workers now had five primary demands: the return of Anna Walentynowicz and Lech Wałęsa to their jobs at the shipyard; a 2,000-złoty pay increase; family allowances similar to those allotted to the police; an assurance that there would be no reprisals against the strikers; and a permanent monument to those killed in December 1970.[13]

Around noon on Saturday, August 16, most of the strike committee agreed to the management's offer of a 1,500-złoty pay increase. Gniech rushed off to announce that all employees needed to leave the shipyard by 6:00 p.m., since the strike was over. But there was trouble in the ranks. Wałęsa was confronted by furious delegates from other striking factories who had come to the Gdańsk shipyard.

"We've won!" Wałęsa had celebrated.

"You've lost," a colleague, Zdzich Zlotkowski, protested. "Just take a look at what's happening in the yard: cables cut and loudspeakers split with axes; they're writing 'Traitor' and 'Informer' on the walls, they're spitting at the very mention of your name. If you go out the door, they'll stone you."

Wałęsa was flabbergasted. "Jesus, what have I done?" he pleaded.

"What have you done?" Zlotkowski replied. "You've sold the lot of us, that's what you've done. You've only looked after yourself. You're among those who'll be getting the 1,500 złoty pay raise!"

"What should I do now?" Wałęsa asked, feeling helpless.

"Get a real strike going, to defend all the small factories that supported you," Zlotkowski implored, not just the Gdańsk Shipyard.

Wałęsa grabbed a microphone and shouted, "If you want to go on with the strike, it will go on! Who wants to go on with the strike?"

"We do!" the crowd thundered.

"Who doesn't want to go on with the strike?" Wałęsa asked.

Silence.

"So the strike goes on!" he shouted to the frenzied crowd. "I'll be the last to leave the yard."[14]

Wałęsa's turnabout was abrupt, but fully in keeping with his character. One of his great gifts was the ability to feel the pulse of a crowd and improvise. The strike would continue, but now as a *solidarity* strike among all those in Poland that had joined the Lenin Shipyard workers. This was a major turning point for the Polish opposition and purged the strike leadership of those motivated primarily to secure pay raises. Pouring into the opposition movement came delegates from some twenty factories in the Gdańsk area and activists from the Young Poland Movement and the fundamental Movement for Defense of Human and Civic Rights (*Ruch Obrony Praw Człowieka I Obywatela*, or ROPCiO).[15] The pen—or, perhaps more appropriately, the printer—was a critical weapon of the opposition movement. The *Strajkowy Biuletyn Informacyjny Solidarność*, or *Solidarity Strike Information Bulletin*, was the official journal of the striking shipyard workers. It contained information about the strikers' demands, along with poetry, interviews, and features.

In the next twenty-four hours, the chain-smoking Wałęsa and other labor activists took two momentous steps. First, they formed an Inter-Factory Strike Committee comprising two representatives from each striking enterprise. Second, they put together a list of twenty-one demands, which were written in charcoal block letters and blood-red numbers on two plywood boards.[16] The boards were mounted on Gate Number Two and became the iconic symbols of the August 1980 strike.[17]

At nine o'clock in the morning on Sunday, August 17, Father Henryk Jankowski, the parish priest at nearby St. Bridget's Church in Gdańsk, celebrated mass at a roughly hewn altar inside Gate Number Two before several thousand workers. After mass, workers planted a wooden cross in front of the gate to honor the fallen shipyard workers of December 1970.[18] There was a carnival atmosphere, and loudspeakers blared out the 1966 Beatles song "Yellow Submarine." Wałęsa was popular because he was one of the workers, the embodiment of the "little man." Each day during his "vespers," he updated workers on their struggle with the authorities (or *władza*).[19]

On Friday, August 22, Deputy Prime Minister Mieczysław Jagielski agreed to open negotiations with the Inter-Factory Strike Committee. He arrived the next day. As Jagielski's bus pulled up to the Gdańsk Shipyard to begin discussions at the Health and Safety Hall, he was met by an angry crowd that raised their fists and shouted "Get out! Walk to the workers! On your knees!"[20] It was an anguishing experience for Jagielski, as he later recalled: "The walk through that lane of shipyard workers was the longest of my life. I felt their hostility, it was horrific . . . I had no support. I was alone, left entirely to myself, and I needed to respond to the questions they were asking. I had no contact with the central authorities, no instructions."[21] But Jagielski had the backing of the security services. If the talks broke down, the army and the ZOMO—the regime's paramilitary police established to deal with riots and other civil disturbances—

were prepared to arrest significant numbers of demonstrators in an operation codenamed "Lato '80" ("Summer '80"). The country was on the precipice.

On Saturday, August 30, workers hung an oversized banner above the main gate that read: "Proletarians of all factories—unite!" About 10:30 a.m., Jagielski arrived and heartily shook hands all around. He accepted many of the demands. Wałęsa smiled and was carried through the sea of workers to the main gate. "*Sto lat, sto lat*" many of them sang ("let him live for a hundred years"), the Polish equivalent of "For he's a jolly good fellow."[22] On Sunday, August 31, representatives of the Inter-Factory Strike Committee and the Communist regime signed what became known as the "Gdańsk Agreement" in the Health and Safety Hall, a short walk from gate number two of the Lenin Shipyard. Wałęsa read a short prepared statement:

> This is a success for both sides. Kochani! [Beloved] We return to work on 1 September. We all know what that day reminds us of, of what we think . . . of the fatherland . . . of the family which is called Poland . . . We got all we could in the present situation. And we will achieve the rest, because we now have the most important thing: Our IN-DE-PEN-DENT SELF-GOVERNING TRADE UNIONS. That is our guarantee for the future . . . I declare the strike ended.[23]

A roar went up from the crowd. Everyone rose and sang the Polish national anthem, with Jagielski and Wałęsa facing each other across a Formica table. Wałęsa thanked Jagielski. "There are no winners and no losers," he remarked, "no victors and no vanquished . . . We have settled, as Pole talks to Pole." Jagielski responded by picking up the phrase "as Pole talks to Pole," and concluded, "I think, and I deeply believe . . . that we wish to serve as best we can the cause of the people, the cause of our nation, our socialist fatherland—the Polish People's Republic."[24]

———

THE GDAŃSK AGREEMENT was a tremendous victory for the workers.[25] A Communist Party state had now authorized independent representation from the working class, which the Communist Party itself claimed to represent. The structure of Solidarity emerged from the summer strikes. Factory strike committees became Solidarity's Factory Commissions. The regional Inter-Factory Strike Committees became Solidarity's Inter-Factory Founding Committees. Other regions followed suit, establishing their own Inter-Factory Founding Committees in a somewhat haphazard process. Examples included the Adolf Warski Shipyard in Szczecin, the Zofiówka coal mine in Jastrzębie-Zdrój, and the Huta Katowice steelworks in Dąbrowa Górnicza.

In this rapidly changing environment, delegates from thirty-six regional trade unions met in Gdańsk on September 17, 1980, and united under the name *Solidarność*. KOR disbanded and Solidarity held a dramatic election on October 2, 1980, during the First National Congress of Solidarity delegates. Wałęsa received votes from 462 delegates, 55.2 percent of the total, and became Solidarity's first democratically elected leader. Over the next year, Solidarity basked in its newfound freedom and Poland enjoyed a period, however short, where opposition literature, media, and culture flourished.

Fulfilling a longstanding goal, Polish workers completed a massive monument to the 1970s workers outside Gate Number Two in Gdańsk in December 1980. The monument was a stunning concession by the regime, since every worker that walked into—and out of—the Gdańsk shipyard would see it as a symbol of successful resistance. The 138-foot steel sculpture was erected where the first three victims of the 1970 riots were killed. It included three crosses that represented three atrocities against workers—in Poznań in 1956, Gdańsk in 1970, and Radom and other cities in 1976. The crosses themselves signified the suffering and sacrifice of the protesters. At the top were large anchors, characteristic of the seafaring city of Gdańsk, which symbolized hope. Near the base of the monument were socialist realist reliefs that depicted struggling workers.[26] Likening the Jaruzelski regime to a whale, Wałęsa referred to the enormous steel structure as "a harpoon driven through the body of a whale. No matter how hard the whale struggles, it can never get rid of it."[27]

U.S. officials were impressed with Solidarity's progress. Leaders like Lech Wałęsa saw their achievements not just as a campaign to support workers' rights and economic improvements, but as the first steps in an *ideological* struggle to advance freedom and democracy.

Chapter 7

POLISH ABYSS

Across the Atlantic Ocean, Americans elected a new president on November 4, 1980. Ronald Reagan was just shy of seventy. During the election campaign, Reagan had scored points against incumbent president Jimmy Carter by lambasting Carter for a lackluster foreign policy, which many saw as being weak on Moscow. "Militarily, our nation was in danger of falling behind the Soviet Union," Reagan warned. "Abroad the Soviet Union was engaged in a brutal war in Afghanistan and Communism was extending its tentacles deep into Central America and Africa."[1] Reagan reminded Americans of Carter's comment during a visit to Poland that "our concept of human rights is preserved in Poland . . . much better than other European nations with which I'm familiar." Carter had also remarked that Poles enjoyed "a substantial degree of freedom of the press" and religion.[2] Reagan strongly disagreed. He condemned the Polish regime for stifling democracy, praised the Polish people for their "courageous and indomitable spirit," and highlighted "how precious freedom is to those who have lost it."[3] For Reagan, the struggle in Poland was stark and vivid, like a Hollywood action movie. It had heroes (Wałęsa and his brave band of Solidarity freedom fighters) and villains (the Communist Jaruzelski regime and their Soviet allies).

Within days of Reagan's election, CIA officials began foreign policy briefings with Reagan and key members of his transition team, including Vice President George H. W. Bush, Bill Casey, Ed Meese, James Baker, and Richard "Dick" Allen. Casey would become Reagan's CIA director to the delight of many of Casey's former OSS colleagues, Meese his counselor and then attorney general, Baker his chief of staff and then Treasury secretary, and Allen his national security adviser. Outgoing CIA director Stansfield Turner, who led the briefings, included a section on Solidarity, noting that the trade union movement had launched a surprisingly successful opposition campaign against the Polish government.[4] CIA intelligence products warned that Soviet intervention in Poland was increasingly possible.[5] Turner had recently sent a note to President Carter explaining that "Soviet military activity detected in the last few days leads me to believe that the Soviet leadership is preparing to intervene militarily if the Polish situation is not brought under control in a manner satisfactory to Moscow."[6]

Soviet documents show that Moscow indeed had contingency plans to mobilize divisions in the western military districts of the USSR for possible use in Poland. On August 25, 1980, less than two weeks after the strike began at Gdańsk, the Central Committee of the Communist Party of the Soviet Union had established a commission under the supervision of Mikhail Suslov, a senior member of the politburo, charged with tracking developments in Poland and recommending courses of action.[7] Three days after the commission was formed, it forwarded to the Central Committee a plan for preparing nine to eleven divisions in the western USSR military districts for possible commitment to Poland.[8] The rationale for this step, according to the Commission, was to ensure that a large "group of [Soviet] forces" would be at "full combat readiness . . . in case military assistance is provided to the Polish People's Republic."[9] The Polish leadership had also established a Ministry of Internal Affairs task force to begin preparations for a forceful suppression of the strikes and protests. The plan, codenamed "Lato-80" ("Summer '80") included storming the Gdańsk Shipyard with the assistance of helicopters. By the end of

August, the Polish Ministry of Internal Affairs task force was ready to conduct operations if called upon.[10]

———

THE MERE POSSIBILITY OF SOVIET INTERVENTION pushed Poland to the top of Reagan and his team's agenda as they prepared to take office. In late November, the CIA's National Foreign Assessment Center, which was later renamed the Directorate of Intelligence, created a task force to monitor the situation in Poland. By December 1980—more than a month before Reagan had taken office—CIA reports were blinking red. The first notices reported that the Soviet Union and its Warsaw Pact allies had agreed to hold a military exercise called "Soyuz-80" in Poland.[11] The situation in Poland grew more precarious when Solidarity leadership insisted that farmers be able to register as an independent union, "Rural Solidarity." A U.S. intelligence community alert memorandum described the situation as "the gravest challenge [to the Polish regime's] authority since the strikes on the Baltic coast ended in August."[12] In December, the CIA disseminated another alert memorandum, this time accompanied by a cover letter from Director Stansfield Turner declaring: "I believe the Soviets are readying their forces for military intervention in Poland. We do not know, however, whether they have made a decision to intervene, or are still attempting to find a political solution."[13]

While U.S. officials in Washington neared a state of panic, U.S. diplomats in Warsaw had a more tempered view. On Sunday, December 7, 1980, the State Department sent urgent instructions to Francis Meehan, U.S. ambassador to Poland. They asked embassy officials to check for unusual activity at key Polish government and party buildings, military installations, communication and transportation facilities, and the Soviet embassy chancery and housing complex. The secret instructions arrived just when U.S. embassy officials in Warsaw were involved in the final stages of an intensely competitive paddle tennis tournament. "Washington would probably not have been greatly

amused," remarked Meehan with a dash of humor, "to know we finished the tournament first before setting about the duties that had been
laid upon us, but I like to think we showed a proper sense of proportion
at a tense moment."[14]

He was right. The Soviets did not invade—at least not yet.

———

By the time Reagan was sworn in as America's fortieth president on
January 20, 1981, Solidarity's membership had grown to nearly ten mil-
lion and the Communist Party was in turmoil.[15] "The basic problem of
Poland today," a CIA report summarized, "is the *total disintegration* of the
Polish Communist Party."[16] In late January, the Reagan administration
established an interagency group on Poland, chaired by Under Secretary
of State David Newsom.[17] By this time, CIA assessments indicated that
Soviet leaders were increasingly concerned about the risks of deploying
Soviet troops to Poland. As one classified CIA memorandum concluded:

> Extensive reporting indicates that Moscow was concerned that
> any intervention might trigger widespread popular opposition in
> Poland, including violent resistance. The Soviet leaders recog-
> nized that, unlike the case of Czechoslovakia in 1968, the Polish
> situation involved a broad popular movement and would be diffi-
> cult to bring under control. Moscow was also concerned that it
> could face direct resistance from the Polish armed forces and was
> eager either to co-opt or to neutralize them. Finally, the Soviets
> were conscious of the international impact direct intervention
> would have, particularly in Western Europe and in the interna-
> tional Communist movement.[18]

Bill Casey, now confirmed as CIA director, neatly summed up the
assessment in a memo to Reagan: "before sending divisions in, [the
Soviets] will move heaven and earth to get the Poles to crack down

themselves."[19] On February 6, Reagan held a National Security Council meeting. Poland, unsurprisingly, was at the top of the agenda. Secretary of State Al Haig told the cabinet that "regarding Poland, the Soviets view the situation there as more critical now than last November. We have a list of contingency actions ready."[20] Administration officials discussed a number of responses, from more aggressive economic sanctions to the deployment of U.S. navy ships to the Baltic Sea.[21] On February 11, Reagan held another National Security Council meeting, in which the council raised the possibility of deploying additional Airborne Warning and Control Systems (AWACs) and other military equipment to Western Europe; sending additional forces to Europe; and beginning a call-up of reservists or National Guard units.[22] Still, some administration officials were skeptical about the benefits of more aggressive measures. NSC staffer William Stearman wrote a controversial memorandum to National Security Adviser Dick Allen—pleading that "I hope this memo is never declassified"—in which he argued that "to be cynical, such Soviet action would probably enhance our national security by having sizeable numbers of Soviet forces tied down in Poland (as well as in Afghanistan) by encouraging our Allies to do more in their defense and by discrediting the USSR throughout the world."[23]

During these discussions, the legacy of Yalta loomed large. Reagan and his inner circle were increasingly uncomfortable with ceding Eastern Europe to the Soviets, as they believed Franklin Roosevelt had done in 1945. A number of prominent U.S. academics and policymakers agreed. In his influential book *Strategies of Containment*, the historian John Lewis Gaddis wrote that during the Cold War the word "Yalta" had become virtually synonymous with "Munich," a reference to the decision by France, the United Kingdom, and Italy in 1938 to allow Nazi Germany to annex portions of Czechoslovakia.[24] The Munich Agreement did not appease Hitler. Nor did Yalta appease the Soviets.

Allen sent a pointed note to Reagan that "since the end of World War II, the West has, indeed, recognized Eastern Europe as falling within the

Soviet sphere of influence and refrained from intervening actively in that area (Hungary, 1956, or Czechoslovakia, 1968)." Allen argued that this needed to change, explaining that "this psychological legacy of the era when it was believed that unethical concessions to Moscow to behave more ethically must be shed for the simple reason that it has not brought the desired results."[25] If previous administrations hoped to change Moscow's behavior through appeasement and cooperation, they had all failed. Like Reagan, Allen believed that the U.S.-Soviet relationship was inherently conflictual as long as the Soviets, in their view, wanted to pursue world domination.

"How do you handle the Soviets?" Allen once asked Reagan.

"Look Dick," Reagan responded matter-of-factly. "I see it this way. We win and they lose."[26]

Still, neither Reagan nor his staff had decided *how* to change Yalta and *what* this meant for U.S. policy and actions in Poland or Eastern Europe. But it was clear that the crisis in Poland was building to a crescendo and that, as the CIA concluded, it constituted "the most serious and broadly based challenge to Communist rule in the Warsaw Pact in more than a decade."[27]

Yet there was one silver lining for the Soviets. Solidarity's success had now outpaced its organizational capabilities, and Wałęsa struggled to establish a single command-and-control arrangement and a coordinated vision for the future. There was growing factionalism among Solidarity's leadership and indiscipline in the ranks, causing Wałęsa to complain that events "were slipping away from us" and warning that it "was much more difficult to keep a tight rein" on Solidarity and the opposition movement.[28] Solidarity leaders disagreed over holding additional strikes, how far to push freedom of the press, and pay raises as the number of local Solidarity committees exploded across the country. By early 1981, the CIA wondered whether Solidarity was fracturing: "Not surprisingly, the leadership—the National Coordinating Commission headed by Lech Wałęsa—is beset by dissension over goals, tactics, and philosophy."[29]

———

SOLIDARITY'S PREDICAMENT PRESENTED a possible window of opportunity for Wojciech Jaruzelski to impose martial law. Jaruzelski had become prime minister in February 1981, though he remained defense minister as well. In his inaugural address on February 12, 1981, Jaruzelski called for a ninety-day moratorium on strikes.[30] U.S. intelligence analysts interpreted these steps as the cautious prime minister desperately trying to de-escalate tensions. As one U.S. Defense Intelligence Agency document concluded:

> Twice previously, in 1970 and again in 1976, Jaruzelski managed to keep regular combat units of the armed forces out of direct conflict with the population, and he argued successfully against their use during strikes last August. In 1970, the military were used to provided support to the Minister of Internal Affairs (MSW) by guarding key government buildings and installations. We are convinced Jaruzelski wants a peaceful settlement to the problems confronting the nation.[31]

But could Jaruzelski deliver? His first major test came from the Soviets—not Wałęsa or Solidarity. On Wednesday, March 4, 1981, Polish leaders were hauled to the Kremlin. Jaruzelski, Stanisław Kania, and others faced some of the most fearsome men in the world, from Soviet leader Leonid Brezhnev to KGB chief Yuri Andropov and politburo member Mikhail Suslov. This intimidating group read them the riot act. Why was the Russian language no longer required in Polish schools? How dare they consider private ownership of land! And why were they dragging their feet instead of crushing Solidarity?[32] Their message sunk in, at least temporarily. At five o'clock the next morning, Polish security forces arrested several opposition leaders like Jacek Kuroń, one of the founders of the Workers' Defense Committee, or KOR, and a staunch critic of the regime's authoritarianism. Reagan administration officials back in Washington were deeply concerned about these developments.[33] Kuroń was held for six hours and informed that he was under investigation for slandering the Polish government.[34]

Polish security agencies had recruited numerous spies within Solidarity. From his perch in the Polish Ministry of Defense, Ryszard Kukliński informed the CIA that Solidarity "was infiltrated by security agents from the beginning" and that the "security forces had very good information on Solidarity."[35]

Still, Jaruzelski was in a precarious position. He tried to balance Soviet demands to act against Solidarity with the historical stigma of using military force against his own population, which might trigger a civil war. Jaruzelski remained deeply scarred from the December 1970 massacre of protestors by the Polish People's Army and Citizens' Militia. Declassified Soviet documents leave no doubt that the Soviet Union exerted relentless pressure on Polish officials, from the deployment of combat-ready troops around Poland's borders, to bilateral military exercises, to angry ultimatums from Soviet leaders to act against Solidarity.[36] Soviet plans also envisaged the use of forces from East Germany, Czechoslovakia, Bulgaria, and Hungary. In addition, a number of hardliners in the Polish Communist Party, such as Stefan Olszowski (who Ryszard Kukliński described as the "principal leader of the Moscow group") and Tadeusz Grabski, pressured Jaruzelski to act.[37]

Soviet browbeating took a toll on Jaruzelski. He had visibly aged and had a flat, inscrutable face with dark circles under his eyes from a lack of sleep. He still wore his trademark dark glasses, and it looked like his tiny head was attached to his body by an immoveable steel pin.[38] A few months before, in November 1980, he came close to a nervous breakdown about the introduction of Soviet and Warsaw Pact forces in Poland.[39] Some of those who worked directly with Jaruzelski, including Kukliński, variously described him as "depressed" and on the verge of resigning.[40] The stakes were certainly high, as Kukliński highlighted:

Defense Intelligence Agency Map of Polish Military Units

There is no doubt, though, that [Jaruzelski] arrived at a conviction, not without certain basis, as it appeared from the veiled comments of his closest friend Siwicki, that the USSR is to repeat in
the [Polish People's Republic] one of its scenarios from Hungary,
Czechoslovakia, or Afghanistan. This conviction solidified with
Jaruzelski still more in 1981 when the USSR undertook further
preparations in this direction.[41]

A few weeks later, it was Moscow's turn to visit Warsaw. As Kukliński
informed the CIA, roughly thirty senior Soviet military and KGB officials flew to Warsaw to get briefed on martial law plans. According to

Kukliński, the Soviets pushed Jaruzelski and Kania to make a number of changes. They argued that when martial law was declared, the Polish constitution should be suspended and supreme authority transferred to a military command. The Soviets also demanded changes in the timing and procedures of the planned arrests for martial law, and insisted that Soviet military and security officers be placed as "advisors" in all components of the Polish national and regional commands.[42] The Polish military had already deployed forces across the country that could be used to move against Solidarity. The map shows the posture of Polish forces according to U.S. intelligence estimates, which were provided to Reagan administration officials.[43]

Reagan administration officials understood that the Soviets were heavily influencing Polish plans for martial law. Reagan, in particular, was furious about Soviet interference in Poland—and even more upset at Soviet imperialism writ large. In 1981, referring to Soviet leaders in his diary he wrote simply, "D–n those inhuman monsters."[44]

Chapter 8

THE CASE FOR COVERT ACTION

In the spring of 1981, Reagan remained as deeply opposed to Communism as he was in October 1947, when he testified before the House Un-American Activities Committee. "The West will not contain communism, it will transcend communism," Reagan remarked to students at the University of Notre Dame in May 1981. "We will not bother to denounce it, we'll dismiss it as a sad, bizarre chapter in human history whose last pages are now being written."[1] In response to Soviet actions in Poland and across the globe, Reagan pushed for a larger defense budget. He also supported a global covert action campaign against the Soviets led by Bill Casey.

Nearly sixty-eight when he took over from Stansfield Turner as CIA director, Casey was now waging a secret war against the Soviet Union.[2] Following a March 9, 1981, situation room meeting on covert operations, Reagan wrote in his diary: "I believe we are getting back on track with a proper approach to 'intelligence' under Bill Casey."[3] Reagan had such faith in him that he appointed Casey as the first director of central intelligence with cabinet rank.

In the spring of 1981, White House officials began to debate covert action options in response to events in Poland.[4] They considered establishing an exiled Polish government in the United States if the Soviets invaded. The United States also considered several outlandish options in response to a Soviet intervention in Poland, including a U.S. invasion and a sea-and-air blockade of Cuba.[5] As Richard Pipes, director for East European and Soviet Affairs on the National Security Council staff, wrote: "In the event of a Soviet invasion, we may consider allowing the formation on U.S. soil of a Polish Government-in-Exile, composed of representatives of the groups presently involved in the Solidarity movement (workers, peasants, intellectuals) as well as those of the church and of the deposed Polish government."[6] Pipes, who had grown up in a Jewish family in Poland and fled the country following Hitler's 1939 invasion, was a staunch conservative and anti-Communist who came to the White House from Harvard University, where he was a Russian history professor.

Pipes argued in a memo to National Security Adviser Dick Allen that it might be worth considering an expansion of "covert action in Afghanistan, Cuba, the Horn of Africa, and the Soviet bloc itself" in the event of a Soviet invasion of Poland.[7] But in the absence of direct Soviet intervention or a significant Polish crackdown, Reagan held off—for the moment—on supporting a new covert action program in Poland.

———

WHILE BILL CASEY AGREED on this cautious approach to Poland, he was increasingly alarmed at the KGB's covert activity around the globe, which was much more aggressive than CIA efforts. The Soviet strategy was best captured in the phrase "active measures" (aktivnyye meropriatia), which was used by the KGB to cover activities designed to influence populations across the globe. The KGB established front groups, covertly broadcast radio and other programs, orchestrated disinformation campaigns, and conducted assassinations.[8] The KGB's use of assassinations made active measures different from CIA covert action, which only involved political measures and propaganda. Casey argued in a sensitive memo that "most of these active measures are not new. Many of them were employed by Lenin and Stalin and by others throughout history. At no time in this century, however, have these techniques been used with more effect or sophistication than by the current Soviet state."[9]

Early in 1981, Casey convened a top secret CIA study group on Soviet active measures. The group was chaired by Dick Malzahn, but Casey took a hands-on role.[10] He would show up at their offices at CIA headquarters and ask for more details and context—peppering them with questions— about papers they had written or programs they were working on. Casey was an action-oriented director and wanted to turn covert action proposals into programs. Yet some in the CIA's Directorate of Operations felt differently. They sneered at Malzahn and his colleagues, and considered covert action a waste of time and money.

Malzahn brushed off the criticism. He had seen the effectiveness of Soviet active measures from the front lines. After returning to CIA headquarters from the Bonn station, Malzahn had worked his way to become the chief of the Soviet–East Europe Group in the International Activities Division (IAD), which oversaw covert action programs within the Directorate of Operations. Soon he was involved in running offensive covert action into the Soviet Union and Eastern Europe, working to thwart Soviet active measures, and distributing information to broader audiences within the U.S. intelligence community. The staff included individuals like Benjamin Fischer from the CIA and Jack Dziak from the Defense Intelligence Agency. Malzahn and his group also worked closely with Mark Palmer, deputy assistant secretary of state for the Soviet Union and Eastern Europe, who supported their covert action programs. Malzahn's "rabbi," a CIA term for patron, was Gardner "Gus" Hathaway, one of the CIA's most aggressive operatives against the KGB. Hathaway instilled in Malzahn a deep appreciation for espionage tradecraft and a relentless drive to outwit the Soviets.

Using a pseudonym, since he was still operating under cover, Malzahn had testified about KGB activities before the Subcommittee on

Oversight of the House Permanent Select Committee on Intelligence.[11] He told subcommittee members that "the Soviet covert action system" was hierarchical and adaptive. "Almost everything is considered at the center, in Moscow, and it is worked up in aspects of Soviet foreign security policy," Malzahn explained. "So the Soviets are in a position to react and act *quickly* if it is something that is in their game plan."[12]

Malzahn's study group started operations in July 1981, just six months after the beginning of the administration.[13] The analysis concluded that "active measures are in essence an offensive instrument of Soviet foreign policy" that "contribute effectively to the strategic Soviet purpose, central to that foreign policy, of extending Moscow's influence and power throughout the world."[14] The report was just what Reagan needed. He used the findings in an August speech to emphasize the magnitude of the Soviet disinformation campaign in areas like NATO's nuclear force modernization in Europe.[15] "We have information that the Soviet Union spent about one hundred million dollars in Western Europe alone a few years ago when the announcement was first made of the invention of the neutron warhead," Reagan said, "and I don't know how much they're spending now, but they're starting the same kind of propaganda drive."[16] The CIA needed to catch up. Casey asked his deputy, Admiral Bobby Ray Inman, to pay closer attention to KGB propaganda, subversion, terrorism, and other less tangible threats to U.S. interests.[17] In addition, Casey tasked the Agency to collect more information on Soviet active measures.[18] All CIA stations were soon required "to submit a monthly report on Soviet covert action ('active measures') in their respective countries as a way of permitting more aggressive counter operations."[19]

———

MEANWHILE, DETERIORATING ECONOMIC CONDITIONS in Poland exacerbated popular discontent with the Jaruzelski regime. Reagan administration officials watched the Polish economy spiral. "Their

THE CASE FOR COVERT ACTION

economy is going bust," Reagan wrote in his diary on July 14, 1981. "Here is the 1st major break in the Red dike—Poland's disenchantment with Soviet Communism."[20] On July 23, the Polish government announced that monthly per capita meat rations would be cut by 20 percent. The government published a list of price increases showing that food items like butter, bread, sugar, and milk had more than tripled in price while others such as flour and ham had more than doubled. A week later, the parliamentary budget commission reported that per capita national income for 1981 was expected to be 15 percent lower than the already dismal 1980 level.[21]

These announcements were a match in the tinderbox. Protests and "hunger marches" erupted almost instantly. Local Solidarity chapters, which had flourished since the establishment of the movement in September 1980, helped organize and supervise some of these marches in an effort to channel the anger away from even more inflammatory reactions like the use of violence.

———

ON SEPTEMBER 15, REAGAN HELD a National Security Council meeting to discuss assistance to Poland. The debate illustrated the high stakes of the situation.

"The Polish people and the West would 'lose' if Solidarity were crushed and the Soviets could boast to all of Eastern Europe that liberalization had failed," said National Security Adviser Dick Allen.

Secretary of Defense Casper "Cap" Weinberger agreed, cautioning against providing long-term economic aid to a Polish regime that was cracking down on its own population. But aid to Solidarity might be another matter. "We should do what we can to encourage Solidarity to resist such Soviet pressures," he said.

CIA director Casey agreed. He favored "financial aid to Poland if there could be assurance that it would not go down the drain." But he said no such assurance could be given.

The discussion then turned to a Soviet invasion.

Does anyone believe "that if the Soviets invade they would not meet resistance," Reagan asked.

"The Poles surely would resist," responded Casey.[22]

Casey's view was partly informed by a highly classified CIA assessment in mid-1981, which concluded that "the Soviet leadership would have to expect a degree of resistance to invasion far surpassing that encountered in Hungary in 1956 or Czechoslovakia in 1968."[23] Soviet forces brutally suppressed revolts in Hungary in 1956 and Czechoslovakia in 1968. But the Polish opposition was much better organized in 1981 than in either Hungary or Czechoslovakia when Soviet forces intervened. CIA analysts presumed that Polish shipyard workers and miners would present a much more formidable adversary if Moscow sent in the Red Army.

While Casey pressed his case, cabinet members around the table struggled to understand his mumbling. "Reagan was partially deaf in one ear," National Security Adviser Dick Allen recounted. "He'd sit there with his head cocked as Bill droned on. He'd look to me desperately and I'd break in: 'Just a minute, Bill—I'd like to emphasize what you just said.' Then I'd repeat Casey's point, and say, 'Now Bill, I know you have more to say.' And he'd start mumbling all over again."[24]

While those around the table may have struggled to decipher Casey, they understood his position: Casey was convinced the CIA needed to ramp up its covert action efforts. From Casey's perspective, the CIA was established to accomplish two main tasks: figure out what was going on in the world, and help make the right things happen covertly when open diplomacy or military action failed or were inappropriate.[25] Back at CIA headquarters, Dick Malzahn and others celebrated Casey's embrace of covert action. The KGB may have been well ahead of the CIA in their global "active measures" campaign, but the Soviets were vulnerable. The growth of a well-organized opposition movement in Poland was fertile ground for CIA action.

———

BACK IN POLAND IN SEPTEMBER 1981, the government continued to lose its grip on society. Protesters carried banners with slogans like "Starving people of the world unite" and "We'll have Kania for breakfast." The latter slogan was a play on words, since *kania* was both a type of forest mushroom and the last name of the general secretary of the Communist Party. People had to stand in line for virtually everything: meat, butter, sugar, potatoes, and rice. Perhaps the two most frequently heard words were "*nie ma*" ("we don't have it"), which became a running joke among Poles. Some called the clumsy architecture prevalent through Poland "repressionist style." Political jokes proliferated throughout the country.

A man walks into a butcher shop and demands pork, went one joke.

"Nie ma" says the butcher. The same goes for beef, lamb, veal, and chicken. "Nie ma" repeats the butcher.

Enraged, the customer asks, "Well what *do* you have then?"

The butcher gestures toward the plastic Polish coat of arms hanging on the wall, and dryly remarks, "Eagle."[26]

Tensions continued to escalate between Solidarity and the Polish regime, with Moscow increasingly aggressive in demanding action against the "counterrevolutionaries." Solidarity leaders then took a provocative step at their first congress in September, publishing a letter to East European labor unions. The letter extended "greetings and expressions of support to the workers of Albania, Bulgaria, Czechoslovakia, the GDR, Hungary, Romania, and all the peoples of the USSR." It then dropped a bombshell: "We support those among you who have decided to enter the difficult path of struggle for a free trade union movement."[27] Moscow viewed the letter as incendiary—an incitement of revolt across the Soviet Bloc and a direct challenge to Moscow's authority. Brezhnev was apoplectic, fuming in a politburo meeting: "It's a dangerous and provocative document. It contains few words, but all of them are aimed at the same thing. The authors of the appeal would like to create confusion in the socialist countries and stir up groups of different types of turncoats."[28]

In mid-September 1981, Poland's Homeland Defense Committee (*Komitet obrony kraju*, or KOK) agreed at Jaruzelski's behest that martial law would be necessary, though they did not settle on a specific date.[29] By now, Soviet officials were reluctant to send troops into Poland as part of "Operation X," Moscow's codename for martial law.[30] At an October Soviet politburo meeting, Andropov noted that "Polish leaders are talking about military assistance from the fraternal countries," but that "we need to adhere firmly to our line—that our troops will not be sent to Poland."[31] This put Jaruzelski in a bind. He was unenthusiastic about imposing martial law without Soviet military assistance or at least a solid guarantee that Soviet troops would help if martial law failed to stabilize the situation.[32]

———

THE CIA SENT OUT A SERIES of alarming intelligence products summarizing the extent of Moscow's fury with the near-anarchy in Poland.[33] The CIA had learned from its source in the Polish Ministry of Defense, the "Polish Viking" Ryszard Kukliński, that the chief of the Polish General Staff, General Florian Siwicki, had told a small group of Polish military officers that Poland was approaching the imposition of martial law. Pressure from Moscow continued to increase in October. Stanisław Kania was removed and replaced by Wojciech Jaruzelski in mid-October 1981. Jaruzelski now held the positions of prime minister, minister of defense, *and* first secretary of the Communist Party—unprecedented in Polish history. On October 20, two days after Kania's removal, police used force and tear gas to disperse thousands of protesters at Katowice, a mining city in southern Poland, who were angry about the arrest of three Solidarity activists for distributing leaflets and the continuing food shortages. A *New York Times* article described the protest as "the worst outbreak of street violence in fourteen months."[34] Strikes persisted into November.

Polish intelligence picked up information from a KGB source in Rome—possibly at the Vatican—that someone in the Polish Ministry of Defense with direct access to martial law preparations had provided classified information to the CIA. There were only a small number of people with the complete set of plans for martial law, referred to as the "final version." Kukliński was one of them. On November 2, Polish general Wacław Szklarski confronted Kukliński and two other Polish military officers about the leak, noting that Polish counterintelligence was conducting an investigation. Terrified, Kukliński sent a message to the CIA station in Warsaw, and the acting station chief, Sue Burggraf, alerted CIA headquarters. After discussing options, Director Casey sent a cable to U.S. Ambassador Francis Meehan in Warsaw, saying that Secretary of State Al Haig had been briefed on the situation. "We appreciate your cooperation," Casey's cable said. "I wish to confirm that the Secretary authorizes you to do all possible in support of our efforts to protect and possibly exfiltrate this valuable man and his family."[35]

On November 7, the CIA helped shuttle Kukliński, his wife, and two sons out of Poland in a dramatic escape after Polish and Soviet intelligence agencies began to close in on him.[36] Kukliński had smuggled out more than 40,000 pages from classified Soviet, Polish, and Warsaw Pact documents—including war plans, military maps, mobilization schedules, allied command procedures, summaries of exercises, technical data on weapons, blueprints of command bunkers, electronic warfare manuals, military targeting guidelines, and allied nuclear doctrine.[37]

In late November 1981, after Kukliński was safely in the United States, the CIA learned that Polish authorities were meeting with high-level military delegations from Moscow to review martial law implementation. A group of nine Soviet and other Warsaw Pact General Staff officers met in Warsaw with the Polish General Staff.[38]

By early December, Polish action appeared imminent.[39]

———

JARUZELSKI WAS NOW UNDER intense pressure from Moscow. Soviet leaders had grown increasingly concerned that a democratic movement in Poland might have a domino effect across Eastern Europe and trigger a wave of revolts against Soviet-backed governments from East Germany to Romania. A coterie of top Communist Party of the Soviet Union (CPSU) officials—Mikhail Suslov, Konstantin Chernenko, Konstantin Rusakov, and Vladimir Rakhmanin—had flown to Poland in early December to consult with Polish leaders on the eve of martial law.[40] Lieutenant General Viktor Anoshkin, adjutant to the Soviet's Warsaw Pact commander-in-chief Marshal Viktor Kulikov, summarized the concerns of Soviet leaders in his personal notebook: "The participation of a large proportion of the working class in strikes shows that the ideas of the counterrevolution are still alive among the broad popular masses. For this reason, the only way to prevent the remaining part of the leading core from resorting to an illegal situation and launching a variety of anti-government actions is by *thoroughly destroying the counterrevolution*."[41]

Despite their insistence that Jaruzelski smash Solidarity, most Soviet leaders were opposed to using Red Army forces to invade Poland. Soviet defense minister Marshall Dmitrii Ustinov agreed: "In general one might say that it would be impossible to send our troops to Poland. They, the Poles, are not ready to receive our troops."[42] It was a devastating blow for Jaruzelski, who felt betrayed. He had been pleading—even begging—for Soviet troops to be sent to Poland. On December 11, Jaruzelski had sent an urgent request to Moscow via the Soviet ambassador in Poland, Boris Aristov.

"Can we count on assistance of a military sort from the USSR—the additional sending of troops?" Jaruzelski flatly asked.

Konstantin Rusakov, the CPSU secretary for interparty relations in the Warsaw Pact, quickly responded: "No troops will be sent."

When Aristov informed Jaruzelski that his request had been turned down, the Polish leader sulked: "This is terrible news for us!! A year-

and-a-half of chattering about the sending of troops went on—and now everything is gone!"[43]

To many who worked with him, Jaruzelski normally appeared relaxed and carefully controlled his emotions.[44] But the deliberations about martial law were tearing him apart. "I spent the weeks prior to taking the decision on martial law as in some horrible nightmare. I entertained thoughts of suicide," he later acknowledged.[45] Internal Soviet accounts of Jaruzelski leading up to martial law painted him as unstable. "Psychologically, [Jaruzelski's] state of mind is very nervous," wrote Lieutenant General Anoshkin in his notebook.[46] Soviet officials that interacted with Jaruzelski said that he seemed "extremely neurotic and diffident about his abilities," "back to his vacillating position," and "in a highly agitated state."[47] General Florian Siwicki, the chief of the Polish General Staff, remarked that Jaruzelski was "very upset and very nervous" and that "psychologically . . . Jaruzelski has gone to pieces."[48]

———

IN THE FACE OF SOVIET PRESSURE TO ACT, but without a commitment of Red Army forces, Jaruzelski began military deployments on December 11. Solidarity members were acutely aware of the gravity of the situation. Wałęsa and other members of the national executive committee met on December 11 and 12 at the Health and Safety Hall in the Gdańsk Shipyard, where Wałęsa had signed the Gdańsk Agreement in August 1980. Around 2:00 p.m. on December 12, Jaruzelski telephoned General Czesław Kiszczak, Polish minister of internal affairs, and instructed him to commence operation "*Jodla*," the army and Citizens' Militia's codename for martial law.

Late in the evening on December 12, 1981, Polish security forces began arresting members of Solidarity and others considered a threat to the state. Jaruzelski sent Polish special motorized security forces into the streets of cities like Warsaw, set up roadblocks and checkpoints, ordered tanks to patrol city blocks, and consolidated power in a Military

Council of National Salvation (*Wojskowa Rada Ocalenia Narodowego,* or WRON). Security forces also rounded up members of Solidarity, raided their offices, and seized radio and television buildings.[49] At 6:00 a.m. the next day, Jaruzelski made his public announcement on national television. Over the next few days, Polish security services imprisoned around 6,000 Solidarity activists in twenty-four internment centers, including most of its leadership.[50] Soviet military and KGB officials had been deeply involved in the planning efforts. Polish officials had opted to impose martial law on a weekend to avoid bloodshed.[51]

Perhaps the archetypal image of martial law came from Chris Niedenthal, a British-Polish photographer whose work graced the pages of such magazines as *Newsweek* and *Time.* While wandering through Warsaw, Niedenthal snapped an iconic picture of a Polish armored personnel carrier sitting in front of a cinema in Warsaw under a light blanket of snow. In the background, there was an oversized white banner advertising Francis Ford Coppola's movie *Apocalypse Now.* Niedenthal was overwhelmed by the symbolism that many Poles felt with the onset of martial law. As he later recalled:

> We were turning and from behind the trees I could see a new, better scene. If it wasn't enough that there was a banner with *Czas apokalipsy* (*Apocalypse Now*) on the cinema building, in front of it, there stood an armored personnel carrier—SKOT—and soldiers around it. The setting looked as if it were staged. I couldn't have asked for a better photo opportunity![52]

———

THE IMPOSITION OF MARTIAL LAW IN POLAND was a defining moment for Reagan, providing an unprecedented opportunity to stand up to the Soviets and embrace the democratic principles of Solidarity. It would launch his declaration of a moral war against the Soviet Union, a war of ideas more than armies. After martial law, demonstrations erupted in Philadelphia, Boston, New York, Washington, and Chicago against the Jaruzelski regime. One CIA estimate suggested the grassroots opposition movement in Poland was potentially catastrophic for the Soviets.[53] By late 1981, Reagan's interest in Poland had become deeply personal— even emotional. Solidarity and its ideology embodied the freedom that America represented. Reagan had often referred to America as a "shining city on a hill"—a beacon of light for oppressed peoples around the globe. Poland had now slipped into the darkness of tyranny.

Reagan also warmly welcomed Polish defectors. On December 19, 1981, the Polish ambassador to the United States, Romuald Spasowski, telephoned Deputy Assistant Secretary of State Jack Scanlan and asked for political asylum. U.S. officials, including Reagan, jumped at the chance. Spasowski spoke in front of news cameras in Washington, condemning the Jaruzelski government for declaring martial law and expressing his support for Wałęsa.[54] On December 22, Reagan invited Ambassador Spasowski and his wife to the White House in an emotional meeting, which sent Moscow and Warsaw into a fury. The next day, two days before Christmas, Reagan addressed the nation from the Oval Office. He sat comfortably at his English-oak desk, a gift from Queen Victoria to President Rutherford B. Hayes in 1880 that was built from the timbers of the British Arctic exploration ship HMS *Resolute*. Reagan wore a dark suit with a seasonal red tie and white handkerchief tucked into his lapel, with his hair slicked back and red cheeks glowing. He spoke with warmth and affection about the holiday season, before turning his attention to Poland.

"As I speak to you tonight," he remarked, growing more solemn, "the fate of a proud and ancient nation hangs in the balance." The Polish population had been betrayed by their own government, he said, and by the Soviet Union. Reagan promised that "if the forces of tyranny in Poland, and those who incite them from without, do not relent, they should prepare themselves for serious consequences." He continued that America would not stand by idly: "I want emphatically to state tonight that if the outrages in Poland do not cease, we cannot and will not conduct 'business as usual' with the perpetrators and those who aid and abet them. Make no mistake, their crime will cost them dearly in their future dealings with America and free peoples everywhere. I do not make this statement lightly or without serious reflection."[55]

Back in Poland, Reagan said, the Polish people had placed lighted candles on their window sills as a symbol that liberty was still alive. Looking into the camera, Reagan urged Americans to do the same during the holiday season in support of Poland. Referencing World War II and the rise of Hitler, Reagan implored Americans to light a candle. "Once, earlier in this century, an evil influence threatened that the lights were going out all over the world. Let the light of millions of candles in American homes give notice that the light of freedom is not going to be extinguished."[56]

Chapter 9

THE BIRTH OF QRHELPFUL

At a December 1981 National Security Council meeting, barely a week after the imposition of martial law in Poland, Reagan urged action. He likened Poland's oppressed workers to the intrepid patriots who had struggled for freedom during America's Revolutionary War. Poland was now at a critical juncture, Reagan believed. He assembled his senior advisors—from Bill Casey to Secretary of State Al Haig—in the Roosevelt Room of the White House. The windowless room had an ornate false skylight perched above the long black conference table, illuminating the intricate triglyph molding. Along the curving east wall of the room stood a mantled fireplace and two sturdy, mahogany-paneled doors. Reagan's advisors gathered beneath bronze low-relief plaques of Theodore Roosevelt and Franklin D. Roosevelt—whom Reagan admired—as the president prepared to begin.[1]

Looking around the table, Reagan spoke deliberately. He characterized the situation in Poland as a struggle between freedom and authoritarianism, good and evil. "Let me say something in the form of a positive question. This is the first time in 60 years that we have had this kind of opportunity. There may not be another in your life-time. Can we afford not to go all out?" He reminded his staff that the Soviets were behind

martial law and argued that the United States could not concede to tyranny any longer. "We have backed away so many times! After World
War II we offered Poland the Marshall plan, they accepted, but the Soviets said no." Now it was time for action to support Solidarity and other
Polish opposition members. "There may never be another chance! It is
like the opening lines in our own declaration of independence. 'When in
the course of human events . . .' This is exactly what they are doing now." [2]

Poland was at a defining period in its struggle for freedom, Reagan
said, and the United States would provide a hand because America had
been there before. While the way Reagan processed information was
often simplistic—perhaps even naïve at times—it enabled him to be deci-
sive. Vice President George H. W. Bush chimed in: "I have thought a lot
about this problem over the weekend," he said. "I agree with the President
that we are at a real turning point." So did Secretary of Defense Casper
"Cap" Weinberger. "I agree," Weinberger reinforced. "This is not a time
for prudence or caution. The world needs to be told that it has a leader."
Bill Casey was equally convinced it was time to act. "We lose credibility
if we fail to follow through now on this situation," he said.[3]

Reagan ended the meeting with a renewed vigor to support Solidarity, a decision that was not lost on Casey.

———

CIA OFFICIALS HAD BEEN DISCUSSING covert assistance to Solidarity
since the beginning of the Reagan administration—and even before.
Casey believed that the United States should examine contingency
options, including covert action.[4] He also believed that covert action
was preferable to other options in a Soviet satellite country because it
would keep the U.S. hand hidden. Overt assistance, Casey feared, might
undermine the legitimacy of Solidarity by tying it too closely to the
United States.

At Casey's request, Reagan created—and chaired—an exclusive,
high-level committee called the National Security Planning Group

(NSPG). It was a restricted subcommittee of the National Security Council composed of such individuals as the vice president, secretaries of state and defense, national security advisor, director of central intelligence, and a small group of Reagan's political aides like the chief of staff, presidential counselor, and deputy chief of staff. It was the only group authorized to consider covert action programs. To prevent leaks, the group did not prepare papers in advance of the meetings, prohibited aides from attending, and collected all papers at the end of each meeting.[5]

U.S. discussions about covert assistance to Solidarity had picked up over 1981.[6] In April 1981, Robert Gates, who directed the executive staff for the director and deputy director of central intelligence, wrote a memo to Casey urging him to think about other options: "I believe we must begin to give some attention to the prospect that the Soviets will not intervene in Poland and that the reform movement will continue." The memo then outlined the dramatic changes toward democratization in Poland. "In my view," Gates continued, "we may be witnessing one of the most significant developments in the post war period which, if unchecked, may foreshadow a profound change in this decade in the system Stalin created both inside the Soviet Union and in Eastern Europe."[7]

In June, Secretary of Defense Weinberger asked Casey to outline possible CIA actions and to draft a presidential "finding" that might include paramilitary measures. In 1974, Congress had passed the Hughes-Ryan Amendment to the Foreign Assistance Act.[8] The amendment prohibited the CIA from conducting covert action unless the president determined that an operation was important to U.S. national security and submitted a classified finding—in writing—to appropriate congressional committees.[9] Later in June, the CIA's Directorate of Operations produced a draft presidential finding outlining CIA training, lethal aid, and nonlethal equipment to Polish opposition. The draft was based, in part, on the CIA presidential finding that supported covert action in Afghanistan.[10]

But there was significant resistance within the CIA to arming the Polish opposition. Several officials from the CIA's International

Activities Division, including Walter Raymond, Jr., argued that infiltrating arms to Solidarity—even after a possible Soviet invasion—would trigger a robust Soviet military response against the United States and other NATO countries. Richard Pipes at the White House also objected to providing weapons to Solidarity, arguing that "Solidarity didn't need or want arms."[11] So did Ed Meese, who argued that "the risks of providing arms to Solidarity was high and the probability of success was low."[12] Some officials also had strong reservations that the CIA could sustain plausible deniability, particularly in the face of heavy casualties if Polish opposition members engaged in combat with Jaruzelski's security forces. Despite these widespread concerns, the CIA did send one of its paramilitary operatives down to the "Farm"—the CIA training facility in southern Virginia—to do an inventory of arms and ammunition just in case the White House approved lethal aid to Solidarity.

While CIA and Reagan officials still remained undecided about covert assistance to Poland, the administration did support assistance to Solidarity from overt sources. As Secretary of State Al Haig explained in a memo to Reagan, the United States was already leveraging the assistance of labor unions (particularly the American Federation of Labor and Congress of Industrial Organizations, or AFL-CIO), private organizations (particularly Polish ethnic organizations), and other sources to assist Solidarity.[13]

It became increasingly clear, however, that this limited assistance might not be sufficient.

———

BACK IN POLAND, JARUZELSKI HAD ARRESTED roughly 6,000 Solidarity members and sympathizers by January 1982, including Lech Wałęsa, bringing the country to the brink of civil war.[14] Catholic leaders—who kept in close touch with Solidarity—became alarmed about the possibility of large-scale violence, particularly involving radical militants within Solidarity.[15] There were demonstrations at the Lenin Shipyard in Gdańsk, the Adolf Warski Shipyard in Szczecin, the Lenin Steelworks in Kraków, and the Huta Katowice Steelworks in southern Poland. The strongest resistance came from the coal mines in Silesia near Poland's border with Germany and Czechoslovakia. Polish security forces had killed nine miners at the Kopalnia Wujek coal mine. At the Piast coal mine in Bieruń, over a thousand miners held a strike two thousand feet underground.

In a message to Jaruzelski, Pope John Paul II asked that the regime lift martial law and return to dialogue with Solidarity to prevent further destabilization. Most Catholic Church officials were sympathetic to Solidarity. As the pope wrote to Reagan: "The solidarity expressed by individuals, social groups and peoples [in Poland] is certainly the very same that inspires the attitudes assumed by many Governments, like your own, on the international level—attitudes which are not directed against the life and development of Poland, but which intend to support her people's aspiration for freedom."[16]

But Jaruzelski was single-mindedly focused on crushing—and discrediting—Solidarity, and he reached out to neighboring states for help. East Germany's Communist Party boss, Erich Honecker, sent a task force—named Arbeitsgruppe 4 ("Workgroup 4")—that was composed of counterintelligence operatives from the Ministry for State Security (MfS) and the Main Directorate for Intelligence (HVA).[17] The MfS controlled all traffic entering and exiting Poland along the East German–Polish border, and searched for printing equipment, radios, and other material smuggled to Solidarity from the West.[18] Arbeitsgruppe 4 recruited its own agent networks, intercepted mail, and conducted physical, audio, and video surveillance of Solidarity leaders and Catholic officials. The HVA's Abteilung X ("Department X"), conducted a black propaganda campaign to discredit Solidarity leaders by producing phony copies of underground publications and spreading defamatory rumors about its leaders.[19] The HVA's disinformation campaign included painting Solidarity as a "Zionist plot," raising doubts about its nationalistic roots and aspirations, and accusing its members of being CIA stooges.[20] The HVA also pursued Solidarity leaders in the West. Using intercepted correspondence, it forged letters suggesting that the exiled activists were enjoying the "good life" while their colleagues were living underground in Poland.[21]

———

REAGAN ADMINISTRATION OFFICIALS grew alarmed as Jaruzelski stepped up attacks and the East Germans joined the effort. One classified National Security Council assessment found that Jaruzelski was unraveling the limited reforms introduced the year before: "The Polish Government is moving quickly and ruthlessly to destroy all vestiges of political reforms introduced in 1980–81. The democratic processes introduced into the party in July 1981 have been abrogated and strict centralism is being restored."[22] Senior U.S. officials worried that these developments would not only destroy the democratic movement in Poland, but also boost Moscow and undermine U.S. global leadership. A top secret State Department paper presented at a February 4, 1982, National Security Council meeting outlined the gravity of the situation:

> Poland relates to so many fundamentals (the future of Eastern Europe, the Alliance, Soviet security, American political and moral leadership) that our objectives must be placed in the context of our overall foreign policy. Our overall objective is to maintain U.S. capacity for world leadership by halting and if possible reversing adverse trends in the world power balance over the last decade or more.[23]

In March 1982, Polish sources told NSC staffer Richard Pipes that the political situation was deteriorating and that hard-liners were gaining strength and pushing Jaruzelski even further toward the right.[24] "The application of the law," Pipes concluded, "is so ambiguous that one may speak of a generalized terror."[25]

Before deciding on controversial steps like covert action, however,

Reagan first wanted to refashion America's national security strategy. In March 1982, an interagency group began to revise U.S. strategy toward Eastern Europe. The goal was, in part, to examine whether the United States should pursue a policy of "differentiation."[26] This meant providing preferential treatment to those Eastern European countries that established a measure of independence from Soviet foreign policy. For instance, did they formally disassociate themselves from Soviet foreign policy initiatives? Did they refuse to grant aid to Soviet ventures in the third world? As Richard Pipes noted, "ever since the introduction of sanctions toward Poland and the USSR," a growing number of Europeans demanded to know the long-term strategy of the United States. There was no Reagan strategy yet. "It seems to me, therefore quite imperative," Pipes wrote in a memo marked urgent to National Security Adviser Bill Clark, "that a decision be made on what our long-term policy toward the Communist Bloc is."[27]

Clark had recently replaced Dick Allen as national security adviser. Clark was a devout Catholic who had a deep contempt for Communism and was concerned that the Catholic Church was in danger of being suppressed by the Jaruzelski regime. Clark lacked the demeanor of a diplomat or a politician. He was aloof and reserved. In his youth, he had spent a year in a seminary that allowed only two hours of speech per day. At fifty, he sometimes spoke considerably less. He was tall, thin, handsome, expressionless, and walked the halls in alligator boots. Clark was by nature a rancher, happiest when riding on horseback over his vast estate in California's San Luis Obispo County. He proudly kept a Colt .45 on permanent display above his desk at the White House. Reagan loved that side of Clark, and occasionally snuck out with him for a few hours in the saddle at Quantico or Camp David. This closeness gave Clark a window into the president's psychology. He understood the way Reagan oversimplified situations and perceived issues in black and white.[28]

Clark had restored morale and efficiency in the National Security Council, firing and hiring as if he were improving stock at his ranch. He hired Robert C. "Bud" McFarlane as deputy national security advisor, a dogged strategy specialist who had impressed Clark at his previous job as deputy secretary of state. Clark had also pressed for direct access to the president, which didn't always sit well with other Reagan advisors. "You can't just *walk* in," Michael Deaver, White House deputy chief of staff, once protested when Clark marched into the Oval Office unannounced. Clark peered down at Deaver from his superior height and replied with some contempt, "Mike if it wasn't for me, you wouldn't be here."[29]

Clark helped spearhead two major directives that impacted U.S. aid to Solidarity. On May 20, 1982, Reagan signed into law NSDD-32, a top secret document titled "U.S. National Security Strategy," which marked a shift in U.S. policy. It authorized a wide range of diplomatic, propaganda, political, and military action to "contain and reverse the expansion of Soviet control and military presence through the world."[30] The document also had a covert action component and supported such efforts as sponsoring "demonstrations, protests, meetings, conferences, press articles, television shows, exhibitions, and the like."[31] Several months later, Reagan signed NSDD-54, titled "United States Policy Towards Eastern Europe." This document went even further than NSDD-32, declaring that it was U.S. policy to unhinge Moscow's grip on Eastern Europe and to reunite it—eventually—with Western Europe.[32] NSDD-54 also formally defined what "differentiation" in Eastern Europe meant. Examples ranged from "encouraging more liberal trends in the region" to "reinforcing the pro-Western orientation of their peoples" and "undermining the military capabilities of the Warsaw Pact."[33] These directives provided the strategic logic and political cover for a more aggressive U.S. policy toward the Soviet Union and its Eastern European satellites, including Poland.

Reagan wasn't done. Immediately after Jaruzelski had imposed martial law, the United States had invoked economic sanctions against Poland. Reagan suspended most-favored-nation trade status and vetoed Poland's application for membership in the International Monetary Fund. He also continued to demonize Soviet ideology in public. On June 8, 1982, Reagan gave the "Westminster Address" before the British Parliament, relegating Marxism-Leninism to the "ash heap of history."[34] The speech predicted that Poland would be a severe test for the Soviet Union. After one reporter asked what he thought of the Berlin wall, Reagan replied unequivocally: "It's as ugly as the idea behind it."[35]

While the British remained a firm ally, not all European governments viewed the Polish crisis in such stark black-and-white terms. West Germany "told us in no uncertain terms that it had no objection to the imposition there of martial law in December 1981, denying us the license to meddle in the 'internal affairs' of countries controlled by Moscow," lamented Richard Pipes at the National Security Council.[36] An exasperated Reagan condemned the "chicken littles" in European capitals who refused to stand up to the Soviets in Poland, and Secretary of State Al Haig bemoaned that European heads were "not the most courageous people."[37] It was a delicate situation for West German leaders, who largely accepted Yalta and conceded Eastern Europe to the Soviets. West Germany bordered the Soviet bloc and had much to lose if there was a major deterioration in East-West relations.

With Lech Wałęsa still in jail, Reagan lobbied for his release. In his concluding remarks at a June 18 National Security Council meeting, Reagan remarked that the "time has come for someone to stand on principle. Maybe the Allies will go to the Soviet Union. If the Soviet Union would only—I said—let Walesa out, and other Polish prisoners . . . that alone would be enough for us to make a complementary act."[38] But Reagan's hope that Jaruzelski might release Wałęsa and other Solidarity members was quickly dashed.

———

WAŁĘSA WAS ONE OF JARUZELSKI'S PRIME TARGETS. The night of martial law, Wałęsa's doorbell rang as anxious Solidarity members shuffled in and out. Wałęsa and his family were living at Pilotów 17d/3 in the Zaspa area of Gdańsk. Zaspa was a housing monstrosity: a square mile of giant steel-and-concrete structures, rising between four and twelve stories high. Wałęsa's apartment wasn't a typical worker's one, however. The local housing committee combined three normal apartments to create a "super flat" for Wałęsa and his growing family. A wave of nervous Solidarity members cycled through Wałęsa's home to offer information on arrests or to seek advice on what to do next. His wife, Danuta, was pugnacious with the security officials who eventually came to arrest Wałęsa, first refusing to let them in and taunting them, saying they would have to break down the door with crowbars. At 5:30 a.m. on the morning of martial law, Wałęsa was taken by military escort from his house to the airport and flown to Warsaw. He was placed under house arrest in Chylice, in the suburbs of Warsaw, at the villa belonging to a former secretary of the Communist Party's Central Committee.[39] Wałęsa's worldwide celebrity status made it politically risky for Jaruzelski to subject him to a show trial or threaten him with the brutality meted out to some other Solidarity members.

The *Służba Bezpieczeństwa* (SB), Poland's security service housed within the Ministry of Internal Affairs, tried to discredit Wałęsa.[40] While he was working as a shipyard electrician in the early 1970s, the SB had apparently been in contact with Wałęsa. Among the SB files discovered after the collapse of the Communist regime, were ones with a source codenamed "Bolek."[41] The files suggest that Wałęsa was a paid SB informant in the early 1970s, well before he helped establish Solidarity.[42] The SB attempted to intimidate Wałęsa after his internment by "reminding him that they had paid him money and received information from him."[43] The SB also resorted to fabrications designed to portray Wałęsa as a greedy, foul-mouthed embezzler.[44] As Jaruzelski explained to Boris Aristov, the Soviet ambassador in Warsaw, the SB had access to—or perhaps fabricated—pornographic material of Wałęsa (presumably with a mistress) and would expose him as "a scheming, grubby individual with gigantic ambitions."[45]

Despite the SB's targeting of Wałęsa, Polish support for Solidarity remained strong. The regime continued to struggle and the economy was in dire shape. There were few raw materials or supplies available, causing Poland to shutter some 40 percent of its industrial capacity. Light industry was especially hard hit. One Reagan National Security Council assessment summarized that "there is fear in Warsaw of mass violence caused not by political motives but by anger over the dramatic drop in living standards."[46] In the spring of 1982, polls conducted by the Jaruzelski government found that 80 percent of Poles wanted to see Solidarity restored to its pre–martial law status.[47] A few months later, a poll by Radio Free Europe found that 76 percent of Poles "fully support Solidarity today."[48]

THE POLISH CRACKDOWNS ON SOLIDARITY throughout 1982 contributed to a lively discussion about covert U.S. support. Some of this discussion occurred in the Polish Monitoring Group, an interagency working group staffed by CIA, State Department, and other U.S. government officials. Mark Palmer, one of the leading Kremlinologists at the State Department who participated in the group, pushed for more pressure on the Polish regime. Palmer had urged the CIA to expand its ongoing intelligence operations in Poland, such as support to *Kultura*. But he was lukewarm about starting a new CIA covert action program, like aid to Solidarity, which would require a new presidential finding and discussions with Congress.[49] Palmer was concerned that members of Congress or their staffs might leak information about a new finding, defeating the whole purpose of "covert" action. Others in the CIA's Directorate of Operations believed that a covert program would have little or no impact on Solidarity's dire situation, and that neither Moscow nor Warsaw would moderate their crackdown in the face of popular outrage—real or manufactured.[50]

In late 1982, Reagan tasked his national security adviser, Bill Clark, to ask the CIA for alternatives. On August 6, 1982, Clark sent CIA director Bill Casey a letter requesting options to provide support to moderate elements of Solidarity. In a memo to Reagan that same month, Clark urged the president to look carefully at "the role of covert action."[51] Despite White House interest, however, some in the CIA's Directorate of Operations still had little enthusiasm for ramping up activities inside Poland, other than small-scale programs like funding *Kultura*. The Soviets wouldn't react well, they insisted. Other CIA officials raised legitimate questions. Would CIA assistance to Solidarity raise false hopes if Jaruzelski was able to effectively crush the underground? Would it be morally wrong to start a covert action program that the White House might order CIA to halt in the future?[52] Some supporters of CIA activity, including Malzahn, wanted only nonlethal support.

Casey replied to Clark's letter in early September, indicating that an expanded program in Poland would require a new presidential finding. But he supported covert political aid to Solidarity, particularly with help from surrogates, or "cut outs."[53] Surrogates referred to the use of non–U.S. government individuals—as opposed to CIA case officers— to provide aid directly to Solidarity.[54] For Poland, this meant that CIA operatives would not work directly with Solidarity, but instead use philanthropists, publishers, smugglers, and others to move materials from Western Europe to Poland.

On September 29, 1982, the White House convened a working group in the Situation Room—or Sit Room—to discuss supporting moderate elements within Solidarity, chaired by Deputy National Security Adviser Bud McFarlane. Built in 1961 by John F. Kennedy, the Situation Room was not one room, but a sprawling 5,000 square foot complex. The small table in the windowless, low-ceilinged conference room fit about a dozen people. Henry Kissinger had once lamented that it was "uncomfortable, unaesthetic, and essentially oppressive."[55] The encrypted audio visual equipment was sometimes unreliable. Various presidents, including Reagan, complained that the equipment would occasionally go black.[56] The *New York Times* termed the complex "something of a low-tech dungeon."[57]

The staff trapped in the "dungeon" that day included Richard Pipes from the National Security Council staff; General Richard Stilwell, deputy to the assistant secretary of defense for international security affairs; Hugh Montgomery, director of the Bureau of Intelligence and Research at the State Department; Walter Raymond, who had moved from CIA to the NSC; David Forden, chief of the Soviet–East Europe Division at CIA; and Robert Magee, chief of the CIA's International Activities Division. The working group concluded that it was important to keep Solidarity alive and that CIA action would be helpful. By this point, senior White House officials supported increasing psychological and information efforts against the Jaruzelski government in Poland.[58] They did not make a final decision to provide CIA support to Solidarity at the late September meeting, but administration officials were converging on a recommendation to the president. And Reagan was more convinced than ever that covert action was important.

After meeting on October 6, 1982, Reagan wrote in his diary: "I've had a top secret briefing on our ability at covert operations abroad. They made it plain we had lost this capacity under the previous admin. If our people only knew the heroism of unsung Americans risking their life every min. of every hour around the clock they'd be as proud as I am."[59] Reagan and other cabinet officials, particularly Bill Casey, believed that the Carter administration had been far too cautious in conducting covert action against the Soviets. Since a direct confrontation between U.S. and Soviet military forces could escalate to nuclear war, Reagan and Casey agreed that countering the Soviets with covert action through local surrogates was a better option. Furthermore, Solidarity leaders were moderate; most didn't support the overthrow of the Jaruzelski government or armed resistance.[60] American military help would be unwelcome.

Yet the Americans saw great potential in the situation. Richard Pipes at the NSC wrote, "Solidarity was the most important development in the Soviet camp because it directly threatened the Soviet system and ideology. Nothing like it existed," he believed. But support to Solidarity was much bigger than one country. "What might happen in Poland could happen elsewhere and help spread opposition to Soviet rule throughout Eastern Europe," Pipes said. "It was not just about Poland.

It was about encouraging a rebellion in the Soviet system. We could not let Solidarity disappear. It would foreclose future possibilities. Solidarity was unique."[61]

And then, on October 8, 1982, Jaruzelski officially banned Solidarity.[62] Brezhnev was thrilled. Reagan was incensed. In an impassioned radio address, Reagan told Americans that it was time to make a stand in Poland. History was on the side of freedom:

> There are those who will argue that the Polish Government's action marks the death of Solidarity. I don't believe this for a moment. Those who know Poland well understand that as long as the flame of freedom burns as brightly and intensely in the hearts of Polish men and women as it does today, the spirit of Solidarity will remain a vital force in Poland . . . Someone has said that when anyone is denied freedom, then freedom for everyone is threatened. The struggle in the world today for the hearts and minds of mankind is based on one simple question: Is man born to be free, or slave? In country after country, people have long known the answer to that question. We are free by divine right.[63]

———

ON NOVEMBER 4, PRESIDENT REAGAN held a National Security Planning Group meeting to discuss covert action in Poland.[64] Reagan sat at one end of the table in the Situation Room and National Security Adviser Bill Clark sat on the other. Secretary of State George P. Shultz, who had replaced Al Haig, sat to Reagan's left and Vice President George H. W. Bush sat to his right. Rounding out the group were a number of other key White House personnel, among them Richard Pipes, Counselor to the President Ed Meese and Chief of Staff Jim Baker, along with CIA director Bill Casey, and the chairman of the Joint Chiefs of Staff, General John Vessey.[65]

After a short discussion, Reagan agreed to sign a presidential finding to provide money and nonlethal equipment to moderate Polish opposition groups through surrogate third parties, hiding the U.S. government's hand. The finding also authorized the CIA to conduct clandestine radio broadcasting into Poland. The goals were limited: to aid the organizational activities of Solidarity and other Polish opposition groups, improve their ability to communicate with the Polish people inside and outside the country, and put more pressure on the Jaruzelski regime to ease its repressive policies. Neither CIA nor White House officials expected U.S. covert assistance to overthrow the Jaruzelski regime or trigger a collapse of Communism in Eastern Europe.[66]

One of the few books that has mentioned CIA support to Solidarity, Peter Schweizer's *Victory*, erroneously reported that Reagan "signed off on the plan but did not issue a covert action finding" which "was deemed too risky."[67] So did Gregory Domber's extensively researched *Empowering Revolution: America, Poland, and the End of the Cold War*, which concluded that "rather than taking the usual step of issuing a covert action finding, the president and his national security adviser Clark informally gave Casey the authority to run the operation as he saw fit."[68]

But Reagan *did* sign a presidential finding. The CIA could not have initiated a new covert action program without a finding that outlined why the operation was important to U.S. national security and that was briefed to the appropriate congressional committees. Like other covert action findings, however, the CIA ensured that the Polish finding remained classified. That night in his diary, Reagan wrote: "Had a Nat. Security Planning Group meeting re activities in Nicaragua & Poland. It was reassuring to find out how effective we can be."[69] With the finding in hand, the CIA then went to Capitol Hill to brief staff members of the Senate Select Committee on Intelligence and House Permanent Select Committee on Intelligence. QRHELPFUL was born.

Chapter 10

STRUGGLING TO SURVIVE

"My wife woke me up at one in the morning," recalled Adam Skwira, recounting the tragic events that unfolded in his apartment block. Skwira worked at the Wujek mine in Katowice, roughly forty miles from Kraków in southeastern Poland. "Actually, the whole housing estate was wide awake, what with the unexpected loud noises. Everyone was looking out their windows to see what was going on."[1] Wearing assault uniforms and armed with sticks and truncheons, members of the Motorized Reserves of the Citizens' Militia, or ZOMO, descended on the house of Jan Ludwiczak, chairman of the mine's Solidarity branch and a strident anti-regime advocate. An assortment of bright blue militia trucks and jeeps clogged the streets, including the dreaded Star police trucks. Colloquially referred to as "refrigerators," or more derogatorily as "kennels," the Star 200 and Star 244 versions could fit up to eighteen ZOMO officers and were equipped with hooks for shields, helmets, and other riot gear. The Star 200 was a regular make, and the Star 244 was the off-road version with four-wheel drive.[2] Both were iconic symbols of Jaruzelski's martial law.

"A little bit later I saw them dragging Ludwiczak out of his house, making a lot of noise, shoving him into their van, people were shouting, of course, and they rushed away," Skwira described. "We kept on standing around, wondering what to do. I went to Ludwiczak's flat, the door had been forced with axes. His wife and children were frightened, they didn't know what was happening. There were smudges of blood by the door."[3]

Ludwiczak's violent arrest exemplified the regime's harsh crackdown on Solidarity members and supporters during martial law. Polish security forces deployed some 1,750 tanks, 1,900 combat vehicles, and 9,000 cars to apprehend opposition figures. The regime set up fifty-two "internment" camps located in jails, prisons, and holiday resorts for the thousands of people that they arrested (see map). Most were placed in detention centers that were run like prisons. The police kept the cells locked, enforced a "lights off" policy at 9:00 p.m. and a "wake-up call" at 5:00 a.m., and frequently searched the prisoners' cells. Inmates were isolated, denied contact with friends and family, persecuted, and beaten. There were also detention centers for high-ranking members of Solidarity and special military centers.[4]

This was the new normal in Poland: internments, arrests, detentions, curfews, searches, beatings, and dismissals from work for belonging to opposition groups. The Jaruzelski regime seized key state enterprises and put them under the control of the Polish Army. Security forces took over Polish radio and television buildings. Some political trials were transferred to military courts, and most were a farce. The public was generally barred from hearings and defendants were prevented from contacting their lawyers. Defense lawyers were subject to surveillance, harassment, intimidation, and reprisals. Pliant prosecutors conducted investigations, and judges that were hand-picked by government officials adjudicated the cases. The government imposed a minimum penalty of three years' imprisonment, prohibited appeals against court rulings,

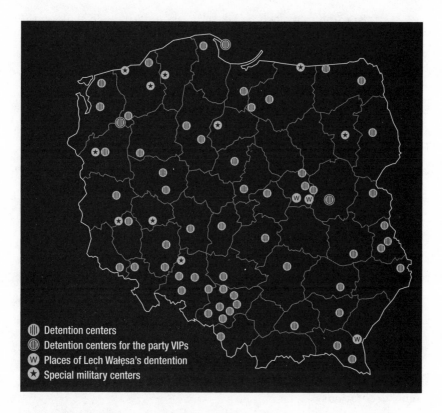

Detention Centers During Martial Law

and allowed the death penalty in political cases. An anonymous poem printed in underground Solidarity newspapers captured the horror of political disappearances:

> *Just look at it, that check shirt*
> *I didn't even have time to wash it for you*
> *Your mother came, and the parish priest*
> *And I'd veal all bought for tomorrow*
> *Christmas round the corner, and you know*
> *I'd found you a present in Chorzow*
> *Some black leather gloves*
> *Oh Jesus, Jesus*[5]

As 1982 came to a close, Solidarity was in peril. Lech Wałęsa, the opposition's charismatic leader, was in prison along with thousands of other Solidarity members. Only about 20 percent of the Solidarity leadership escaped arrest and internment.[6]

———

WHEN MARTIAL LAW BEGAN, Wałęsa realized the situation had dramatically changed. "I knew our movement had been stopped cold, for the time being," he remarked. "It was something I had to accept, like the rules of a game."[7] After initially living under house arrest in Chylice, on the outskirts of Warsaw, Wałęsa was moved to the Otwock Grand Palace about twenty miles southeast of Warsaw. It was a surreal location to house a leading regime opposition member. Not only did Wałęsa escape a drab prison cell, he was sequestered in an architectural treasure. The former summer home of a Polish aristocratic family, the palace's white façade, protective moat, oval towers, and red roof gave it a castle-like appearance. The interior was adorned with elaborate frescoes and bas-relief decorations.

The rooms where Wałęsa stayed were closed off from the rest of the palace, where curators continued their restoration work. He could fish on the palace grounds, and he also zealously listened to broadcasts of Radio Free Europe, Voice of America, and the BBC—initially on a shortwave radio. But after his guards eliminated shortwave reception, Wałęsa used a miniature transistor radio that a supporter had smuggled to him. He lived a solitary life at Otwock, with occasional visits from interrogators, Catholic Church officials, and family. "It was my faith, together with an unshakable belief that Solidarity would win out in the end," he recalled, "that helped me through this period."[8] Pope John Paul II penned an emotional letter, urging Wałęsa to remain hopeful. "I wish to assure you that in these difficult times," the pope wrote, "I am heart and soul with you and your family and with all those who suffer."[9]

His family certainly suffered. On one occasion after visiting Wałęsa, his wife, Danuta, was stopped on the way home and dragged to a police station with two of their children, Anna and Magda.

"I know why you've brought me here," Danuta shouted, "and I'm not getting out of the car. Or rather, I'll get out and take the children with me; we'll walk the rest of the way."

She wasn't expecting the police to use force.

"Don't be stupid," the policeman warned and stood in her way.

Danuta jumped out of the car and tried to dash away with her kids, but a policeman grabbed her and dragged her back inside.

"Let me go," she screamed, as her children began to sob.

"We're going in here," he yelled. Danuta continued to resist, and one of the men pushed her so hard he knocked Anna down as well.

"Shut your mouth, you bitch," one of the policemen thundered.

"Shut your own!" she responded furiously. "And who do you think you're talking to! Haven't I any rights?"

Apparently she didn't. A policeman then inquired whether she had any messages or other items that Wałęsa wanted smuggled out.

"I'm not carrying anything of that sort," Danuta responded.

"Then we'll have to search you," he said.

The search lasted two hours, and the police confiscated a train ticket, photos, religious pictures, a copy of the newspaper *Słowo Powszechne*, and two checks. When the police finally left her, she told the lead policeman that it didn't matter how fancy his uniform was. He was still a filthy pig.[10]

———

JARUZELSKI'S GOAL WAS STRAIGHTFORWARD: to break Wałęsa. But rather than grant him martyrdom through beatings or torture, the regime gave him palatial quarters and sent government visitors to see him. Some visitors offered concessions in exchange for the expulsion of specific "troublemakers" in Solidarity. "Listen, Solidarity can continue to operate," one outlined, "but you've got to drop this guy, and that one, and these others."[11] Several Catholic Church officials also visited him, including Father Alojzy Orszulik and Father Henryk Jankowski, and begged him to be conciliatory for the sake of Polish society. Wałęsa remained implacable, refusing to sacrifice his colleagues or alter the principles of Solidarity. Referring to the Jaruzelski regime, Wałęsa had angrily shouted at Orszulik during one of their first visits: "They'll come to me on their knees!"[12] While most Catholic Church officials supported Solidarity, some were critical of its leaders for being intransigent. Józef Glemp, the archbishop of Warsaw, excoriated Wałęsa for being "inflexible" and "an inexperienced politician."[13]

In March 1982, Wałęsa was moved from the Otwock Grand Palace to a remote hunting lodge in Arłamów, near the Soviet border in southern Poland. During his year of confinement, Solidarity had established a Temporary Coordinating Commission (or *Tymczasowa Komisja Koordynacyjna*, TKK) that spoke on behalf of Solidarity and coordinated activities designed to convince the Jaruzelski regime to end martial law, release prisoners, restore civil rights, and legalize Solidarity. Its members included Zbigniew Bujak, an electrician who had organized strikes at the Ursus tractor factory near Warsaw; Bogdan Lis, a founding member of Solidarity; and Władysław Frasyniuk, a leading Solidarity member from Lower Silesia. To mark the sixty-fourth anniversary of Polish independence, the TKK threatened to hold a large demonstration on November 11, 1982. But Wałęsa worried that the only result would be another round of arrests and detentions.

Despite his obstinacy, Wałęsa was committed to peaceful change in Poland. Over the course of his confinement, Wałęsa believed that strikes were unlikely to help Solidarity's cause, but would provoke an even harsher crackdown by Poland's security forces. "I have no intention of inciting a riot or organizing more strikes," he wrote in a letter to Jaruzelski. "I want to help find a way out of the paralyzing effects of the general strike, because I realize that society can only be weakened by continued stress and shock."[14] This conciliatory tone marked a departure from his comments during Solidarity's meeting at Radom in the fall of 1981, just before martial law, where he briefly acknowledged the possibility of violent confrontation with the regime.[15]

Wałęsa penned a letter to Jaruzelski, which opened the door for his release.

Arlamow, November 8, 1982

> General Wojciech Jaruzelski
> Warsaw
> It seems to me that the moment has come to take a good look at our problems and to reach some kind of understanding. Enough time has passed for it to be widely known now where we stand and what our options are. I propose that we meet for a serious discussion on these matters which concern us all, and I'm sure that with goodwill on both sides, we can come to an agreement.
> Corporal Lech Walesa[16]

Polish newspapers printed the text of the letter the next day. "I wanted the letter to be a proposal, not a plea," Wałęsa explained. "I decided to sign it 'Corporal.' Of course I realized that some people might think it was some kind of joke, but I went ahead anyway."[17] Less than a week later, the Polish government released him. The government's spokesman, Jerzy Urban, announced that Wałęsa was "no longer a threat to internal security."[18] On the night of November 15, 1982, Wałęsa arrived at his apartment at Pilotów 17d/3 in the Zaspa neighborhood of Gdańsk. Thousands of frenzied supporters greeted him, and he addressed them from his window.

"We'll win," he told the cheering crowd. Several shouted that he was their "general," a promotion from his letter to Jaruzelski, which they had read in the press.

———

EVEN BEFORE WAŁĘSA'S RELEASE from Arłamów, Solidarity had managed to stay alive during martial law—though barely. As the political scientist Davis Ost noted, 1982 was not a year for political thought or even political action, it "was a year to survive."[19] Publications were their chief weapon. The Poles referred to underground publishing as *bibuła* ("tissue paper") or as "second circulation" (illegal circulation). Martial law had initially been a major setback for opposition publishing, since Jaruzelski ordered the closure of independent publishing houses, confiscation of printing equipment, and arrest of opposition leaders. But Solidarity and other opposition movements quickly rebounded. During the first year after martial law, roughly 800 illegal periodicals surfaced, many of them associated with Solidarity.[20] By late 1982, there were approximately forty opposition publishing houses that printed a wide variety of books and other publications.[21]

Some of the first underground bulletins began appearing in late December 1981, just days after martial law. While the Jaruzelski regime banned *Tygodnik Solidarność* (*Solidarity Weekly*), the union's official legal bulletin, others like *Tygodnik Mazowsze* surfaced. (*Tygodnik* meant "weekly" and *Mazowsze* referred to the geographical area around Warsaw.) Printed in six different underground shops, the four-page paper eventually reached a circulation of 50,000.[22] In addition to subsequent CIA aid, *Tygodnik Mazowsze* also received funding from the American investor George Soros, who donated money to buy computers.[23]

Before aid from the West arrived, printing capabilities were limited. Sometimes activists were able to illegally use state-operated presses and expropriate state-owned paper supplies.[24] Otherwise, they had to rely on duplicators using alcohol and crude stencils.[25] A duplicator was a machine used extensively in the Polish underground that could print off hundreds of copies of magazines and newspapers from a revolving drum covered in ink. In some cases, printing was done with homemade frames for silk screening or even with modified washing-machine wringers.[26] There were never enough machines, and they often broke down and could not be easily repaired for lack of spare parts.[27] One Solidarity member summed up their travails: "As far as printing equipment was concerned, we simply didn't have anything to conceal. We were barely getting by. Our guys had taken bits and pieces from ancient machines to make new ones so that we'd have something to print with."[28]

Beyond printing, Polish resistance took numerous other forms. Activists painted anti-regime slogans on walls, placed lighted candles in windows on the thirteenth day of each month to remember the onset of martial law, and laid flowers in the form of crosses at the base of monuments or in front of churches. In July 1982, spectators in Spain defiantly waved oversized Solidarity flags during Poland's World Cup soccer match against the Soviet Union, which was captured on television before a worldwide audience.[29]

Dark humor pervaded Polish society. Jokes, poems, and songs were an important component of the struggle. Poles ridiculed Citizens' Militia officers, censors, and Party officials. Cartoonists drew caricatures of government press spokesman Jerzy Urban with large, protruding ears. With power formally transferred during martial law to the Military Council of National Salvation, or WRON, Poles constantly poked fun at the acronym by calling it *wrona* ("crow"). Graffiti on buildings read: "The eagle won't be beaten by the crow." The lyrics of one song ran: "It doesn't matter that the crows are croaking." Political cartoons presented Jaruzelski as a black bird in uniform with the big dark glasses on his beak. "What's the lowest rank in the army?" asked one joke. "A TV presenter," was the answer.[30] An old tune from the German occupation of Poland also made the rounds, with a revised refrain that emphasized the Soviet Union's influence in Poland: "It was on the 13th of this dreadful month / That the crow hatched out of its red shell."[31]

Chapter II

GETTING OFF
THE GROUND

Despite the persistence of Polish opposition, Solidarity was cash- and material-starved. CIA help was critical. Armed with Reagan's presidential finding and with support from the House and Senate intelligence committees, Dick Malzahn and other CIA officers worked to get the covert program off the ground. Two of their most important initial tasks were building an organizational structure and enlisting CIA case officers to join the effort. One of Malzahn's best catches was Cecilia "Celia" Larkin, a sharp Polish-speaker who had been working on Polish radio programs at the Foreign Broadcast Information Service, or FBIS. The service was a part of the CIA that monitored, translated, and disseminated news and information from foreign newspapers, radio stations, and other open sources outside the United States. Larkin understood Polish culture but she had no background in operations and needed training, so the CIA sent her to an accelerated operations course. Covert program managers like Malzahn often encountered dilemmas like this. Seasoned operations officers sometimes knew little about the countries they were tasked to work in. Others understood the country but had no background in operations. It was hard to find those who had both skill sets. Despite her lack of operational experience, Larkin learned quickly.

In January 1983, John Stein, the CIA's deputy director for operations, sent a memorandum to the CIA comptroller asking for an immediate release of $1 million from the Contingency Reserve Fund to jump-start covert aid to Solidarity. Congress's annual budget appropriation to the CIA allowed the director of central intelligence to have this pot of money to address "unforeseen emergencies" around the world, particularly covert action programs.[1] Overall, Stein asked for several types of support to help Solidarity, which totaled roughly $2 million: $600,000 for communications equipment, $300,000 for printing material, $100,000 to assist the families of Solidarity prisoners, over $500,000 for Solidarity members living outside of Poland, and more than $400,000 for propaganda.[2] Unlike the CIA program in Afghanistan, where the United States provided paramilitary material like the famous "Stinger" missiles that neutralized Soviet helicopters, CIA support to Solidarity included only nonlethal assistance. Solidarity, after all, was a *political* movement.[3]

At CIA headquarters, the Polish program initially came under the oversight of the Soviet–East Europe Branch of the Special Activities Group in the International Activities Division (or IAD/SAG/SEB)—a mouthful. When CIA aid to Solidarity began, Robert Magee was chief of the division.[4] In 1983, CIA director Bill Casey divided the International Activities Division into two offices, the Political-Psychological Staff (PPS) and the Counterterrorism, Paramilitary, and Narcotics Staff (CPNS).[5] From then on, the PPS oversaw the Polish program, led by Malzahn, who headed the Soviet–East Europe Branch. Malzahn was committed to implementing the Polish project and to conducting covert action programs against the Soviets across Europe. He viewed Communism with contempt and loathed the KGB. Malzahn was now one of the U.S. government's foremost experts on Soviet active measures and understood better than almost anyone the KGB's ambitious global information campaign. Now was the time to strike, Malzahn believed.

Casey had helped get the Polish program approved, but he had limited time to monitor it because he was busy with other CIA activities including covert action programs against the Soviets in Latin America, Africa, Asia, and other areas of Europe. "He would be briefed periodically," recalled Robert Gates, "but he certainly did not devote the attention to it that I would see in other areas, especially in the Third World."[6] Casey left the execution to Malzahn and others, with some minor exceptions. Casey regularly kept in touch with Zbigniew Brzezinski, President Carter's former national security advisor, about developments in Poland. At one of their meetings, Brzezinski complained that funding had been cut off for a high-profile project. Casey asked how much it would take to remedy the problem and Brzezinski replied, "about $18,000." The next day, an individual showed up at his office without an appointment and asked to see him. The man handed him a briefcase with $18,000 in cash for the project.[7]

———

ON MARCH 1, 1983, THE CIA assigned the Polish program a cryptonym, QRHELPFUL, along with its own file and financial authorization numbers.[8] CIA headquarters, back in the United States, ran QRHELPFUL. But the CIA's Paris station, based out of the U.S. embassy, was a key hub.[9] Other CIA stations in Western Europe and Latin America were also involved in Solidarity support activities, especially London and Bonn. However, the CIA's Warsaw station had virtually no role, since it was under constant surveillance by Polish and Soviet intelligence agencies. Since the Polish program was sensitive, even within the CIA, most analysts and case officers—including those serving in Europe and those working as Polish analysts in the Directorate of Intelligence—did not know much about it. Malzahn visited CIA stations in Europe every few months to check in with case officers. The CIA also held annual confer-

ences for those staff working on QRHELPFUL in such European cities
as London and Stuttgart, Germany, during which they discussed their
efforts across Europe.[10]

When operating overseas, especially on covert action programs, the
CIA had to make choices about whether to collaborate with other intelligence services. Since QRHELPFUL was a unilateral, not a joint, operation, there was little cooperation with European intelligence agencies.
Malzahn and the London station did coordinate with British agencies,
particularly MI6, the United Kingdom's external spy agency. Mossad,
Israel's external intelligence agency, had long maintained a network of
spies that ran from the Middle East into the Balkans, through Poland, and
into the Soviet Union. CIA director Casey wanted to piggyback on this
network for intelligence on Solidarity and help in getting material into
Poland, which Mossad agreed to.[11] The West Germans were generally
aware of CIA support to Solidarity, as were the Swedes, though Malzahn
and others did not provide much detail to them. Malzahn had worked
in the CIA station in Bonn, retained good contacts with West German
intelligence agents, and relied on West German territory to smuggle supplies into—and out of—the Soviet bloc. But he did not partner with the
West Germans for QRHELPFUL. Malzahn and CIA stations across the
continent also didn't coordinate with other European agencies, including the French—and French intelligence agencies generally didn't ask. As
long as Paris believed that Malzahn and the CIA weren't working *against*
France, French officials didn't protest—even if they suspected the CIA
was working with émigrés like Jerzy Giedroyc.

Now that Malzahn and other CIA officials had established an organizational structure for QRHELPFUL and pulled together a team of
case officers, they needed to recruit a stable of assets.

———

ONE OF THE MOST IMPORTANT early catches for the Paris station was a
Polish émigré whom I will call "Stanisław Broda." Broda's CIA code-

name was QRGUIDE. He was born in Poland and joined the nascent opposition movement in the late 1960s. He was a teetotaler, a rarity in the Polish underground. Broda became involved in Poland's illicit press, and he printed and distributed thousands of copies of books, newspapers, and magazines. He mastered the art of printing and built homemade presses with printing matrices—a structure like a wood block or metal plate where the design has been formed and which is used to make an impression on a piece of paper—smuggled from overseas. Broda also hired and trained printers to help with the work, creating an underground army of illicit publishers. Infuriated by the Polish government crackdowns in 1970 and 1976, he was a strident anti-Communist. In the 1970s the SB, Poland's secret police, took an interest in Broda because of his anti-regime activities. SB agents closely monitored his movements and occasionally searched his house in Poland. The establishment of Solidarity in 1980 was a boon for Broda because there was a dramatic rise in interest in the material he published. When martial law finally occurred, Broda was traveling overseas. He did not return to Poland, but settled in Paris among the likes of Jerzy Giedroyc and other Polish émigrés.[12]

Broda was a tremendous help for the CIA and understood the publishing world better than almost any one. He was known to some in the underground as the "boss" because of his authoritative personality and unparalleled network within the Polish underground. While the CIA used the term "assets" to describe individuals like Broda who were clandestine human sources, they were not CIA stooges.[13] Broda was motivated by a desire to aid Solidarity and usher a new era of freedom into Poland. He constantly worried that money would dry up, and he was willing to receive money and other support from the CIA to further those goals. The CIA, in turn, was willing to provide money—bags of it. Cash was the lubricant of the underground, and Broda and other assets used CIA money to purchase duplicators, fax machines, and anything else Solidarity needed to survive. Yet Broda and other assets didn't take daily direction from CIA case officers—and would never have accepted it anyway.

———

ASSETS LIKE BRODA AND THEIR NETWORKS were essential to the success of the CIA's covert action program in Poland. Celia Larkin and other CIA case officers began a sustained effort to recruit individuals like Broda, including human rights activists, underground smugglers, and philanthropists. The CIA gave them codenames like QACARROTTOP and QTOCCUR. To hide the hand of the U.S. government, CIA officials didn't recruit American citizens as assets since they might be easier for the KGB or SB to identify as spies. The CIA also refused to send bulk cash to Poland, which would have increased the likelihood that the Soviets could track serial numbers and identify the origins of the money.[14] Instead, case officers gave the money to assets in Western countries like France to purchase materials and smuggle them to Poland.

By mid-1983, QRHELPFUL had increased to roughly twenty assets.[15] Over the next year, the number of assets rose to around thirty. These assets were divided into three categories. The first were covert action assets, who conducted a broad set of activities from overseeing the identification and movement of material into Poland to helping recruit additional activists.[16] The next were media assets, who were primarily focused on increasing media attention to Solidarity's plight. These individuals were involved in influencing day-to-day media coverage by publishing articles or talking to reporters, as well as organizing political demonstrations in Europe and other locations on significant dates in Polish and Solidarity history. The final category included the surrogate funders, who helped raise money and moved it through clandestine human networks to Solidarity offices and individuals in Poland, Belgium, and other countries throughout Europe.[17]

All three types of assets had important roles to play. The CIA now began devoting funds to diverse purposes like buying communications equipment for the Solidarity underground, printing and infiltrating uncensored publications in Poland, and supporting jailed activists and their families. CIA case officers also began to identify black market routes that already existed and that transported material—including banned goods—into Poland.[18] As Robert Gates explained: "Most of what flowed out of CIA and through the intermediaries to Solidarity was printing materials, communications equipment, and other supplies for waging underground political warfare."[19]

———

EVEN AS THE CIA FORMALLY LAUNCHED QRHELPFUL, Reagan came under fire for not doing enough in Poland. There was growing pressure in the president's Republican Party for stronger action to support Solidarity. In a scathing letter to White House Deputy Chief of Staff Michael Deaver, Terry Dolan, chairman of the National Conservative Political Action Committee, remarked: "Conservatives have been critical of the Reagan Administration's handling of the Polish crisis for two reasons. First, it is bad policy, signaling to the Russians that they can get away with virtually anything," since, in Dolan's view, the Reagan administration had done little in response to martial law.[20] He then referenced a column by George Will, the conservative pundit, who criticized the administration for its mishandling of the Poland situation because the administration "loves commerce more than it loathes communism."[21] Will and other conservatives chastised Reagan for allowing huge grain sales to the Soviet Union, despite the Polish crackdown. This was a terrible mistake, Dolan argued. "Second, the Administration's handling of the Polish crisis has been bad politics. Americans support firm action on Poland, but the administration has attempted to downplay the problem."[22]

The administration was in a no-win situation.[23] Though Reagan had taken some public steps against the Jaruzelski regime, including imposing economic sanctions, the CIA's covert aid to Solidarity was secret. Conservatives like Dolan would never know about QRHELPFUL. The program had to be secret, Reagan concluded, because public awareness of CIA support could severely undermine Solidarity's legitimacy.

By this time, Reagan had developed a genuine curiosity about Polish culture. He viewed members of Solidarity as venerable heroes who stood up to the Jaruzelski regime and the Soviet Union. At the White House, Reagan watched one of the last Polish movies smuggled out after martial law, *Man of Iron*, which was set during the Lenin Shipyard strike in Gdańsk in August 1980. Directed by Andrzej Wajda, the movie depicted Solidarity's initial success in persuading the Polish government to recognize the workers' right to an independent union. "It was most moving & made all of us more determined than ever to help these people," Reagan wrote in his diary, clearly touched.[24]

Reagan showed the ninety-minute television program *Let Poland Be Poland* to a group at the White House. The program was produced by Charles Wick, who was director of the United States Information Agency, a U.S. government organization established by President Dwight D. Eisenhower in 1953 to streamline the government's overseas information programs. Reagan respected Wick's ability to communicate messages. "The genius of Charlie Wick," remarked Reagan, "lies in his ability to recognize how changing information technology, especially satellite communications, has transformed the international political landscape."[25] *Let Poland Be Poland* celebrated Poland's resistance to the Soviets. Bob Hope, Charlton Heston, Kirk Douglas, and Henry Fonda offered statements in support of Solidarity, and Frank Sinatra even sang the Polish folk tune "Wolne Serce" ("Ever Homeward") in Polish.[26] "I think it had a lot of class & must have sent the Russians up the wall," Reagan wrote that evening.[27] The broadcast was beamed by satellite into fifty countries, including in the United States on PBS, though Polish television refused to show it.[28]

Reagan also reached out to imprisoned Solidarity members, reading a message over Voice of America:

I have recently received a moving message from a group of Solidarity trade union members interned in a Polish prison . . . The Polish well-wishers said that they were in prison because they

have been willing to struggle for the same ideals that we celebrate on July 4th. I would like on this occasion to thank these
brave people for their good wishes. Our thoughts and hearts are
with them. The ideals of liberty are eternal and indestructible. I
am confident the day will come when Poland, too, will be able to
celebrate them.[29]

Building on these comments, Reagan remarked in a speech in the
East Room at the White House that Poles—and Americans—needed
to become stronger in the face of adversity. "Lech Walesa not long ago
spoke of the 'wheat that grows from stones,'" Reagan said, "of how freedom sometimes grows from repression of how repression only serves
to strengthen the determination of those living in the darkness of tyranny to someday be free." He urged Americans to pray that "wheat will
someday grow from stones in Poland and other suffering lands and that
the brutal repression of today will be remembered only as a prelude to a
time of freedom, peace and independence." Reagan closed by quoting
Isaiah 40:31:

> But they that wait upon the Lord shall renew their strength;
> they shall mount up with wings as eagles;
> they shall run, and not be weary[30]

Despite Reagan's determination to aid Solidarity, CIA operatives
like Dick Malzahn still faced challenges in executing the program. For
example, how would they smuggle aid to Solidarity members in Poland?

Chapter 12

RATLINES

"An evangelical minister and a politician arrived at Heaven's gate one day together," Reagan said with a wry smile, his eyes twinkling and eyebrows slightly raised. It was just after 3:00 p.m. on a warm spring afternoon in Orlando, Florida, on March 8, 1983. Throngs of supporters crammed into the Citrus Crown Ballroom in the Sheraton Twin Towers Hotel, located along south Orlando's bustling International Drive. Reagan spoke from a lectern emblazoned with the presidential seal, and he was flanked on stage by more than two dozen clergy and politicians. There was a gallant blue curtain behind the stage and an over-sized white sign that advertised the event: "41st Annual Convention of the National Association of Evangelicals." Reagan had the crowd mesmerized. He pressed on.

"And St. Peter, after doing all the necessary formalities, took them in hand to show them where their quarters would be. And he took them to a small, single room with a bed, a chair, and a table and said this was for the clergyman. And the politician was a little worried about what might be in store for him. And he couldn't believe it then when St. Peter stopped in front of a beautiful mansion with lovely grounds, many servants, and told him that *these* would be his quarters," Reagan said, extending forward his left arm, opening up the palm of his hand, and sweeping his arm upward to imitate St. Peter's gesture to the bewildered politician. "And he couldn't help but ask. He said, 'But wait, how—there's something wrong—how do I get this mansion while that good and holy man only gets a single room?' And St. Peter said, 'You have to understand how things are up here. We've got thousands and thousands of clergy. You're the first politician who ever made it.'"[1]

The room erupted. Long after he left Hollywood, Reagan never stopped performing. His sense of humor was infectious. He began this speech with a light, jocular tone, but Reagan quickly moved to the Soviet Union. "During my first press conference as President, in answer to a direct question, I pointed out that, as good Marxist-Leninists, the Soviet leaders have openly and publicly declared that the only morality they recognize is that which will further their cause, which is world revolution," he remarked. Reagan's critique of the godless Communists was red meat for his audience of evangelical Christians. He then criticized those who failed to see the Soviet Union for what it was: a totalitarian state that eschewed religion, oppressed its own population, and supported global expansion. He also warned those promulgating a nuclear weapons freeze, a hotly debated political topic, that such a deal with the Soviets would be tantamount to appeasement:

> So, in your discussions of the nuclear freeze proposals, I urge you to beware the temptation of pride—the temptation of blithely declaring yourselves above it all and label both sides equally at fault, to ignore the facts of history and the aggressive impulses of an *evil empire*, to simply call the arms race a giant misunderstanding and thereby remove yourself from the struggle between right and wrong and good and evil.[2]

The words "evil empire" hung in the air like a snowflake, drifting down to the audience. The remarks that afternoon would go on to become one of Reagan's most famous and celebrated speeches, and the phrase "evil empire" would come to define the Soviet Union for many Americans. Reagan's characterization was deliberate, but also heartfelt. In the president's black-and-white worldview, America was involved in a global struggle with the Soviet Union that pitted right versus wrong and good versus evil.

It was from this outlook that Reagan authorized covert action against the USSR around the world, including in Poland. The Carter administration had been cautious about authorizing covert action following the Church Committee investigations in the 1970s, which found that the CIA had perpetrated a series of abuses and assassinations. Reagan saw covert action as an essential instrument. Still, there was a significant logistical hurdle to launching QRHELPFUL. To wage what Robert Gates described as "underground political warfare," the CIA had to find a way to transfer money and goods to Poland.

———

DICK MALZAHN AND OTHER CIA OPERATIVES overseeing QRHELP-FUL now had assets. But how would they infiltrate money and material into Poland? There were at least two major challenges. First, Soviet, Polish, and other Warsaw Pact governments were acutely aware that Western governments and nongovernmental organizations were conducting clandestine efforts to send money and material to dissidents. Some outside support came from labor unions like the AFL-CIO.[3] Some came from religious groups like the Catholic Church.[4] Some came from humanitarian organizations.[5] Some came from intelligence agencies like the CIA. Polish authorities, who viewed these clandestine programs as subversive attempts to undermine their power and legitimacy, were aggressive in collecting intelligence on infiltration routes, identifying smugglers, and seizing personnel and materials. So any CIA assistance had to be provided under the watchful eyes of the KGB and Warsaw Pact intelligence agencies.

Nevertheless, Malzahn and the CIA team ran assets in places like Sweden, West Germany, Norway, France, Italy, and other European countries. The CIA had mastered the art of smuggling books and other literature across the Iron Curtain throughout the Cold War. As one official remarked, "[B]y the 1980s the Agency had accumulated a great deal of experience, stretching back to the 1950s, in smuggling things into and out of Poland."[6] Moving currency would be a challenge, to be sure, but it would be much harder to move larger items—from typewriters and photocopiers to duplicators—that required trucks and transport beyond one of the most formidable borders in the world.

Second, and more difficult, the CIA wanted to smuggle materials in such a way that Solidarity members—as well as the Soviet and Polish governments—never definitively knew the CIA was providing aid. Solidarity's legitimacy would have been severely undermined if there was unequivocal evidence of CIA assistance. After all, Solidarity was a Polish—not an American—populist movement. The capture of a CIA case officer who was meeting with a Solidarity member, for example, would have handed Jaruzelski a perfect excuse to delegitimize the movement as a tool of foreign intelligence agencies, arrest Solidarity's remaining leaders, and destroy the movement. As former director of central intelligence Robert Gates acknowledged, "Our people thought that deniability was important for Solidarity, and so we worked through third parties or other intermediaries in Western Europe."[7]

Since a direct hand-off of aid from CIA to Solidarity would have risked discovery, case officers and their assets used "ratlines," in CIA parlance. Ratlines referred to routes used to covertly smuggle material, people, and money from one location to another. The operatives utilized smugglers, philanthropists, publishers, and others to move supplies into Poland. A few knew they were working with CIA case officers. Many did not, though some suspected that the CIA or other Western intelligence agencies were involved. Most of the smugglers, including Stanisław

Broda, or QRGUIDE, were already transporting large amounts of material into and out of Poland. By the time the goods made it to Solidarity, they had moved through such a complex web of people, companies, foundations, and geographic locations that it was difficult for anyone—including Solidarity members, the Polish government, and perhaps even the CIA—to keep track of where it was going. The use of assets maximized secrecy by hiding the hand of the CIA, and it protected Solidarity by ensuring that CIA case officers were not working directly with Solidarity members.

But the use of assets and their networks entailed some costs, which all covert action programs faced. CIA assets were often reluctant to reveal the details of ratlines and recipients to protect their sources. Consequently, CIA case officers did not always have a complete understanding of how their money and material were being used, where they were going, who was receiving them, and how useful they were for Solidarity.[8] For example, Broda discussed broad strategic and operational issues with case officers like Celia Larkin, based out of the Paris station, such as what types of material to infiltrate into Poland. He also had to provide receipts to case officers from purchases using CIA funds. But the CIA didn't know all the specifics regarding who Broda worked with, what routes he used, and where the money or material ended up. Broda, who was strong-willed and fiercely independent, would never have provided that type of information anyway—even to the CIA—to protect his network.

As one CIA operative pointed out, since "most intelligence services insist on control over their agents and operations," the decision to suspend the normal rules of tradecraft meant that CIA was "operating on a wing and a prayer that aid would get through." Fortunately, he concluded, "most aid reached its intended destination."[9] In addition, distributing equipment through the underground was not always quick, but could take months or longer.[10] Some CIA officials worried that infiltrating money and material would be problematic because Poland

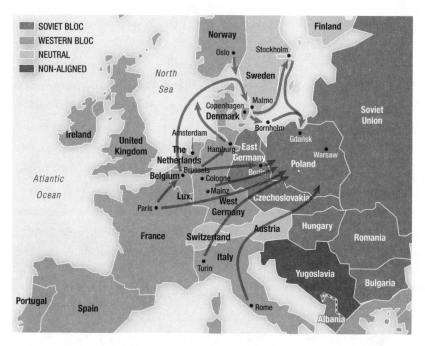

Example of CIA Ratlines into Poland

didn't share a common border with a Western European country. But the Polish border was porous, as Malzahn and others realized. Because of its shaky economic situation, Poland needed goods and humanitarian assistance from Western Europe. CIA case officers used both amateur and professional smugglers.

Many of the infiltration routes were ingenious. Broda had an arrangement with a Turkish émigré who owned a coat factory near Warsaw. The Turkish owner bought sheepskins in Italy for use in his company's coats. When his trucks arrived in West Germany, his workers added Solidarity material to its cargo. Once the trucks arrived in Poland, the Turkish owner and his network distributed the propaganda material to Solidarity activists. On Poland's northern coast, sailors picked up shipments of material during port calls in West Germany and other European coastal cities while their ships were in dry dock. The material was hidden in legitimate cargo and distributed to Solidarity sympathizers when it arrived in Poland. It was too dangerous to place phone calls to recipients, making it difficult to arrange specific pickups once trucks, ships, or individuals delivered equipment in Poland. Instead, Broda would often send a coded postcard that a shipment was on its way.

The map provides an overview of key ratlines, which originated or passed through cities like Malmo and Stockholm, Sweden; Bornholm and Copenhagen, Denmark; Turin and Rome, Italy; Oslo, Norway; Paris, France; West Berlin, West Germany; and Brussels, Belgium.

———

SWEDEN WAS A PRIMARY POINT OF ORIGIN for QRHELPFUL infiltration. Somewhere between one quarter and one half of all material entering Poland arrived from Sweden. West Germany was next at roughly 15 percent.[11] While Sweden was not a NATO member, many of its government officials were sympathetic toward Solidarity. Sweden's southern coastline was also ideal for infiltration. It was just north of Poland on the Baltic Sea, and Sweden was the second state, after the Soviet Union, to sign a trade agreement with Poland after World War II. Sweden and Poland traded machine tools, equipment for steelworks and ships, coal, vegetables, furniture, and textiles—plenty of industries and marketplaces to find holes in.[12]

In 1983, Bill Casey flew to Sweden to ask Prime Minister Olof Palme for assistance. Casey wanted to establish a pipeline to funnel supplies to Solidarity on a regular basis. Because Sweden maintained neutrality, however, many doubted Casey's trip would be successful. "He planned to persuade the Swedes to go along and help out in the effort to support Solidarity," remarked one of his aides. "No one thought he could pull it off."[13] Casey hinted to Palme that he could have simply conducted the operation without alerting the Swedish government, but working together would be much more productive. Palme agreed to help.[14] The CIA now had top cover to use ports, ships, and smugglers in Sweden to move material to the Solidarity underground. To help ensure the goods reached Poland, individuals working in the underground paid off port officials to look the other way when boats docked at Polish ports.

CIA assets and their broader network of smugglers showed great creativity in moving supplies across the Baltic Sea. The CIA provided money to individuals like QRGUIDE who, in turn, purchased materials and sent them through European cities like Brussels. From there, the goods might be repackaged and shipped to Stockholm. Once in Sweden, the containers would be relabeled and placed on crates in ships marked as "tractor parts," "machine tools," or "fish products."[15] In some cases, smugglers shipped Solidarity publications through Bornholm, Denmark—a Danish island in the Baltic Sea south of Sweden—hidden in automobiles. A fireman named Bogarski had the ingenious idea of using fire extinguishers. Polish border guards never suspected that fire extinguishers could be filled with illegal propaganda![16]

Marian Kaleta, a Swedish optometrist based in Malmo, was a particularly active smuggler. He had left Poland after the student riots in the late 1960s, settled in Sweden, and set up an optometry business. Sweden attracted him because it had a robust network of Polish émigrés, and the city library in Malmo had stacks of books in Polish for him to read.[17] Inspired by the formation of the Workers' Defense Committee, or KOR, Kaleta established the Society for Friends of *Kultura*, which drew support from the large Polish émigré community in southern Sweden and provided funds to Jerzy Giedroyc's magazine in Paris. Kaleta paid professional smugglers to move items by boat and brought printing devices, copiers, paint, books, and other materiel—including the first Gestetner stencil duplicating machine—from Sweden to ports along Poland's Baltic coast. He also worked with Jerzy Giedroyc to infiltrate *Kultura* and other magazines into Poland, along with his legitimate eye-examination equipment. The Solidarity office in Brussels used Kaleta's services as well. Kaleta began using a commercial truck with hidden compartments that transported optometry equipment.[18]

———

Stanisław Broda, or QRGUIDE, recruited legal travelers, from mountain climbers to academics, who moved small amounts of cash and messages to—and from—Poland. Broda and others sent items through the mail since Polish authorities often failed to catch letters and care packages with money or small amounts of contraband. CIA assets also hid material in food and other containers. Ink or silkscreen emulsion, for example, could be concealed in cans of food and containers of Hershey's chocolate syrup. Broda's most common technique, however, was to send concealed material on trucks, boats, ships, and tour buses arriving in Poland.[19] One of Broda's most ingenious inventions was a reconfigured refrigeration truck, which had a dividing wall and a hidden compartment that could fit up to ten offset printers.

Broda also used sea routes. He worked closely with the Mainz Solidarity office, which had access to Polish barges. The barges brought coal to West Germany and returned with iron ore and other raw materials. A sympathetic West German businessman who sold artificial fibers in Poland allowed Broda and the Solidarity network to include contraband in his shipments, which entered the country without scrutiny. Solidarity sympathizers were informed of the shipments and removed the contraband while unloading the West German trucks when they arrived in Poland.

Broda and others also hid or camouflaged contraband in legitimate humanitarian aid shipments. Using a Polish shipping firm whose trucks operated under the TIR, or *Transports Internationaux Routiers* (International Road Transports) system, Broda could dispatch small parcels in four days. The TIR system was an international agreement instituted after World War II to facilitate international transport between participating European countries. TIR established a coordinated system of customs control that helped protect the revenue of each participating country. It allowed companies to move goods in sealed vehicles or containers from a customs office of departure in one country to a customs office of destination in another country. The trucks did not require extensive and time-consuming border checks since customs checks were performed at the points of origin and destination, not at border crossings.[20] Using trucking firms that operated under TIR was invaluable for CIA operatives, since Warsaw Pact border agencies did not scrutinize the cargo at the border.

CIA assets and their networks generally loaded smuggled goods onto trucks after they were inspected by customs officials at the point of origin in countries like West Germany and Sweden, and took them off the trucks before they arrived at the final destination in Poland. In some of these trucks, they disguised the contraband as food shipments. Broda and his colleagues sometimes sealed publications in waterproof wrapping and inserted them into tins of "soup." They also smuggled communications equipment into Poland so that Solidarity could maintain contact with the West and with each other.[21] As Reagan advisor Robert "Bud" McFarlane explained, the equipment gave Solidarity "the means of communication with their own membership and the country at large and the means of staying in touch with each other and avoiding compromise."[22]

Overall, the CIA obligated nearly $1.5 million to Solidarity in fiscal year 1983, not quite the $2 million that John Stein, the CIA's deputy director for operations, had requested. QRGUIDE led the way. He sent approximately $50,000 to the leadership of the Temporary Coordinating Commission, or TKK, through a legal traveler and infiltrated 30,000 copies of opposition journals.

———

ANOTHER CIA PARIS STATION ASSET, whom I will call "Artur Kowalski," moved books, magazines, printing equipment, and supplies like book staplers and stencils into Poland. He also organized financial aid for a Polish journal. Kowalski had been a student at the Catholic University of Lublin and a KOR activist involved in underground printing who moved to Paris. After trying to publish banned books by taking photographs of their pages and reprinting them, which looked unprofessional since the pages were barely readable, he switched to duplicators. Kowalski and his colleagues even purchased a small spirit duplicator, disassembled it, and worked with a theater group traveling to Poland to smuggle it into the country. Kowalski utilized a network of individuals in countries like France, Sweden, West Germany, and East Germany to smuggle material into Poland. He was an entrepreneur and raised money by smuggling vodka out of Poland and into France, selling it, and using the proceeds to buy printing equipment for the Polish underground.[23]

Kowalski was a natural target for the CIA since he already had a deep network of smugglers and substantial experience in underground printing. Like most assets involved in QRHELPFUL, Kowalski didn't take much direction from CIA case officers and ran his underground networks with little interference. What he needed—and what the CIA was willing to give him—was money.

In Bonn, a German CIA asset whom I will call "Erhardt Brauer," codenamed QACARROTTOP, passed CIA money from his foundation to a Catholic clergyman. Church officials were not subject to border controls and therefore could carry in money without much risk of search and seizure. QACARROTTOP also gave funds to the Solidarity offices in Paris and Brussels using CIA money masked as foundation donations. For several years, the CIA tried—and ultimately failed—to send an industrial printing press into Poland through QACARROTTOP.[24] Another agent, codenamed QTOCCUR, lived in Oslo and was married to a Norwegian woman. He made frequent business trips to Poland, giving him cover as a legal traveler. A CIA asset in Mexico City, whom I will call "Ryszard Nowicki," sent another $20,000 through his contacts. As one CIA official summarized, "legal travelers to and from Poland served as couriers who carried small amounts of cash and sometimes messages. Though slow and cumbersome, it was secure."[25]

As the CIA recruited assets like Broda, Kowalski, and Brauer, the Polish regime made sure that Wałęsa and his family suffered for their continuing opposition.

Chapter 13

THE UNDERGROUND

B y 1983, Wałęsa was back at home in Gdańsk. But managers at the Lenin Shipyard where he led the August 1980 strike refused to let him return to his job, almost certainly at the insistence of the Jaruzelski regime. Jaruzelski hoped to turn Wałęsa into a "nonperson" and assumed that Solidarity could not function without his active, charismatic leadership.[1] But while the regime might be able to slow down the Solidarity movement, they couldn't weaken Wałęsa's spirit. He told Western journalists in 1983 in an impromptu news conference that the authorities were "arrogant" and "ill willed." Solidarity had a peaceful and realistic program: "It was a moral force without whose participation Poland could not get out of the crisis." His key theme was that "we do not want to overthrow the Government. We do not want to push the party aside. We do not want to undermine our country's alliances. What we want is to improve workers' living conditions within the framework of pluralism."[2]

It was a difficult time for Wałęsa and his family. To witness the regime's oppression, all they needed to do was open their front door. In the spring of 1983, for instance, there were clashes between the police and young demonstrators outside the Wałęsas' mammoth housing development at Pilotów 17d/3 in the Zaspa area of Gdańsk. Militia forces arrived to disperse the demonstrators with tear gas. In response, neighbors leaned out their windows, jeered the police, and pelted them with flowerpots and glass jars. But the regime wouldn't back down. Wałęsa was a constant target.[3] It was disconcerting enough for Wałęsa to see the government publicly slander him. It was doubly disturbing that his wife and children had to see it too. "Week after week they watched how the government spokesman spat on me with total immunity by repeating lies and distortions," Wałęsa recalled, lamenting that his children endured constant abuse. "I was called a bourgeois laborer who couldn't muster the support of a hundred workers, an ignorant fool with too many children, a religious zealot led around by the nose by priests, a CIA agent . . . a tax evader."[4] The list went on.

Though there is no evidence that Wałęsa ever was involved with QRHELPFUL or had any relationship with the CIA, the Jaruzelski regime still disparaged him as a spy. The Polish government often blamed the CIA for dissident actions and accused Solidarity of being manipulated by Western intelligence agencies. It was a tactic the Poles had borrowed from the Soviets, who incessantly complained that the CIA was involved in widespread efforts to subvert Soviet power. Moscow and Warsaw were accurate in assuming the CIA was involved in aid to opposition groups, though they often exaggerated the CIA's influence. But CIA case officers like Celia Larkin were careful enough to provide assistance to the Polish underground without Solidarity's firsthand knowledge.

———

SOLIDARITY NEEDED MONEY TO OPERATE, and its members tirelessly tried to raise funds from U.S. and European labor unions, philanthropists, and the Polish émigré population. CIA operatives like Larkin were well aware of underground needs. Activists involved in printing the four-page weekly *Tygodnik Mazowsze*, which received some covert assistance from CIA, were open about their reliance on international support. "The question of money?" asked one activist, named Maria. "It's not touchy at all. The weekly supports itself with individual contributions, and the only difference is that they are mostly collected from Poles abroad." Another activist, named Paweł, lauded the support from Jerzy Giedroyc's journal: "The Paris *Kultura* sends us a thousand dollars a month of Polonia's contributions, and we make about 200,000 [złotys] from selling the weekly's matrices and sheets of metal, and the rest are contributions from Poland. The income more or less covers our monthly expenses, which range around one million."[5] It wasn't just money that *Tygodnik Mazowsze* needed, explained a Solidarity activist named Andrzej, it was also material like "machines and parts [that] began to arrive from the West."[6]

With a number of Solidarity publishers arrested or exiled, the task for restarting Solidarity presses fell to veteran underground journalists like Halina Łuczywo and Joanna Szczęsna. They used leftover portable presses to print *Tygodnik Mazowsze*, though they desperately needed an infusion of money and equipment.[7] At the center of the underground was the Temporary Coordinating Commission. It created a network of clandestine institutions connected to Solidarity, which constituted the underground's infrastructure.[8] The commission's first leader was Zbigniew Bujak, a gritty former electrician and foreman at the Ursus tractor factory near Warsaw who successfully evaded Poland's secret police for several years. Bujak wrote countless statements and manifestos that were published by the underground press, and he organized press conferences for foreign reporters.[9]

Solidarity sympathizers set up underground printing shops across the country. The CIA made lists of these sites. One of the most important was in Oliwa, a suburb of Gdańsk, in the home of Lechosław Witkowski. It was built by several people, including Zbigniew Nowek, a member of the Independent Students' Union, the student arm of Solidarity. Witkowski and others introduced Nowek as a "cousin from the countryside." Under this cover, Nowek constructed a print shop to publish

Tygodnik Mazowsze and Solidarity's regional bulletin. Entry to the shop was in the basement, and activists accessed it through a trap door located under the refrigerator. Although the house was frequently searched, Nowek's print shop was never discovered.[10] Another printing shop, near Gdańsk, was located in the cellar of a small house, and Solidarity sympathizers used concrete, lumber, steel beams, and a 380-volt electric line to build the shop. They registered the shop as a "small business," a frequent cover for illegal printing shops. Many shops also had fake walls, entrances through wardrobes, partition walls with false chimneys, and other ways to conceal the existence of clandestine shops.[11]

There were large and small print shops. Many like Nowek's shop included some combination of typewriters, fax machines, and photocopiers. Some used duplicators like the Rex-Rotary 1050 duplicator made in Denmark or the AB Dick 8400 offset duplicating press. Duplicators were pervasive in the underground. "A professional printing team could be trained in just four hours," explained one Solidarity member. Many duplicators were small enough that they could be placed in a kitchen or bathroom, and individuals could make dinner or bathe their children during breaks in the printing cycle.[12] In addition to duplicators, there were other ways to copy material. Some print shops used a screen printing frame to copy underground publications. The frame could be easily made at home in less than an hour.[13]

Moving the dissident publications from print shops to their intended audiences, from workers in Polish shipyards to students at Polish universities, required a separate clandestine network. Underground distributors frequently traveled in the dim, poorly lit streets of Polish cities and towns carrying material in rucksacks, suitcases, bags, and sacks. A distributor in Bydgoszcz, for example, tied printed material to his shoulders with string, hidden under his coat.[14] Distributors used multiple routes to avoid detection and employed the old spy technique of drop boxes, or "dead drops," which involved leaving material in a secret location so the distributor and the recipient never met directly. Solidarity members conducted dead drops in drains, tree holes, and under church pews.[15]

Distributing material was a dangerous business. One distributor, named Paweł Bąkowski, ran from police officers after being identified and jumped out of a moving train at the Warszawa Stadion station, located on the east bank of the Vistula near Warsaw's city center. Bąkowski had with him a bag of Tomasz Jastrun's books of underground poems, *Na skrzyżowaniu Azji i Europy* (*On the Crossroads of Asia and Europe*). He sprinted to the Vistula, stashed his bag in the bushes, and retrieved it the next day.[16] Another distributor named Maria Ostrowski recalled a similar, harrowing encounter. "When it got dark, I packed three small bags—dozens of copies of essays by Tadeusz Niczek about the poets of the 1968 generation. We drove to Sielecka Street in Warsaw," she explained. The situation then became dangerous. "On Sobieskiego Street we were stopped by a militia patrol. A soldier, Government Protection Bureau functionary, or a ZOMO, I don't remember, in a camouflage uniform came up to us. His eyes swept the taxi's interior, he leaned towards me, kissed my hand, saluted, handed back my identity card and walked away. I was shocked."[17] So was the driver. Ostrowski was fortunate, since a less sympathetic ZOMO officer might have handcuffed her and thrown her in jail for distributing illegal materials.

RADIO WAS ALSO AN IMPORTANT WEAPON for the underground. Overt programs like Radio Free Europe, Voice of America, Vatican Radio, BBC, and Solidarity's own underground transmitters filled the airwaves with messages from the underground.[18] Covert CIA funds were also used for the purchase of portable radio transmitters. On April 12, 1982, four months after the crackdown, citizens in Warsaw heard the inaugural broadcast of Radio Solidarity, which was broadcast from the roof of a building on Grojecka Street.[19] Zofia and Zbigniew Romaszewski, members of Solidarity's Warsaw leadership, were responsible for the program. On May 9, they broadcast a brief appeal for a general strike.[20] Supported by covert CIA funds, Radio Solidarity went on the air from multiple, roving locations.[21] Like the underground newspapers, the radio showed Poles that Solidarity was still alive and that the Soviet-backed Jaruzelski regime could not eliminate it.[22] But not all U.S. allies were enamored. The West German government refused to allow the CIA to operate a clandestine radio station on German territory, concerned about the Soviet response.

Radios were also used for counterintelligence purposes. Zygmunt Błażek, an activist in the underground, used radio parts to construct a device for listening in on the ZOMO. The radio helped identify the location of units deployed against demonstrators. One of the listening stations was located in Gdańsk, in Błażek's home. The antenna was fitted onto the window frame so that it would not be identified by suspicious militia officers. Błażek and his colleagues then recorded and decrypted the intercepted messages.[23]

———

BY THE MID-1980s, Solidarity's Coordinating Bureau in Brussels, which had been thoroughly penetrated by Polish and Soviet intelligence, had taken in roughly a half a million dollars per year of overt funds. Approximately $300,000 per year came from the AFL-CIO, $100,000 from the International Confederation of Free Trade Unions (ICFTU), and smaller amounts from labor unions in Europe, Canada, Australia, and Japan.[24]

Two CIA-supported publications, *Kultura* and *Aneks*, opened their pages to debates within the émigré and underground communities on strategies and tactics for creating political change in Poland. The underground press, with substantial assistance abroad, flourished as never before. In 1983, there were at least 1,500 uncensored publications in circulation. *Tygodnik Mazowsze* was among the most influential, and it was also Solidarity's largest underground paper. Its pages were filled with news reports, editorials, Solidarity events, and columns by well-known writers and activists. One of its main purposes was to remind Poles that a unified opposition continued to exist.

Irena Lasota, a Polish activist who emigrated after 1968 and formed a Solidarity support committee, summed up the role of illegal publishing by noting that it "allowed Solidarity to survive during martial law. It kept people informed. It also gave Solidarity activists a sense of unity and comradeship and a purpose . . . For some in Poland, the only sign that Solidarity was alive came through the press."[25] Wiktor Kulerski, one of the Temporary Coordinating Commission's founders, put it succinctly: "The printing presses we got from the West during martial law might be compared to machine guns or tanks during war. The importance of the press cannot be overemphasized."[26]

The CIA's success, however, made the opposition press much more prominent and visible. No strangers to propaganda, Polish and Soviet intelligence agencies now moved to expose and crush outside aid, and reassert control over the message.

Chapter 14

HARDBALL

In early 1983, Polish police and intelligence units conducted raids against Solidarity across the country. They arrested members of the underground and ransacked clandestine printing shops. They also seized radios, printing presses, and leaflets with "anti-state content." Jaruzelski's government was expansive in their operations. They targeted print shops in Warsaw, Kraków, Wrocław, Lublin, Katowice, Olsztyn, and Rzeszów. According to internal records from the SB, Poland's secret police, agents seized 1.3 million leaflets, 10,160 posters, 828,050 copies of journals and books, 9 offset presses, 7 Xerox machines, 101 duplicators, 252 silkscreen frames, 297 typewriters, and 4,696 reams of paper in 1982 and 1983 alone.[1] Polish state-controlled television and radio stations prominently trumpeted the arrests and confiscations. Among the most important figures detained by the police was Zbigniew Bełz, a member of Solidarity's former national commission from Gorzów in western Poland. Bełz had been hiding from authorities since martial law in December 1981.[2]

Perhaps most concerning for the CIA, the Polish government attempted to expose the hidden hand of Western governments in aiding the underground. "In *all* cases," the Polish government publicly

announced after one of the arrests, "Western-made equipment and materials were used."³ On the evening news, television announcers explained
that Western intelligence agencies had provided radios and printing
presses to Solidarity members. Polish and Soviet government officials
had long suspected that the CIA was providing assistance to Solidarity,
and Warsaw and Moscow desperately tried to counter QRHELPFUL.

Before his death, Soviet leader Leonid Brezhnev—whom Wałęsa
affectionately referred to as a "heap of rusting iron"—had written a
scathing letter to Reagan demanding that the United States "end at last
the interference in the internal affairs of a sovereign state—the Polish
People's Republic." Brezhnev bluntly noted that "this interference in the
most diverse forms—overt *and covert*—has been underway for a long
time, already."⁴

KGB officials knew Poland was just one front in the war of ideas.
Secret KGB documents assessed that the CIA was fighting a broad
ideological war to subvert the Soviet Union and its satellite countries.
One document with an unwieldy title, "Plan for Basic Counterintelligence Measures to Step Up Still Further the Effort to Combat the Subversive Intelligence Activities of the United States Special Services,"
established priorities for KGB residences abroad and warned that "the
United States special services are continually increasing their subversive intelligence activities against the USSR and expanding the scale
on which hostile methods are used to undermine the military and economic potential, defense capability and preparedness for mobilization
of our country." Alarmed, KGB leaders made it a priority to obtain
intelligence on "operations planned by the American special services
and centers of ideological sabotage associated with them and designed
to step up psychological warfare."⁵

———

ONE OF THE MOST DRAMATIC RAIDS occurred at the summer cottage of
Mariusz Dmochowski, a burly Polish actor who appeared in more than

forty-five films, including popular Polish films like *The Doll*, *A Woman's Decision*, and *The Scar*. In addition to his work as an actor, Dmochowski was a deputy in the Polish parliament, director of a Warsaw theater, and chairman of the Union of Cultural and Artistic Employees. But he handed over his Communist Party membership card in disgust after the imposition of martial law and resigned his posts. Dmochowski became increasingly active in the Polish opposition and used his cottage in Popowo, a fashionable area of country houses south of Warsaw in the woods along the Vistula, to publish underground material. After conducting twenty-four-hour surveillance of Dmochowski, police raided his house and, as Poland's official press agency triumphantly announced, caught him "red-handed while printing illegal materials."[6] Police also seized a duplicator, the blueprint for a radio transmitter, and 16,000 copies of "anti-state" publications.[7] The Polish government newspaper *Rzeczpospolita* then devoted a long editorial to what it described as Dmochowski's traitorous and "disgusting political volte-face."[8]

The SB also conducted an aggressive effort to infiltrate smuggling networks. An SB informant codenamed "Boro" successfully penetrated a route used by the underground to move printing equipment from Sweden to Poland's Baltic coast. Boro secretly recorded conversations on the boat; collected intelligence on the individuals, routes, methods, and material like duplicators on board; and filmed smugglers unloading the goods in Poland. The SB then arrested the ringleaders, Stanisław Kotowski and Andrzej Karpinski, and threw them in prison.[9]

For every raid like the ones against Dmochowski, Kotowski, and Karpinski, the SB conducted a detailed analysis of each book, pamphlet, journal, typewriter, and duplicator seized. SB bureaucrats recorded and described the particulars of each item in their *Index of Anonymous Documents* (*Kartoteka Dokumentów Anonimowych*, or KDA). The SB then used this information to conduct further investigations and as court evidence against individuals charged with illegal publishing.[10]

Polish and Soviet security agencies were now convinced that the CIA was behind the opposition, though they couldn't prove it. As one KGB

official remarked: "Ideologically it made sense" that the CIA was providing support to Solidarity, "but we had no evidence." Over time, however, "the telltale evidence began to appear. They were well funded. They
had sophisticated means for carrying out their activities. We knew then
they were getting something from someone."[11] The Soviets also openly
published several newspaper articles about CIA activity in Poland and
other Eastern European countries, in part to alert U.S. officials they
were watching. An article in the Soviet newspaper *Pravda*, for example,
outlined Soviet suspicions: "Facts show that the aggressive circles of the
imperialist states, above all the United States, are conducting a subversive policy against the socialist countries. The subversive actions conducted in the framework of this policy . . . are assuming ever more acute
forms." The *Pravda* article continued that "the psychological warfare"
waged by Washington was "without precedent in peacetime."[12]

Tensions spilled out into the open when Polish police roughed up
two American diplomats: John William Zerolis, a scientific and technical affairs officer; and James Daniel Howard, the first secretary for cultural affairs. The diplomats were accused of undermining the stability of
the Polish state by encouraging anti-government activity, declared to be
personae non gratae, and promptly expelled from Poland.[13] The Jaruzelski regime also sentenced several "CIA collaborators" to death in absen-
tia for treason. One was Zdzislaw Najder, who was director of the Radio
Free Europe Polish Service in Munich.[14]

As part of its disinformation campaign, the KGB forged allegedly
official or semiofficial U.S. documents. One was a U.S. State Department telegram suggesting that the Reagan administration's Project
Democracy, a multiyear information campaign coordinated by the U.S.
Information Agency, was training covert operatives to overthrow ruling communist and socialist regimes. Another was a forged letter from
the AFL-CIO's chief of international operations, Irving Brown, to an
Italian union member which suggested the labor organization and CIA
were supporting Solidarity. In addition to forgeries, Warsaw and Moscow orchestrated a propaganda blitz delegitimizing Reagan. In early

1983, CIA director Bill Casey wrote a sensitive memorandum to National Security Adviser William Clark saying, "Warsaw continues to mount a vitriolic anti-U.S. campaign, complete with posters ridiculing President Reagan."[15] The KGB sketched out plans to sabotage Reagan's coming reelection campaign by branding him as a warmonger. The KGB's Service A, which was responsible for foreign intelligence operations, devised the slogan "Reagan Means War!"[16]

To assist Jaruzelski, KGB headquarters dispatched a large contingent of spies, including many of its Polish-speaking officers, to the Soviet embassy in Warsaw and Soviet consulates in Gdańsk, Kraków, Poznań, and Szczecin. The KGB also sent intelligence operatives posing as tourists to develop contacts within Solidarity and to gather information.[17] Using a venerable Soviet technique, the KGB spread disinformation in the form of anti-Semitic propaganda and rumors to tarnish Solidarity.[18] These KGB operatives worked closely with the Polish SB, who alerted Moscow about actions against Solidarity.

———

ON NEW YEAR'S DAY IN 1983, the Polish police seized a Solidarity underground printing plant near Poznań, arresting fifteen activists. Polish officials uncovered two underground political cells that produced and distributed leaflets in Gdańsk, arresting at least nine individuals. Polish police raided two other locations used for storing and distributing literature in Warsaw, arresting three individuals. The police rounded up at least five more Solidarity underground members in Leszno and raided a Solidarity radio station in the southwestern city of Kędzierzyn-Koźle. Among the most high-profile arrests was Solidarity leader Stanisław Zabłocki, who headed the strike committee in the Szczecin shipyards.[19] Distribution of literature became more difficult for Solidarity as arrests proliferated.

During the year after martial law, the SB had identified 701 underground opposition groups, 430 of them associated with Solidarity. They also reported that they had arrested 10,131 individuals and dispersed over 400 demonstrations.[20] The SB kept a close eye on family members and friends of suspected CIA assets like Artur Kowalski, who had family in Warsaw. SB operatives mapped out the networks of notable individuals suspected of involvement in the underground, tapped their phones, recruited informants close to them, and conducted surveillance. The SB never found definitive evidence that Kowalski or others, such as Stanisław Broda, or QRGUIDE, were working with the CIA. Broda had a close call when Polish authorities arrested one of his smugglers, who drove a refrigeration truck transporting underground material. The regime announced the arrest immediately but could not link the operation directly to the CIA. Still, smuggling was a tense business for individuals like Broda, who suffered several heart attacks. As one member of the underground remarked, "everyday stress played a part . . . To be active in a small center was like being naked on an open beach. One felt watched all the time, and one constantly expected to be arrested."[21]

Polish security agencies, including the Ministry of Internal Affairs, stepped up their aggressive disinformation and intimidation tactics. With help from the KGB, they denounced some opposition leaders as homosexuals. They told the wives of other Solidarity activists that their husbands were philanderers who were using their political activities as a cover to have extramarital affairs. They forced selected Solidarity leaders to publicly recant their views and denounce their colleagues on radio and television as members of a "terrorist" organization. Ministry of Internal Affairs agents also painted crosses on the houses of selected army officers and spread rumors that Solidarity had targeted them for liquidation.

———

THE CIA KNEW THAT THE Polish countermeasures were having an impact. In early 1983, CIA director Casey shared an intelligence report with Reagan which concluded that despite recent Polish government "conciliatory" actions, the Jaruzelski regime had become more repressive and had achieved a "clear victory over the Solidarity underground." The report depicted the situation as grim for thousands that remained under arrest while "persecution and defiance persist."[22] Jaruzelski had released a number of individuals from internment, but the CIA saw these as tactical maneuvers—not substantive concessions. Based on intelligence from an underground activist, the CIA reported that Solidarity internees who were released were systematically harassed and urged to leave the country. One in five suffered significant job demotions.[23] Poland's parliament, the Sejm, passed a new trade union law that explicitly outlawed Solidarity and provided the regime with numerous controls over future trade unions. The Sejm also passed an "anti-parasitism" law which was used to punish regime critics, or "social parasites."

CIA analysts concluded that these and other steps indicated the regime's "increased confidence that they have crushed the will to resist" among Poles. The CIA deduced that "there is no reason to believe that, in the coming months, the nervous security-minded authorities will ease their efforts to quash the underground press, arrest fugitive leaders, and generally prevent underground organizational work."[24] Some members of Congress like Barry Goldwater, who chaired the Senate Intelligence Committee, also grew anxious that Polish or Soviet intelligence agencies might find incontrovertible evidence that the CIA was providing covert assistance to Solidarity.

In August 1983, Goldwater sent a note to Bill Casey summarizing his counterintelligence concerns.[25] Goldwater, who not-so-affectionately referred to Casey as "flapper lips," was frustrated because he believed Casey was deceitful with Congress about CIA covert action programs and Casey's own involvement in potentially questionably business deals that had come under congressional scrutiny.[26] Goldwater complained to Casey that he was troubled by "the lack of counterintelligence information being provided" to the Senate Select Committee on Intelligence, which he chaired, and demanded that Casey "instruct appropriate members of your staff to provide the Committee with information regarding these counterintelligence issues."[27] Poland was a useful example for Goldwater. If Polish or Soviet intelligence agencies found proof of CIA aid to Solidarity, which would have been a counterintelligence failure, it could seriously damage America's—and the CIA's—reputation overseas and at home less than a decade after the Church Committee investigations into CIA improprieties.

Would QRHELPFUL remain covert? And, even if so, would it be enough to keep the underground alive? Secretary of State George Shultz was skeptical in 1983 of Solidarity's chances for survival. "[I]t is becoming increasingly evident," Shultz warned Reagan, "that prospects for a revival of the Solidarity period are dim for the foreseeable future."[28] Administration officials knew that the Soviets were urgently trying to piece together CIA activity in Poland. "I think it would be foolish to believe that they didn't have a reasonable idea of the things we were doing," said Admiral John Poindexter, Reagan's deputy national security advisor. "They had informants that were telling them what was going on. And so I think our assumption when we planned operations was that they knew in general terms what we were doing. They fussed about it and raised threats, but it never got to a threshold where we even considered changing our policy."

Despite losing ground in the ideological battle, Reagan and other officials, including Dick Malzahn, maintained their position that the CIA should refrain from providing weapons, ammunition, and other lethal aid to Solidarity, as the administration was doing with the mujahideen in Afghanistan. The CIA pointedly refused to provide aid to "Fighting Solidarity" (Solidarność Walcząca), led by Kornel Morawiecki. Its main goal was to regain independence for Poland, and Morawiecki supported the use of armed violence for self-defense purposes—such as in response to a brutal regime crackdown. Weapons in Eastern Europe would have been a red line for Moscow. "We tempered what we would do for Solidarity," recalled Poindexter, "by not doing those things that would provide the trigger that would provoke the Soviets into military intervention."[29]

CIA DIRECTOR CASEY SAW THE SETBACKS to Solidarity as part of a much bigger problem. He waged a public relations war inside the administration, arguing that the Soviets had developed an increasingly assertive policy to expand power and undermine U.S. influence across the globe. Casey ordered CIA analysts to carefully document KGB and other Soviet actions—including "active measures"—and then brief the results to U.S. government and congressional leaders. By 1983, Casey had settled in as one of Reagan's closest confidants. Reagan relied heavily on the CIA and approved huge budget raises for the organization—22 percent per year for the first three years of his administration. Under Casey, personnel soared by an average of almost 8 percent per year during the same period.[30] Casey had now vaulted to national attention, recognizable by his stooped physique, heavy glasses, and virtually indecipherable speech. He chewed the end of his ties during meetings and occasionally picked his teeth with paperclips. He sounded like a shortwave radio broadcast with bad reception. His tired eyes, stiffened gait, and drooped head made him look like Ebenezer Scrooge from *A Christmas Carol*. Undisciplined wisps of hair fluttered on the edges of his bald head.[31]

Yet Casey had a thoughtful, probing, and educated mind. He was a voracious reader and had amassed an impressive knowledge of guerrilla movements a few years earlier while researching his book on the American Revolutionary War, titled *Where and How the War Was Fought*.[32] Published in 1976, the book was emblematic of Casey's approach to intelligence. It was carefully researched and supplemented by on-site inspections of the terrain, fortifications, harbors, hallowed taverns, and meandering streams of revolutionary war sites from Lake Champlain to Yorktown. The book exemplified what Casey expected of his analysts at CIA: detail and objectivity. Casey became notorious within the CIA for his hard-driving management style, which his critics often termed confrontational. But he was also praised for improving the CIA's standards for analytical work.[33]

Casey's examination of revolutionary war fighting—particularly the American use of guerrilla warfare tactics against better-equipped and better-trained British regulars—informed his approach to the global proxy war against the Soviets. From Casey's perspective, diplomacy and conventional military operations were not ideal options against the Soviets, particularly since conventional campaigns that pitted American and Russian forces facing each other across a field of battle risked escalation to nuclear war. Covert action was the mechanism for rolling back the Soviets and limiting U.S. involvement. Reagan supported Casey's vision. With the president's backing, the CIA expanded its ability to take military and political action outside the United States, while also supporting a wider range of anti-Communist insurgent organizations in developing countries.

Over the course of 1983, Casey wrote several alarming "eyes only" memos to Reagan and Clark about Soviet expansionism.[34] In one memorandum to Reagan, for example, a vexed Casey pleaded: "I must draw your attention to the acute danger that we may be on the brink of a great failure in Central America. This could not only bring permanent damage to our security and geopolitical position in this hemisphere but could also reverse what has been achieved in checking the advances the Soviets had made in Asia, Africa and Latin America before your presidency."[35] Casey was particularly concerned about Nicaragua. "We are losing in Central America," he warned Reagan in another top secret letter, and "there is a good chance that the national security and geopolitical position of the United States will have been permanently worsened. This would represent an historical failure."[36] The Soviets were creeping ever closer to the U.S. homeland, Casey asserted, and U.S. action had been far too cautious. "[The Soviets] have their spheres of influence nailed down," he wrote to Clark, and "they are presently targeting and expanding other areas which we have shown little capacity to defend."[37]

Casey's view of a world besieged by Soviet operatives extended even to domestic politics. Casey and Reagan worried about clandestine Soviet activity in supporting the nuclear freeze movement in the United States.[38]

A classified FBI memo noted that "the Communist Party, USA (CPUSA) is actively involved in furthering these Soviet causes" like peace and disarmament, and "KGB officers in the United States have instructed their contacts to report on meetings of disarmament and peace groups, participate in demonstrations and the planning of demonstrations, and distribute leaflets and their publications to add fuel to the movement."[39] While some Americans understandably wanted to rid the country of nuclear weapons to prevent catastrophic war, FBI intelligence indicated that the Soviets covertly funneled resources to the peace movement.[40] The KGB cared little about disarmament, but its operatives wanted to strengthen domestic opposition in the United States and sow discord, if possible.

Yet even as the KGB tried to influence domestic politics in the United States, Moscow now had a problem back in Poland—Wojciech Jaruzelski.

Chapter 15

CRACKS IN THE FOUNDATION

Jaruzelski was in a bind. The KGB demanded *more* action, and many KGB officials wondered whether Jaruzelski had backbone enough to crush Solidarity. Moscow pressured him to suppress the underground and protect the ideological purity of Communism in Poland. But Jaruzelski knew Polish society would revolt against continual martial law or true Soviet-style Communism. His dilemma did little to console KGB agents who grew increasingly exasperated. One KGB agent in close contact with Jaruzelski described him as "the offspring of rich Polish landowners" with little sympathy for working people. "His tendency is pro-Western," the agent noted, "and he surrounds himself with generals who are descendants of Polish landowners and are anti-Soviet in inclination." He accused Jaruzelski of being a "Zionist" that "virtually ignored" the advice of the flamboyant Soviet ambassador to Poland, Boris Aristov.[1] The reports of both the KGB mission in Warsaw and the Soviet embassy repeatedly condemned Jaruzelski's tolerance of men with revisionist tendencies in the Polish leadership.

Vadim Pavlov, head of the KGB mission in Warsaw, and Ambassador Aristov pressed for more arrests and trials of opposition members, irritated at what they considered the glacial pace of the Polish government. At a meeting with General Czesław Kiszczak, minister of internal affairs, Pavlov denounced Kiszczak's ministry and the SB as "weak and indecisive." Kiszczak defensively replied that there were 40,000 Solidarity activists, and it was impossible to prosecute them all.[2] He was in a good position to know. Kiszczak had been battling anti-Communist forces for much of his life.[3] As a teenager during World War II, he was banished to work in the coal mines of Silesia and later sent to perform forced labor in Vienna. After the war and Yalta's division of Europe, Kiszczak joined the Polish army and fought local guerrilla forces that resisted the Soviet-backed government. In the summer of 1946, his father was captured by a guerrilla cell that spared his life only after Kiszczak's mother begged for leniency. Kiszczak later explained that those struggles, particularly the bloodshed caused by Polish rebels after World War II who fought their own government, had inspired his response to Solidarity and his desire to squelch internal resistance that could tear the country apart. "Experiences linked with that drama, that fratricidal struggle, are among the major reasons that shaped my role" in combatting Solidarity, Kiszczak later recalled. "I did not want that tragic history to repeat itself."[4]

Soviet ambassador Aristov delivered to Jaruzelski a personal message from Soviet leader Leonid Brezhnev which repeated the Soviet demand for more prosecutions. But Jaruzelski stood firm, responding that to try high-profile individuals like Lech Wałęsa would trigger a backlash not only in Poland, but around the world.[5] Jaruzelski told the Soviets that he had to be particularly careful with the Catholic Church. Individuals like Józef Glemp, the archbishop of Warsaw, were willing to work with the Polish regime to prevent further bloodshed. But Jaruzelski worried that the church could turn on the government if he adopted a more confrontational approach toward Solidarity. Since at least the 1970s, some Catholic officials had worked with Polish intellectuals and labor union activists to support Poland's opposition movement. In a testy letter to Aristov, Jaruzelski wrote:

> We cannot continue martial law as if we were living in a bunker; we want to pursue a dialogue with the people ... Glemp's latest statements are such that they could even be printed in *Trybuna Ludu* [the Communist Party newspaper]. He appeals for calm, restraint and realism ... We are, of course, playing a game with the Catholic church; our aim is to neutralize its harmful influence on the population. The aims of the church and my aims are still different. However, at this stage we must exploit our common interest in stabilizing the situation in order to strengthen Socialism and the positions of the Party.[6]

Jaruzelski's attitude toward Moscow had become less deferential over time. The KGB mission reported that Jaruzelski had declared: "The Soviet comrades are mistaken if they think that the ... CPSU Central Committee will make Polish policy as in the days of Gierek. This will not happen. [Those] days are over."[7] The Soviets wielded considerable influence over Warsaw while Edward Gierek was the Polish leader, but Jaruzelski increasingly attempted to assert his independence. After a meeting in Moscow with Yuri Andropov, former head of the KGB and Brezhev's successor, Jaruzelski told Kiszczak:

> This was a genuine conversation on an equal footing between the leaders of the two Parties and countries, not a monologue as was the case earlier with Brezhnev. In a conversation lasting three hours, Andropov said that all Socialist countries must take account of the specific conditions of Poland. The Polish problems were not the concern of one country alone; it was a world problem.[8]

KGB distrust of Jaruzelski continued to grow throughout 1983. The KGB's Warsaw mission reported that Jaruzelski had given a dangerously defeatist address in early 1983 to the central committee of the Polish Communist Party (Poland United Workers' Party, or PUWP). Jaruzelski remarked that "we have a multi-party system" in Poland and that "Gierek's slogans about the moral and ideological unity of the Poles, the development of Socialism—all this is a fantasy and dreamworld."[9] Even Lenin, Jaruzelski claimed, had engaged in tactical retreats. Poland must do the same. Vadim Pavlov believed that Jaruzelski intended to retreat even farther. According to Pavlov: "The episcopate, and right-wing forces within the PUWP and country at large, seek to influence Jaruzelski and intimidate him with the might of the church. There are many signs that the right wing and church are succeeding in this."[10]

For KGB leaders, Jaruzelski all too often bent to bourgeois or capitalistic pressure, such as when he supported a constitutional amendment, which passed the Sejm, that Poland's 2.8 million private farmers could keep their land without fear of government seizure.[11] Moscow saw counterrevolutionary forces and Western influence at every turn. The Soviet embassy condemned a report presented to the Polish Communist Party's politburo on "The Causes and Consequences of Social Crises in the History of the Polish People's Republic" as the product of "bourgeois methodology." As a Soviet cable concluded:

> [The report] reduces the essence of the class struggle in the Polish People's Republic to conflicts between the authorities and society, thereby deliberately excluding the possibility of analyzing the actions of anti-Socialist forces, and their connections with the West's ideological sabotage centers. There is not a word about the USSR's help in restoring and developing Poland's economy.[12]

After extensive lobbying from the Soviet embassy, which had received an advance copy, the politburo rejected the report and prepared a revised version, emphasizing Poland's supposed achievements in Socialist construction under the leadership of the Communist Party.[13] Aristov complained that "ideological work remains a most neglected sector of the

PUWP's activity," and that the Communist Party leadership was failing to overcome "the revisionist right-wing opportunist bias in the Party." Moscow had ideological concerns about almost every aspect of Polish culture. Soviet leaders expressed frustration that Polish translations of Soviet textbooks were openly disparaged: "Currency has been given to the idea that the Soviet model is unsuitable for Poland; the PUWP is incapable of solving contradictions in the interests of the whole of society, and a 'third path' needs to be worked out. There is increasing criticism of real Socialism."[14]

Despite these frustrations, the KGB still viewed the political environment in Poland as an improvement over the near-anarchy of 1980 and 1981. Jaruzelski may have been weak, but at least he had contained Lech Wałęsa.

———

JARUZELSKI HAD DECLINED TO PUNISH Wałęsa harshly, for fear of turning him into a martyr. He had sequestered the Solidarity leader in a palace, not a prison, and released him in exchange for open dialogue—thus preserving the pretense of cooperation while moving swiftly to repress the rest of the opposition. But Jaruzelski and the SB had no reservations about attacking Wałęsa's reputation. Though it was never successful in undermining Wałęsa's legitimacy, the SB's disinformation campaign was aggressive and devious.

Armed with a hidden camera, the SB took film footage of Wałęsa eating with his older brother, Stanisław, and used it as the basis of a sham documentary called *Money*. The thirty-minute film, which aired on prime-time Polish television, suggested that Wałęsa had stashed $1 million in the West that he wanted to place in the Vatican bank with the help of the pope. The SB constructed the dialogue by joining together some of Wałęsa's public statements, mixed with extracts from the stolen tape recordings of his meal with Stanisław and words by a Warsaw actor imitating Wałęsa's voice. The film dialogue included a fabricated exchange about Wałęsa's fictitious fortune in the West.

"You know all in all it is over a million dollars," said Wałęsa at one point in the scratchy recording. "Somebody has to draw it all and put it somewhere. It can't be brought into the country, though."

"No, no, no!" responded his brother Stanisław.

"So I thought about it and they came here and this priest had an idea that they would open an account in that bank, the papal one," Wałęsa continued. "They give 15 percent there . . . Somebody has to arrange it all, open accounts in the Vatican. I can't touch it though or I'd get smashed in the mug."

Wałęsa had become an international celebrity in the West for his willingness to stand up to the Communist regime. By 1983, rumors swirled in the press that the Nobel Committee was considering Wałęsa for the Nobel Peace Prize, a development that the Soviet and Polish governments worried would undermine their effort to destroy Solidarity. Part of the purpose of the SB's propaganda campaign was to sabotage Wałęsa's prospect of winning the Nobel, which ultimately failed when Wałęsa received the prize later in the year. The actor impersonating Wałęsa explained that the prize was worth a lot of money.

"I'd get it if it weren't for the church!" said Wałęsa. "But the church is starting to interfere."

"Yeah," says his brother Stanisław, "because they've put up the pope again."[15]

Beyond the false documentary *Money*, the smear campaign included planted newspaper stories that Wałęsa—and Solidarity more broadly—received over a billion dollars in aid from the Vatican and the United States.[16] The SB and KGB hoped that tying Wałęsa to U.S. and other Western assistance would destroy his credibility as a Polish patriot. The campaign was a failure but Solidarity supporters were outraged to see their reputations sullied in public.

Wałęsa also had to deal with constant surveillance. Poland's security services codenamed him "Ox" and developed a straightforward remit:

The goal of the observation is to monitor the subject's behavior, the addresses he visits, determining the persons he comes in contact with and determining the visitors to the subject's residence. . . . The observation is to be carried out by intelligence agents in a four-shift system (round the clock). Three radio cars are to be used in the observation operation. A signaling point has been organized in a private apartment in order to ensure the correct surveillance of the subject and the secrecy of the observation group.[17]

The unwanted attention taxed Wałęsa and his family, and made a target out of anyone that Wałęsa met with. "Every step I took was scrutinized by several pairs of vigilant eyes," recalled Wałęsa, who had to plan every movement in advance and weigh its consequences. "It's this kind of tension that makes the burden of leadership a heavy one."[18]

As Wałęsa and his family suffered under Polish surveillance, Reagan instructed his National Security Council staff to write a comprehensive strategy designed to counter the Soviet Union across the globe. National Security Advisor William Clark led the charge, though Casey was strongly supportive. Up to now, the United States lacked an overall strategy toward the Soviet Union, Clark explained in a secret note to Reagan. "Although our relations with the Soviet Union lie at the heart of our foreign policy and military strategy," Clark wrote, "we do not, at present, have any formal guidelines capable of guiding us in the pursuit of these relations." He suggested to Reagan that the goal of U.S. strategy would be to "show concern not only for Soviet political and military *behavior,* but also for the *system* that makes behavior of this kind possible."[19] The document was published in 1983 as National Security Decision Directive (NSDD)-75, "U.S. Relations with the USSR."[20] It built on previous national security directives that focused on U.S. national security (NSDD-32), propaganda (NSDD-45), U.S. policy toward Eastern Europe (NSDD-54), and economic instruments like sanctions (NSDD-66).

With Clark's oversight, the new strategy, NSDD-75, was prepared by an interdepartmental group. The lead author was Richard Pipes.[21] "NSDD-75 was a clear break from the past," Pipes later reflected. It was the first document which "said our goal was no longer to coexist with the Soviet Union but to change the Soviet system. At its root was the belief that we had it in our power to alter the Soviet system through the use of external pressure."[22] Senior officials in the State Department considered Pipes' drafts too belligerent and aggressive, but that's what Reagan liked about the document.[23] NSDD-75 bluntly stated that U.S. policy toward the Soviet Union would now consist of three inter-related objectives: to reverse Soviet expansionism by competing on a sustained basis in all international arenas, promote change in the Soviet Union toward a more pluralistic political and economic system, and engage in negotiations with the Soviet Union which protect and enhance U.S. interests.

To accomplish these objectives, NSDD-75 put all options on the table. It argued that the United States should use a broad panoply of military, economic, political, and other instruments—including ideological ones: "U.S. policy must have an ideological thrust which clearly affirms the superiority of U.S. and Western values of individual dignity and freedom, a free press, free trade unions, free enterprise, and political democracy over the repressive features of Soviet Communism."[24] In addition, the document named Eastern Europe as an essential battleground: "The primary U.S. objective in Eastern Europe is to loosen Moscow's hold on the region while promoting the cause of human rights in individual East European countries."[25]

When Reagan signed NSDD-75 in 1983, the document contained the core of his views on combatting Communism. With its audacious and comprehensive strategic plan to undermine Soviet power, it would become one of the most important foreign policy documents of the Reagan administration.

—

REAGAN'S WILLINGNESS TO STAND UP to the Soviets was an inspiration to Poles. The U.S. embassy in Warsaw was flooded with letters from imprisoned Solidarity members. One came from a group of internees in Lowicz prison who thanked Reagan for his support. Another letter included pictures of a young boy and girl holding signs that read: "Our father is 'sitting in prison' for Solidarity," "I am the daughter of an extremist," and "What does the SB want with our father?" As National Security Advisor William Clark noted to Reagan: "These mementos clearly manifest the defiant and proud spirit of the Polish people."[26]

Still another flicker of hope came from the Catholic Church. As Reagan and other U.S. government officials realized, most church officials were disturbed by the Jaruzelski regime's repressive policies. Yet Soviet leaders were generally dismissive of the church. "How many divisions has the pope?" Stalin had once famously asked.[27] The Soviets quickly found out that the church was developing into a powerful ally of Solidarity.

Chapter 16

HOLY ALLIANCE?

A half mile from Gate Number Two, the hallowed site where Lech Wałęsa and the Gdańsk Shipyard workers rose up against the government in August 1980, stood St. Bridget's Church. It was underwhelming both in size and grandeur, particularly compared to St. Mary's Church, just a ten-minute walk away. Whereas St. Mary's was one of the largest brick churches in the world, capable of holding nearly 25,000 people, St. Bridget's was much smaller and older. Originally erected in the fourteenth century, it had been reduced to rubble during World War II. The rebuilt structure had a Gothic-style façade lined with neat rows of rust-colored bricks and topped like an ice cream cone with a cinnamon roof.

St. Bridget's was a blue-collar church with simple, if elegant, decorations. Red brick columns lined the nave and continued across the ceiling like an ethereal spider web. In the afternoons, light streamed into the church through its great windows, producing a rose-colored hue from the red brick. Five black, wrought-iron candle holders clung to each column in the nave, along with black circular chandeliers that held fourteen candles. The floor was composed of large irregular-sized slabs of taupe gray and sand-colored limestone. In the sanctuary at the front of the church, there was a large amber altar flanked by bronze figures of St. Bridget and Blessed Elizabeth Hesselblad, reformer of the Order of St. Bridget.

What St. Bridget's lacked in extravagance, however, it made up in symbolic importance. To the side of the grand altar, a haunting chapel contained a sculpture devoted to the memory of Katyn, where the Soviets murdered thousands of Polish officers in 1940. An epitaph honored those Polish officers that were killed with the inscription "God—Honor—Homeland," along with the Knight's Cross, Poland's highest military medal. Another chapel in St. Bridget's honored the Polish army's resistance fighters, who fought the Communists after World War II.[1]

Father Henryk Jankowski served as the church's provost. But he was much more than that. He was a resistance leader, outspoken friend of Lech Wałęsa, and perpetual thorn in the side of the government. Jankowski held mass for the shipyard workers during the August 1980 strike and was now providing support and inspiration to the underground. Those who passed through the entrance of his unpretentious church saw Solidarity banners hanging along an internal wall and an elaborate stainless steel sculpture to the country's political prisoners.[2] Writers, artists, poets, musicians, journalists, and Solidarity activists held clandestine meetings in its cloistered rooms and alcoves.

Even during the darkest days of martial law, St. Bridget's nurtured the spirit of Solidarity. Its members provided aid, shelter, and ideological fortitude. CIA officials like Bill Casey, who was a Catholic himself, were acutely aware of the Catholic Church's importance in Poland. As Casey would soon witness, the church and several of its key figures—like Jankowski and Pope John Paul II—would become major players in the Solidarity struggle.

IN THE IMMEDIATE AFTERMATH of the Cold War, *Washington Post* reporter Carl Bernstein (of Watergate acclaim) and Italian journalist Marco Politi argued that the CIA and the Vatican formed a secret "holy alliance" to support Solidarity. Casey and Reagan, they asserted, believed that "there was a potential third superpower in the world—the twenty-block-square Vatican city-state—and that its monarch, Pope John Paul II, had at his command a remarkable arsenal of unconventional weapons that might help tip the balance in the cold war." Bernstein and Politi also contended that Poland was the most important prize. "The highest priority of American foreign policy was now Poland . . . Solidarity and the pope, as [Reagan and Casey] saw it, were the levers with which Poland might begin to be pried loose."[3]

According to Bernstein, the new Polish pope wanted to free his homeland from Soviet rule, and had teamed with a cabal of Catholics on Reagan's national security team—including CIA director Casey and National Security Advisor Bill Clark—who were inspired by "the teachings of their church, combined with their fierce anti-communism."[4] Communist antipathy toward religion fueled their abhorrence of the Soviet Union. "Religion is the sigh of the oppressed creature, the heart of a heartless world, and the soul of soulless conditions," Karl Marx had famously written. "It is the opium of the people."[5]

My interviews with Reagan administration officials and review of information released from U.S. archives indicate that there was no veritable holy alliance. But this vision proved deeply compelling to some Americans, even if it was revealed to be hyperbolic and, in some cases, simply wrong.[6] U.S. and Vatican officials did not develop a joint strategy or conduct mutual planning to undermine Communism in countries like Poland, nor did the CIA significantly utilize Catholic officials in QRHELPFUL.

The reality was less conspiratorial and complex, though, in some ways, more intriguing. As CIA officials monitored events in Poland, they certainly appreciated the power of the Catholic Church. Indeed, the election of Cardinal Karol Wojtyła, archbishop of Kraków, as pope in October 1978 gave the Vatican a particular interest in Polish affairs.[7] While Reagan was a Protestant, he was the son of a working-class Irish-Catholic father and reserved a compassionate place in his heart for the

Catholic Church. He won the lion's share of the Catholic vote in the 1980 presidential election. It didn't take long for Reagan to forge a bond with the pope, in part because both survived assassination attempts weeks apart: Reagan on March 30, 1981, and the pope on May 13, 1981.

After the assassination attempt against John Paul II, Reagan sent an eloquent note to the pope: "All Americans join me in hopes and prayers for your speedy recovery from the injuries you have suffered in the attack. Our prayers are with you."[8] Their near-death experiences united them during their face-to-face visit at the Vatican on June 7, 1982. Meeting in the gilded papal library, with Perugino's famous painting *Resurrection* hanging behind them, Reagan told the pope "that they had been spared by God, for a purpose. And that purpose was freeing Poland."[9] They discussed issues which, as Reagan described, they shared "both spiritually and politically."[10] John Paul II professed his admiration for the American commitment to liberty and for "how the moral and spiritual values transmitted by your Founding Fathers find their dynamic expression in the life of modern America. The American people are indeed proud of their right to life, liberty and the pursuit of happiness."[11]

Reagan found the pope warm, charismatic, and well informed about world events. The pope also had a group of young American priests sing "America the Beautiful" during the June visit, bringing Reagan and Nancy to tears.[12] As a parting gift, John Paul II gave Reagan an ivory statue of the Madonna to watch over them.[13] The meeting had been a smashing success, even though Reagan had nodded off at one point during the meeting to the amazement—and embarrassment—of his staff.[14]

CIA OFFICIALS HAD LONG DEBATED the possibility of cooperation with Catholic Church officials. CIA director Casey met with the pope several times to discuss world events.[15] As Casey's widow, Sophia, later remarked, "they would ask each other to pray about things," including Poland.[16] For Casey, it was more than a coincidence that the Polish pope had come to power right at the moment of Solidarity's birth. John Paul II's emergence was perhaps God-ordained, he believed.

In the summer of 1983, CIA, State Department, Pentagon, and White House officials met to discuss covert U.S. assistance to Poland. Malzahn, State Department officials Dennis Kux and Mark Palmer, and Walter Raymond, Jr., from the National Security Council were among the attendees. Raymond was a propaganda expert who had come to the National Security Council from the CIA. The group discussed cooperation with the Catholic Church, among other issues, and agreed that U.S. and Vatican interests overlapped in some areas, including their mutual desire to support Solidarity. But their interests did not overlap in other areas, such as sanctions against Poland, which many church officials wanted partially or entirely lifted. Malzahn believed that the United States, including the CIA, could work with Vatican officials on issues where they shared a common interest. But they would go their own way when their interests diverged.[17]

When it came to cooperation on Poland, the Reagan administration and the Vatican began by maintaining diplomatic ties similar to those U.S. officials held with thousands of other leaders and influential figures. This meant holding discussions with the pope and other Catholic leaders on issues like U.S.-Soviet relations to arms control, space exploration, the war between the British and Argentina in the Falkland Islands, and U.S. foreign policy.[18] They passed diplomatic messages, made telephone calls, and met with formal and informal representatives that passed through Washington, the Vatican, and neutral locations.[19] Poland was an important focus of U.S.-Vatican discussions, especially the issues of Polish refugees in the United States, the role of Solidarity, martial law, and sanctions. Most of these exchanges involved routine conversations or letters.

In addition, the CIA and other Reagan administration officials attempted to leverage the Catholic Church's influence in Poland and support for Solidarity. Following martial law, for example, Reagan wrote to the pope and asked him to "draw on the great authority that you and the church command in Poland to urge General Jaruzelski" to peacefully negotiate with Solidarity.[20] Reagan understood the tremendous political power the pope waged in Poland and across the globe, asking him to use his "suasion throughout the West" and "influence with the church" to pressure Jaruzelski and support Solidarity.[21] In response, John Paul II vowed to use his power on the "moral plane" to support the Polish people in their struggle for liberty.[22] In the eyes of CIA and other U.S. leaders, the Catholic Church was one of several potential organizations—along with labor organizations like the AFL-CIO and Eastern European émigré populations—that could be called upon to support Solidarity because of their abhorrence of the Soviets.[23]

In terms of spycraft, the CIA entrusted only a few Catholic officials—always working through surrogates—to bring money and material into Poland as part of QRHELPFUL. Catholic Church officials were not subject to border controls and could carry money and equipment into Poland with little risk of being searched. These individuals likely had no idea they were carrying CIA money or contraband, since they weren't getting it directly from CIA case officers. Case officers like Celia Larkin were prohibited from working directly with clergy. The CIA asset named "Erhardt Brauer" passed $25,000 in CIA funds from his foundation to a Catholic clergyman who, in turn, delivered it to Solidarity. Still, CIA's use of Catholic Church surrogates to move money was minimal, probably less than $50,000, or 0.25 percent, of a program that totaled nearly $20 million.[24] Congressional staffers from the House Permanent Select Committee on Intelligence, who occasionally received updates on QRHELPFUL, raised few objections to the CIA's use of Catholic officials. When a congressional investigation found that the CIA had used "a minor channel" to deliver between $20,000 and $30,000 to Solidarity through a Catholic organization, however, they ordered it closed for fear of political backlash.[25]

For the CIA, a successful QRHELPFUL covert action program meant understanding the power of the Catholic Church in Polish society and cajoling church leaders to support Solidarity. But the CIA didn't need to convince the Vatican to help. Most Catholic officials were already on their side.

———

EVEN BEFORE THE INCEPTION OF SOLIDARITY, Catholic officials had supported opposition efforts in the 1970s that fused together labor union members, artists, and intellectuals. Just after martial law, John Paul II proclaimed, "the church is on the side of the workers." Yet he also exchanged private handwritten letters with Jaruzelski.[26] On December 18, 1981, John Paul II penned a letter to Jaruzelski with copies addressed to Lech Wałęsa and Primate Józef Glemp, the archbishop of Warsaw. The pope expressed hope that no blood would be spilled, the regime would release political prisoners, and Poland would soon return to normalcy. Jaruzelski replied on January 5, 1982, noting that martial law had been a "shock to our society" and that "many people feel disappointed in their hopes, crushed by circumstances, embittered."[27] He assured John Paul II that he would not return to pre-Solidarity days, presumably a reference to the violence by Polish forces in Gdańsk in December 1970. In response, the pope told Jaruzelski that the "shock" triggered by martial law was also a result of the "internment of thousands of leading Solidarity militants, including Lech Wałęsa, along with a number of painful sanctions in relation to the worlds of labor and culture ... It is not only necessary to remove the shock, but, above all, to rebuild trust."[28]

Despite the inclination of many church officials to support Solidarity, however, some were more cautious. One classified U.S. State Department cable suggested: "There are differences within the Polish Catholic church leadership on relations with the Jaruzelski regime."[29] Some individuals like Glemp took a conciliatory tone toward Warsaw and Moscow to prevent the possibility of civil war, however remote. A U.S. State Department intelligence report reasoned that "Moscow and the Vatican apparently developed a tacit understanding last winter that the Catholic church would use its influence in Poland to discourage civil turmoil or activity against the Polish Communist Party or the USSR."[30]

Primate Glemp would become a divisive leader of this conciliatory faction.[31] Born on December 18, 1929 in Wrocław, a cultural and commercial hub in southwestern Poland, Glemp decided at a young age to become a priest. But his schooling was interrupted when the Nazis invaded Poland. During the German occupation of Poland, Glemp—along with his mother, two younger brothers, and sister—was forced into slave labor. Ordained in 1956, Glemp served as a parish priest and a teacher before earning doctorates in civil and canon law in Rome. He returned to Poland in 1964 and became the adviser for Stefan Wyszyński, archbishop of Gniezno and Warsaw, as well as primate of Poland. John Paul II appointed Glemp as Poland's fifty-sixth primate in 1981 after Wyszyński's death. Glemp developed a reputation as a consensus builder with homespun modesty and a soft-spoken personality. With a stocky build and warm, dark eyes, he was genuinely humble and modest. When Glemp received visitors in his ornate residence on Miodowa Street in a vast, wood-paneled reception room under the gaze of grim-faced paintings of earlier primates, he preferred to sit at a table to one side rather than on the elevated, crimson-backed throne.[32]

Yet some Catholics wanted Glemp to be a fighter—a strong-minded, iron-fisted leader like his predecessor, Stefan Wyszyński. Many wanted him to stand up to Jaruzelski and martial law, rather than embrace appeasement. Some Catholics quietly referred to him as "Comrade Glemp."[33] Glemp saw Jaruzelski as a force for moderation in the Polish government, and he was deeply concerned about the prospects of civil war in Poland.[34] He worried incessantly that his priests might get involved in "extremist activities."[35] And he criticized Solidarity leaders like Wałęsa for, in his view, refusing to seriously negotiate with the government. "He wants the government to come to him on its knees," Glemp told U.S. ambassador to Poland Francis Meehan, referring to Wałęsa.[36]

By 1983, however, the vast majority of Catholic officials either supported Solidarity or looked the other way at underground activity.

The Bishop's Palace in Kraków, St. Martin's Church in Warsaw, and St. Bridget's Church in Gdańsk all aided Solidarity. A clandestine network of nuns and priests provided money, distributed literature, offered sanctuary, and delivered material to the Solidarity underground. Even these supporters, however, were occasionally caught by surprise. Sister Ruth Woziek was preparing dinner with a can of tomatoes and soy she had set aside from a food shipment, only to find it contained anti-Soviet press clippings. Hanna Federowicz, a volunteer in the St. Martin's Church distribution effort, opened an oversized jar of jam from the family of one imprisoned Solidarity leader and discovered that it contained printer's ink.[37]

Many church officials who weren't directly involved in aiding Solidarity simply shrugged. Bronisław Dembowski, St. Martin's rector, told workers, "Don't tell me what you're doing, I don't want to know."[38] On at least two occasions, he entered his confessional and found secretly delivered messages from Zbigniew Bujak, head of Solidarity's Temporary Coordinating Commission, or TKK, thanking him for the flow of supplies to the underground.[39] The Vatican also provided limited financial aid to Solidarity and other opposition groups through the Institute for Religious Works, the principal Vatican financial institution.[40] Solidarity leaders explained later that the organization's survival during and after martial law never hinged on great sums of money or material. Instead, the most important contribution from the Catholic Church was its moral and political support.[41]

A key figure in this support was Father Jankowski, who continued to use St. Bridget's Church as a virtual safe house for Solidarity activity. When Jankowski heard that the pope was coming to Poland, he was elated. While the pope had visited Poland in 1979, the country had changed dramatically since then with the birth of Solidarity and the imposition of martial law. John Paul II was, by far, the most important foreign dignitary to visit Poland since martial law. Jankowski saw the pope's 1983 visit as a potential watershed—a chance to break the impasse and perhaps to shake the very foundations of regime power.

Ronald Reagan and Nancy Reagan on a walk at Camp David. The stroll on the morning of December 12, 1981, was one of Reagan's last peaceful moments before Polish prime minister Wojciech Jaruzelski declared martial law. (REAGAN PRESIDENTIAL LIBRARY)

Lech Wałęsa speaking at the Gdańsk Lenin Shipyard gate in August 1980. The feisty electrician was a charismatic figure around the shipyard and helped negotiate the agreement that authorized independent, self-governing labor unions, giving birth to Solidarity. (GETTY IMAGES)

St. Bridget's Church in Gdańsk, Poland, was a sanctuary for the underground. Solidarity activists held clandestine meetings in its cloistered rooms and alcoves.

Lech Wałęsa (left) is blessed by Bishop Henryk Jankowski during the strike in August 1980. Jankowski was the parish priest at St. Bridget's Church in Gdańsk, which would become a bastion of support for Solidarity. (Getty Images)

Polish workers completed this 138-foot monument in Gdańsk in December 1980 in memory of three atrocities against workers—in Poznań in 1956, Gdańsk in 1970, and Radom and other cities in 1976. (GETTY IMAGES)

President Reagan meets with CIA Director William Casey in the Oval Office. With Reagan's support, Casey expanded CIA covert action programs across the globe—including in Poland. (REAGAN PRESIDENTIAL LIBRARY)

Statue of Ryszard Kukliński, the "Polish Viking," in Gdynia, Poland. In 1972, Kukliński, a lieutenant colonel on the Polish General Staff, offered his services to the United States. Over the next decade, he provided more than 40,000 pages of classified Soviet, Polish, and Warsaw Pact documents.

Polish leader Wojciech Jaruzelski declares martial law on December 13, 1981, in a televised announcement. Jaruzelski sent Polish special motorized security forces into cities, arrested Solidarity leaders, and consolidated power in a Military Council of National Salvation. (GETTY IMAGES)

President Reagan addresses the nation from the Oval Office on December 23, 1981, about martial law in Poland. Reagan urged Americans to place a candle in their windows as a sign of support to the Polish people. (REAGAN PRESIDENTIAL LIBRARY)

CIA Director William Casey speaks at the American Society of Newspaper Editors. Casey was tall, stoop-shouldered, and partially bald, with wisps of white hair. But he was an energetic CIA director with an affinity for covert action. (GETTY IMAGES)

Do Czytelników

Więc w końcu jest. Oto masz Czytelniku w ręku pierwszy numer „Tygodnika Solidarność". Pierwszy numer ogólnopolskiego pisma naszego związku.

Przyszło nam długo na nie czekać. Do ostatniej też chwili nie wiedzieliśmy czy uda nam się wydać je w ustalonym terminie. Ten pierwszy numer został zamknięty w nocy z 30 na 31 marca. Nikomu w Polsce nie musimy tłumaczyć w jakich to się działo okolicznościach i w jakiej atmosferze koherycliśmy pracę. To już historia. Nie chcemy się usprawiedliwiać trudnościami. Chcemy tylko stwierdzić fakt oczywisty: wydarzenia, jakie rozegrały się w kraju w ostatnich dwóch tygodniach i to, że do ostatniej chwili nikt nie wiedział, czy można będzie przyznać estetyczne do druku, wszystko to sprawiło, że pierwszy nasz numer przedstawia się inaczej, niż był zaplanowany. Z pewnością gorzej.

To była sprawa decyzji: czy odłożyć start o tydzień, albo dwa i wydać pierwszy numer dopracowany, napięty na wszystkie guziki, czy też machnąć ręką na elegancję i dokonałość, dotrzeć do naszych Czytelników nazajutrz po wielkim kryzysie, w którym ważyło się wszystko.

Wybraliśmy te drugą możliwość, bo sądziliśmy, że taki był nasz obowiązek.

Dlatego idziemy do Was z dziełem niedoskonałym, które właściwie dopiero się rodzi i będzie stopniowo ulepszane. Dużą część miejsca zajmują materiały informacyjne. Staraliśmy się uwzględnić najważniejsze wydarzenia ostatnich tygodni, a działo się przecież tak wiele. W kąt poszły różne pomysły redakcyjne, jakie dwa tygodnie temu wydawały się jeszcze niezbędne. Przyjdzie na nie stosowniejsza pora.

Zostało natomiast zachowanych kilka najważniejszych zasad, które stanowią dla nas sens tego pisma i jego rację istnienia. Po pierwsze, chcemy, aby ono było możliwie najściślej związane z życiem polskiego społeczeństwa. Po drugie, chcemy aby mówiło prawdę, jeśli zaś nie zawsze mogłoby powiedzieć całą prawdę – aby nie kłamało.

Pismo nasze podlega cenzurze. Ukazuje się ono na podstawie Porozumień Gdańskich i zostało mniejszone opublie z zawarunkami nich możliwościami. Tygodnik będzie nazem podlegał ograniczeniom, to prawda, na to nikt nie będzie mógł niczego nam narzucić. Czasami nasze milczenie będzie również wymowne, jak zachowane strony.

Czego jeszcze chcemy? Chcemy dobrze służyć naszemu związkowi, wałczyć z jego zasady, programem i idee. Chcemy uczestniczyć w tworzeniu trwałych warunków życia dla całego naszego społeczeństwa, życia godniejszego, sprawiedliwszego i swobodniejszego, mówili dotąd. A także brać udział w trudnym dziele naprawy życia publicznego, gospodarczego i kulturalnego w naszym kraju, w przezwyciężeniu w naszym kraju kryzysu i jego nastał pogromów. Chcemy bronić praw ludzi pracy i praw ludzi więcej, walczyć o lepsze szanse dla młodych, o spokój i szacunek dla starszych. Domagać się, aby wszyscy mieli jednaki prawa i aby prawa jednako obowiązywało wszystkich. Aby uznawana i szanowana była godność i kultura. Aby obywatelo Polski byli prawdziwymi gospodarzami swego kraju, aby uczestniczyli w rządzeniu i ponosili za nie odpowiedzialność.

Chcemy służyć idei porozumienia społecznego, propagować ją i bronić. I chcemy się przeciwstawiać wszystkiemu, co jej zakłóci, a w szczególności pogardzie dla ludzi, nietolerancji i fanatyzmowi, wszelkim przejawom niedemokratycznym. Stawiamy obowiązując w Polsce konstytucję i chcemy, aby jej postanowienia były realizowane w praktyce.

Chcemy więc służyć zasadom i ideom „Solidarność", która wyrasta z wielkich demokratycznych tradycji naszego polskiego, z jego umiłowania prawdy i sprawiedliwości.

Chcemy uczestniczyć we wszystkich ważnych sprawach naszego kraju. Pragniemy nic być pismem otwartym dla wszystkich, dopuszczającym na swe łamy różne poglądy, nie obawiającym się kontrowersji.

Wierzymy, że w tej pracy będziemy mieli stałe przy sobie wielkie rzesze członków naszego związku, ludzi ograniczonych lepszego, który poprawia życie w Polsce.

Smaka dziś swojej nowej drogi rzie społeczeństwo, szukają drogi związki zawodowe, szukać będzie i nasze pismo. Idzie o to, by było to poszukiwanie wspólne, Solidarne.

„Nie będziemy w tym piśmie używać wielkich słów „Solidarność" ich nie używa. „Solidarność" je czuje i rozumie.

REDAKCJA

TYGODNIK

Solidarność

Wzywam Was, abyście nie zapomnieli...,
Wzywam Was, żeby Polska stawała się coraz bardziej mieszkaniem ludzi...

(LECH WAŁĘSA – z przemówienia wygłoszonego na odsłonięcie Pomnika Poległych Stoczniowców)

Fot. ERAZM CIOŁEK

POCZĄTEK ROZMÓW

TADEUSZ MAZOWIECKI

Każdy człowiek i każdy naród potrzebuje nadziei. Nie można żyć bez nadziei. W historii rzadkie są jednak momenty kiedy coś na naszych oczach staje się wyrazem nadziei całego narodu.

Przeżyliśmy najpierw taki moment w ciągu dziewięciu dni 1979 r. Kiedy Jan Paweł II modlił się na placu Zwycięstwa w Warszawie słowami psalmu: „Niech zstąpi Duch Twój i odnowi oblicze ziemi, tej ziemi" – czuliśmy, że słowa te mówi on od nas i za nas. Wiedzieliśmy, że wyrażają one naszą wspólną potrzebę nadziei i czuliśmy jej siłę. Było to wydarzenie nie tylko religijne ale i społeczne, narodowe, o wielkiej, nieporównywalnej z niczym skali. Odradzało ono i prostowało postawy ludzkie, stanowiło lekcję samozognizowania się społeczeństwa, skupienia i zespolenia wokół wartości dla nas najważniejszych. I było także wskazaniem drogi jak dochodzić naszych uprawnień bez nienawiści, a z poczuciem praw moralnych, że świadomością siły płynącej z ludzkiej godności.

Latem 1980 stała się rzecz, która zmieniła sytuację społeczeństwa i obraz Polski: protest społeczny przebił sobie drogę. Po raz pierwszy wielki strajk łączący cele obywatelskie i pracownicze zakończony został porozumieniem, a nie rozlewem krwi; otwarta została droga do stworzenia naprawdę niezależnego i samorządnego ruchu związkowego. Zmienił się układ sił kraju. W konsekwencji tego co wtedy nastąpiło – „Solidarność" jako ruch społeczny stała się wyrazem naszej zbiorowej polskiej nadziei. Losy „Solidarności" stały się sprawą Polski, jej przyszłości.

Czas, jaki upłynął od sierpnia 1980 r. nie był czasem spokojnym. Co najmniej pięć lub sześć razy konflikt przybrał rozmiary groźne dla całego kraju. Działo się tak dlatego, że słuszne żądania społeczne napotykają liczne bariery, które pokonywane nie dopiero sięgając po broń ostateczną, jaką stanowi strajk. W ostatnich dwóch tygodniach po wydarzeniach bydgoskich które wywołały tak ogromną falę protestu, przetoczył się przez Polskę konflikt, który groził niebezpieczny w dalszych dla losów kraju konsekwencjami.

Czy więc warto dziś mówić o nadziei? Czy możemy dziś wrócić do niej, jako do podstawy spokojniejszego już spojrzenia w przyszłość?

Wydaje mi się, że istnieją trzy podstawowe źródła nadziei łączonej z tym co się stało w Polsce od sierpnia 1980.

Pierwsza z nich sięga samych korzeni „Solidarności". Wiemy co zaczyło nasz ruch, nadało mu rozmach i siłę. Czynnikiem tym jest poczucie godności ludzkiej, świadomość praw przynależnych człowiekowi tak w sferze obywatelskiej, jak pracowniczej. A także bunt przeciw niesprawiedliwości.

Potrafiliśmy jako społeczeństwo przetworzyć to poczucie kształtujące dotąd jedynie postawy niezadowolenia, rzadziej zaś protestu – w masowy ruch społeczny. Pytanie, które przed nami teraz stoi, brzmi: czy to społeczeństwo zdobyło, ten obszar niezależności, potrafimy teraz wypełnić naszą inicjatywą.

Drugim źródłem naszej nadziei – jest zmiana o modelowym znaczeniu, jaką powodować musi fakt powstania „Solidarności" – masowego związku zawodowego o rzeczywiście niezależnym i samorządnym charakterze. Otwarło to kwestię dopasowania organizmu państwowego do tej nowej sytuacji. A zarazem stworzyło – odmiennie niż w roku 1956 czy 1970 – sytuację, w której na straży dokonanych zmian stoi niezależna siła społeczna.

I trzecie wreszcie źródło nadziei, które w tych dniach może najbardziej zasługuje na refleksję. Myślę o szanowanej przez cały świat dojrzałości polskiego sposobu rozwiązywania konfliktów w drodze porozumienia – bez rozlewu krwi.

Toczy się nieraz w „Solidarności" spór czy osiągany na tej drodze kompromis jest sukcesem czy porażką, owszem pięć lub sześć naszej siły czy słabości. Różnice poglądów w konkretnych sytuacjach nie mogą dziwić. Ale zasadą: większość albo nic, łatwo może prowadzić do stawiania losu narodowego na jedną kartę.

Jako społeczeństwo i jako związek idziemy drogą nie przetartą przez nikogo. Żadne wzory do naszej sytuacji nie pasują, wszystkie musimy tworzyć na nowo. Tym bardziej musimy być wierni tej nadziei, która się wśród nas zrodziła.

W numerze m.in.: ● WYDARZENIA BYDGOSKIE ● Bożena Wawrzewska i Krzysztof Lenglewicz: NA CHŁOPSKI ROZUM ● Kazimierz Dziewanowski: NIE ZA POŹNO, NIE ZA WCZEŚNIE ● Waldemar Kuczyński: UDZIAŁ „SOLIDARNOŚCI" ● Bohdan Cywiński: TYLKO MOCĄ WŁASNEGO WYBORU ● Wojciech Adamiecki: STOP. KONTROLA ● Janusz Beksiak: CENA REFORMY GOSPODARCZEJ ● Leon Bójko: PRZEŻYĆ PRZEDNÓWEK ● Rozmowa ze Zbigniewem Bujakiem: PRAWDA RAZ POWIEDZIANA ● CZEGO OCZEKUJESZ OD „SOLIDARNOŚCI"

President Reagan and Nancy Reagan meet with John Paul II during a visit to the Vatican. Reagan administration officials, including the CIA, attempted to leverage the Catholic Church's influence in Poland and its support for Solidarity. (Reagan Presidential Library)

Soviet leader Mikhail Gorbachev and Polish leader Wojciech Jaruzelski in Warsaw. Gorbachev's support for perestroika and glasnost helped set the stage for greater liberalization in Eastern Europe at the end of the Cold War, including in Poland. (GETTY IMAGES)

John Paul II addresses a large crowd in Gdańsk, home of Solidarity, in June 1987. The pope speaks at Lech Wałęsa's housing development, paying homage to its leader and openly embracing Solidarity. (GETTY IMAGES)

In 1989, the Polish government and opposition leaders, spearheaded by Solidarity, conduct the Round Table Talks. The agreement led to the relegalization of independent trade unions, including Solidarity, and elections that Solidarity won handily. (GETTY IMAGES)

GŁOSUJ NA

BRONISŁAWA GEREMKA
KANDYDATA DO SEJMU

LECH WAŁĘSA

Lech Wałęsa's approval rating before the 1989 Polish elections was 74 percent, and Solidarity lever-aged Wałęsa's popularity by photographing him with most of Solidarity's candidates—including this one, Bronisława Geremka—for the Sejm and Senate. Solidarity's strategy was to present oppo-sition candidates as members of "Lech's Team." (European Solidarity Centre)

Lech Wałęsa addresses a joint session of Congress in November 1989, while House Speaker Tom Foley and Vice President Dan Quayle applaud in the background. Wałęsa entered the chamber to a boisterous reception, and Republicans and Democrats greeted him with a deafening ovation that lasted several minutes. (GETTY IMAGES)

Statues of John Paul II and Ronald Reagan in Gdańsk. Both men played significant roles in supporting Solidarity and democratization in Poland.

Chapter 17

AN EMOTIONAL VISIT

Wojciech Jaruzelski approached the pope's arrival with trepidation. Before agreeing to the visit, Jaruzelski placed several conditions on the Vatican. He requested that the trip be exclusively religious and that the pope not mention Solidarity, which was still outlawed. Jaruzelski also asked that the pope not visit the Baltic cities of Gdańsk and Szczecin, the cradles of Solidarity, out of concern that explosive anti-government demonstrations and civil unrest would erupt.[1] John Paul II agreed.

But when he arrived in Warsaw on June 16, 1983, the pope did not hide his anguish at the condition of Poland. "I ask those who suffer to be particularly close to me," he solemnly remarked after kissing Polish soil in an emotional ceremony at Warsaw's Okęcie airport. "I myself cannot visit all those in prison, all those who are suffering. But I ask them to be close to me in spirit to help me, just as they always do."[2] On June 17, John Paul II held the first of two meetings with Jaruzelski, who appeared stiff, pale-faced, and expressionless—a stark contrast to the gregarious and magnetic pope. As Jaruzelski later recounted, he was uncharacteristically nervous, and his hands and legs trembled as he greeted the pope. For every Pole brought up in Catholicism—even

Jaruzelski—the pope was a mythical figure. "It was a very emotional moment," said Jaruzelski. "I felt it was a great moment, [but] I noticed that he was rather cold toward me." As Jaruzelski recalled, the pope warmly smiled at Henryk Jabłoński, Poland's president, "while I was the man of martial law."[3] The pope, Primate Glemp, President Jabłoński, and Jaruzelski then retreated to a small room in the Belweder Palace, where the pope raised the subject of Solidarity.

"The state must think of the individual," said John Paul II in a reflective tone. "All trade unions have the right to exist.

"General," the pope continued, "for me the dissolution of the trade unions is more painful than the introduction of martial law in December 1981."

Jaruzelski respectfully disagreed. He told the pope that the decision to impose martial law was "very dramatic for me, very painful; we were in a catastrophic situation which truly endangered Poland." Jaruzelski argued that his action had prevented civil war and a Soviet military invasion. Jaruzelski then turned to the pope's visit, asking him to "use his influence to help us isolate the most extreme wing within Solidarity, to help us lift the Western embargo, especially by the Americans."

John Paul II suggested that martial law should be lifted. "I am anxious to reach a certain state of normalcy as soon as possible," the pope said. "Then Poland will be regarded differently by other countries," he continued.[4]

The conversation became more relaxed and even collegial, and Jaruzelski felt at ease in explaining to the pope how "indignant" he was over Reagan's demands that Poland enter into a dialogue with Solidarity and even the Catholic Church as a condition for lifting the sanctions.

"We are not establishing contacts with Solidarity," Jaruzelski remarked. Instead, he emphasized the continuing relationship between the church and the regime. He pointed out that the circulation of Catholic publications and bulletins had risen from 800,000 to 1.9 million, and argued that contacts with the church were "never interrupted" and had even grown "stronger."[5] The meeting was cathartic for Jaruzelski:

For me, it was a deep personal experience. I am a non-believer, but, you know, something remains in the genes from one's youth. So the pope, this figure in white, it all affected me emotionally. Beyond all reason . . . I was deeply moved by that encounter. I was even nervous. . . . It was our first conversation, a get-acquainted conversation, but, at the same time, very important in substance.[6]

Jaruzelski reflected on his childhood and his mother, Wanda, who had raised him in a staunchly Catholic household, sent him to church on Sundays, and packed him off to a Jesuit boarding school outside of Warsaw at the age of ten. The meeting had a powerful impact on his psyche:

In that first encounter, I had the subconscious sense that this is something special, that I am in the presence of greatness. Especially after I had seen those crowds, these millions falling on their knees. I have seen people, bishops, writers kneeling, kissing his hand. So it is a contagious mood. Of course, I am rationally very, very sober in such situations, and I have the consciousness of his human dimension . . . But it was a very deep experience for me. And when you add his personality, his charisma, you can imagine the impression.[7]

After the meeting, the pope continued onward in Warsaw, Częstochowa, Poznań, Wrocław, Katowice, and Kraków.[8] Massive crowds thronged him. As Jaruzelski recalled, John Paul II was "in a very difficult position, under pressure from the crowds that almost expected him to lead them to the barricades." While Jaruzelski understood that the pope didn't want to trigger violence and encourage civil war, he nonetheless detected the pope's latent sympathy toward Solidarity. "He felt convinced inside," Jaruzelski remarked, referring to the pope, "that he must support this movement and all these national social aspirations, that he must keep them alive, and reinforce this hope in some fashion, but without crossing certain frontiers."[9] For his part, John Paul

Pope John Paul II's Visit to Poland, June 16–23, 1983

II avoided major confrontations, though the visit sparked a handful of opposition protests.

Despite their differences, Jaruzelski and John Paul II managed to develop a personal connection and a degree of trust. They held a second meeting on June 22 in Kraków's royal Wawel Castle. "It was a very important conversation," Jaruzelski later observed. The pope spoke of "his appreciation of the peaceful atmosphere of the visit and the cooperation of the authorities." Upon further reflection, Jaruzelski divided his interaction with the pope into two nearly contradictory levels:

> One level was that of a friendly feeling; here I was welcoming a great man, a guest who was also our compatriot. But at the same

time there was this other level . . . where we had to present our respective reasons which didn't always coincide. Sometimes they were totally different. . . . Even when we came to a controversial point that we couldn't resolve on the spot we decided to study it further in future meetings with the primate and the government, and try to find a good solution.[10]

The comity between these two powerful figures would prove important in avoiding violence. But there was one point the two could never resolve: whether the pope should meet with Lech Wałęsa.

———

IN DISCUSSING THE TERMS OF THE POPE'S VISIT, Polish authorities initially said they would never allow it. They refused to let Wałęsa leave Gdańsk during the pope's visit, and then threatened to arrest him if he left the city without their permission.[11] But the Vatican had bluntly communicated to the Jaruzelski regime that the pope would not come to Poland if he couldn't meet with Wałęsa. Jaruzelski was in a no-win situation. Rather than risk cancelling the visit and facing a massive domestic backlash, he eventually agreed to a compromise: the pope and Wałęsa would meet, but it would be away from the press and television cameras. Jaruzelski hoped that a meeting away from journalists and with no photo opportunities would dampen Solidarity's ability to use the visit for propaganda purposes. But he was wrong.

Wałęsa was overjoyed to meet with John Paul II. Two years before, in January 1981, Wałęsa had trekked to the Vatican and sat with the pope. "I believe the cornerstone of your venture, which began in August 1980 in the coastal region and in other great centers of Polish industry," the pope told Wałęsa, "was a common impulse to promote the moral good of society."[12] For Wałęsa, the Polish pope was more than just a spiritual inspiration. "I had felt a profound spiritual communion with the Holy Father" from the first day of the strike, Wałęsa recalled.[13]

The Polish regime selected a village near the holiday resort town of Zakopane in the foothills of the Tatra Mountains for the June 1983 meeting, where the pope had enjoyed hiking and climbing as a child.[14] Bishop Tadeusz Gocłowski later wrote that the meeting, which lasted forty minutes, covered the security situation in the country and the prospects for Solidarity's survival. There was also an aura of "certainty about the victory of the ideal [of Solidarity], which had become so dominant all across Poland. They were in full agreement that, difficult as things might be, the facts were irreversible."[15] Wałęsa described the meeting as one with an "atmosphere of openness and simplicity." He also noticed "the pope's large feet" and his "steady, measured, and confident" steps as he walked.[16]

Jaruzelski, who attended the meeting, had a different recollection. The visit "lasted only twenty minutes," recalled Jaruzelski. "They got through with the introductions, there were heaps of [Wałęsa's] children about." The meeting occurred in a largely "symbolic dimension," but nothing of substance transpired. "Wałęsa wasn't happy about that, and I understand why," Jaruzelski said. "But it seems that at the time the people thought that the most important thing was to preserve peace and calm in Poland. He perceived the goodwill of the authorities . . . and I think this was a sort of freezing, a hibernation of Wałęsa while waiting for future developments."[17]

In reality, the pope's visit was a coup for Wałęsa and a welcome development for Solidarity. Wałęsa was euphoric, arguing that it helped Solidarity "enormously."[18] The pope did not publicly refer to the banned organization Solidarity during his visit, as the Vatican had pledged. But he snuck variants of the word into his speeches. "It is up to you," he proclaimed at Częstochowa, to assert the "fundamental *solidarity* between human beings."[19] Opposition demonstrations erupted across Poland, though they remained nonviolent. During the pope's second meeting with Jaruzelski, for instance, thousands of Poles marched in Kraków and nearby Nowa Huta in support of Solidarity, as police peacefully dispersed them.[20] Jaruzelski recalled that the pope energized Poles across the country:

We, the authorities, began to discern certain disturbing things, which might destabilize the situation. . . . The pope, of course, never said anything that might have actually created a controversy with us. But he knows how to speak so splendidly, to modulate the mood, and to create perceptions in such a way that a word spoken at random could open the way to a situation that might be hard to control.[21]

Such a reinvigoration of Solidarity is exactly what Warsaw had feared—and exactly what U.S. officials hoped might occur.

———

BACK IN WASHINGTON, Reagan was ecstatic about John Paul II's visit to Poland. So were the CIA and U.S. military. According to one top secret U.S. Defense Department report, "the papal visit has served to at least temporarily buoy the spirits of Poles." The report continued that "the spirit of Solidarity is not dead and Poles were eager—especially in the safety of numbers—to display the spirit."[22] Church leaders who met with Reagan and other administration officials lauded the trip. One church official told Reagan that the visit highlighted that "the spirit of Solidarity will never die; water cannons, tear gas and other repressive instruments can be used on them but their spirit will never cease."[23] Clergy said the visit helped bolster Solidarity, encourage reconciliation, and weaken the government's stranglehold on the country.

Perhaps the clearest sign of easing tensions was Jaruzelski's decision to lift martial law on July 22, 1983, a month after the pope's visit. In ending martial law, however, Jaruzelski still threatened that he would crush any resistance. "There will be no return to anarchy," he told the Polish Sejm. "Any attempts at antisocialist activities will be muzzled no less decisively than before."[24] The same day, the Sejm also passed legislation permitting the government to declare a state of emergency in the event of future disorder and unrest.

With the end of martial law, Catholic Church officials pressed

Washington to reconsider several of its policies, including economic sanctions. After martial law, the Reagan administration had cancelled scientific exchanges between the United States and Poland, banned the Polish airline LOT from landing in the United States, suspended most favored nation trading status, and vetoed Poland's bid to join the International Monetary Fund. While Soviet aid to Poland offset some of the economic pain, the sanctions nonetheless weakened Poland's already-struggling economy.

In a meeting with Reagan after John Paul II's visit, Cardinal John Krol, the archbishop of Philadelphia, remarked that the "Administration should make some kind of gesture to acknowledge the Polish government's consent to the Papal visit." Krol suggested that the United State lift a "low cost" sanction like restrictions on LOT Polish Airlines.[25] Over the next several months, Catholic Church officials lobbied the United States to ease additional measures, taking a slightly critical tone toward Washington. As the Vatican explained in one letter to the White House: "In view of these developments the Holy See would look upon with great favor some corresponding sign of openness by the government of the United States, such as the lifting of some of the economic restrictions and the removal of obstacles that do not permit the participation of the government of Poland in the International Monetary Fund."[26]

In February 1984, Vice President George H. W. Bush traveled to the Vatican, where the pope asked him to ease sanctions and reduce Polish suffering. As Bush reported back to Reagan: "The Holy Father said the people are getting hurt. 'This must be changed.' He said the Holy See and I agree that there should be a change in sanctions, that the people themselves are looking for a relationship with the United States."[27] The Vatican believed that it was fruitless to attempt to unseat Jaruzelski. "The government cannot be changed," said John Paul II, speaking softly, leaning gently across his desk towards Vice President Bush. "Therefore you must influence Jaruzelski to have a more human face."[28]

Reagan officials took these requests seriously.[29] Even Lech Wałęsa joined in the fray, arguing that it would be reasonable to lift some sanctions. "Above all, there are really small amounts, more symbolic, more propagandistic. If you speak about restrictions on flights or fish and so forth, that's really not a big matter. And in my opinion, in our opinion, we should not any longer avail ourselves of them."[30] Catholic leaders also prodded Reagan administration officials to allow more Polish refugees and asylum seekers into the United States. In one letter, the Vatican explained that "numerous requests for political asylum, made at different periods of time to the competent United States Authorities, have apparently not yet been taken into consideration, thus leaving the petitioners faced with an uncertain future and even obliging many of them to prolong their illegal stay in the United States; many other requests have unfortunately had a negative response."[31]

In late February, Reagan wrote a letter to John Paul II, explaining that "we are prepared to lift the ban on regularly scheduled LOT flights to the United States, permit the resumption of travel," and "begin an official—but highly confidential—dialogue" with Jaruzelski. Reagan also told the pope that "I am also conveying to the General my strong interest in the situation of Lech Walesa and his family and my concern that they not be subjected to officially-inspired harassment."[32] Reagan eventually eased some sanctions. He restored scientific exchanges and lifted the ban on American landing rights for LOT. Most Solidarity members were happy to see sanctions eased, though U.S.-Polish relations remained cool. Larry Speakes, Reagan's spokesman, said that the United States remained "concerned" about the Polish situation and that the president was maintaining a "step-by-step approach."[33]

———

WHILE U.S. OFFICIALS WERE GENERALLY PLEASED with the Catholic Church's activities in Poland, Soviet leaders were incensed.[34] A top secret KGB memo concluded that "in recent years the Head of the Catholic church and right-wing circles in the Vatican have been stepping up subversive activity against the socialist countries and the national liberation and anti-war movements."[35] The KGB disdained John Paul II, who its leaders accused of being both anti-Communist and anti-Soviet. They blamed the church for using Poland as a launching pad for subversive activity across Eastern Europe: "The Vatican also assumes that the action of the Polish church to strengthen its position in the state can be extended to other socialist countries."[36] According to the KGB, which asked its operatives to recruit spies in Catholic organizations and the Vatican, the pope's strategy was simple: to exploit church officials across the region as ideological shock troops that could intensify anti-Communist and anti-Soviet sentiments among the masses.

Yuri Andropov, the general secretary of the Communist Party of the Soviet Union who had succeeded Brezhnev, wrote a ferocious letter to Jaruzelski warning that the "church is reawakening the cult of Wałęsa, giving him inspiration and encouraging him in his actions. This means that the church is creating a new type of confrontation with the Party."[37] Wałęsa, who had won the Nobel Peace Prize in October 1983, gave the prize money to a Catholic Church fund to help private farmers modernize the countryside. Andropov wrote to Jaruzelski:

> Today, the church is a powerful opposition force against socialism, appearing in the role of patron and defender of the underground and defender of the idea of Solidarity. . . . In this situation, the most important thing is not to make concessions, but to establish firmly a line of restricting the activity of the church to the constitutional framework, and narrow the sphere of its influences on the social life.[38]

Soviet leaders wanted Jaruzelski to muzzle the church. In April 1984, two months after Andropov's death, Soviet officials summoned Jaruzelski to a railway car meeting in Brest-Litovsk, this time with Foreign Minister Andrei Gromyko and Defense Minister Dimitri Ustinov. They were livid at Jaruzelski's account of state-church relations. As Gromyko told the Soviet politburo: "Concerning the attitude of the Polish church, [Jaruzelski] described the church as an ally, without whom progress is impossible. He did not say a word about a determined struggle against the intrigues of the church."

Presiding over the politburo review on April 26, 1984, Konstantin Chernenko, Andropov's successor, noted sternly, "The counterrevolutionary forces continue their activities, the church leads the offensive, inspiring and uniting the enemies of communism and those dissatisfied by the present system."

"Generally, if one may say so, the matter of building the [Communist] Party is out of line with Jaruzelski's soul," said Gromyko.

"I'm of the opinion that he was insincere with us," Ustinov responded.

"It turns out," said Mikhail Gorbachev, who had carefully reviewed the notes of the railway car meeting, "that Jaruzelski undoubtedly wanted to present the situation as better than it really was. It seems to me that we don't yet understand the true intentions of Jaruzelski." Gorbachev then paused: "Perhaps he wishes to have a pluralistic system of government in Poland."[39]

For Jaruzelski, the whole encounter had been a nightmare. As he later remarked:

> You can't imagine what I had to live through . . . Not quite half-a-year after Andropov's letter, there is more pressure on us [from Moscow], critically assessing our policy toward the church. And we were caught in the middle. From one side, the West was attacking us, applying sanctions. And from those [in the East] whom I was asking for economic assistance, they were refusing it. They were attacking us over our relations with the church.[40]

But Jaruzelski's tensions with Moscow and the Catholic Church were about to grow much worse with the shocking assassination of one of Poland's most outspoken priests.

———

IN OCTOBER 1984, Father Jerzy Popiełuszko did not arrive at his church for morning mass in Żoliborz, a blue-collar district in Warsaw that stretched from the banks of the Vistula to the northern cusp of the city. Popiełuszko was chaplain of the Huta Warszawa steelworks outside of Warsaw and a resident vicar at the St. Stanislaus Kostka Church, a Solidarity stronghold. He also had close ties to the pope. It soon emerged that he had been killed by the SB. Pressed to do more, the Jaruzelski regime overreacted. The brazen slaying further isolated the government from many church members.

Popiełuszko was a slight, somber thirty-seven-year-old priest hated by the regime because of his firebrand anti-Communist rhetoric and his enthusiastic support for Solidarity. He drew thousands of listeners from around the country to his sermons, which he delivered with a slow cadence in a low, rumbling voice. He did not mince words, harshly criticizing the government for its ruthlessness. This verbal campaign was unprecedented. Almost nowhere else in Eastern Europe, from East Berlin to Moscow, had anyone disparaged their government like Popiełuszko did in Poland. His sermons were broadcast in Poland and across Eastern Europe by Radio Free Europe, much to Warsaw and Moscow's ire. A few months before, Popiełuszko had given a rousing, fiery sermon at the St. Stanislaus Kostka Church that infuriated the regime:

> Two years ago I said that Solidarity had received a wound that continues to bleed, but one which was not mortal, because one cannot murder hopes. Today you can see and feel this even more clearly as we marvel at the faith of our brothers returned from prison. We see and feel more clearly that the hopes of 1980 are alive and are bearing fruit. Today they are even dearer to us because they have entered into human hearts and minds. That which is in the heart, that which is deeply tied to man, cannot be liquidated with this or that regulation or statute.... We have to fight our way out of the fear that paralyzes and enslaves reason and the human heart.[41]

Popiełuszko encouraged his listeners to demand the freedoms that Lech Wałęsa and others had been fighting for since August 1980. This assault on the regime was too much for a small cabal of SB officers. On October 19, Popiełuszko's driver, Waldemar Chrostowski, stumbled barefoot and bleeding into a church in Torun and told stunned listeners that he and Popiełuszko had been kidnapped by Polish security agents. Popiełuszko was beaten, tied up, and stuffed into the trunk of a Polish-built Fiat. Chrostowski was shoved into the front but managed to open the door and roll out of the speeding car. Four policemen were soon arrested. One of them—Leszek Pękala, the most junior of the officers arrested—broke under questioning and led investigators to a reservoir on the Vistula, where they fished out Popiełuszko's corpse. The SB officers had tied rocks to his body and then tossed him into the water. One newspaper report described his body as looking "like a porpoise, flopped on the shore."[42]

The regime's initial response to Popiełuszko's disappearance was to shrug its shoulders. The government's spokesman, Jerzy Urban, told inquisitive journalists that the government could not keep track of every priest across the country. Everyone knew, Urban said with a mischievous grin, that some priests vanished for brief periods to escape from their vows of chastity. But government officials did not laugh long. "This time the poisoned dwarf has gone too far," remarked one Pole, referring to the diminutive Urban, after word surfaced that SB officers had assassinated Popiełuszko.[43] At the trial, four police officers from the SB's Department IV, which conducted surveillance against outspoken priests, were convicted and received sentences from two to fourteen years.[44] Yet no higher-ups were ever tried, even though one of the defendants confessed in court that the kidnapping had been authorized by his superiors in the Ministry of Internal Affairs.[45]

Poles held vigils for Popiełuszko in virtually every city across the country. At St. Bridget's in Gdańsk, supporters erected a ghastly memorial: a life-size, cast bronze statue of Popiełuszko in which the priest lay grotesquely on the ground with his mouth slightly open, hands wrenched and tied behind his back, and feet shackled—as he apparently was found in the Vistula. A steady flow of visitors lit candles and prayed for him in the small chapel dedicated to his memory. Wałęsa and other Solidarity members embraced a poignant song inspired by the death of Popiełuszko:

My Country,
so many times swamped in blood,
how deep your wound is today,
and how endless your suffering.
How many times have you sought freedom,
How many times been strangled by the hangman;
But then it was always by the hand of a foreigner,
while today, brothers are killing brothers. [46]

———

ANGUISH AT THE DEATH of Father Jerzy Popiełuszko, and antipathy towards the regime that killed him, were not confined to Poland. More than a quarter of a million Poles attended an open-air requiem mass for Popiełuszko in Warsaw on November 3, 1984, pictures of which were splashed across newspapers and television screens around the globe. Catholic officials and opposition figures praised the slain priest as a national hero.

Józef Glemp, the archbishop of Warsaw, conducted the service from a balcony at St. Stanislaus Kostka Church. The white twin-spired building's façade was adorned with hundred-foot-long diagonal ribbons. Popiełuszko's coffin rested gently on a white bier below Glemp. A wide swath of silk, adorned in Poland's red and white colors, ran from the coffin up the length of the church façade. Loudspeakers broadcast the mass to the oversized crowd that filled the square and packed the side streets outside the churchyard's flower-covered fences. Glistening Solidarity banners fluttered above the crowd. Some mourners crowded

onto rooftops and balconies around the church, or climbed into surrounding trees, straining to catch a glimpse of the proceedings. Wałęsa
addressed the crowd, declaring to thunderous cheers: "Solidarity lives
because Popiełuszko shed his blood for it."[47] Wałęsa was greeted by a sea
of people flashing the "V" sign with their fingers for victory, and chant-
ing "Solidarność."

While the Jaruzelski regime denied U.S. senator Edward Kennedy
a visa to attend the funeral, other international figures paid homage to
Popiełuszko in Poland. John Morgan, the British ambassador to Poland,
and Malcolm Rifkind, a Foreign Office official and later secretary of
Britain's foreign and defense ministries, laid a wreath at Popiełuszko's
grave in a solemn ceremony captured on BBC.[48] Rifkind attached a
card to the wreath, which read: "With expressions of deepest sorrow
and respect from Her Majesty's Government and the entire British
nation."[49] Rifkind was effusive in his praise for Popiełuszko and the virtues he espoused, noting: "We hope that the values he stood for will continue to flourish in accordance with the wishes of the Polish people."[50]
A classified U.S. Department of Defense document sent to the White
House praised Rifkind for his actions after the funeral, urging U.S.
allies to "model their conduct in Warsaw on that of British Undersecre-
tary Rifkind, who openly received Solidarity leaders and laid a wreath at
Father Popiełuszko's grave."[51]

Back in the United States, the Polish community in Chicago erected
a monument to Popiełuszko in the "Garden of Memory" at the Basilica of
St. Hyacinth in the northwest neighborhood of Avondale. It was a symbolic gravestone in the shape of a cross. St. Hedwig's Catholic church
in Trenton, New Jersey, also constructed a bust of Popiełuszko with a
chain wrapped around his neck. In Rome, the rock that was allegedly
used to kill Popiełuszko was placed among the relics of modern martyrs
in the Basilica of St. Bartholomew. The pope weighed in from the Vatican, speaking of Popiełuszko's death as a beginning—a resurrection.[52]
Hollywood eventually followed suit. Columbia Pictures released a
movie several years later, titled To Kill a Priest, starring Christopher

Lambert as Popiełuszko and Ed Harris as a police captain involved in
the assassination.

————

SOON THE CIA GOT INVOLVED. Recognizing the symbolic value of
Popiełuszko's death, the CIA provided aid which enabled the underground to print roughly 40,000 postcards with the priest's image, along
with texts of his sermons.[53] Radio Free Europe also broadcast audio seg-
ments of his sermons. In Popiełuszko's death, the CIA had discovered a
sharp wedge it could drive between the Jaruzelski regime and the Polish
population. One classified CIA assessment concluded: "In essence, the
chasm between the government and society remains as wide as ever.
Although the government's tools of repression effectively crush any outright resistance, society continues to defy the government whenever it
can, such as the use of the Popiełuszko funeral to demonstrate its continued loyalty to the ideals of Solidarity."[54] Even more damning, a classified
CIA report deduced that the KGB may have been involved—at least
indirectly—in the assassination of Popiełuszko. "By encouraging hard-
line factions in the Polish party and police to push for harsher measures
against Solidarity," it noted, the KGB "helped create the climate in which
such an act could occur."[55]

By the time of Popiełuszko's death, one of the Polish government's
main objectives was to suffocate media coverage of the underground
movement inside Poland and, as much as possible, outside the country.
Jaruzelski had censored all forms of publication, printing, and copying
materials. In Bill Casey's opinion, the reforms instituted by the Jaruzelski regime had largely been window dressing: "General Jaruzelski has
created the trappings of public participation in decision-making, while
concurrently enacting legislation and taking repressive action to prevent
a genuine national dialogue from developing."[56] The task for CIA officers
involved in QRHELPFUL, then, was to expose Jaruzelski's reforms as a
sham. At a cabinet meeting in 1984, Casey told Reagan, "political con-

trol has remained General Jaruzelski's top priority." But, he said, the CIA now had an extraordinary opportunity. Popieluzko's death had triggered a global outpouring of support. Jaruzelski's censors would have an uphill battle keeping this story from creating worldwide sympathy for Solidarity. Especially if the CIA could develop a sophisticated and coordinated global ideological campaign.

Chapter 18
A GLOBAL CAMPAIGN

In the face of Jaruzelski's actions, Dick Malzahn told senior U.S. government officials that Solidarity was still capable of surviving, but needed covert support to continue. By late 1984, QRHELPFUL's infrastructure was operating at full capacity. Within the International Activities Division at CIA headquarters, Dick Malzahn remained head of the Political-Psychological Staff's Soviet–East Europe Group (PPS/SEG), though he would eventually be replaced by Boyd Bishop. With a strong team in place, the CIA ramped up its media campaign to aid Solidarity. The CIA's International Activities Division boasted a worldwide covert action infrastructure of media assets and outlets to distribute a pro-Solidarity message. Malzahn's group aimed to organize political demonstrations inside—and outside—Poland. The CIA wanted to further increase global awareness of the Polish regime's crackdowns and generate additional funding and other aid to Solidarity. For the CIA, this strategy was an ideological one.

The CIA promoted the Solidarity logo around the world and helped manufacture and distribute Solidarity buttons, T-shirts, key chains, and other items—much like a public relations firm. Malzahn and his team also identified significant dates in Polish history—including

Solidarity's history—that could be used to raise media and public awareness. Examples included August 31, the day Solidarity members signed the Gdańsk Agreement in 1980; December 13, the day Jaruzelski declared martial law in 1981; May 1, Labor Day in Poland; and May 3, the anniversary of the day that the Great Sejm, or parliament, adopted the Polish constitution in 1791. With Malzahn's oversight, CIA case officers and assets helped organize demonstrations in roughly twenty countries during these dates to increase global awareness of Solidarity's cause.[1]

The CIA stations in Mexico City and Paris were particularly active. CIA case officers and their networks helped place articles in over two dozen Mexican newspapers; provided financial assistance for pro-Solidarity demonstrations; organized a half dozen television and radio interviews with Miroslav Domińczyk, one of Solidarity's founders; helped arrange a dozen press conferences with Domińczyk; and distributed over 70,000 bulletins across the country, including in such cities as Mexico City, León, and Torreón.[2] While Mexico did not have as large a Polish émigré population as the United States, it did have an active one. Some of the first Polish immigrants arrived in Mexico in the late nineteenth century. During World War II, Mexico received thousands of refugees from Poland, primarily of Jewish ethnicity, who settled in the states of Chihuahua and Nuevo León. The Catholic Church was also a powerful force in Mexico and a helpful ally in organizing demonstrations.

The overseas hub of QRHELPFUL remained Paris, where QRBERETTA—the covert action program that began in 1950 to support Jerzy Giedroyc and *Kultura*—had been one of the CIA's first-ever political programs. The CIA asset Stanisław Broda, or QRGUIDE, who worked closely with CIA case officer Celia Larkin, helped plaster Metro stations with 40,000 stickers urging Parisians to write protest letters to the Polish ambassador. Broda also arranged for French television to broadcast taped interviews with Solidarity leaders still living underground.[3] One of the most interesting demonstrations was organized by a CIA Paris station asset, Artur Kowalski, in cooperation with the French labor confederation Force Ouvrière (Workers' Force). Five trade unionists boarded the Paris-Warsaw-Moscow express train at the Gare du Nord train station on the right bank of the Seine, changed into prison garb, hung placards around their necks with the names of Solidarity prisoners, and handcuffed themselves to the train.[4] Other participants plastered the train with Solidarity stickers and held up banners reading "This Train to Warsaw and Moscow and to the Gulag" and "Solidarity Lives." French police were slow to respond to the situation, which allowed some media coverage. Thanks to these and other efforts, Poland and the plight of Solidarity continued to be covered in newspapers, magazines, and radio and television programs.[5]

In addition to Mexico City and Paris, several additional CIA stations played roles in supporting QRHELPFUL. They included Rome, London, Brussels, and Bonn, as well as smaller CIA offices in West Berlin, Hamburg, Munich, and Frankfurt. Other CIA hubs

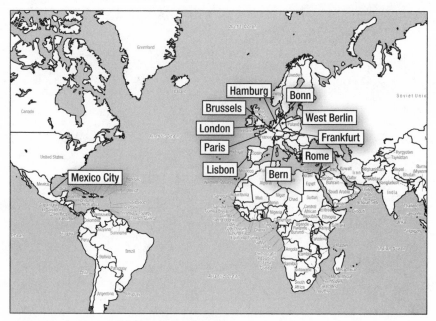

CIA Hubs for QRHELPFUL

included Lisbon, Portugal and Bern, Switzerland—which had mostly supporting roles.

Several wealthy Europeans provided cover for the large sums of money flowing into Poland and Poland-related activities. The CIA recruited a Portuguese businessman whom I will call "Afonso Coutinho"

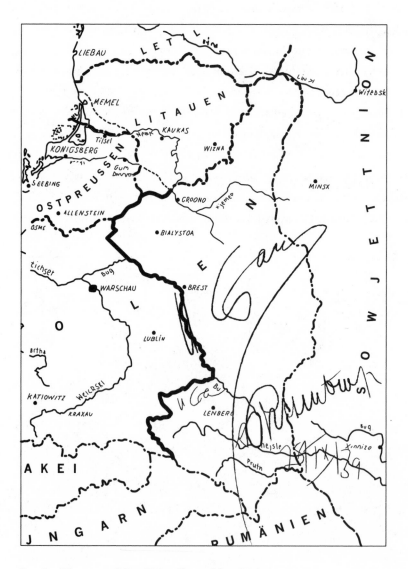

Soviet-German Map Distributed by CIA

who mounted pro-Solidarity demonstrations and served as what the CIA called an "agent of influence."[6] CIA sources also distributed copies of a map that Stalin and Hitler's foreign minister, Joachim von Ribbentrop, had initialed in September 1939 after German and Soviet forces invaded Poland. The Soviet Union and Germany divided Poland, Lithuania, Latvia, Estonia, Finland, and Romania into German and Soviet spheres of influence. Polish territory east of the Narew, Vistula, and San rivers would fall under Soviet control.

As the CIA's Robert Gates said, "We made hundreds of miniaturized copies and arranged for their infiltration into Poland."[7] The map identified the respective German-Soviet occupation zones and the partition of the former Polish state. A Polish-language translation of the secret Nazi-Soviet accord appeared on the reverse side of the map.[8] CIA assets also helped organize pro-Solidarity demonstrations during high-visibility events like soccer games, especially when they were broadcast on television. "On one occasion," a CIA official noted, "the CIA sponsored a demonstration in which a Solidarity banner displayed at a Poland-Belgium football (soccer) game was prominently displayed during television coverage of the event."[9]

The CIA's information campaign helped draw Solidarity back into the global spotlight. Reagan was elated.

———

HEADING INTO THE 1984 ELECTION YEAR, Reagan heightened his ideological rhetoric against the Soviets. His Democratic opponent, Walter Mondale, a former senator from Minnesota, had served as Jimmy Carter's vice president. Unlike Mondale, who adopted a more conciliatory policy toward the Soviet Union, Reagan told America he did not want reconciliation with Moscow, but rather the *end* of Communism.[10] Reagan had announced a proposed missile defense system, termed the Strategic Defense Initiative (nicknamed "Star Wars"), designed to protect the U.S. homeland from attack by shooting down Soviet ballistic missiles. He warned the American people that "in Poland, the Soviets denied the will of the people and in so doing demonstrated to the world how their military power could also be used to intimidate."[11] For Reagan, Poland still served as a microcosm of Moscow's global ambitions. He went after Soviet ideology again and again on the campaign trail.

"I'm reminded of a story about a conversation between one of our citizens and a Soviet citizen," he told guests at a White House luncheon in August 1984, marking the fortieth anniversary of the Warsaw uprising. "The American described the freedom of speech that we have here in the United States, and the citizen of the Soviet Union said, 'Well, we're free to speak in the Soviet Union just like you are in the United States.' He said, 'The only difference is you're free *after* you speak.'"[12]

The same month, Reagan made his most explicit public statement yet that Yalta was an anachronism, no longer confining his words to top secret National Security Decision Directives and classified presidential findings. "[L]et me state emphatically that we reject any interpretation of the Yalta agreement that suggests American consent for the division of Europe into spheres of influence," Reagan said. He argued that the permanent subjugation of the people of Eastern Europe was not an acceptable alternative, and he highlighted Solidarity's struggle:

> The rise of Solidarity is a matter of historic significance. It continues to be an inspiration of all free people that the Marxist-Leninist myth of inevitability is crumbling. Communism has brought with it only deprivation and tyranny. What happened in Poland is one sign that the tide is turning. The Polish people, with their courage and perseverance, will lead the way to freedom and independence, not only for themselves but for all those who yearn to breathe free. The battle cry of the Polish Home Army still rings true: "Poland is fighting. Poland will live. Poland will overcome."[13]

QRHELPFUL remained essential in this environment. One CIA report concluded that "the continued circulation of some 1,000 underground publications" suggested that Polish society continued to defy the government. The CIA painted Jaruzelski as a "consensus man" who attempted "to preserve the standard Communist framework and will continue his attempt to preserve the standard Communist system of rule from above."[14] Another CIA document judged, almost triumphantly, that "Jaruzelski continues to be unable to stifle the influence of the church or Solidarity but simultaneously rejects any role for them in arranging a genuine national reconciliation program."[15]

U.S. Department of Defense documents painted an even darker picture of Jaruzelski's Poland. One classified analysis at the end of 1984 argued that Jaruzelski's government was "fundamentally repressive, intent on gaining a grip over every facet of Polish life as tightly and as quickly as internal opposition and Western attitudes will allow. Thus, in our view, Jaruzelski's . . . notion of dialogue is not of one with Polish society about compromise but with Western governments about credits."[16] In the view of Defense Department analysts, Jaruzelski's reforms were designed to loosen the West's economic asphyxiation of Poland and were not the result of an enlightened view of Poland. Dissidents were regularly harassed. Private shopkeepers and small businesses were burdened with restrictive regulations. Poland's security apparatus continued to conduct routine beatings and even murders. These realities made it particularly important, according to Department of Defense officials, to continue with a covert action program to support Solidarity and find other ways to aid anti-regime dissidents.

As one classified Pentagon document concluded: "[W]e believe the USG should pursue a policy of low-key but firm support for the opposition. Such support should range from protesting human rights violations to helping supply paper and printing materials to legal, church-affiliated publications." It ended by highlighting what was on the line in Poland: "Ultimately it is the strength of the internal opposition that will determine the level of repression in Poland. We should, of course, be careful not to incite exaggerated hopes, but we must not by our actions leave the activists in the East with the feeling that they have no friends in the West."[17]

Secretary of Defense Cap Weinberger was particularly critical of Jaruzelski, referring to him as "a Soviet general in a Polish uniform."[18]

Jaruzelski took offense at this comment. He ordered his diplomats to tell Weinberger—and every U.S. diplomat they could reach—that Jaruzelski had suffered in Soviet exile, his father had died in a Siberian camp, and he considered himself to be a Polish patriot not a Soviet stooge. Still, Polish underground cartoonists couldn't resist mocking Jaruzelski's stiff demeanor and pink-faced visage. He was reviled by the opposition and disliked by Soviet leaders. Michael Kaufman, the *New York Times* bureau chief in Warsaw, quipped that it was a no-win situation for Jaruzelski: "He was proving to be too much of a Communist to win the trust of Poles, but too much of a Pole to maintain the full trust of the Kremlin."[19] The Soviets wanted him to be harsher—a dreaded autocrat—and Poles wanted him to shed his Soviet marionette image and embrace reform.

For Reagan, the unpopularity of Jaruzelski and persistence of Solidarity signaled that the U.S.'s strategy toward Poland—and the Soviet Union more broadly—was working, albeit slowly. Throughout the 1984 election campaign, Reagan excoriated Mondale for being weak on the Soviet Union and too eager to appease Soviet leaders. At seventy-three, Reagan was the oldest president ever to hold the office, and there were numerous questions about his ability to serve another grueling four-year term as president. Reagan's first debate with the fifty-six-year-old Mondale didn't help dispel these concerns. Partway through the debate, Reagan confided to panelist Fred Barnes, a national political correspondent for the *Baltimore Sun*, that he had started going to church "here in Washington"—even though the debate was in Louisville, Kentucky. Reagan also referred to military uniforms as a "wardrobe," and sheepishly admitted near the end of the debate—after a question from panelist Barbara Walters—that "I'm all confused now."[20] In the second debate, however, Reagan landed one of his best jokes of the campaign after a question from Henry Trewhitt, diplomatic correspondent for the *Baltimore Sun*, about his age.

"I will not make age an issue of this campaign," Reagan told Trewhitt. "I am not going to exploit, for political purposes, my opponent's youth and inexperience."[21]

The packed audience in Kansas City exploded with laughter and applause. Mondale himself laughed at the joke, and later admitted that Reagan had effectively neutralized the age issue: "[I]f TV can tell the truth, as you say it can, you'll see that I was smiling. But I think if you come in close, you'll see some tears coming down because I knew he had gotten me there. That was really the end of my campaign that night, I think."[22]

AS REAGAN ZIGZAGGED ACROSS the United States on the campaign trail, there were elections in Poland. The CIA sensed an opportunity to undermine the regime. The local People's Council elections and the Sejm elections were scheduled for 1984 and 1985, respectively. According to the Polish Constitution of 1952, Sejm elections should have been held every four years. But since the political situation was still considered unstable—even after Jaruzelzki repealed martial law—the Sejm elections were pushed from 1984 to 1985. The elections were not democratic, and only candidates approved by the Communist Party could run. Still, the regime hoped for a high turnout, which they could claim as evidence of strong popular support. Recognizing the regime's goals, Solidarity decided to boycott the elections.

The CIA opted to help. QRHELPFUL's goals were still modest: to keep the spirit of Solidarity alive. Before the People's Council and Sejm elections, CIA case officers provided money to make and distribute roughly 350,000 mini-posters on sticky-back labels urging Poles to boycott the elections. The CIA also supported efforts to organize commemorative demonstrations on major dates leading up to the elections. Polish security forces responded to many of these demonstrations with force, quickly and firmly dispersing them with armor-clad police.[23]

Back at CIA headquarters in McLean, analysts argued that several issues "could increase the strains between the regime and the opposition."[24] One was the elections, which the CIA concluded was "shaping up as a new test of wills. Solidarity has announced a boycott strategy and chances are that the church might support the boycott if the regime continues to use its current heavy-handed tactics."[25] While it is impossible to conclusively judge how significant CIA efforts were, voter turnout was uncharacteristically low. In previous elections, only 1 to 2 percent of eligible Polish voters refused to participate. But the numbers jumped to between 25 and 40 percent in the 1984 People's Councils elections and the 1985 Sejm elections, depending on whether the government or Solidarity's estimates could be believed.[26] Regardless of which estimate was closer to the truth, it was a striking shift.

Another potential friction point was the economic situation. The Polish economy was in dire shape. "Poland's recovery from its economic crisis of the early 1980s has stalled," one classified National Intelligence Estimate concluded, "and prospects for sustained improvement over the last year's disappointing performance appear slim for the rest of the decade."[27] The report listed a litany of problems, including an inability to meet consumer demands, an unproductive labor force, and a failure to secure funding from Western creditors. The CIA also monitored the dramatic rise in the number of strikes led by Wałęsa and other opposition members, which were becoming "a test of the regime's will."[28]

———

QRHELPFUL WAS HELPING KEEP SOLIDARITY AFLOAT, as were other CIA programs. CIA began channeling funds to small, private ventures called Polonia companies. The London-based Polonia Book Fund published Polish-language books and smuggled them into Poland. Editor in chief Jan Chodakowski edited *Puls* (*Pulse*), a literary journal published in Warsaw and Stockholm. Together, *Kultura* and Polonia received about $450,000 per year in CIA funds. In 1985, CIA assets infiltrated a total of roughly $900,000 into Poland, more than doubling the amount during the previous year. Assets also sent roughly 500,000 publications to Poland.[29]

In Paris, Stanisław Broda, or QRGUIDE, began making opposition videocassettes as the number of VCRs in Poland increased. He made a video history of Solidarity and sent 2,500 cassettes to Poland in 1985. The

CIA asset Artur Kowalski issued two editions of his quarterly (2,000 regular and 10,000 miniature format); moved roughly 42,000 books into Poland; and infiltrated 163,000 items to the underground. Kowalski's smuggling operation was especially adept. He bought a small factory that packaged food, which was sent to Poland as humanitarian aid. Underground members wrapped the publications in waterproof material and inserted them in the food packages. The underground created a verification system using coded references to food items in phone calls or in newspaper articles, or using couriers to indicate receipt of shipments. Most of the books that Kowalski sent over covered Polish history and Communism. They included volumes on the rise of Solidarity, the 1940 Soviet massacre of Polish officers and soldiers in the Katyn forest, and the role of Polish forces in World War II. Kowalski and Broda also helped organize pro-Solidarity demonstrations in France with French political figures and labor unions.[30]

CIA analysts gradually became more optimistic as Solidarity showed signs of strength. One estimate concluded that "Solidarity is making gains in recovering from the heavy blows of 1981 and 1982."[31] CIA assistance to Solidarity complemented other aid that eventually poured in from the AFL-CIO, Catholic organizations, the National Endowment for Democracy, and countless other nongovernmental organizations. The National Endowment for Democracy was a congressionally funded organization established by the Reagan administration in 1983 to support the growth and strengthening of democratic institutions around the world. Each year, it provided grants to support the projects of nongovernmental groups abroad who were working for democratic goals. The CIA had to coordinate with the State Department, however, to avoid duplicating assistance from the National Endowment for Democracy.

———

REAGAN WAS SWORN INTO OFFICE for a second term on January 21, 1985. The day was sunny and bright, but bitterly cold with polar gusts and wind chill temperatures hovering between minus ten and minus twenty degrees Fahrenheit. Over sole mousse and champagne in the Capitol's Statuary Hall following the inauguration, the Democratic speaker of the U.S House of Representatives, Tip O'Neill, congratulated Reagan, telling him that he was "very conscious" of the size of his win. "In my fifty years in public life," O'Neill remarked, "I've never seen a man more popular than you are with the American people."[32] Reagan carried forty-nine of the fifty states, losing only Mondale's home state of Minnesota.

Reagan didn't waste any time continuing his crusade against Communism. On February 5, 1985, he took one final swing at Yalta on the fortieth anniversary of the agreement, warming the hearts of CIA case officers involved in QRHELPFUL. "Forty years ago this week, the leaders of the United States, Great Britain and the Soviet Union met at Yalta, to confer on the approaching end of World War II and on the outlines of the post war world," Reagan said. "Since that time, Yalta has had a double meaning. It recalls an episode of cooperation between the Soviet Union and free nations, in a great common cause. But it also recalls the reasons that this cooperation could not continue." He ticked off several items: Soviet leaders broke their promises, they refused to hold elections, and Europe remained divided by an Iron Curtain. He continued that the United States would *never* recognize a dividing line between freedom and repression. "I do not hesitate to say that we wish to undo this boundary," Reagan said. "Long after Yalta, this much remains clear: The most significant way of making all Europe more secure is to make it more free. Our 40-year pledge is to the goal of a restored community of free European nations. To this work we recommit ourselves today."[33]

Time and technology were not on Warsaw or Moscow's side. Reagan's election coincided with a telecommunications revolution, in which consumers shifted from print to electronic media across the globe. The CIA seized on the new opportunities, and QRHELPFUL entered a new phase.

PART III

Chapter 19

THE TIDE TURNS

One balmy evening in 1985, *New York Times* journalist Michael Kaufman visited Solidarity members in the Warsaw suburb of Legionowo to witness a display of the underground's newfound technological prowess. Situated a dozen miles north of Warsaw, Legionowo was a tough blue-collar community that had been a hub for Polish resistance during World War II against the Nazis. The town was wedged between the Narew and Vistula rivers, the commercial lifeblood of central Poland. Massive Soviet-style eight- and ten-story complexes dominated the skyline. Kaufman described buildings ringed by patches of dirt and trampled grass, with weathered stucco and cement walls that highlighted their decrepitude.

Kaufman's friends led him to one of these apartments, plopped him in front of an aged television set, offered him a steaming cup of tea, and waited. Not long after the 7:00 p.m. evening news began, the words "Solidarity lives" in Polish flashed over the head of the television announcer, who was blissfully unaware that his program had been hijacked. After a few minutes, another message flashed on the screen that instructed viewers in Polish to "Listen to Radio Solidarity in half an hour" and provided a radio frequency to tune into. "My hosts," recalled Kaufman, "who were members of the firm that sent the signal, were proud of the skills that enabled them to literally break into the television."[1] After a few minutes, police sirens shattered the evening's silence. Kaufman and his hosts watched a large blue truck move deliberately through the neighborhood with a disc mounted on top, searching for the source of the radio signal. "It's driving the police crazy," said one of the Solidarity members. "They can't believe we can penetrate their television. They are trying to pinpoint our transmitter, but they won't find it."[2]

The words on the television screen could only be seen by viewers within a one-mile radius of the mobile transmitter. Only a few thousand families may have seen "Solidarity lives" appear on the screen that evening. But Solidarity conducted hundreds of these break-ins, inserting slogans that flashed on television screens across Poland. Television was now another medium—along with print and radio—for Solidarity to spread its message. The audacious technological hack also had an implicit message: Solidarity was creative and thriving, and the Jaruzelski regime was powerless to stop it.

What Kaufman did not know was that the CIA was partly behind Solidarity's new technology and tactics. The agency had helped Solidarity leap into the information age. In Washington, CIA officials like Soviet–East European division chief Burton Gerber, head of the Political-Psychological Staff David Gries, and national intelligence officer George Kolt briefed the results to Zbigniew Brzezinski, the Polish-born national security advisor who had served under President Carter. They were thrilled about Solidarity's new capabilities. The CIA had helped Solidarity with numerous successful overrides under QRHELP-FUL, and were planning more.[3]

———

BY 1985, ONE OF THE MOST IMPORTANT GOALS of QRHELPFUL was to provide video and other advanced equipment to Solidarity, marking a shift away from purely conventional printing and literature distribution.

Poland was experiencing widespread economic troubles. There were shortages of production and consumption of goods and a slowdown in productivity. Yet the country nevertheless witnessed a rise in televisions, VCRs, and, to a lesser extent, personal computers.[4] Home VCRs had become widely available in the West, and CIA operatives from the Political-Psychological Staff recognized the implications for Poland. There was an opportunity to shift their information campaign to the powerful realm of video.

Television was one of the Jaruzelski regime's most important ideological weapons. State-owned television content was heavily politicized, and journalists were encouraged to "be propagandists who day after day conveyed Marxist-Leninist theories, agitators who day after day spoke about the international political situation and about the Party's and people's government policies, and organizers who day after day mobilized the forces for their active part in Socialist construction."[5] For the 9.5 million viewers, shows and news programs reinforced the economic and political accomplishments of the regime, and denounced Solidarity, in ways both subtle and brazen.[6] Jaruzelski used Solidarity as a scapegoat.[7] Television programs blamed the underground for the deteriorating situation.[8] But impugning Solidarity for the growing economic crisis was an increasingly untenable argument for most Poles, who felt the government, not Solidarity, was in charge of Poland and thus responsible for its fate.

For the CIA—and the Reagan administration more broadly—television and video communications became an important new medium to wage political warfare. Solidarity still devoted resources to producing and distributing newspapers and magazines like *Tygodnik Mazowsze*, which the CIA continued to aid under QRHELPFUL. In a letter to Jerzy Giedroyc on his eightieth birthday, CIA director Casey had even thanked the Paris-based publisher for his contributions and his untiring work for *Kultura*.[9] "As traditional avenues of communication became more heavily watched, we tried new approaches," explained the CIA's Robert Gates. The CIA turned to a technique for clandestine broadcasting that its case officers had developed for Iran: overriding government programming. "We provided a good deal of money and equipment to the Polish underground for this—actually to take over the airwaves for a brief time," Gates continued. "The effort was effective, and in June 1987 the underground overrode Warsaw's evening television news with a message urging Solidarity activists to participate in public demonstrations."[10]

CIA case officers and assets leveraged the evolution in communications technology to infiltrate videocassettes, computers, floppy discs, and communications equipment into Poland using many of the traditional ratlines. Stanisław Broda, among others, now took advantage of less stringent border controls in countries like Hungary to bring in money and material like photocopiers and duplicators. In 1986, for example, CIA assets sent more than $1 million to the Solidarity underground. A growing percentage of this aid was video-related equipment.[11]

Broda used $40,000 in QRHELPFUL CIA funds to buy print and video equipment for Solidarity's educational and information programs. Solidarity broadcasts, announced during overrides of Polish national television programs, became more frequent. Polish officials complained that 10 million Solidarity videos—all illegal—were in circulation. There were now 15,000 satellite antennas.[12] CIA operatives also arranged satellite telecasts into Poland from Western Europe of labor unrest and other issues.[13]

Movies served an important role in undermining government support. The independent publishing house NOWA, for example, illegally distributed an explosive movie titled *Przesluchani* (*The Interrogation*), directed by Ryszard Bugajski. Set during the pro-Soviet Polish regime in the early 1950s, the plot was blatantly anti-Communist. The protagonist, Tonia, was a flighty cabaret singer after World War II, who was arrested after performing for Polish soldiers. The police threw her into a political prison, where they tortured her until she confessed to crimes she did not commit. While the Jaruzelski regime banned the film, it was clandestinely distributed by the underground, viewed by thousands of Poles, and discussed in hushed tones at dinner tables around the country.[14]

CIA's assistance in overriding government programs complemented its support to Radio Solidarity and other components of QRHELPFUL by helping break the regime's monopoly on the media. Throughout 1985 and 1986, the CIA provided funds for demonstrations, protests, meetings, conferences, press articles, television shows, and exhibitions to focus worldwide attention on Poland. On May 1, 1985, while the government celebrated the official May Day holiday, more than 15,000 people in Warsaw and 2,000 in Gdańsk spilled onto the streets to support Solidarity. It was the largest display of defiance since the declaration of martial law in 1981.[15] CIA assets and their networks also mobilized participants in anti-Soviet activities in cities like Geneva, Switzerland during a visit by Soviet leaders.[16]

Half a decade after martial law, Poland's vibrant intellectual community created an environment unprecedented in Eastern Europe. "Nowhere in Communist Europe except in Poland were groups of people doing so many things independent of party or state," remarked Michael Kaufman of the *New York Times*. "I had to remind myself almost continually that the illicitly produced books, magazines, and films, innocuous as they might appear by Western standards, were without parallel in the East bloc."[17]

———

IN RESPONSE TO THE CIA'S USE of video and other mediums, the KGB doubled down on its own propaganda campaign.[18] In a top secret memo to the Polish Ministry of Internal Affairs, KGB director Viktor Chebrikov chided Poland for being the "weakest link" in the Soviet bloc and for tolerating opposition. He encouraged the Polish secret police to more aggressively infiltrate the underground and recruit informants. Chebrikov also committed more KGB resources to uncover "provocateurs" that were threatening Poland and "funding subversion."[19] The KGB forged U.S. documents and attempted to jam radio stations like Radio Liberty and Radio Free Europe, which the Soviets accused of broadcasting "openly anti-Soviet character" and focusing on "malicious slander."[20]

Under greater pressure from the KGB, the Jaruzelski regime struck back against Solidarity. Robert Gates wrote, "As Solidarity's activities increased, so, too, did the aggressiveness of the Jaruzelski regime in cracking down on underground publishing and opposition activities. Several of our shipments were seized early in 1986."[21] In February 1986, Polish law enforcement agencies interdicted one of Artur Kowalski's clandestine shipments and reported it in the Polish press. In March, the police stopped, searched, and seized underground material on two trucks from Turin, Italy, that were operating under the TIR system and carrying contraband to Solidarity. Around the same time, Polish authorities intercepted several shipments from Stockholm and the port of Ystad in Sweden. Polish officials were waiting dockside when the shipments arrived, suggesting they had informants in the underground.[22] In July, Polish police seized additional shipments from CIA assets. Polish press articles reported an uptick in foreign aid assisted by the CIA. These seizures and the Jaruzelski regime's public relations campaign set off alarm bells at CIA headquarters.

In late 1986, Polish customs officials stopped a forty-ton truck when it arrived on a ferry from Sweden at the Polish port city of Świnoujście, nestled on the Baltic Sea along Poland's northwestern border with East Germany. Acting on a tip from a Swedish customs official that had been recruited by the SB, Polish officials discovered aid to Solidarity worth $200,000 hidden in secret compartments on the truck.[23] They confiscated 23 offset duplicators from German, British, and Japanese manufacturers; 420 six-pound cans of printer's ink; 49 photocopiers; 16 fax machines; Tandy and IBM computers; 12 small NL-10 printing calculators; radio scanners to listen to the radio communications of security officials from the ministries of internal affairs and defense; radio transmitter assembly kits; and 5,000 copies of pamphlets and books of "subversive texts."[24] Security officials off-loaded the contraband and brought it to a nearby athletic stadium, where Polish television broadcast the seizure. Aleksandr Makowski, a Polish intelligence officer who was in charge of Section 11, the group that targeted Western intelligence services suspected of aiding Solidarity, said the shipment was too large to let it pass without going public.[25]

As the Polish government worked harder to intercept contraband going to Solidarity, they also continued to harass Solidarity members and Catholic Church officials.[26] Over the first several months of 1986, Polish authorities arrested over 300 activists. The biggest arrest came in June, when they seized Solidarity underground leaders Bogdan Borusewicz and Zbigniew Bujak. Bujak ran the organization, oversaw the bank accounts, and distributed resources. The arrest thrust the movement into temporary disarray. The structure of Solidarity's Provisional Coordinating Committee was purposefully decentralized, and few leaders knew specific details about what others were doing. But Bujak knew more than most. A CIA report sent to director Casey following Bujak's arrest concluded that the Solidarity "underground has clearly had great difficulties operating against the regime's many instruments of coercion."[27] But it warned that the regime still faced widespread opposition across Poland. In August, the SB raided a Solidarity printing shop run by Stefan Dąbek, who hid leaflets celebrating Solidarity's anniversary in his basement. The SB brought in a television crew that filmed the discovery and aired it on national television.[28]

The Jaruzelski regime also outed Ryszard Kukliński, the CIA spy who had defected to the United States. The Polish government identified Kukliński, whose name had not been publicly released, in an effort to undermine the Reagan administration. Government officials claimed that since Kukliński had access to the martial law plans, Reagan officials could have prevented the crackdown. "The U.S. administration could have publically revealed these plans to the world and warned Solidarity," government spokesman Jerzy Urban said. "Had it done so, the implementation of martial law would have been impossible."[29] Urban continued that the failure of the United States to publicize martial law "gave us an insight into Reagan's actions and sayings. Much of the love which he professes for Solidarity is insincere."[30]

CIA officials were initially concerned about the leak. The United States *did* have information on Warsaw's plans for martial law, and some in the CIA worried that Solidarity sympathizers would be incensed that the U.S. failed to alert them. Much like at Yalta, it might look like the U.S. government had sold Poland out. A classified memo to Casey expressed alarm: "Paralleling its efforts to link Solidarity with 'foreign elements,' especially CIA, the regime has sought to use the Kukliński case to invoke 'Yalta fears' of U.S. duplicity. In both areas the campaign has met with some success."[31] An article in the July/August 1986 issue of Jerzy Giedroyc's *Kultura* criticized the United States for withholding information on martial law, picking up some of the themes that Jerzy Urban had raised.[32]

The best way to respond, the United States ultimately decided, was to let Kukliński speak. The former spy responded in an interview published in *Kultura*. Kukliński said the military crackdown was inevitable by the time he fled the country, and that warnings by him or the United States about it would only have led to more bloodshed. He also argued that if Jaruzelski and former Communist Party leader Stanisław Kania had strongly opposed martial law, Soviet leaders would have backed down. "If the U.S.S.R. had been confronted with open resistance of the party leadership supported by the population . . . we would have had a war of nerves, and had the Polish side stuck to its guns, Moscow most likely would have been forced to retreat."[33]

An infuriated Jerzy Urban lashed out at Kukliński as a "traitor" and said the publication of his recollections was composed of "half-truths, distortions and outright lies" and was the work of U.S. intelligence officials seeking to disrupt Poland's internal politics and relations with the Soviet Union.[34] But Kukliński's response seemed to work. It dispelled most of the criticism leveled against the United States and reflected criticism back on Jaruzelski, whose situation was about to get much worse than he realized.

———

CHANGES AFOOT IN THE SOVIET UNION began to work against Jaruzelski and for Reagan. Several years before, Reagan had quipped about Soviet leaders: "How can I be expected to make peace with them, if they keep dying on me?"[35] Leonid Brezhnev, Yuri Andropov, and Konstantin Chernenko all cycled through the top office in Moscow. As Reagan's biographer, Edmund Morris, recalled, Chernenko's "ill health—the wheezing and disorientation, the slow shuffle, the inability to stand up without help—seemed to signal a sort of sickly continuity with *genseks* of the past."[36] But Chernenko's death sent a tremor across the Soviet empire.

"Awakened at 4 A.M. to be told Chernenko is dead," Reagan wrote in his diary. "Word has been received that Gorbachev has been named head man."[37] Though some in the CIA worried that the draft intelligence assessments about Gorbachev "read like campaign flyers," CIA leaders were generally "enthusiastic" that Gorbachev might replace Chernenko for several reasons.[38] First, the CIA judged that Gorbachev was "prepared to make tough decisions" to address the political, economic, and social challenges facing the Soviet Union. Second, several CIA products indicated that Gorbachev was also likely to make reductions in military expenditures. Third, some CIA leaders hoped that Gorbachev "might cool things down," which would be a relief as the Cold War had grown increasingly hotter through proxy wars in Latin America, the Middle East, Africa, and Asia. Fourth, as Robert Gates remarked, Gorbachev was more fun for the CIA: "After long years of watching every move of a group of aging, colorless, uninteresting Soviet leaders, here was one of flesh and blood, of energy and action, of emotion, a man seemingly determined to change things."[39]

Few Americans realized how decrepit the Soviet Union really was.

Gorbachev had received information that the Soviet Union's gross national product was half that of the United States, while its economic development was lagging "ten to fifteen years behind the capitalist countries." The economic data suggested a "further weakening of the USSR's international position, and its decline into a second-rate power."[40] Since at least the time of Brezhnev, Soviet realists recognized that computers were becoming more pervasive in the West, while Russian shopkeepers in central Moscow were still using the abacus.[41] On top of all these crises came the 1986 explosion in the Chernobyl nuclear power plant, one of the most significant environmental disasters of the century.

Gorbachev understood better than most Soviet leaders that change was essential in the country and its satellites, including Poland. Among his most influential advisors was Alexander Yakovlev, who was born to a peasant family in a tiny village on the Volga River northeast of Moscow. In 1986, Yakovlev became secretary of the central committee in charge of ideology and he later vaulted to become a full member of the politburo. In private memos to Gorbachev, Yakovlev urged him to consider greater freedom of the press, political openness, and democratization.[42] Yakovlev helped Gorbachev institute the policies of glasnost and perestroika, which set the stage for fundamental political change in Poland and across the Soviet empire. "Perestroika has brought up the issue of democratization," Yakovlev wrote in a position paper for a politburo session of the Communist Party's Central Committee. While some worried that democratization might lead to a weakening of society, Yakovlev said that it would be a stabilizing factor. "In reality, democracy is discipline, the strengthening of the rule of law, and the development of self-discipline." He continued that "democracy and glasnost are advancing their historical cause" and change was now inevitable. "This is why we should not stop," Yakovlev insisted.[43]

Years later, some of Gorbachev's harshest critics in Russia alleged that he and Yakovlev had been CIA assets. "They weren't, and it's a good thing," remarked Robert Gates. "We could not possibly have guided him to engineer the destruction of the Soviet empire."[44] They did it themselves.

———

BASED ON THESE DEVELOPMENTS in the Soviet Union, the Jaruzelski regime was increasingly on its heels. As one CIA assessment summarized, Warsaw was "an island in a sea of opposition."[45] The government showed a two-part series, *Polish Aide Ties Solidarity, CIA*, on Polish National Television. But most Poles considered the series pure government propaganda and ignored it. Then some of the Polish Ministry of Internal Affairs' secret instructions to monitor Catholic Church officials were leaked to Radio Free Europe and picked up in the press, embarrassing the regime. The Ministry of Internal Affairs concluded that the United States had "informants within the circle of people who had access to the referenced material."[46] The regime also could not disrupt Solidarity's ratlines. The Sejm appointed a commission to study Western infiltration operations several years later. It concluded that Polish intelligence and security forces had little success in infiltrating the underground. The regime failed to intercept virtually all the money and 70 percent of the equipment sent to Solidarity from outside the country.[47]

As Moscow's grip on Eastern Europe started to weaken, Jaruzelski now began to jettison some of his most extreme, hard-line advisors. He ousted General Mirosław Milewski, a fifty-seven-year-old career officer in the state security police. Milewski headed the Ministry of Internal Affairs until July 1981, when he was elevated to the politburo and handed the job of national party secretary responsible for the police and the security services. Milewski had come under fire for overseeing security at the time of the assassination of Father Jerzy Popiełuszko. Jaruzelski also removed Stefan Olszowski as foreign minister, once widely believed to be a favorite of the Soviets. In addition, Minister of Internal Affairs Czesław Kiszcak forced several hundred policemen out in a substantial purge.[48]

Jaruzelski then summoned some of his top advisors to his office and declared that Zbigniew Bujak had to be released. The government declared a general amnesty. Most political prisoners were freed, including Bujak.[49] The Polish regime's days appeared numbered. Reagan was ecstatic, but progress in Poland coincided with increasing troubles at home.

———

COVERT ACTION HAD BEEN A CORNERSTONE of Reagan's foreign policy. With support from Casey and other administration officials, the United States conducted covert action programs around the world, from Poland and Afghanistan to Central America. While there were some encouraging programs, such as QRHELPFUL, U.S. activity in Nicaragua led to one of the most significant crises of the Reagan presidency. Congressional oversight committees had become alarmed about U.S. intelligence activities in Central America, particularly CIA aid to the Contra rebels in Nicaragua. Congress then enacted restrictions, referred to as the Boland amendments, which placed limits on aid to the Contras. In late 1986, congressional committees learned that Reagan had approved a covert action finding the previous year, which the administration never shared with Congress and which authorized arms sales to Iran to secure the release of Americans held hostage in Lebanon. Congressional investigators then discovered that proceeds from the arms sales were used to provide assistance to the Contras, which appeared to violate the Boland amendments aimed at limiting U.S. government aid to the rebels.[50]

According to U.S. attorney general Ed Meese, the blood drained from the president's face when he told Reagan in 1986 that some of the money paid by Iran for tube-launched, optically tracked, wire-guided (TOW) missiles had been siphoned off by National Security Council staffer Oliver North and funneled, through a Swiss bank account, to the Nicaraguan Contras.[51] As Reagan biographer Lou Cannon summarized, the Iran-Contra scandal had an impact on Reagan's reputation. The president "was no longer the magical sun king, no longer the Prospero of American memories who towered above ordinary politicians and could expect always to be believed." Still, by admitting that Iran-Contra had been wrong, Reagan ultimately "regained his political footing" and "made it possible to get on with the real foreign policy business of his presidency."[52] But moving on wouldn't be easy.

Reagan and his Republican Party had also lost the Senate to the Democrats in the 1986 midterm elections, which meant the Democratic Party controlled the House of Representatives *and* the Senate during his final two years in office. Reagan's ratings plummeted to nearly 40 percent approval by the American public in late 1986, a stark contrast from the nearly 70 percent approval he enjoyed at the beginning of the year.[53] Reagan was also consumed with rescuing U.S. hostages in Lebanon, defending the Strategic Defense Initiative (or "Star Wars"), and reducing nuclear and conventional weapons.

Despite these challenges, Reagan was still revered by some of his staff as a visionary and a charismatic leader.[54] "Never—absolutely never in my experience—did President Reagan really lose his temper or utter a rude or unkind word," Chief of Staff Donald Regan remarked. "Never did he issue a direct order, although I, at least, sometimes devoutly wished that he would. He listened, acquiesced, playing his role and waited for the next act to be written."[55]

But Reagan now had a horde of detractors. Al Haig, who had resigned as secretary of state in 1982 after constant battles with other cabinet members, blasted Reagan as incompetent. "I don't blame Ronald Reagan" for the administration's challenges, Haig remarked. "I blame his kitchen cabinet, those men who believed that the man was qualified to be President of the United States. They thought they could run him. But some sharpies around the President took over, and they ran him instead. With Ronald Reagan, you were dealing with an amorphous mass that had no substance, no opinion."[56] Others complained that the president failed to hold his staff accountable. As Bill Casey told journalist Larry King during a luncheon at the Palm Restaurant in Washington: "The President has one big weakness. He's incapable of firing anybody.

He can't dress anybody down. He never blows up over a failure. Call somebody into the office and give him a chewing out? He just can't do it. It's beyond him."[57]

———

REAGAN KEPT HIS SENSE OF HUMOR in the face of political turbulence. At one point in a briefing on the Soviet Union, Reagan popped out of his chair in obvious discomfort. "I was seated closest to him, and about two minutes into my comments I heard a piercing electrical hum," the CIA's Robert Gates recalled. "Reagan's eyes got very wide, and he reached up to his ear to adjust his hearing aid. A couple of minutes later, the hum returned and, since I could hear it, I could only guess how loud it must have been in his ear. At that point, in some disgust, he reached up, pulled the hearing aid out of his ear, and pounded it on the palm of his hand a couple of times. As he replaced it in his ear, he looked at me, smiled, and said, 'My KGB handler must be trying to reach me.'"[58]

By now, Reagan and Casey's global campaign to roll back the Soviets was producing results, despite the troubles with the Iran-Contra affair. Much of the success was covert aid. In an influential *Time* magazine article, journalist Charles Krauthammer described what he termed the "Reagan Doctrine." Outlined in foundational documents like National Security Decision Directive-75 ("U.S. Relations with the USSR") and National Security Decision Directive-54 ("U.S. Policy towards Eastern Europe"), the "Reagan Doctrine proclaims overt and unashamed American support for anti-Communist revolution," Krauthammer wrote. "Only a few months ago, a Nicaraguan friend, an ex-Sandinista who still speaks their language, said in near despair that the struggle of democrats around the world was doomed by the absence in the West of what he called 'democratic militance.' The Reagan Doctrine represents a first step toward its restoration."[59] Reagan lauded Krauthammer's interpretation, explaining that he was trying to "send out a signal that the United States intended to support people fighting for their freedom against Communism wherever they were."[60]

With the ascendancy of Gorbachev and a deteriorating Soviet economy, Reagan now saw an opportunity to shift the balance of power in
favor of the United States. Reagan's initial impression of Gorbachev
had been dismissive. "Gorbachev will be tough as any of their leaders,"
Reagan wrote in his diary. "If he wasn't a confirmed ideologue he never
would have been chosen by the [politburo]."[61] But Reagan soon warmed
up to the Soviet leader. They had first met in Geneva in November 1985,
where they held deeply personal "fireside chats." Reagan and Gorbachev
met again in October 1986 in Reykjavik. The Americans and Soviets
could not agree on concrete arms control measures or whether to cooperate on such developments as Star Wars at Reykjavik. But the meeting
did provide an unprecedented opportunity for Reagan and Gorbachev to
present their views to each other.

A few months after Reykjavik, Reagan conducted a blistering assault
on Gorbachev and challenged him to take down the Berlin Wall—the
iconic symbol of a divided Europe. "There is one sign the Soviets can
make that would be unmistakable, that would advance dramatically the
cause of freedom and peace," Reagan declared in a June 1987 speech in
West Berlin. "General Secretary Gorbachev, if you seek peace, if you seek
prosperity for the Soviet Union and Eastern Europe, if you seek liberalization: Come here to this gate! Mr. Gorbachev, open this gate! Mr.
Gorbachev, *tear down this wall!*"[62]

While Gorbachev could not see it yet, his country's plight would
soon send significant ripples across Eastern Europe and the globe. The
Cold War was coming to an end, and Poland was at the epicenter. At
this moment, Pope John Paul II made a dramatic return visit to his home
country that would alter the course of history.

Chapter 20

THE RETURN OF SOLIDARITY

On June 12, 1987, Pope John Paul II held an open-air mass before nearly a million people in Gdańsk's enormous Zaspa housing development. Since his previous visit four years before, the pope had become a vocal supporter of freedom and human rights around the globe. He was increasingly opposed to Communism, eventually condemning it for its inherent "mistakes and abuses."[1] The day was cloudy, with intermittent sunshine. Nearly every apartment window in Zaspa bore the pope's image or insignia, and residents draped the building façades with ribbons of papal yellow and Polish red and white. The pope spoke from an altar atop a three-story model of a seventeenth-century vessel. With a towering mast that reached toward the sky and a massive white sail that curved outward as if filled with a gusting wind, the structure was a reproduction of a *koga*, a ship frequently used by Gdańsk traders. A few supporters waved Solidarity banners that looked like bright red boats floating in a sea of Poles.[2] In his homily, John Paul II made an unprecedented and historic break from his 1983 visit, where he had been politically cautious. The pope hadn't visited Gdańsk and hadn't publicly discussed the Solidarity movement. This time, however, he was unabashed.

"The 'Gdańsk Accords,'" the pope said, referring to the August 1980 agreement that Solidarity brokered with the Polish regime, "will remain in the history of Poland a manifestation of this growing awareness of the working people in regards to the entire socio-moral order in the Polish land. Their genesis dates back to the tragic December of 1970. And they still remain a task to be fulfilled."[3] The crowd, which was surrounded by high-rise apartment buildings that looked like mountain peaks, gave a deafening roar of approval. The pope extolled the virtues of pluralism, free association, and human rights, and sprinkled his comments with religious parables and Gospel citations. As he concluded his homily, John Paul II put aside his prepared text, took a deep breath, and reinforced his support for Solidarity. "Every day I pray for you, in Rome and wherever I am," he said. "Every day I pray for my country and I pray for men at work, and I pray for this particularly significant Polish symbol: 'Solidarity.' I pray for those who are linked to that legacy, particularly for those who had or have to make sacrifices for it."[4] The crowd went into a frenzy—weeping, applauding, praying, and raising clenched fists.[5] By identifying himself with Solidarity and the cause of democratic freedom, John Paul II was now challenging the Jaruzelski regime.

The pope's speech was extraordinary in several respects. First, he had traveled—and been allowed by the regime to travel—to the epicenter of Solidarity: Gdańsk. It was a forbidden city during his last visit in 1983. Second, the housing development of Zaspa was home to Lech Wałęsa, who still lived with his family in an apartment at Pilotów 17d/3. Not only was John Paul II speaking to the masses in Solidarity's heartland, his choice of venue paid homage to its leader. Third, the pope openly embraced Solidarity and its goals. It was a stunning development with repercussions that most Poles—and government officials in Warsaw, Moscow, and Washington—did not fully comprehend. Within a year, strikes broke out across Poland, signaling the possible end of

Communist rule in Poland, Jaruzelski's iron grip on the country, and the Soviet empire.

———

THE POPE'S PILGRIMAGE LASTED FROM JUNE 8 TO 14, 1987, and he spoke to formidable gatherings in Gdańsk, Gdynia, Warsaw, Lublin, Tarnów, Kraków, Szczecin, Częstochowa, and Łódź. For Wałęsa and other Solidarity leaders, the visit catalyzed the resurrection of Solidarity and led to Poland's own perestroika and glasnost. "The most important event of 1987 for Solidarity, and for all of Poland, was the pope's third visit," Wałęsa said confidently, referring to John Paul II's previous visits in June 1979 and June 1983. "While some people might want to interpret the history of Solidarity differently—and emphasize its autonomy from any external influence—the pope's visit was undeniably a turning point in the national mood."[6]

During John Paul II's visit to Zaspa, Wałęsa put on his best white church suit and inspected his children before meeting the pope. All of Zaspa had been decked out in flowers for the celebration. Wałęsa knelt, kissed the pope's ring, cleared his throat, and presented his children. The pope commented on each one. "Brygidka? The youngest?" the pope inquired. "Her name makes her a true daughter of Gdańsk. Victoria? It all began with her, and she is the one they show to the world."[7] The pope then made the Solidarity "V" sign for victory with his fingers, and Wałęsa gave him a copy of the first part of his autobiography bound in white leather. The pope leafed through the pages and then lifted his head.

"I wouldn't have come to Poland if the government hadn't allowed me to visit Gdańsk," he said.

The pope then asked: How were the Polish people managing to survive the crisis, which put their future in such doubt? How did people cope while living in the grip of a government in which they played no part?

Wałęsa responded that change could only occur by reform *without violence*.

The pope agreed, noting that Solidarity's methods recalled those of Mahatma Gandhi, leader of the Indian independence movement in British-ruled India. "If the world grasps what you are trying to do, if it sees in your movement hope and a way to resolve conflicts, it is precisely because you have renounced violence."[8] It was an extraordinary visit. As Bishop Tadeusz Gocłowski recalled:

> The pope loved Gdansk, loved Solidarity and knew well what it stood for. He was a man who had a fantastic vision about Solidarity's value as a movement which was to have an impact on Europe. He was perfectly aware of this. It was apparent that communism was badly wounded. It was first wounded by the pope's election, then with his first pilgrimage to Poland in 1979. When he stepped up on the ship-altar in Zaspa, the pope said, "This is a ship under construction." That was a clear suggestion. The mood formed itself. The organizers wanted to force the pope to sit behind a bullet-proof pane away from the people. And he said, "Right reverend bishop, I go where the Bible is read, so I'm going to the captain's bridge." And from that moment on, the crowd was his.[9]

At other stops on his visit, the pope chiseled away at the regime's legitimacy by publicly extolling the virtues of Solidarity. At the port of Gdynia, the pope used the word "solidarity" seven times in three minutes. He concluded his address by challenging all Poles to spread the word:

> In the name of the future of mankind, this word solidarity must be pronounced. Today, it is spreading like a wave throughout the world, signaling that we cannot live according to the principle of "all against all," but only according to the principle of "all with all," "all for all." This word has been pronounced here in a new way and in a new context. And the world cannot forget.[10]

John Paul II's words had an electrifying impact on the Polish population, emboldening Solidarity and fueling a sense of indignity with the regime. Poland was slowly waking up from its slumber under Communism, and the pope's 1987 visit was a critical turning point. Still, the government remained defiant. In Gdańsk, helmeted riot policemen shut down much of the city during the pope's visit, conducted military-style sweeps using convoys of police trucks, and clashed with placard-carrying Solidarity sympathizers. The government's spokesman, Jerzy Urban, perhaps the most hated man in Poland, remained steadfastly pro-regime. "Political provocateurs can thwart the activities of the church within socialist countries when they exploit religious occasions to air expressions antagonistic to socialism," he remarked.[11] Jaruzelski was also irritated. "Your holiness, you will soon bid farewell to your homeland. You will take its image with you in your heart, but you cannot take with you its problems," he said. "Poland needs truth. But the truth about Poland is necessary too. How often in recent days has it been the victim of outside manipulation so offensive to the common sense of our people?"[12]

For the CIA, the pope's visit boosted morale among the QRHELP-FUL team. After fighting against Soviet and Polish counterintelligence tactics, they suddenly had a tailwind of support from one of the world's most admired figures. But back in Washington, the momentum was moving in the opposite direction.

———

BY THE LATE 1980s, THE U.S. CONGRESS was in a foul, budget-cutting mood. The Gramm-Rudman-Hollings Balanced Budget Act mandated automatic spending cuts to trim the federal budget deficit, which had a second-order impact on QRHELPFUL. Congress authorized approximately $2 million for QRHELPFUL for fiscal year 1987, but CIA program managers and desk officers now had to micromanage every activity. CIA leaders recommended that $775,000 be allocated to the general fund for QRHELPFUL. But they also advised that the Mexico City seg-ment of QRHELPFUL and Stanisław Broda's operations out of the Paris CIA station should be terminated.[13]

Some members of Congress began to question the need to con-tinue QRHELPFUL since the U.S. government provided a growing amount of overt funding to Solidarity. Indeed, the Polish underground had now endured long enough to attract the sympathy—and increas-ingly the financial support—of U.S. government agencies and private institutions other than CIA. The National Endowment for Democracy, for example, with its recently approved congressional funding, had sent roughly $600,000 to Solidarity in 1985.[14] The endowment took a partic-ular interest in supporting the Polish journal *Aneks*, which also received assistance from the CIA. The CIA, in turn, had to spin off *Aneks* into a separate project.[15]

Still, there was a small cadre of U.S. officials that lobbied to preserve QRHELPFUL—at least for now. One was David Baad, who was chief of the CIA's Political-Psychological Staff, which oversaw QRHELPFUL. He was in that position from December 1986 until the spring of 1988, when he handed over the reins to Peter Raudenbush. The CIA in this period remained focused on providing communications equipment and technological know-how to Solidarity. Robert Gates wrote:

> In October 1988, CIA arranged the first satellite telecast into Poland from Western Europe, a ten-minute program covering recent labor unrest in Poland. We got a strong, positive reaction from Solidarity leaders. By November we were advised that nearly every factory committee in Poland had the capability to publish a newsletter and that recent labor unrest had led to increased publishing requirements that were pushing the equip-ment to the limit.[16]

Another supporter of QRHELPFUL was John Davis, the U.S. chargé d'affaires and then ambassador to Poland. Milt Bearden from the CIA's

Soviet–East European division was another. Even European Division chief Burton Gerber, who had counterintelligence and security concerns about QRHELPFUL, argued against termination of the program for the time being. Part of the reason for continuing QRHELPFUL, its proponents argued, was that Solidarity was not entirely out of the woods yet. It still needed assistance, particularly with elections on the horizon, which brought the tantalizing possibility that Solidarity might run a slate of viable candidates against the Communist Party. For some at CIA, now it was even *more* important to provide assistance to Solidarity to ensure that it didn't lose the gains it had already made.[17]

THE CIA WOULD HAVE TO FINISH QRHELPFUL without Bill Casey. After suffering two seizures several months earlier, Casey died on May 6, 1987, in Glen Cove Community Hospital on Long Island. He was seventy-four years old. The Iran-Contra scandal had tarnished his reputation, but he was spared the immediate fallout of the scandal. The first witness in the Iran-Contra Congressional hearings, Air Force major general Richard V. Secord, named Casey as having helped provide arms to Nicaraguan rebels. Casey died less than twenty-four hours after Secord took the stand.

Despite Casey's reputation for controversial actions like Iran-Contra, most CIA officials venerated Casey. He was more than just a run-of-the-mill CIA director. He had been a rabid anti-Communist, which earned him a close relationship with the president. That partnership—which extended to Reagan's first presidential campaign—gave the CIA virtually unprecedented access to the White House.[18] After Casey's death, Reagan offered a heartfelt tribute. "His nation and all those who love freedom honor today the name and memory of Bill Casey," Reagan remarked. "In addition to crediting him with rebuilding America's intelligence capability, history will note the brilliance of his mind and strategic vision, his passionate commitment to the cause of freedom and his unhesitating willingness to make personal sacrifices for the sake of that cause and his country."[19]

Reagan appointed William Webster, who had previously served as FBI director, to replace Casey as the director of central intelligence. By the time Webster took over, the Polish regime was about to lose its grip on the country.

———

BY 1987, CARTOONS DISPARAGING THE REGIME had grown commonplace. An opposition member named Dariusz Paczkowski created a famous stencil titled *Lenin with a Mohawk*. The simple image rebranded the Communist founder, adding a punk haircut that mocked the regime's bureaucrats. Paczkowski printed the stencil on leaflets with a quotation from Lenin: "When young people cease to be revolutionaries, it will spell trouble for the young and the revolution." The drawing was meant to be ironic. As Paczkowski explained: "We had to act in the underground, so for many years I was not known as the author of that template . . . for me it was a way to ridicule communism, my blow right at the heart of the system."[20] The stencil quickly became a cult symbol of Solidarity.

After the pope, one of the next major international figures to visit Poland was U.S. vice president George H. W. Bush, who paid a four-day visit to Poland in September 1987. Bush said he had long wanted to visit Poland. He praised the Poles for helping the United States win independence from Great Britain, thanks to Tadeusz Kościuszko and Kazimierz Pułaski who had fought on the side of George Washington during the Revolutionary War. Bush and Wałęsa also visited the grave of Father Jerzy Popiełuszko, who had died at the hands of the secret police. Bush told Wałęsa that President Reagan had decided to resume diplomatic dialogue with the Polish government.[21] Earlier that year, Reagan had lifted some sanctions against Poland following pleas from both Wałęsa and the Pope. Reagan confided in his diary that the sanctions "were beginning to hurt the Polish people & that was never our intention."[22] But Bush also told Wałęsa that the administration refused to normalize relations until Jaruzelski's government loosened its restrictions on Solidarity and made greater progress toward democratization.

———

ON OCTOBER 25, 1987, AT A JOINT SESSION of the Solidarity Provisional Coordinating Board and the Provisional Council, members appointed a new leadership and christened it the National Executive Board.[23] They held another meeting on November 7. Wałęsa opened the meeting by urging his fellow members to be prepared for action. "We meet at a time when something significant is taking place throughout the Eastern Bloc and particularly at its center," he told them. "Events are rendering obsolete the way the economy has been managed and the government has been organized up to now. These events will change Poland, and these changes have begun. But we want actions, not words."[24]

Solidarity was still illegal, and a surveillance team continued to monitor Wałęsa's movements, tap his phones, and bug the rooms where he met visitors. Despite these obstacles, Wałęsa met almost daily with journalists, politicians, and famous foreign visitors like New York mayor Ed Koch and actress Jane Fonda.[25] The *Washington Post*'s Jim Hoagland interviewed Wałęsa around this time at St. Bridget's Church and remarked that ideas "tumble out, end over end" from his head "like a wobbly pass" in American football. But Hoagland was in awe of Wałęsa. "He continues to be the living symbol of and spokesman for the most important revolt against communist rule in this generation, despite a totalitarian empire's efforts to break and discredit him."[26]

But even as world attention swung towards Poland, Solidarity had evolved. Its membership had declined from as many as ten million members to less than two million. Membership in the Gdańsk region, a hotbed of Solidarity support, was only one-quarter the level of 1981. Many members had lost their initial enthusiasm, and the government forced others to join industry unions.[27] Solidarity also had to deal with distracting problems like the interminable search for a headquarters. Krzysztof Pusz, Wałęsa's chief of staff, recalled, "Wałęsa would become irritated and make a fuss about not having anywhere to work, not to mention where to host the delegations which were arriving in increasing numbers."[28] Eventually, Solidarity secured the Projmors Maritime Construction Design Office in the center of Gdańsk, a 1950s-era building constructed on top of a huge air-raid shelter.[29]

Just when Solidarity needed a boost, Jaruzelski inadvertently gave one to Wałęsa. In February 1988, the government announced new price increases for food and consumer goods. Solidarity's National Executive Board had vigorously decried the regime's price hikes, though had stopped short of calling for mass demonstrations. But events spiraled out of their control. In April 1988, the first crippling strikes in more than six years broke out across Poland. On April 25, a day-long strike paralyzed public transportation in Bydgoszcz, roughly a hundred miles southwest of Gdańsk. The next day, workers at the Lenin Steelworks in Nowa Huta went on strike and presented a list of seven demands. Each one involved raising salaries and rehiring fellow workers fired for engaging in government-prohibited union activity.[30] The participants in these strikes were primarily young workers, many of whom were not in the workforce during the 1980–1981 period of Solidarity's birth—and were not even Solidarity members. Facing a new generation of opposition members, the regime was temporarily paralyzed, unsure how to respond.

Wałęsa's activism and declining economic conditions transformed Poland into a powder keg. It only needed a match.

Chapter 21

THE TRUMP CARD

On the afternoon of April 30, a division of the ZOMO took positions in front of the Nowa Huta factory, where workers were on strike. On May 1, spontaneous and violent clashes erupted in a dozen Polish cities. Solidarity quickly responded. Wałęsa considered himself, in his own words, as "the trump card, the matador, who, after the toreadors have finished enraging the bull with their jabs and pokes, enters the arena carrying his sword and *muleta*." He continued: "My job was to goad when things got stagnant, to add water when the vine was withering, to keep up morale, to encourage, to soothe."[1] Standing in front of several thousand people who had assembled for Sunday mass at St. Bridget's Church, Wałęsa demanded that the government enact emergency political and economic reforms. He then asked for their undivided assistance. "Show your solidarity with those in Nowa Huta," Wałęsa thundered. The crowd responded: "Tomorrow we strike!"[2] Protestors stored money, food, blankets, medicine, and other items at St. Bridget's. When riot police cut the shipyard off from the rest of the city, young boys and girls, nicknamed "kangaroos," smuggled letters and small packages to striking workers by hiding them in their pockets and jackets.[3]

CIA leaders recognized that it was essential now—perhaps more than ever—to ramp up ideological efforts in Poland.[4]

———

IN MAY 1988, THE STRIKE COMMITTEE at the Lenin Steelworks in Nowa Huta used CIA-funded radio equipment to communicate over Radio Solidarity with striking workers at other locations.[5] Reagan remained supportive. In May, he wrote in his diary that the "Polish govt. is getting rough on the strikers."[6] Senior officials in the Jaruzelski regime realized they were losing the image war. "Reports on the continuing strikes in Poland remain a main theme for Polish-language Western broadcasters," one classified Polish government document summarized, hinting at CIA and other U.S. government activity. "Just as in 1980–1981, the broadcasts aim to encourage and shape ongoing events, in some cases by putting on the air Polish opposition activists to mobilize the broad mass of Polish society to radicalize pay demands and spread the strikes."[7] The document concluded that Western propaganda presented the strikes as a major success for Solidarity and ultimately hoped to change the social, political, and economic fabric in Poland.

Reagan saw the wheels of history turning. "In Poland," he reflected in his autobiography, "a people stubbornly determined to rid itself of tyranny was rising up in a final historic upwelling of freedom that would mark the beginning of the end of the Soviet empire—and yes, it was an evil empire."[8] Earlier that year, Reagan had celebrated when Gorbachev announced that he was withdrawing Red Army forces from Afghanistan. The first troops started coming out in May 1988, and the Soviets completed their withdrawal in February 1989.[9] Poland, in Reagan's view, was now facing an unambiguous reversal of the domino theory, which assumed that if one country in a region came under the influence of Communism, others would follow like a line of dominoes. Communism was losing allies across the globe. What's more, the Soviet Union was faltering in the ideological war as well. In a war, as Reagan put it, "between one system that gave preeminence to the state and another that gave preeminence to the individual and freedom," democracy and capitalism were winning.[10] Reagan loved to needle Gorbachev about the differences between the United States and the USSR. During a meeting in Washington, Reagan interrupted the Soviet Premier with a joke. "Reminds me of the one about our two educational systems," Reagan said, grinning. "Here, you ask a college graduate what he's gonna do, he says: 'Haven't decided yet.' In Russia, kids say: 'We haven't been told.'"[11]

Despite progress against Communism, 1988 was bittersweet for Reagan. His second term was nearly over. It was an election year, and his vice president—George H. W. Bush—was involved in a hard-fought presidential campaign against Michael Dukakis, the Democratic challenger and liberal governor of Massachusetts. On November 8, Election Day, Reagan watched the results roll in. Just after 11:00 p.m., Dukakis conceded defeat and congratulated Bush. "About 11 P.M. to bed—happy," Reagan wrote in his diary.[12] He was elated, in part, because his legacy— including his Cold War crusade against the Soviets—would now be directed by his trusted vice president, who, he hoped, could take it across the finish line.

———

EVENTS IN POLAND CONTINUED TO UNRAVEL. On the night of May 4, a division of the ZOMO forced their way through the gates of the Lenin Steelworks at Nowa Huta. After tossing in small explosives and tear-gas grenades, they stormed the factory wielding clubs and nightsticks, ordered the workers to lie face down on the floor, and kicked and berated them. Jaruzelski's regime continued to take swipes at Wałęsa and Solidarity. Jaruzelski's spokesman, Jerzy Urban, was relentless:

Had Lech Walesa . . . undertaken to respect the law instead of create organizations to oppose it, had he sincerely and openly admitted that the union he led had made some mistakes, had he made unambiguous his willingness for entente . . . had he not concealed slogans calling for his brand of pluralism and for plotting against our regime, *were he not so obviously in cahoots with Western forces hostile to Poland*, then the following statement might be applied to this man in whom we once had confidence: "It doesn't matter where he stood before. What matters is where he stands now."[13]

Despite the condemnations of Wałęsa, however, Jaruzelski knew that he and the regime were in serious trouble. In July 1988, Gorbachev visited Poland. "We've got two lines that we cannot cross, just as the Red Army could not retreat from Moscow or from the line of the Volga River," Jaruzelski explained. "Those lines were trade union pluralism and political parties. The West is putting pressure on us to recognize Wałęsa."[14] With Gorbachev's support for glasnost and perestroika, Jaruzelski recognized that democracy—in some form—was likely part of Poland's future. Jaruzelski could not turn the clock back to 1981.

As Gorbachev explained, the Soviet Union desperately needed Western technology and credits to overcome economic travails. The cost of maintaining its "empire"—the military, KGB, and subsidies to foreign client states like Poland—staggered the moribund Soviet economy. Anatoly Chernyaev, a top Soviet advisor to Gorbachev, wrote in his private diary that the leadership understood that Soviet-style Communism was dying. Nowhere in Eastern Europe was this more evident than in Poland. At a meeting of the Soviet politburo, Soviet ambassador to Poland Vladimir Brovikov used an old Leninist expression to capture the mood. "Poland is the weakest link in the socialist community," he said emphatically.[15]

Events would soon prove Brovikov correct, perhaps even more than he realized. On August 15, 1988, miners in Silesia went on strike, upset by the previous month's wage "adjustment." Topping the miners' list of grievances was a demand for free unions. Over the next few days, over a dozen mines went on strike and all of them demanded legalization of Solidarity. A CIA report concluded that the labor unrest was "potentially the worst crisis for the government since the imposition of martial law in 1981."[16]

———

IN THE EARLY SUMMER OF 1988, Czesław Kiszczak, the head of Poland's Ministry of Internal Affairs, had approached Wałęsa through an intermediary, Władysław Siła-Nowicki. Kiszczak wondered if Wałęsa was ready to talk. Wałęsa agreed in a letter dated July 21, 1988. On August 26, Kiszczak officially announced on television the government's willingness to open dialogue with Solidarity. On August 31, Solidarity members and government officials began preliminary meetings about a way forward. The "Round Table Talks," as the formal discussions would eventually become known, would birth the Third Polish Republic.

For the government, the top priority was to force the opposition to end the strikes. For Solidarity, however, there was some disagreement about how to proceed. Bogdan Borusewicz, a prominent Solidarity leader, did not want Wałęsa to meet with senior Polish officials. "Our view was that the strike should be continued," he recalled. "That the right moment for communicating with the authorities had not yet arrived. That the next wave, which would come in the autumn at the latest, would sweep Jaruzelski away. I considered us still too weak to hold talks on an equal footing."[17] Borusewicz and others preferred to continue putting pressure on the regime. "Of course, politics isn't mathematics, where one plus one makes two. The next strike might not have been strong enough, it might have taken place even a year or eighteen months later. But in my opinion the mood was becoming more radical. The thing to do was wait."[18]

But Wałęsa was undeterred. Overcoming internal dissent, Wałęsa bullied his way to the negotiating table. Throughout the fall of 1988, he and other Solidarity members met with regime representatives to hammer out specifics like the proposed dates, topics, the number and names of attendees at the meetings, as well as broader issues like whether Solidarity could be legalized.[19] On September 16, 1988, Wałęsa, Kiszczak, and nearly two dozen other negotiators agreed to terms at a luxury estate owned by the Ministry of Internal Affairs in Magdalenka, near Warsaw.[20]

Despite these discussions, the situation remained perilous. In November 1988, the new CIA director, William Webster, was given a confidential report that declared the Polish government "was pursuing an aggressive course against Solidarity which could lead to violence and national crisis." It continued that this crisis would be a "potentially explosive test of strength" for the rulers in Warsaw. "[T]he stage has been set for a major confrontation between the Jaruzelski regime and Solidarity"[21]

Chapter 22

ROUND TABLE TALKS

Just before 9:00 p.m. on January 11, 1989, Ronald Reagan sat at his desk in the Oval Office for his final address to the nation. It was the same desk, built from the gnarled oak timbers of the HMS *Resolute*, he used while addressing the nation on December 23, 1981, shortly after the declaration of martial law. Coarse-grained from Arctic exposure, and discreetly shimmed to accommodate Reagan's taller frame, the desk was uncluttered, except for a glossy black folder to his right, a glass pen and pencil holder to his left, and two plaques in front of him with the mottoes "It can be done" and "There is no limit to what a man can do or where he can go if he doesn't mind who gets the credit." As he glanced around the room, the Oval Office looked pristine.[1] Reagan wore a dark blue suit with a clean, neatly pressed white dress shirt, burgundy-colored tie, and white pocket square tucked into the breast pocket of his jacket.

Staring into the camera, he spoke sentimentally. "My fellow Americans, this is the 34th time I'll speak to you from the Oval Office, and the last," he said. "We've been together eight years now, and soon it'll be time for me to go. But before I do, I wanted to share some thoughts, some of which I have been saving for a long time." As the camera zoomed in on

Reagan, his facial features became more visible. Less than a month away from his seventy-eighth birthday, he looked dramatically older than at the beginning of his presidency. His hair was grayer and the wrinkles on his face and neck were more pronounced.

Reagan highlighted his chief foreign policy and domestic accomplishments. Above all, he emphasized his "two great triumphs, two things that I'm proudest of. One is the economic recovery, in which the people of America created—and filled—19 million new jobs. The other is the recovery of our morale: America is respected again in the world, and looked to for leadership." In nations like Poland, he had stood by Solidarity and supported the nascent grassroots democratic movement. "Countries across the globe are turning to free markets and free speech—and turning away from the ideologies of the past," he continued.

Reagan then spoke of America as a shining city on a hill—a New Jerusalem. "I've spoken of the shining city all my political life, but I don't know if I ever quite communicated what I saw when I said it," he remarked, his eyes now gleaming and cheeks flushed. "But in my mind, it was a tall proud city built on rocks stronger than oceans, wind swept, God blessed, and teeming with people of all kinds living in harmony and peace—a city with free ports that hummed with commerce and creativity, and if there had to be city walls, the walls had doors, and the doors were open to anyone with the will and the heart to get here."

Reagan paused and peered intently into the camera. "And how stands the city on this winter night?" he asked rhetorically. "More prosperous, more secure and happier than it was eight years ago," he answered, furrowing his brow. "But more than that, after 200 years, two centuries, she still stands strong and true on the granite ridge, and her glow has held steady no matter what storm."

Slightly tilting his head, he continued: "And she's still a beacon, still a magnet for all who must have freedom, for all the Pilgrims from all the lost places who are hurtling through the darkness, toward home."

Reagan was clearly proud. "We've done our part," he said. "And as I walk off into the city streets, a final word to the men and women of the Reagan Revolution—the men and women across America who for eight years did the work that brought America back. My friends, we did it."

Reagan was thrilled that his vice president, George H. W. Bush, who would be sworn in a week later as the forty-first president of the United States, would have a chance to oversee the final realization of his vision. But he was more interested now in looking backward. "We weren't just marking time, we made a difference. We made the city stronger—we made the city freer—and we left her in good hands."[2]

The speech was a fitting end to Reagan's tenure as president, and he was buoyed by approval ratings north of 60 percent. His address combined optimism with his trademark smooth delivery forged on Hollywood movie sets and General Electric television programs. Back in December 1981, Reagan had likened Solidarity members to America's founding fathers.[3] Since that time, Solidarity had not only survived martial law and nearly a decade of repression, but had emerged as a viable, authentic political force. That summer, in June 1989, Poland would participate in its first national elections.

———

By THE BEGINNING OF 1989, the Polish Communist Party was in disarray. Jaruzelski recognized that the disastrous performance of Poland's economy had put the regime in an untenable situation. "The economic failures of 1987–1989 convinced us that our methods were ineffective," he concluded. "Without letting into the power system the so-called constructive opposition, we were unable to overcome social resistance to necessary economic reforms."[4] Jaruzelski and several of his closest advisors, including Minister of Internal Affairs Czesław Kiszczak, had discarded their false triumphalism after martial law and lessened their contempt for Solidarity, which had proven impossible to dislodge with coercive and ideological instruments.[5] They also realized that the Red

Army was unlikely to intervene in Poland. Moscow had threatened to invade in 1981, but Gorbachev's embrace of perestroika and glasnost ended that possibility. Declassified Polish documents show that Polish diplomats supported negotiations with Solidarity to prevent further domestic unrest and to increase the possibility of economic relief from the West.[6]

Still, Jaruzelski was embittered, remarking sarcastically that the West believed "that all the democracies that we've been promising, second chambers, etc. will fall from heaven once Solidarity is installed because Solidarity will take care of everything, including communism and socialism." He continued: "How dare they! They are exploiting our weakness in a cynical way."[7] But Jaruzelski was resigned to his fate. On January 16, 1989, at the Tenth Plenary Session of the Communist Party, Jaruzelski bluntly confided to his comrades: "There is a growing awareness that the difficulties that beset us cannot be solved by a miracle, but only by joint efforts and mutual compromise."[8]

On January 27, Czesław Kiszczak, Lech Wałęsa, and others met at Magdalenka to discuss the imminent Round Table Talks. They reaffirmed their willingness to negotiate and they finalized the broad outline of the talks, which would begin on February 6.[9] One of the biggest issues was elections. Wałęsa and others demanded that Poland hold national elections in which Solidarity could participate as a legal political entity. Democratic elections would be unprecedented in the Soviet Bloc. Solidarity wanted to be recognized as a legitimate—and perhaps the only legitimate—opposition party to the government.

Jaruzelski was willing to compromise if it meant giving Solidarity more influence, but only if the Communist Party remained in overall control of Poland. Yet Jaruzelski was met with a wave of opposition and a heated rebuke from some within the party who were vehemently against reforms, negotiations, and power sharing. Most of these hardliners overestimated popular support for the regime and underestimated support for Solidarity.[10] Some had already conducted an intense subversive media campaign through leaks and newspaper articles, warning that the regime would never legalize Solidarity.[11] In response, Jaruzelski, Kiszczak, Prime Minister Mieczysław Rakowski, and Defense Minister Florian Siwicki threated to resign if the Central Committee refused to accept the legalization of Solidarity. The hard-liners, who lacked a strong leader in the politburo, backed off.

Opposition to the negotiations also arose from within Solidarity. Some Solidarity members, such as Kornel Morawiecki, considered negotiations with the regime a betrayal of everything they had worked for over the past decade. They did not want to compromise *at all* with the government and pushed for a revolution in which Solidarity gained full political power. They also accused Wałęsa of embracing a dictatorial management style, monopolizing negotiations with the government, and adopting unnecessarily conciliatory policies toward a regime that had attempted to eradicate them.[12] Morawiecki had established a group called Militant Solidarity, and rejected any suggestion of detente with the government.

Wałęsa was undeterred. "The time is past for fighting among ourselves or indulging in recriminations. It is time to seek agreement," he told supporters on a cold, damp evening in the southeastern city of Stalowa Wola. "We will overhaul our country gradually, through civilized, *nonviolent* methods."[13] For Wałęsa, peaceful opposition was the essence of Solidarity's position, and it was particularly important to maintain that stance during this fragile period. He knew that at some point negotiating with the regime would become necessary. Now was that time, Wałęsa believed. Solidarity member Adam Michnik agreed. "Those who favor the peaceful way of resolving conflict are always faced with similar questions and charges. How can one think about making a pact with an enemy?" he asked.[14] The need to compromise, as Wałęsa and Michnik recognized, was the result of the relative weakness of both sides. The Jaruzelski regime was too weak to crush Solidarity, and Solidarity was too weak to topple the government. "And out of those two weaknesses," noted Michnik, "a new chance arose for a new compromise solution."[15]

———

NOT UNLIKE THE COMMUNIST HARD-LINERS and the militant laborers, CIA analysts in Washington were deeply conflicted about where
Poland was going. They had supported Solidarity steadily for years, but
there was some concern that Solidarity was not strong enough to prevail
against the Soviet-backed regime. Only a year before, a National Intelligence Estimate warned that Poland could be on the verge of a popular
upheaval "involving a broad-based challenge to party supremacy and
ultimately to Soviet control."[16] But it argued that upheaval was highly
unlikely since "the challenge posed by Solidarity in Poland had been
successfully contained...and the Jaruzelski regime had made some
progress toward restoring party control and neutralizing its domestic
opposition."[17] One reason for the skepticism among CIA analysts may
have been that most knew little—or nothing—about QRHELPFUL
and U.S. support to Solidarity. Few in the CIA, even those working on
Poland, were given access to the details about QRHELPFUL because of
its sensitivities.

   Back in Poland, Solidarity was about to prove the CIA analysts wrong.

———

ON FEBRUARY 6, 1989, FIFTY-FIVE DELEGATES—twenty-nine from the
government and twenty-six from the opposition—sat down in Warsaw's
Presidential Palace, along with three observers from the Catholic
Church. The donut-shaped roundtable was remarkable for its size. Nearly
twenty-eight feet in diameter, the rough-hewn oak table had been built in
record time by twenty craftsmen working twelve-hour days. No sooner
had its fourteen pieces been assembled in the Hall of Columns at the palace than the jokes began.[18] "Why was it twenty-eight feet wide?" went
one joke. "Because the world's spitting record distance was only twenty-
five feet."[19]

   The roundtable negotiations took place in small groups, where official representatives were joined by issue-area experts. The three major

groups focused on relegalization of Solidarity, political changes, and social and economic reforms. The group on social and economic reforms had several additional working groups that focused on legal and judicial improvements, education, housing policy, agriculture, mining, and health care. On April 5, 1989, participants signed a historic agreement that relegalized independent trade unions, including Solidarity; created the office of president, which eliminated the Communist Party general secretary; and formed a Senate.

Political power was vested in a newly created bicameral legislature, which included the Sejm and Senate, and a powerful president. To fill these spots, Poland would hold elections. The participants agreed that 65 percent of the seats in the Sejm, or lower house, would be left in the hands of the Communists. But the remaining 35 percent would be filled following a free, competitive election held six weeks later, as would all the seats for the newly created Senate. The parties also agreed to establish the office of president, who was elected by both houses of parliament to a six-year term and would have strong powers. The president, who the Communists expected would be Jaruzelski, had the power to impose martial law and to dissolve the Sejm in the event it was unable to appoint a government or pass a budget over a three-month period.

With Solidarity now legal, Wałęsa and Jaruzelski met for the first time in seven years in a deliberately low-key session on April 17. When a journalist queried Wałęsa about the meeting, he answered smugly. "Oh, I got rid of emotions a long time ago. Our meeting marked the end of the phase of struggle and the beginning of a period of cooperative reconstruction." While Wałęsa still did not fully trust Jaruzelski, Poland had dramatically changed. "Sure, I had some fears," Wałęsa acknowledged, "since it was General Jaruzelski who had declared martial law, interned thousands of people, and blocked political reforms for many years, but what would we gain by opening old wounds? I agreed to talk with him because in my mind it was already the future. We discussed entente."[20]

The roundtable agreement paved the way for the first partially free elections in Eastern Europe in fifty years. It also helped launch tectonic changes in Eastern Europe. As Wałęsa remarked at the conclusions of the Round Table Talks:

> No freedom without Solidarity—armed with that truth we came to the Round Table. We have come to this table from prisons and from under the clubs of the ZOMO, carrying with us the living memory of those who shed their blood for Solidarity . . . We realize that the Round Table negotiations have not lived up to every expectation. But for the first time, we have talked among ourselves using the force of arguments and not the arguments of force . . . So we look to the future with courage and hope. We look to the words inscribed on the monument at Gdansk: "The Lord gives strength to His people; And to his people the blessings of peace."[21]

The Communist hold over Poland was loosening. On May 8, the inaugural issue of Poland's first independent daily paper since before World War II, *Gazeta Wyborcza*, appeared on newsstands. Adam Michnik, a Solidarity member and renowned Polish writer, was the editor in chief. Solidarity's slogan became its motto: "No freedom without Solidarity." On May 17, the Polish parliament passed a law legalizing the Catholic Church and restoring a number of privileges that had been revoked following World War II. Once again the church could buy and sell land, establish and run schools and hospitals, and operate radio and television stations.

This was the Poland many had dreamed might emerge: a country with a democratic political foundation that respected the Catholic Church's long history in the country and began to unshackle itself from Soviet influence. Yet because these changes uprooted the Communist Party and the security apparatus, which had exercised near-complete control of Poland since World War II, the country was now entering an extremely fragile period.

Chapter 23

FINISHING THE JOB

With the national elections fast approaching in Poland, the CIA remained active. QRHELPFUL had one last job to do. CIA operatives led by Peter Raudenbush, now the chief of the Political-Psychological Staff, attempted to offset the Jaruzelski regime's media advantage by supporting Solidarity's information campaign. During the Round Table Talks, CIA assets like Stanisław Broda, or QRGUIDE, sent $105,000 worth of copiers, fax machines, election materials, and cash for paper, posters, and stickers to Solidarity for the six-week campaign.[1] The CIA also established contacts with Eastern European intelligence services to lay the foundation for future cooperation and to lure them away from the KGB.[2] Now the Soviets had to face the prospect of espionage and subversion behind the Iron Curtain as former allies became conduits for the West.[3]

The White House, with President George H. W. Bush at the helm, supported steps to jump-start the Polish economy. Bush signed National Security Directive 9, "Actions to Respond to Polish Roundtable Agreement," which outlined eight measures to support a new Poland, such as "substantial rescheduling of Poland's official debt with the Paris Club," supporting a new financial aid package from the International Monetary

Fund, and eliminating tariffs on a variety of products.[4] As Bush had promised on his September 1987 visit to Poland, the United States agreed to help Poland's ailing economy now that Solidarity was legal again.

U.S. ambassador to Poland John Davis held frequent, informal gatherings with Solidarity members at his residence where they socialized, watched American movies, and consumed hefty servings of beef stroganoff and lasagna.[5] Davis had become a close confidant of Solidarity's leadership and had an unusually deep understanding of the complex situation. A few weeks before the elections, Davis sent a cable to Washington warning that Jaruzelski and the regime "are more likely to meet total defeat and great embarrassment." The Communist Party, Davis contended, was not well organized to run an election campaign and was "vastly disliked and nearly incapable of persuading an electorate through traditional campaign techniques, with which it has had no experience."[6] He also argued that Communist-style propaganda tactics were unlikely to be effective in a free and open election.

Solidarity, on the other hand, was adapting much quicker than the regime. Davis, who was aware of QRHELPFUL and CIA aid to Solidarity, remarked that there "are signs that Solidarity's inexperience and disorganization are being overcome; preparations for full and unified Solidarity participation in the elections are well advanced."[7] The Jaruzelski regime had indeed underestimated Solidarity's ability to organize. The democratic movement had a vast army of local supporters through its civic committees, which selected local opposition activists to run as candidates and help organize their campaigns. Tens of thousands of volunteers, including young people and representatives of the Catholic Church, pitched in to help. Solidarity also overcame the government's propaganda advantage by printing more than two thousand regional bulletins and supplementing them with a newspaper and radio blitz.[8] Radio Free Europe's Polish Service provided ample coverage of Solidarity candidates, who were not given access to official media.

Rather than exult in Solidarity's momentum, however, Davis became alarmed that a Solidarity victory might actually destabilize Poland. In a

June 2 cable, two days before the election, Davis predicted a "nearly-total Solidarity victory," with the Communist Party winning only two or three Senate seats. Such a rout by Solidarity, Davis surmised, would likely trigger "a sharp defensive reaction from the regime" which had "committed the sin of most decaying power elites" and "vastly underestimated the depth and strength of the opposition facing it." The reform wing of the Communist Party could be humiliated and lose its fragile hold on power, raising the possibility of "a military coup d'état, civil war, or both." Some Solidarity members, like sociologist and Sejm candidate Jacek Szymanderski, believed they had the Communist Party by the throat "and should slit it 'with a long, sharp knife.'"[9]

After years of instability because of Solidarity's relative weakness, Poland was now in a precarious position because of Solidarity's unexpected strength. "The stakes are enormous," Davis wrote. "One senses that the historical force of a vast and powerful current is about to transform Poland's topography forever."[10]

———

SOLIDARITY SPRINTED TO THE ELECTION, while the regime limped along. Wałęsa's approval rating a month before the elections was an extraordinary 74 percent, and Solidarity leveraged Wałęsa's popularity by photographing him with most of Solidarity's candidates for the Sejm and Senate.[11] The photographs then appeared on billboards with pithy captions like: "Get the message? Vote for the guy standing next to Wałęsa."[12] Solidarity's strategy, which had been conceived by Solidarity members Andrzej Wajda and Bronisław Geremek, was to present opposition candidates as members of "Lech's Team."[13]

Among the most iconic symbols of the election was a poster by Tomasz Sarnecki that drew inspiration from the 1952 American Western film *High Noon*, with Academy Award–winning Gary Cooper as the marshal.[14] The poster featured a rugged, debonair Cooper wearing a Solidarity insignia above his badge, grasping a voting card instead of a six-shooter, and walking with a cool swagger. Since the CIA had provided some funding, its lawyers demanded that Gary Cooper's gun be removed out of concern that it might incite violence during the election. Emblazoned with a blood-red "*Solidarność*" logo in the background, the poster combined American cool with Solidarity's righteousness. It also tacitly characterized the Jaruzelski regime as the villain and Solidarity as the hero bringing justice at "high noon" on election day.[15] Solidarity signs were ubiquitous during the campaign—on walls, in store windows, hanging from trees, and draped on cars. The Catholic Church was also supportive. According to Wałęsa, Bishop Ignacy Tokarczuk had told his parishioners, "You know very well how the Good Lord Himself would vote in these elections."[16]

Poles cast their ballots on June 4, 1989. Two weeks later, Poland held a second round of elections. As U.S. ambassador Davis predicted, Solidarity swept the elections, winning 99 of 100 seats in the Senate and 160 of 161 contested seats in the Sejm. The only seat that Solidarity lost in the Sejm was secured by Henryk Stokłosa, a millionaire from Pila who owned a salvaging firm with 210 employees, more than 100 trucks, a gas station, and a plane. He had spent a fortune on his campaign, but still only won 2.8 percent more votes than his Solidarity opponent.

That evening, the actress Joanna Szczepkowska announced on television: "Ladies and gentlemen, on 4 June communism has come to an end in Poland."[17] Poland had done what no other Warsaw Pact country had yet done: hold successful democratic elections. On June 4, the same day as Poland's elections, Chinese troops in Tiananmen Square, armed with assault rifles and tanks, killed hundreds of unarmed demonstrators who had been pushing for political and economic reform.

———

To WASHINGTON'S HORROR, Ambassador John Davis's worry proved correct. Solidarity's landslide victory created a crisis over the post of president. Demonstrations broke out in Kraków as Poles called for

Jaruzelski to resign from the government. Polish military and police officials started to panic. As one classified U.S. State Department cable
noted, embittered members of the Communist Party leadership complained that Polish security officers "would feel personally threatened if
Jaruzelski were not president and would move to overturn the Round-
Table and election results."[18] Minister of Internal Affairs Kiszczak also
told Catholic officials that if Jaruzelski "was not elected president then
we would be facing a further destabilization and the whole process of
political transformation would have to end. No other president would be
[listened to] in the security forces and in the army."[19]

As the situation spiraled, Ambassador Davis met with leading Solidarity members over dinner on June 22. According to a secret cable sent
the following day, Davis reported that some Solidarity leaders believed
"if Jaruzelski is not elected president, there is a genuine danger of civil
war." The frank assessment by Solidarity leaders created a problem,
since many of them had publicly pledged *not* to vote for Jaruzelski during the election campaign. Davis jotted down numbers on the back of
an embassy matchbook to explain the "arcane Western political practice
known as head-counting." As Davis pointed out, the quorum required
for the presidential election was two-thirds of the combined membership
of the Sejm and Senate. Of those present, they needed only a majority of
votes. So, as Davis explained, if a large number of "Solidarity senators
and Sejm deputies are ill or otherwise unable to attend the session," the
government coalition majority could get Jaruzelski elected. But it would
require Solidarity politicians to stay at home and abstain from voting.[20]

The great irony was the U.S. ambassador was now actively advis-
ing Solidarity members about how to *elect* Jaruzelski only a few weeks
after they had trounced the regime in the elections. But there was a
new problem, as Davis explained in a classified U.S. State Department
cable. Jaruzelski was increasingly reluctant to run for office. "The General," Davis wrote, "is determined that he will not 'creep' into the presidency. He is understandably reluctant to face another public humiliation
after the defeat of Party reformers on the National List in round one

of the elections."[21] Jaruzelski was doing his own head-counting of pro-government Sejm and Senate members to weigh his chances of winning. Privately, Jaruzelski confirmed Davis's fears, when, during the Thirteenth Plenum of the Communist Party Central Committee, he voiced his unwillingness to run.[22]

———

PRESIDENT BUSH NOW WALKED into this storm. On the evening of July 9, Bush landed in Warsaw for a two-day visit that included private meetings with Jaruzelski and Lech Wałęsa.[23] In a private conversation at Belweder Palace on the morning of July 10, Bush encouraged Jaruzelski to run for president to ensure a smooth transition and stability in the country. As Bush recalled:

> Jaruzelski opened his heart and asked me what role I thought he should now play. He told me of his reluctance to run for president and his desire to avoid a political tug-of-war that Poland did not need. I told him his refusal to run might inadvertently lead to serious instability and I urged him to reconsider. It was ironic: Here was an American president trying to persuade a senior Communist leader to run for office.[24]

Jaruzelski listened intently but made no commitment. Bush then spoke before the Polish parliament and laid out a six-point program for American aid to Poland. He traveled to Wałęsa's new house at 54 Polanki Street.[25] After a short walk around Wałęsa's garden, they drove to the center of Gdańsk to the 1970s monument outside Gate Number Two at the Gdańsk Shipyard. A speaker's platform, protected on two sides by bulletproof glass, had been set up for Bush. An estimated 30,000 to 40,000 people came to the monument, waving Polish and American flags. Father Henryk Jankowski dispatched five hundred oblates from St.

Bridget's Church.[26] Bush thanked Solidarity for serving as a beacon of hope for democracy around the world:

> Poland has a special place in the American heart and in my heart. And when you hurt, we feel pain. And when you dream, we feel hope. And when you succeed, we feel joy.... This special kinship is the kinship of an ancient dream—a recurring dream—the dream of freedom. "They are accustomed to liberty," wrote a Byzantine historian about the Slavic people more than a thousand years ago. And the spirit of the Poles has been conveyed across the centuries and across the oceans, a dream that would not die.... Your time has come.[27]

Audience members cheered "President Bush! President Bush! President Bush!"[28] Wałęsa spoke next, and hailed the United States—and Ronald Reagan—as longstanding allies: "From the very moment martial law had been declared, on December 13, 1981, the United States had taken a radical and very tough attitude toward the Communist regime in Poland. They had condemned from the very beginning the military takeover, the violation of human rights, and the lack of compromise."[29]

A week after President Bush departed, key Solidarity senators followed the advice of Ambassador Davis and abstained from voting. Jaruzelski was elected president of Poland, winning just over 50 percent of the votes.

———

MUCH TO WASHINGTON'S EMBARRASSMENT, Poland then slipped into another crisis, this time surrounding the question of a prime minister and the creation of a government. The U.S. Embassy had assumed that the Communist Party and its coalition partners would utilize their majority to create a Communist coalition government. Adam Michnik, a leading Solidarity intellectual, had proposed an agreement that would allow the Communist Party to retain the presidency while a member of Solidarity would become prime minister.[30] The Communists countered this offer with their own compromise to create a "grand coalition" in which Communist Party delegates would maintain control over key power ministries like the Ministry of Internal Affairs, the Ministry of Defense, and the Ministry of Foreign Affairs. In return, Solidarity delegates would receive key positions in economic and social ministries, as well as a deputy prime minister position.[31]

At the beginning of August, however, Wałęsa openly rejected the idea of a "grand coalition" government. Solidarity delegates would not approve Czesław Kiszczak, who had the support of Jaruzelski, for prime minister. Moreover, Lech Wałęsa and Solidarity leaders began to court members of the Communist Party's coalition partners to join a Solidarity-led coalition. Although a few U.S. cables had mentioned the possibility of members of the coalition parties breaking ranks with the Communist Party and voting with Solidarity, the reality of the situation seems to have taken Ambassador Davis by surprise.[32] As he recalled:

> What I didn't predict, what I couldn't predict was that the two satellite [Communist] parties would be willing to break away and form a government with Solidarity . . . It was an item of doctrine with [the Solidarity leadership] that these were contemptible satellites that had no independent views of any kind and should never be treated as anything separate from the Party itself. That was the general view that prevailed for many, many years. And it misled us in the end, because [the United People's Party and Alliance of Democrats] turned out to have their own interests. Walesa and some of his people saw this and knew how to exploit it . . . It was a brilliant political maneuver.[33]

Wałęsa's coup was effective, and, by August 7, he had paralyzed Kiszczak's efforts to create a government. Four days later, on August 11,

Davis met with Kiszczak at the peak of the crisis. According to a classified U.S. State Department cable from Davis, Kiszczak explained "that
Solidarity's latest proposal that it take over the government in coalition
with the Peasant Party [United People's Party] and Democratic Party
[Alliance of Democrats] . . . was unacceptable to the senior officers of
the army and police and to the Czechs, East Germans, and Soviets."[34]
The minister continued by explaining that a Solidarity coalition was
"regarded as breaking the deal made at the round table," and he made a
thinly veiled threat that there could be serious implications—perhaps a
coup d'état—at a time when there was a "very delicate balance in Poland."
Kiszczak noted that "100 senior officers of the Interior Ministry and
Ministry of Defense have been meeting and have expressed deep fears
concerning future developments," implying Polish military intervention
and possibly even Soviet interference.[35]

Washington took Kiszczak's warnings seriously and requested analysis from Jack Matlock, the U.S. ambassador to the Soviet Union. In a
sensitive cable back to Washington, Matlock concluded that Moscow
was unlikely to intervene:

> The Soviet response to the Polish political crisis has thus far
> been restrained, and barring a major misstep by Solidarity is
> likely to remain so. In keeping with Soviet "new thinking" in
> foreign policy, a strong reaction to Polish events does not seem
> to be appropriate . . . in the final analysis, although Solidarity
> may be a bitter pill to swallow, our best guess is that the Soviets
> will do so, if it comes to that, after much gagging and gulping.
> Their essential interests in Poland will be satisfied by any regime,
> Solidarity-led or not, that can promote domestic stability and
> avoid anti-Soviet outbursts.[36]

Unlike CIA assessments in 1980 and 1981, Matlock believed that
Soviet intervention in Poland was highly unlikely. The Brezhnev
Doctrine, which affirmed Moscow's right to intervene in the affairs of

Communist countries, was now dead. With reassurances from Moscow that the situation was not as dire as Kiszczak had hinted, the U.S. Embassy in Warsaw took no new action, though U.S. officials continued to worry about the outcome. Nevertheless, the Solidarity leadership was now exclusively in control of its own destiny and quickly reached an agreement with the regime to appoint a Solidarity prime minister.

On August 21, Jaruzelski designated as his prime minister Tadeusz Mazowiecki, a Solidarity member. Mazowiecki was a veteran politician and editor of *Tygodnik Solidarność*.[37] In his speech to the Sejm, Mazowiecki promised that there would be no witch hunts: "What has happened in the past must be dropped. What we must deal with now is the state of collapse in Poland *today*."[38] With the appointment of a Solidarity prime minister, Poland peacefully ended nearly a half century of Communist rule. On September 28, a new government spokesperson appeared on television to replace the loathed Jerzy Urban: Małgorzata Niezabitowska, formerly a reporter for *Tygodnik Solidarność*. That same day, the government announced that it had disbanded the ZOMO. For decades Poles had lived in fear of midnight arrests, character assassination, disappearances, torture, and imprisonment. On September 29 that fear melted into thin air.

———

IN NOVEMBER 1989, LECH WAŁĘSA traveled to the United States to pay tribute to his American friends. It was an emotional trip, highlighted by his November 15 address to a packed joint session of Congress. As Wałęsa walked into the House Chamber, the doorkeeper bellowed: "Mr. Speaker, the leader of Solidarity."[39] Wałęsa was only the third person to address a joint session of Congress who was not a sitting head of state.[40] Wałęsa entered the chamber to a boisterous reception, and Republicans and Democrats greeted him with a deafening ovation that lasted several minutes. Some wept.[41] As Wałęsa made his way down the center aisle, members of Congress jockeyed to shake his hand. Standing before a large

American flag, Wałęsa began to tremble. "The welcome made my knees go weak and my mouth go dry," he recalled.[42] House Speaker Tip O'Neil, one of Reagan's staunchest opponents, introduced Wałęsa to the raucous chamber. Members leapt to their feet and gave him a clamorous welcome with whoops, whistles, and thunderous applause.

Wałęsa paused and cast his eyes around the room. Normally a confident speaker, he now had to overcome his nerves. He had aged over time, but his portly figure, walrus-style mustache, and ruddy cheeks were still hallmarks. Wałęsa then focused on the text before him. "We the people," he began, quoting the U.S. Constitution. Members erupted. Even in the United States, Wałęsa had a gift for firing up a crowd, like he had done so many times in Poland. He continued:

> With these words I wish to begin my address. I do not need to remind anyone here where these words come from. And I do not need to explain that I, an electrician from Gdansk, am also entitled to invoke them. "We the people...." I stand before you as the third foreign non-head of state invited to address the joint Houses of Congress of the United States.
>
> The people in Poland link the name of the United States with freedom and democracy, with generosity and high-mindedness, with human friendship and friendly humanity....
>
> I, a shipyard worker from Gdansk, who has devoted his entire life—alongside other members of the Solidarity movement—to the service of this idea: "government of the people, by the people, for the people." Against privilege and monopoly, against violations of the law, against the trampling of human dignity, against contempt and injustice. Such in fact are the principles and values— reminiscent of Abraham Lincoln and the Founding Fathers of the American republic, and also of the principles and ideas of the American Declaration of Independence and the American Constitution—that are pursued by the great movement of Polish Solidarity; a movement that is effective. I wish to stress this point

with particular strength. I know that Americans are idealistic but at the same time practical people endowed with common sense and capable of logical action. They combine these features with a belief in the ultimate victory of right over wrong.[43]

Wałęsa explained that after many long years of struggle, Solidarity had brought Poland the freedom and democracy its people had yearned for since Yalta. "[W]e were being locked up in prison, deprived of our jobs, beaten and sometimes killed," he said, yet Solidarity had achieved victory "without resorting to violence of any kind." He concluded by reminding members of Congress that "the ideals which underlie this glorious American republic and which are still alive here, are also living in faraway Poland." The tide of history was now changing. "Together with Poland, other nations of Eastern Europe are following this path. The wall that was separating people from freedom has collapsed. The nations of the world will never let it be rebuilt."[44]

———

THAT SAME MONTH, THE BERLIN WALL FELL. The East German opposition, following the Polish example, began talks with the Communist regime. With Solidarity victorious and the Iron Curtain crumbling, the CIA could now close the book on QRHELPFUL after a remarkably successful eight-year run. One CIA estimate concluded that "Communist party rule in Eastern Europe is finished, and it will not be revived. This and the lifting of Soviet hegemony create new opportunities for establishing representative democracies and self-sustaining market economies."[45]

On January 9, 1990, the National Security Council issued new guidance that QRHELPFUL would receive $830,000 in fiscal year 1991 to allow the CIA to shut it down. The CIA's Operational Resources and Management Staff also recommended approval of $1.7 million to terminate such publications as *Aneks*. QRHELPFUL formally came to an end in 1991 when the Soviet–East European Division took it over from the Political-Psychological Staff. Throughout the year, the Soviet–East

European Division terminated assets and operations. Celia Larkin, the Polish-speaking case officer in charge, began calling herself "Terminator II," after the villain in the Arnold Schwarzenegger movie. Artur Kowalski and Stanisław Broda, among the first to join, were among the last to leave. Broda, or QRGUIDE, finished two CIA-funded documentaries and sold them to Polish television.[46] Dick Malzahn was gone. He had moved from covert action to counterintelligence in 1985, and then retired from the CIA in 1991.

During the early debates within the Reagan administration about whether to approve a covert action program to support Solidarity, those who fought for it—including Reagan himself—had hoped that an ideological campaign might strengthen "reformist forces inside the Communist bloc" and help weaken the Soviet empire.[47] Most U.S. officials had low expectations. Virtually no one imagined what would transpire at the end of the 1980s, and few predicted that the Soviet empire would crumble as quickly as it did. At a cost of less than $20 million, CIA helped the Poles—without arms—resist and defeat the Moscow-backed regime in Warsaw and set in motion the momentous events that followed.

Chapter 24

THE WHITE EAGLE

The afternoon of July 17, 2007, was pleasant at the Ronald Reagan Presidential Library, with a light breeze out of the west and temperatures in the eighties. Visitors to the Simi Valley campus that day had sweeping views of the valley below. Polish president Lech Kaczynski had traveled to Simi Valley to award Reagan, who had died three years before on June 5, 2004, posthumously with Poland's highest honor: The Order of the White Eagle.

Reagan's wife, Nancy, received the honor on Reagan's behalf. The star of the order is an exquisite enameled Maltese cross with golden rays, superimposed on a white eagle with spreading wings and adorned with a magnificent golden crown. Instituted in the early eighteenth century, the order had only been bestowed on Poles until this moment. Kaczynski, neatly dressed in a navy-blue suit and a gold-splashed tie, thanked Reagan for his support to Solidarity and help in overthrowing the Communist regime. In a ceremony attended by over a thousand guests, Kaczynski declared that the ouster of Jaruzelski's government "would not have been possible without the resoluteness and determination, without the sense of mission of President Ronald Reagan." Kaczynski then recalled that tense moment in late 1980, before Reagan had been sworn in as president and while there were growing concerns of a Soviet military invasion:

> When for the first time there was almost certainty that the Russians would intervene in Poland, Ronald Reagan had only been elected President. He had not assumed office yet but it was known he would do it. And in Moscow they knew who the U.S. president would be six weeks later. It was known that the period of softness was over. That power in the world's mightiest country would be taken by a genuine anticommunist—with all due respect to the achievements of President Carter. It must be remembered that this awareness was extremely important as regards the decision to back off and not intervene. When the threat of intervention appeared again a few months later Ronald Reagan was already president. And it is doubtless that the awareness of the Soviet authorities of the fact that U.S. policy would now be tough kept them again from intervening. Moreover it indeed eradicated any such plans.[1]

Poland's decision to award Reagan The Order of the White Eagle was a testament to Reagan's Cold War stance, but also to his method of fighting. Reagan knew the battle between the American system and the Soviet one was an ideological struggle. His decision to authorize CIA aid to Solidarity gave support to the nascent democracy movement in its most dire moment. Reagan's vision for Poland was embodied in the inscription on his tomb in Simi Valley: "I know in my heart that man is good. That what is right will always eventually triumph. And there's purpose and worth to each and every life."

———

THE CIA'S COVERT ACTION PROGRAM, QRHELPFUL, was a gamble that risked a confrontation with Moscow. CIA officers had to recruit

assets, establish covert networks, clandestinely move material, and provide aid to a resistance movement behind the Iron Curtain and under the
noses of the KGB and Polish security agencies. Reagan's decision, which
he signed as a presidential finding on November 4, 1982, was particularly
bold because the United States had conceded Eastern Europe to the
Soviets since Yalta in 1945. But Reagan wanted a clean break with the
past and vowed to roll back—not contain—the Soviet Union and its satellite countries. His presidential finding authorized the provision of
money and nonlethal equipment to Polish opposition groups through
surrogate third parties, hiding the CIA's hand.

What's more, Reagan's 1982 document "U.S. National Security
Strategy," NSDD-32, authorized a wide range of diplomatic, propa-
ganda, political, military, and covert action to "contain and reverse the
expansion of Soviet control and military presence through the world."[2]
Several months later, Reagan signed NSDD-54, "United States Policy
Towards Eastern Europe." It declared that the United States would
loosen Moscow's grip on Eastern Europe and reunite it with Western
Europe.[3] These documents provided the strategic logic and political
cover for a more aggressive U.S. policy toward the Soviet Union and its
Eastern European satellites.

Poland, of course, was not the only covert battlefield during the
Cold War. The CIA oversaw a paramilitary covert action program in
Afghanistan, started under President Jimmy Carter. Unlike the political program in Poland, however, the one in Afghanistan was larger and
more militarized. U.S. aid to the Afghan mujahideen began at a relatively
low level, but then increased as the prospect of a Soviet defeat appeared
more likely, totaling as much as $5 billion between 1980 and 1992.[4] The
CIA provided about $60 million per year to the Afghan mujahideen
between 1981 and 1983, which was matched by assistance from the Saudi
government. Beginning in 1985, the United States increased its support to the Afghans to $250 million per year. This shift culminated in
National Security Directive 166, which was signed by Reagan and set a
clear U.S. objective in Afghanistan: to push the Soviets out.[5] The United

States provided money, arms (including heavy machine guns, Stinger missiles, and Oerlikon anti-aircraft cannons), technical advice on weapons and explosives, strategic advice, intelligence, and sophisticated technology such as wireless interception equipment. Most of this assistance went through Pakistan's Directorate for Inter-Services Intelligence (ISI), rather than directly from the CIA to the mujahideen.[6]

But the results were controversial. After the Soviet withdrawal, Afghanistan collapsed into a civil war in the 1990s. The Taliban eventually seized the capital and allowed Osama bin Laden and al Qa'ida to establish a sanctuary.[7] Several of Reagan's other Cold War efforts were also contentious, including in Latin America. Reagan administration officials used money from the sale of weapons to Iran, which was under an arms embargo, to fund the Nicaraguan Contras. These efforts violated congressional amendments that placed limits on aid to the Contras.

In Poland, however, Solidarity was victorious and, crucially, Lech Wałęsa and the opposition ushered in freedom and democracy to Poland. QRHELPFUL remains one of the nation's greatest covert action programs. It is also a reminder of the importance of information and propaganda campaigns.

Lech Wałęsa, Solidarity, and the Polish people ultimately won their own freedom—not the CIA, Reagan, or anyone else from the outside. Members of the underground risked their lives to distribute literature, establish an organizational structure, and conduct strikes and demonstrations against the regime. Solidarity members were aided by declining economic and social conditions in Poland and the Soviet Bloc, as well as a robust support network made up of Catholic officials, intelligentsia, and Polish workers. Yet it is still important to examine the impact of QRHELPFUL.

————

THE SPREAD OF FREEDOM ACROSS EASTERN EUROPE and the crumbling of the Iron Curtain were truly inspiring. But what impact did

QRHELPFUL have? To answer this question, it is first important to understand QRHELPFUL's objectives. The available evidence suggests that Reagan and his staff wanted to keep Solidarity alive and weaken a Soviet satellite country in Moscow's backyard. These goals were limited. During the internal Reagan administration debates in 1982, QRHELP-FUL's primary supporters did not expect that the program would lead to the Jaruzelski regime's demise, let alone the collapse of the Soviet Union or its empire. Reagan's hope was perhaps best captured in his address to the nation in October 1982, shortly after Jaruzelski officially banned Solidarity: "There are those who will argue that the Polish Government's action marks the death of Solidarity. I don't believe this for a moment. Those who know Poland well understand that as long as the flame of freedom burns as brightly and intensely in the hearts of Polish men and women as it does today, the spirit of Solidarity will remain a vital force in Poland."[8] The November 1982 finding was aimed at supporting Solidarity as a "vital force," albeit in limited ways. Its goal was to aid the organizational activities of Solidarity and other groups, improve their ability to communicate with the Polish people inside and outside the country, and pressure the Jaruzelski regime to ease its repressive policies.

Did QRHELPFUL achieve these objectives? Questions about overall impact are difficult to assess. As Harvard historian Mark Kramer argued: "Far too often, journalists and scholars studying [Radio Free Europe], [Radio Liberty], and other U.S. Cold War–era political warfare entities have been wont to characterize the organizations as extremely effective without actually demonstrating this was the case."[9] In examining QRHELPFPUL, one of the most significant challenges is trying to disentangle CIA aid from other outside assistance. U.S. labor organizations like the AFL-CIO; humanitarian groups like Catholic charities; and U.S. government programs like Radio Free Europe, Voice of America, and the National Endowment for Democracy provided assistance and information to Poles. Outside of the United States, other groups—from the Vatican to labor unions and non-governmental organizations in Europe, Canada, Australia, and Japan—also offered support.

Unfortunately, there is limited data on how much money each of these organizations provided to Solidarity, what specific types of material they provided, and how it was used.

In addition, there are no publicly available data on the specific types and amounts of aid the CIA provided through its assets, which Solidarity members received it in Poland, and how it was used by Solidarity. What's more, it is unlikely that the CIA *ever* had this level of fidelity. The nature of covert action programs like QRHELPFUL, which relied on assets and informal ratlines, meant that CIA case officers had limited control over the program. CIA assets were often reluctant to reveal the details of their infiltration routes and recipients to protect their sources.[10]

Despite these challenges, a proper understanding of QRHELPFUL's impact needs to address several questions. How significant was CIA aid, compared to other types of assistance to Solidarity? How helpful to Solidarity was CIA aid? How concerned were Soviet and Polish authorities about CIA support to Solidarity? Based on answers to the above questions, what was the net impact of QRHELPFUL?[11]

It is important to examine each of these questions in turn.

———

FIRST, QRHELPFUL WAS LIKELY the single largest source of external aid to Solidarity, based on available evidence. The CIA spent roughly $20 million on assistance to Solidarity. The National Endowment for Democracy, the next largest, funded approximately $9 million for Polish programs between 1984 and 1989.[12] But most of this aid came at the *end* of the 1980s (over one-third came in 1989 alone), too late to help Solidarity survive during its darkest days after the imposition of martial law. The National Endowment for Democracy also supported a wide range of programs like Polish conferences; not all of its funding went to Solidarity. Most funding from the AFL-CIO, which totaled more than $4 million, was subsumed under the National Endowment for Democracy.[13] Between 1980 and 1981, the AFL-CIO raised roughly $250,000 through the Polish

Workers Aid Fund, which AFL-CIO leader Lane Kirkland established to support Solidarity.[14] After martial law, the National Endowment for Democracy provided grants to the AFL-CIO's Free Trade Union Institute of roughly $300,000 in 1984, $540,000 in 1985, $304,163 in 1986, $412,750 in 1987, $1,375,000 in 1988, and $1,435,000 in 1989.[15] There are few reliable figures on assistance from most other outside organizations and private donors.[16]

Consequently, the CIA provided roughly double the amount of assistance as did the National Endowment for Democracy, particularly in the immediate years after martial law when there was comparatively little assistance from outside. For example, the CIA obligated nearly $1.5 million to Solidarity in 1983. CIA assistance may have been particularly crucial after martial law when the Jaruzelski regime attempted to decimate Solidarity and there was little other outside aid coming to the Polish opposition.

Second, Solidarity benefited from CIA aid. The CIA provided funding and other assistance to Polish magazines like *Tygodnik Mazowsze*, a four-page weekly produced by Solidarity; Polish journals like *Aneks* and *Kultura* that were smuggled into Poland; and Radio Solidarity. CIA assets and surrogates like Stanisław Broda and Artur Kowalski smuggled everything from typewriters and photocopiers to money and duplicators through key European countries like France, Sweden, Denmark, Italy, Norway, Belgium, and West Germany. Outside aid was critical for Solidarity. "Neither the editors nor the printers could function without Western money," remarked one activist from *Tygodnik Mazowsze*. "This whole business of ours is based on huge help. We cannot survive on the weekly's cover price or dues, but on what the West is giving us."[17] Many of the parts required for printing were not available in Poland and had to be imported from outside the country. "Our dependence on the West is simply driven by needs. Pressure-sensitive offset sheets are simply not produced in Poland," said another activist from *Tygodnik Mazowsze*.[18] CIA assets also helped Solidarity break into Polish television programs.

These sources of information were influential in reaching Solidarity's support network. *Tygodnik Mazowsze*, for example, was the main opposition newspaper. As one history of Solidarity summarized: "*Tygodnik Mazowsze* became the most widely produced and circulated publication, serving as the major outlet for pronouncement from the remaining Solidarność structures."[19] Radio Solidarity also had an important impact on the underground.[20] "Solidarity Radio went on the air from multiple, roving locations" in the spring of 1982, one analysis concluded, and it helped "persuade Poles that Solidarity lived, and that the communists could not stamp it out."[21] While it is unclear how beneficial CIA aid was for Solidarity, the available evidence suggests that it was undoubtedly helpful for an opposition movement that was cash- and material-starved to run an underground political movement—especially in the initial years after martial law.

Third, Soviet and Polish authorities were seriously concerned about CIA assistance to Solidarity. Section 11 of the Ministry of Internal Affairs collected information on Western aid to Solidarity. Ministry operatives identified Solidarity sympathizers involved in printing and distributing opposition media and then planted moles in the underground, made arrests, and intimidated their families.[22] Over the course of the 1980s, Polish police and intelligence units conducted thousands of dramatic raids against the Solidarity underground, seizing people, radios, printing presses, leaflets, and other material. As the table below highlights, SB internal records indicate that they confiscated millions of leaflets, journals, and other items, though they barely made a dent in underground publishing. The Jaruzelski regime also aired a two-part series, *Polish Aide Ties Solidarity, CIA*, on Polish National Television in February 1985.

Polish agencies often trumpeted the materials seized in these raids as examples of CIA support, though Polish agencies never showed definitive proof. A Sejm investigation into Western intelligence efforts concluded that the Jaruzelski regime failed to intercept virtually all the money and nearly three quarters of the equipment sent to Solidarity from outside the country.[23] One SB report that summarized activities from December 1981 to December 1983 noted that "despite our intense operations and achieving significant results confiscating printing equipment and arresting people involved in these activities, illegal journals are persisting and improving their conspiratorial methods in preparing and editing texts, and organizing locales for duplication and systems of distribution."[24] The report blamed "far reaching aid from the West" on the underground's survival and eventual expansion.[25]

The KGB was equally concerned about CIA activity in Poland. As outlined in a secret KGB document with the bulky title "Plan for Basic Counterintelligence Measures to Step Up Still Further the Effort to Combat the Subversive Intelligence Activities of the United States Special Services," the KGB assessed that the CIA was involved in a broad ideological war designed to subvert the Soviet Union and its satellite countries—including Poland.[26] According to one KGB official, Moscow believed that the CIA was providing aid once it became clear that Solidarity was well funded and had access to foreign technology and parts

SB SUMMARY OF CONFISCATED ITEMS, DECEMBER 13, 1981 TO DECEMBER 31, 1988[27]

	1981	1982	1983	1984	1985	1986	1987	1988	Total
Leaflets	9,591	793,422	460,951	907,217	999,968	371,283	235,083	198,750	3,979,265
Posters	35	4,302	5,858	7,656	4,214	651	2,283	980	25,979
Copies of journals and books	2,107	440,362	387,688	439,559	530,106	359,900	208,367	44,620	2,412,709
Offset presses	-	4	5	14	2	20	2	1	48
Xerox machines	-	2	5	1	5	3	1	-	17
Duplicators	-	52	49	43	32	107	13	4	300
Silkscreen "frames"	-	164	88	134	170	120	41	30	747
Typewriters	-	209	88	117	68	40	9	3	534
Papers (reams)	-	3,414	1,282	7,168	2,048	1,122	2,240	1,924	19,198

unavailable in Poland to carry out their activity.[28] Vadim Pavlov, head of
the KGB mission in Warsaw, was convinced that the CIA was providing
assistance to Solidarity.[29] The Soviets viewed such activity with alarm,
interpreting it as a campaign to destabilize Poland and other Eastern
European countries and to undermine Soviet influence in its backyard.
According to one top secret KGB report: "The [KGB's] foreign intelligence service has sought to thwart the crude interference by the USA and
other NATO countries and their special services in the internal affairs of
Poland."[30] In a top secret memo to the Polish Ministry of Internal Affairs,
KGB director Viktor Chebrikov ordered the ministry to maximize its
efforts to "expose material support coming from imperialist circles in
the West."[31]

Fourth, answers to the previous questions suggest that CIA assistance was useful, though it is impossible to know *how much* it helped
Solidarity survive and ultimately prosper. CIA aid likely ensured that
neither Jaruzelski nor the KGB could crush the Polish opposition movement, even during the bleakest days of persecution after martial law. The
CIA helped generate media coverage and provided money and resources
to help Solidarity organize demonstrations, distribute newspapers and
leaflets, run radio stations, and break into Polish television programs
that boosted the opposition's local support, morale, and effectiveness.
QRHELPFUL was also cost-effective. The total bill amounted to less
than $20 million. What made QRHELPFUL particularly notable was
that it didn't create anything. Reagan and the CIA had a ready-made ally:
a popular democratic movement whose power came from the country's
vast trade unions. The long, grinding patience of Reagan and the CIA
helped Solidarity survive its darkest days. And when Solidarity's opportunity finally came, as the Soviet Union and Warsaw Pact neared an economic and military precipice, the Polish people embraced democracy.

Public knowledge that the CIA was involved in a covert program to
aid Solidarity would have been a severe blow to Solidarity's legitimacy in
the 1980s. But concrete evidence never leaked. In Poland, QRHELPFUL
suffered few losses and no major operational or security setbacks. The

CIA's decision to use surrogates as channels to the Polish underground and to create its own operations and infrastructure—bypassing Solidarity's designated representatives in the West—was vindicated. The program showed that covert action could be a critical U.S. foreign policy tool in cases where the U.S. government's role needs to be hidden to protect the United States and its local allies. While the American public often focuses on the role of CIA paramilitary activity—including the use of drone strikes in such countries as Pakistan and Yemen—covert action remains critical in such areas as political action.

In the end, QRHELFPUL was helpful to Solidarity's success, though it was still only one program among many. Solidarity members like Lech Wałęsa were unquestionably the true heroes.

EPILOGUE

Wojciech Jaruzelski was not as fortunate as the leaders of Solidarity. After serving only one year of his six-year term, Jaruzelski resigned in 1991 and opened the way for a new presidential election, which was won by Lech Wałęsa. Jaruzelski spent the last decade of his life in relative obscurity, attempting to salvage his reputation. He wrote several books, gave some public interviews, and became engaged in a few heated exchanges when he felt that he was unjustly maligned.[1] Among the most entertaining debates was a response to declassified documents on martial law released by the Cold War International History Project at the Wilson Center in Washington. Mark Kramer, a Harvard historian, wrote a scathing essay that suggested "a full-scale reassessment" of the "lenient treatment of Jaruzelski" and "his place in history" because of Jaruzelski's involvement in martial law and his alleged support of Soviet military intervention.[2] Jaruzelski wrote an acrimonious response disputing the allegation. "We imposed and carried out martial law *alone*," he said, arguing that he never asked for Soviet military aid.[3]

Jaruzelski died on May 25, 2014, at the age of ninety. His reputation in Poland remains a complicated one. To his supporters, Jaruzelski epitomized pragmatism at a time when Poland was torn between internal and external political, social, military, and economic forces. In Jaruzelski's own words, "I served the Poland that existed."[4] Jaruzelski pleaded to Richard Pipes, National Security Council staffer and Harvard professor, that he "was a Polish patriot" because he "had saved Poland from a Soviet invasion." Jaruzelski believed that "the alternative to martial law—a Soviet invasion—would have been much, much worse."[5]

In a letter to the Sejm's Commission of Constitutional Oversight, Mikhail Gorbachev defended Jaruzelski's actions. He noted that it was "obvious to any unprejudiced person" that Jaruzelski's decision to enact martial law was a difficult one based on Poland's unraveling economic and social fabric, as well as tense Polish-Soviet relations. "Under such conditions," Gorbachev continued, "Gen. Jaruzelski was forced to take upon himself this altogether difficult decision, which at the time was, in my opinion, the choice of a lesser evil."[6] Solidarity leader Adam Michnik also remarked that Poland under Jaruzelski was not a full dictatorship, but was "totalitarianism with some teeth knocked out."[7] Opinion polls suggested that Poles were deeply divided about Jaruzelski. A 2009 poll found that 46 percent of those interviewed said Jaruzelski would be remembered negatively, while 42 percent responded that he would be remembered positively. Another poll in 2011 showed that 44 percent of Poles surveyed agreed with the imposition of martial law, while 34 percent opposed martial law.[8]

Some of Jaruzelski's fiercest political enemies tried to nail him for past crimes, and court cases from the Communist era dogged him in his final years. Prosecutors from the Institute of National Remembrance, a state body that investigated Communist-era crimes, charged Jaruzelski with violating Poland's constitution for his imposition of martial law. They accused him of creating a criminal military organization with the aim of carrying out acts like illegally imprisoning Poles. Separately, Jaruzelski faced charges stemming from the shooting of the Gdańsk Shipyard workers in 1970. But Jaruzelski avoided trial at the end of his life, claiming ill-health.

Despite his escape from punishment, Jaruzelski led a government that was deeply unpopular in Poland throughout most of the 1980s. For decades before that, as a career officer and party official, he dutifully worked to entrench Soviet Communism in Poland.[9] Under martial law, Jaruzelski established an authoritarian Military Council of National Salvation. The council banned Solidarity, arrested its leaders, prohibited public gatherings, censored publications, and unfairly detained thousands of people. Many risked their lives to end Communism's grip on Polish society, not blunt its edges. These freedom fighters were Poland's true heroes, and they did it through peaceful means.

Jaruzelski was not one of Poland's heroes. He will forever be remembered for his decision to enact martial law, which cast a pall across the country. "In accordance with the Constitution," Jaruzelski announced in the early morning hours of December 13, 1981, "the State Council has imposed martial law all over the country."[10] For the next eight years, Poles lived in darkness.

———

LECH WAŁĘSA WAS DIFFERENT. He and his intrepid band of opposition members deserve most of the credit for Solidarity's victory and the collapse of Communism in Poland. On December 9, 1990, Wałęsa won the presidential election, defeating Prime Minister Tadeusz Mazowiecki and other candidates to become the first freely elected president of Poland in over six decades.[11] During his presidency, Wałęsa guided Poland through privatization, the transition to a free-market economy, Poland's first completely free parliamentary elections, and a redefinition of the country's foreign relations. Wałęsa negotiated the withdrawal of Soviet troops from Poland and won a substantial reduction in foreign debts. He also supported Poland's eventual entry into NATO and the European Union, both of which occurred after his presidency. Poland became a member of NATO in 1999 and the European Union in 2004.

Despite his monumental achievements, Wałęsa remains a controversial figure. As Solidarity member Bogdan Borusewicz remarked when asked how he graded Wałęsa's tenure as president: "Not bad at the beginning; after that, terrible."[12] Wałęsa's bombastic, in-your-face style alienated some Poles. He established a political party, the Nonpartisan Bloc for Support of Reforms, which performed poorly in the 1993 parliamentary elections. His support dwindled and he narrowly lost the 1995 presidential election to Aleksander Kwaśniewski from the Democratic Left Alliance party. Wałęsa's fate was sealed by his poor handling of the media and his gruff demeanor. During the election campaign, Wałęsa appeared incoherent and rude. After one of the presidential debates, he refused to shake Kwaśniewski's outstretched hand and told him to "shake his leg" instead.[13] Wałęsa threw his hat into the ring for the 2000 presidential elections, but received a paltry one percent of the vote. His political career was officially over.

Wałęsa was also hounded by accusations that he had served as an informant for the Polish security services in the 1970s, despite his vehement denials and the ruling of a special court in 2000 that cleared him of the allegations. The controversy resurfaced in 2008 with the publication of a book with new documents purportedly showing that Wałęsa had been a paid informant for the security services from 1970 to 1976 using the codename "Bolek."[14] In 2016 and 2017, the Institute of National Remembrance released analysis and files seized from the widow of former minister of internal affairs Czesław Kiszczak, shortly after his death, which allegedly provided further evidence that Wałęsa had cooperated with the SB.[15]

While it is plausible that a young, unemployed Wałęsa with a wife and growing family may have agreed to briefly serve as an informant, Wałęsa's pivotal role in undermining Communism during the Cold War is incontrovertible. He led Solidarity during the August 1980 Gdańsk Agreement, suffered immensely during martial law, remained a bitter opponent of the Jaruzelski regime after he was released from confinement in November 1982, steered Solidarity through the Round Table Talks, and became Poland's first democratically elected president in the modern era. The 1983 recipient of the Nobel Peace Prize won countless state decorations and awards, including the Order of the Bath from the United Kingdom, Order of Merit from Germany, Legion of Honor from France, European Human Rights Prize from the European Union, and Liberty Medal from the United States. He was awarded dozens of honorary doctorates by universities around the world.

In his hometown of Gdańsk, Wałęsa remains one of the city's great heroes. Among many honors, the city renamed the airport Gdańsk Lech Wałęsa Airport and incorporated Wałęsa's signature into the airport's logo.

———

Today in Gdańsk, which once served as the hub of Solidarity, memories of Cold War heroes are preserved throughout the city. One site is in Ronald Reagan Park, situated along the Baltic coastline northwest of downtown Gdańsk. Built between 2003 and 2006, the hundred-acre park honors Reagan and Pope John Paul II. Bronze statues of Reagan and the pope, walking side by side and thoughtfully engaged in conversation, greet visitors at the park's entrance. The statues are modelled on a famous photograph taken by Scott Stewart of the Associated Press when Reagan and the pope met in Miami in 1987. The park itself offers a serene sanctuary for Poles to walk, jog, ride bikes, or frolic on the playground. The engraving on Reagan's statue sums up Polish appreciation for his commitment to freedom: "Grateful for the independence of Poles."

Elsewhere in the city, reminders of the Cold War struggle persist. Statues of Father Jerzy Popiełuszko, Anna Walentynowicz, Father Henryk Jankowski, and even the CIA spy Ryszard Kukliński in nearby Gdynia dot the landscape. St. Bridget's Church remains a shrine to Solidarity and a home to its memorabilia. Next to Gate Number Two at the Gdańsk Shipyard sits the European Solidarity Centre, opened in 2014 and devoted to the history of Solidarity and other opposition movements in Eastern Europe. As the Polish academic Jacek Kołtan summarized, "the Solidarity movement in Poland and the peaceful revolutions in most countries of Central and Eastern Europe were all part of the tradition of seeking peaceful solutions to social and political conflicts." Ronald Reagan and the CIA both recognized the importance of keeping Solidarity a peaceful opposition movement. Indeed, nonviolent opposition was the secret to their success. "Their history, and especially the history of countries whose fate unfolded in a dramatically different way, indicates that to this day non-violence is not the obvious choice, but rather a delicate fabric, with which we must constantly sew the culture of peaceful coexistence," Kołtan wrote.[16]

Nowhere is this message of peace as raw as near Gate Number Two in the Gdańsk Shipyard, which has been preserved for visitors. There is a plaque dedicated to the memory of those killed by Polish forces in 1970. It reads:

> *A token of everlasting remembrance of the slaughter victims.*
> *A warning to rulers that no social conflict in our country can be resolved by force.*
> *A sign of hope for fellow-citizens that evil need not prevail.*

Acknowledgments

"If you want to write, if you want to create, you must be the most sub-lime fool that God ever turned out and sent rambling.... You must lurk in libraries and climb the stacks like ladders to sniff books like per-fumes and wear books like hats upon your crazy heads."

—Ray Bradbury, American author and screenwriter

I first began to consider writing a book about U.S. support to Solidarity in early 2013. Over the next several years, I fell victim to Ray Bradbury's description of writing. I visited libraries and archives from the Ronald Reagan Presidential Library in Simi Valley, California, to the William J. Casey papers at the Hoover Institution in Stanford, California, climbing the "stacks like ladders" and "sniffing books like perfumes." Rarely a day went by when I wasn't reading, writing, editing, taking notes, or other-wise thinking about the book.

I owe an enormous debt of gratitude to my agent, Eric Lupfer, and my editor, Tom Mayer, for helping conceptualize the book from the beginning. Their wisdom, advice, and friendship were essential along the way. Eric did an outstanding job sifting through a litany of topics and settling on U.S. assistance to Solidarity. Tom's diligence and constructive criticism were unparalleled. I came to expect—and sometimes dread— Tom's thorough review of each draft of the manuscript. He would often send a dozen or so pages of single-spaced, typed notes and handwritten comments on virtually every page of the manuscript, with additional instructions about what to read.

Thanks to the CIA's History Office and Public Affairs Office for their cooperation—including their comments on the manuscript. Thanks also to those individuals who read through one or more drafts of the manuscript. They included Ross Johnson, Ben Fischer, Jim Dobbins, Rich Girven, Richard Malzahn, Arturo Muñoz, David Robarge, Jim Thomson, and Mike Vickers. Nathan Chandler was extraordinarily helpful at several points along the way, including hunting down facts, documents, and people involved in the Polish program. After leaving the Reagan Library after one visit to the archives, Nathan and I had a close call with a brush fire on our way from Simi Valley to Santa Monica as we hopped onto Interstate 405. I'm glad it didn't deter him from continuing to help! Bruce Hoffman and his wife Donna, who also spent considerable time at the Reagan Library and Hoover Institution archives, were helpful in exchanging information and discussing aspects of the Reagan administration. In addition, I would like to extend a hearty thanks to those individuals who agreed to take time out of their busy schedules to discuss the Reagan administration, Poland, and the Soviet Union. They included Zbigniew Brzezinski, Edwin Meese III, Mark Kramer, Paula Dobriansky, Frank Carlucci, Burton Gerber, Richard Pipes, Ian Brzezinski, Michael Warner, John McLaughlin, Steve Steiner, Mircea Munteanu, and John Lenczowski. There are many others that did not wish to be identified, but I thank them nonetheless.

Among the most important people were those who helped track down sources. In Poland, the European Solidarity Centre was instrumental in allowing me to peruse their museum and archives. The European Solidarity Centre was a goldmine of information. It had a door from the Gdańsk Shipyard hospital with bullet holes from the December 1970 riots, offset plates from the Solidarity Strike Information Bulletin, the sweater worn by Lech Wałęsa when he signed the August 1980 agreements, the forklift that served as a platform during the 1980 Gdańsk strikes, duplicator machines, police trucks, postmarks from the internment of political prisoners, and many other valuable items that brought Solidarity's struggle to life.

At the Reagan Library, Ray Wilson helped steer me through the archives and suggested new avenues to look for information. He saved me from wasting countless hours. I also thank Carol Leadenham at the Hoover Institution. In addition, library personnel at the following institutions were friendly and accommodating in helping track down information and documents: the National Archives at College Park, Maryland (particularly the CIA Records Search Tool, or CREST); Wilson Center Digital Archive; Cold War International History Project; and Churchill Archives Centre (which houses the Mitrokhin Archive).

At CSIS, I would like to thank several people who provided support as I finished the manuscript, including John Hamre, Kathleen Hicks, Olya Oliker, Andrew Schwartz, Mike Hayden, and Craig Cohen. At RAND, I owe an enormous debt of gratitude to several managers and researchers who offered support along the way. They included Michael Rich, Andy Hoehn, Jack Riley, Charlie Ries, Laura Baldwin, John Parachini, Steve Larrabee, Bill Courtney, Chris Chivvis, Mike McNerney, Stuart Johnson, Jim Dobbins, James Bruce, Mike Mazarr, Andrew Radin, and Austin Long. My assistants, Katrina Griffin-Moore and Joy Merck, played critical roles in getting the document off the ground and over the finish line.

The W. W. Norton team was stellar. Tom Mayer led the way. Rachel Salzman was a true professional and an outstanding publicist. I'm grateful as well for the hard work by Sarah Bolling, Emma Hitchcock,

Rebecca Homiski, Julia Druskin, Ingsu Liu, Sierra Stovall, Steven Pace, Meredith McGinnis, Avery Hudson, and everyone else who helped make this book possible.

My parents (Alec and Sethaly) and three brothers (Alex, Josh, and Clark) have always been my backstop. I can't thank you enough. Finally, I would like to thank my wonderful wife (Suzanne) and two daughters (Elizabeth and Alexandra). They are my constant source of joy, and I dedicate this book to them.

Map Credits

p. 27   Gdańsk Lenin Shipyard: Map courtesy of European Solidarity Centre in Gdańsk.

p. 109   Major Units Allocated to Operational Forces: Defense Intelligence Agency, "Intelligence Appraisal Poland: Martial Law and Operational Forces," March 30, 1981. Available in Executive Secretariat, NSC, Poland to Romania, Box 18, Ronald Reagan Presidential Library.

p. 143   Detention Centers during Martial Law: The data is from the European Solidarity Centre in Gdańsk.

p. 234   Soviet-German Map Distributed by CIA: Robert Coalson, "Molotov-Ribbentrop: The Night Stalin and Hitler Redrew the Map of Europe," Radio Free Europe / Radio Liberty, August 21, 2009. Available at: http://www.rferl.org/a/MolotovRibbentrop_The_Night_Stalin_And_Hitler_Redrew_The_Map_Of_Europe/1804154.html.

Notes

PROLOGUE

1. On the weather for December 12, 1981, see "Weather History for Hagerstown, MD," December 12, 1981, Weather Underground (www.wunderground.com).
2. Ronald Reagan, *The Reagan Diaries, Vol. I, January 1981–October 1985*, ed. Douglas Brinkley (New York: HarperCollins, 2009), p. 16.
3. See Reagan's diary entry for October 3, 1981, in Reagan, *The Reagan Diaries, Vol. I*, p. 71.
4. Quoted in W. Dale Nelson, *The President Is at Camp David* (Syracuse, NY: Syracuse University Press, 1995), p. 15.
5. Nancy Reagan, *My Turn: The Memoirs of Nancy Reagan* (New York: Random House, 1989), p. 255.
6. Marilyn Berger, "Ronald Reagan Dies at 93; Fostered Cold-War Might and Curbs on Government," *New York Times*, June 6, 2004.
7. Lawrence K. Altman, "Doctor Says President Lost More Blood than Disclosed," *New York Times*, April 3, 1981.
8. Nancy Reagan, *My Turn*, p. 6.
9. Central Intelligence Agency, "Soviet Goals and Expectations in the Global Power Arena," National Intelligence Estimate, NIE 11-4-78, July 7, 1981. Available from the National Security Archive.

10. Central Intelligence Agency, Memorandum For: The Director of Central Intelligence and the Deputy Director of Central Intelligence, From: Redacted, Subject: Polish Preparations for Martial Law, December 7, 1981, p. 3. Available from the CIA (http://www.foia.cia.gov/collection/preparing-martial-law-through-eyes-colonel-ryszard-kuklinski).

11. The discussion at CIA headquarters comes from Douglas J. MacEachin, *U.S. Intelligence and the Confrontation in Poland, 1980–1981* (University Park: The Pennsylvania State University Press, 2002), p. 209.

12. John Darnton, "In Poland, Well-Worn Tightrope Snaps at Last," *New York Times*, December 13, 1981.

13. The Proclamation of Martial Law by the State Council, December 13, 1981.

14. See, for example, Polish Ministry of Internal Affairs, Assessment of the Present Situation in the Country as of 25 November 1981, Supplement No. 2: Planned Activity of the Interior Ministry, November 25, 1981. Available from the National Security Archive.

15. Lieutenant-General V. I. Anoshkin, "The Anoshkin Notebook on the Polish Crisis, December 1981," p. 24. Availabe in *Cold War International History Project Bulletin*, No. 11, Winter 1998.

16. John Tagliabue, "Lech! Lech! Lech!" *New York Times*, October 23, 1988.

17. Quoted in Timothy Garton Ash, *The Polish Revolution: Solidarity*, Third Edition (New Haven, CT: Yale University Press, 2002), p. 275.

18. Quoted in Ash, *The Polish Revolution*, p. 276.

19. Quoted in Peter Schweizer, *Victory: The Reagan Administration's Secret Strategy That Hastened the Collapse of the Soviet Union* (New York: The Atlantic Monthly Press, 1994), p. 68.

20. Memorandum from Alexander M. Haig, Jr., to the President, "Subject: The United States and Poland," November 12, 1981. Available in Executive Secretariat, NSC, Country Files: Poland, Box 17, Ronald Reagan Presidential Library.

21. Reagan, *The Reagan Diaries, Vol. I*, p. 95.

22. Ronald Reagan, *An American Life: The Autobiography* (New York: Simon and Schuster, 1990), p. 301. Emphasis added.

23. Among the most accurate accounts of the program are the short mentions in Robert M. Gates, *From the Shadows: The Ultimate Inside Story of Five Presidents and How They Won the Cold War* (New York: Simon and Schuster, 1996), pp. 358–359; William J. Daugherty, *Executive Secrets: Cover Action and the Presidency* (Lexington: University of Kentucky Press, 2004), pp. 193–211; and

Benjamin B. Fischer, "Solidarity, the CIA, and Western Technology," *International Journal of Intelligence and Counterintelligence* 25, no. 3 (2012), pp. 427–469.

24. Notable exceptions include Gates, *From the Shadows*; Daugherty, *Executive Secrets*; and Fischer, "Solidarity, the CIA, and Western Technology."

25. H.W. Brands, *Reagan: The Life* (New York: Doubleday, 2015), p. 343.

26. Andrzej Paczkowski, "Playground of the Superpowers, Poland 1980–1989: A View from Inside," in Olav Njolstad, ed., *The Last Decade of the Cold War: From Conflict Escalation to Conflict Transformation* (London: Frank Cass, 2004), p. 321.

27. Reagan, *An American Life*, p. 715.

CHAPTER 1: THE PEOPLE'S MAN

1. Lech Wałęsa, *A Way of Hope* (New York: Henry Holt and Company, 1987), p. 98.

2. For an overview of underground printing during the 1970s and 1980s see, for example, Gwido Zlatkes, Paweł Sowiński, and Ann M. Frenkel, *Duplicator Underground: The Independent Publishing Industry in Communist Poland, 1976–89* (Bloomington, IN: Slavica, 2016); Joanna M. Preibisz, ed., *Polish Dissident Publications: An Annotated Bibliography* (New York: Praeger, 1982); Jane L. Curry, *The Black Book of Polish Censorship* (New York: Vintage, 1984); Michael H. Bernhard and Henryk Szlajfer, eds., *From the Polish Underground: Selections from "Krytyka," 1978–1993* (University Park: Pennsylvania State University, 1995).

3. See, for example, the description of Lech Wałęsa in "Time Man of the Year: Poland's Lech Wałęsa," *Time*, Vol. 119, No. 1, January 4, 1981. Also see the description of Charles Howard in Laura Hillenbrand, *Seabiscuit: An American Legend* (New York: Random House, 2001), p. 3.

4. Wałęsa, *A Way of Hope*, p. 109.

5. Wałęsa, *A Way of Hope*, p. 104.

6. Lech Wałęsa, *The Struggle and the Triumph: An Autobiography* (New York: Arcade Publishing, 1991), pp. 16–17.

7. Wałęsa, *A Way of Hope*, p. 14.

8. Rebecca Stefoff, *Lech Wałęsa: The Road to Democracy* (New York: Ballantine Books, 1992), pp. 25–27; Wałęsa, *A Way of Hope*, p. 26.

9. Wałęsa, *A Way of Hope*, p. 31.

10. Wałęsa, *A Way of Hope*, p. 29.

11. Wałęsa, *A Way of Hope*, p. 29.

12. Alfred, Lord Tennyson, *Maud, and Other Poems* (London: King, 1876).

13. Key documents include U.S. Department of State, *Foreign Relations of the United States* [hereinafter cited as *FRUS*]: *The Conferences of Malta and Yalta 1945* (Washington, DC: United States Government Printing Office, 1955); John L. Snell, ed., *The Meaning of Yalta: Big Three Diplomacy and the New Balance of Power* (Baton Rouge: Louisiana State University Press, 1956).

14. Norman Davies, *God's Playground: A History of Poland*, Vol. I and II, Revised Edition (New York: Columbia University Press, 2005).

15. Marc Trachtenberg, *A Constructed Peace: The Making of the European Settlement* (Princeton, NJ: Princeton University Press, 1999), pp. 4–5.

16. "Letter from President Roosevelt to Stalin on Acceptable Compromise Regarding the Composition of the Postwar Polish Government, 6 February 1945," February 6, 1945. Available from the History and Public Policy Program Digital Archive, Woodrow Wilson International Center for Scholars.

17. *FRUS: The Conferences of Malta and Yalta 1945*, pp. 968–983.

18. Melvin Leffler, *A Preponderance of Power: National Security, the Truman Administration, and Cold War* (Stanford, CA: Stanford University Press, 1992); Diane Shaver Clemens, *Yalta* (New York: Oxford University Press, 1970); Robert Dallek, *Franklin D. Roosevelt and American Foreign Policy* (New York: Oxford University Press, 1979).

19. Leffler, *A Preponderance of Power*; Clemens, *Yalta*; Dallek, *Franklin D. Roosevelt and American Foreign Policy*.

20. On the broader Cold War implications of Yalta see, for example, John Lewis Gaddis, *The United States and the Origins of the Cold War, 1941–1947* (New York: Columbia University Press, 1972); Daniel Yergin, *Shattered Peace: The Origins of the Cold War and the National Security State* (Boston: Houghton Mifflin, 1978); Leffler, *A Preponderance of Power*.

21. Davies, *God's Playground*, Vol. II, p. 570.

22. Wałęsa, *A Way of Hope*, p. 3.

23. Quoted in Davies, *God's Playground*, Vol. II, p. 574. Also see Hugh Thomas, *Armed Truce: The Beginnings of the Cold War, 1945–46* (New York: Atheneum, 1987), p. 254.

24. Davies, *God's Playground*, Vol. II, p. 556.

25. Davies, *God's Playground*, Vol. II, pp. 579–581.

26. Czeslaw Milosz, *The Captive Mind* (New York: Vintage International, 1990), p. 11.

27. Wałęsa, *A Way of Hope*, p. 39.

28. See, for example, P. M. H. Bell, *The Origins of the Second World War in Europe*, Second Edition (New York: Longman, 1997), pp. 298–300.

29. Paweł Huelle's *Cold Sea Stories* offer a collection of short stories incorporating the history and mythology of Gdańsk and the Baltic Coast with contemporary political events. See Paweł Huelle, *Cold Sea Stories* (Manchester, England: Comma Press, 2012).

30. Nicholas Kulish, "Historic Polish Shipyard Struggles in a New Age," *New York Times*, August 26, 2007.

31. Wałęsa, *A Way of Hope*, p. 36.

32. Timothy Garton Ash, *The Polish Revolution: Solidarity*, Third Edition (New Haven, CT: Yale University Press, 2002), pp. 13–15.

33. Roman Laba, *The Roots of Solidarity: A Political Sociology of Poland's Working-Class Democratization* (Princeton, NJ: Princeton University Press, 1991), p. 117; Wałęsa, *A Way of Hope*, p. 40–42.

34. Wałęsa, *A Way of Hope*, p. 44.

35. Laba, *The Roots of Solidarity*, p. 117.

36. Wałęsa, *A Way of Hope*, p. 48.

37. Piotr Adamowicz, Andrzej Drzycimski, and Adam Kinaszewski, *Gdańsk According to Lech Wałęsa* (Gdańsk: Morze możliwości, 2008), p. 14.

38. Adamowicz, *Gdańsk*, p. 15.

39. Wałęsa, *A Way of Hope*, p. 50.

40. Wałęsa, *The Struggle and the Triumph*, pp. 16–17.

41. Ash, *The Polish Revolution*, p. 13.

42. Ash, *The Polish Revolution*, pp. 13–15.

43. Michael Dobbs, *Down with Big Brother: The Fall of the Soviet Empire* (New York: Vintage Books, 1996), p. 35.

44. Wałęsa, *A Way of Hope*, p. 70.

45. Dobbs, *Down with Big Brother*, pp. 35–36.

46. Poland's national anthem is "Poland is Not Yet Lost." The lyrics were written by Józef Wybicki in July 1797. Emphasis added.

47. Wałęsa, *A Way of Hope*, p. 71.

48. U.S. Department of State, Subject: RFE Broadcasts to Poland, From: Ambassador Walter Stoessel, Embassy Dispatch No. 192, January 21, 1971. Available

from the History and Public Policy Program Digital Archive, Woodrow Wilson International Center for Scholars.

49. "Report by KGB Chairman Andropov on Radio Free Europe and Radio Liberty," October 29, 1971. Available from the History and Public Policy Program Digital Archive, Woodrow Wilson International Center for Scholars.

50. Robert D. McFadden, "Edward Gierek Dies at 88," *New York Times*, July 30, 2001.

51. Ash, *The Polish Revolution*, p. 15.

52. Quoted in George Blazynski, *Flashpoint Poland* (New York: Pergamon Press, 1979), p. 45.

53. Ash, *The Polish Revolution*, p. 15.

54. Wałęsa, *The Struggle and the Triumph*, p. 15.

55. Wałęsa, *The Struggle and the Triumph*, p. 33.

56. "Institute for the Study of Contemporary Problems of Capitalism, 'Propaganda of Western Broadcasting Stations about the So-Called Workers' Defense Committee and the Supreme Sentence on the Seven Participants of the Ursus Events,'" October 1976. Available from the History and Public Policy Program Digital Archive, Woodrow Wilson International Center for Scholars.

57. Ash, *The Polish Revolution*, p. 19.

58. Dobbs, *Down with Big Brother*, pp. 35–36.

59. Oliver MacDonald, ed., *The Polish August: Documents from the Beginnings of the Polish Workers' Rebellion* (San Francisco: Ztangi Press, 1981), p. 81.

CHAPTER 2: THE GENERAL

1. Quoted in Tina Rosenberg, *The Haunted Land: Facing Europe's Ghosts After Communism* (New York: Random House, 1995), p. 141.

2. Wojciech Jaruzelski, 105th Landon Lecture, Kansas State University, March 11, 1996.

3. Ryszard Kuklinski, "Jaruzelski's Attitude, Behavior, and Style," Paper Prepared for the Central Intelligence Agency, January 7, 1982. Available from the Central Intelligence Agency at: https://www.cia.gov/library/readingroom/docs/1983-01-01.pdf.

4. Hella Pick, "General Wojciech Jaruzelski Obituary," *Guardian*, May 25, 2014.

5. See the descriptions of Jaruzelski in Michael T. Kaufman and Nicholas Kulish, "Gen Wojciech Jaruzelski, Solidarity's Foil, Dies at 90," *New York Times*, May 25, 2014.

6. Quoted in Rosenberg, *The Haunted Land*, p. 129.

7. Jaruzelski, 105th Landon Lecture.

8. Wojciech Jaruzelski, *Les chaines et le refuge* [*The Chains and the Refuge*] (Paris: Lattes, 1992), p. 50; Michael Dobbs, *Down with Big Brother: The Fall of the Soviet Empire* (New York: Vintage Books, 1996), p. 70.

9. Dobbs, *Down with Big Brother*, pp. 68–69.

10. Dobbs, *Down with Big Brother*, p. 70.

11. See Rosenberg, *The Haunted Land*, p. 132.

12. Jaruzelski, *Les chaines et le refuge*, p. 44.

13. See the descriptions of Jaruzelski in Kaufman and Kulish, "Gen Wojciech Jaruzelski, Solidarity's Foil, Dies at 90"; "Wojciech Jaruzelski," *Economist*, June 14, 2014.

14. See Rosenberg, *The Haunted Land*, p. 133.

15. See Rosenberg, *The Haunted Land*, p. 135.

16. Quoted in Rosenberg, *The Haunted Land*, p. 136.

17. See the descriptions of Jaruzelski in Kaufman and Kulish, "Gen Wojciech Jaruzelski, Solidarity's Foil, Dies at 90."

18. Ryszard Kuklinski, "Jaruzelski's Attitude, Behavior, and Style," Paper Prepared for the Central Intelligence Agency, January 7, 1982, p. 49. Available from the Central Intelligence Agency at: https://www.cia.gov/library/readingroom/docs/1983-01-01.pdf.

19. Jaruzelski, 105th Landon Lecture.

20. See, for example, Jaruzelski, *Les chaines et le refuge*; Jaruzelski, *Stan wojenny dlaczego* [*Why Martial Law*] (Warsaw: BGW, 1992).

21. Rosenberg, *The Haunted Land*, p. 141.

22. Rosenberg, *The Haunted Land*, p. 142.

23. The dialogue comes from notes taken by U.S. diplomat H. Freeman Mathews at Yalta. "Notes on Meeting at Yalta Between the Big Three," 4–8 pm, Livadia Palace, Yalta, February 6, 1945. Available from the National Security Archive at: www.nsarchive.gwu.edu/coldwar/documents/episode-2/05.pdf. Emphasis added.

24. In April and May 1940, the Soviet secret police executed thousands of Polish nationals in the Katyn Forest, near the Russian city of Smolensk.

25. Quoted in Dobbs, *Down with Big Brother*, p. 307.

26. William D. Leahy, Memorandum for the Secretary of State, White House, May 11, 1945. Available from the National Security Archive at: http://nsarchive.gwu.edu/coldwar/documents/episode-2/10.pdf.

27. Leahy, Memorandum for the Secretary of State, White House, May 11, 1945.

28. Winston Churchill, "The Sinews of Peace," March 5, 1946, Westminster College, Fulton, Missouri.

29. Rosenberg, *The Haunted Land*, p. 146.

30. Quoted in Rosenberg, *The Haunted Land*, p. 141.

31. Stephen Engelberg, "Jaruzelski, Defending Record, Says His Rule Saved Poland," *New York Times*, May 20, 1992.

32. Wojciech Jaruzelski, *Jaruzelski: Prime Minister of Poland: Selected Speeches* (New York: Pergamon Press, 1985), p. xii.

33. Engelberg, "Jaruzelski, Defending Record."

34. *FRUS 1946: Eastern Europe; the Soviet Union,* Volume VI (Washington, DC: United States Government Printing Office, 1969), p. 697.

35. "Telegram from Nikolai Novikov, Soviet Ambassador to the U.S., to the Soviet Leadership," September 27, 1946. Available from the History and Public Policy Program Digital Archive, Woodrow Wilson International Center for Scholars.

36. Christopher Andrew and Vasili Mitrokhin, *The Sword and the Shield: The Mitrokhin Archive and the Secret History of the KGB* (New York: Basic Books, 1999), p. 224.

37. Katherine L. Herbig, *Changes in Espionage by Americans: 1947–2007*, Technical Report 08-05 (Washington, DC: Defense Personnel Security Research Center, U.S. Department of Defense, March 2008); Michael Warner, *The Rise and Fall of Intelligence: An International Security History* (Washington, DC: Georgetown University Press, 2014), p. 157.

38. Woodford McClellan, "Molotov Remembers," *Cold War International History Project Bulletin*, No. 1, Spring 1992, pp. 17, 19.

39. On the expansion of Soviet power see, for example, John J. Mearsheimer, *The Tragedy of Great Power Politics* (New York: W. W. Norton, 2001), pp. 199–201.

40. Earl F. Ziemke, *The U.S. Army in the Occupation of Germany 1944–1946* (Washington, DC: Center of Military History, 1975), p. 320.

41. Simon Duke, *United States Military Forces and Installations in Europe* (New York: Oxford University Press, 1989), p. 60.

42. Rosenberg, *The Haunted Land*, p. 146.

43. Kuklinski, "Jaruzelski's Attitude, Behavior, and Style," p. 54.

44. Eric Bourne, "Wojciech Jaruzelski—A General Shaped by World War II," *Christian Science Monitor*, April 11, 1984.

45. Kuklinski, "Jaruzelski's Attitude, Behavior, and Style," p. 8.

46. Rosenberg, *The Haunted Land*, p. 148.

47. Rosenberg, *The Haunted Land*, p. 145.

48. Kuklinski, "Jaruzelski's Attitude, Behavior, and Style," p. 36.

49. Kuklinski, "Jaruzelski's Attitude, Behavior, and Style," p. 37.

50. Rosenberg, *The Haunted Land*, p. 125.

51. Kuklinski, "Jaruzelski's Attitude, Behavior, and Style," p. 54.

52. Rosenberg, *The Haunted Land*, p. 156.

53. Rosenberg, *The Haunted Land*, p. 155.

54. Kuklinski, "Jaruzelski's Attitude, Behavior, and Style," p. 7.

55. Kuklinski, "Jaruzelski's Attitude, Behavior, and Style," pp. 58–60.

56. Rosenberg, *The Haunted Land*, p. 157.

57. Rosenberg, *The Haunted Land*, p. 159.

58. Jaruzelski, 105th Landon Lecture.

59. Adam Zagajewski, *Polen: Staat im Schatten der Sowjetunion* (Hamburg: Rowohlt, 1981), p. 164.

CHAPTER 3: THE SPYMASTER

1. Joseph E. Persico, *Casey: From the OSS to the CIA* (New York: Viking, 1990), p. 178.

2. Persico, *Casey*, pp. 178–179.

3. James Conaway, "Spy Master: The File on Bill Casey," *Washington Post*, September 7, 1983.

4. Conaway, "Spy Master."

5. Persico, *Casey*, p. 41.

6. Remarks of William J. Casey, Director of Central Intelligence at United States Securities and Exchange Commission Golden Anniversary, Washington Hilton, Washington, DC, June 29, 1984. Available at: https://www.cia.gov/library/readingroom/docs/DOC_0001446248.pdf.

7. Persico, *Casey*, p. 15.

8. Persico, *Casey*, p. 17. On the descriptions of Casey's childhood, including the influence of Catholicism and the Democratic Party, also see pp. 10–18.

9. Persico, *Casey*, p. 44.

10. Persico, *Casey*, p. 41.

11. William Casey, "The Hidden Struggle for Europe," Draft Manuscript, 1976, p. 11. Available in the William J. Casey Papers, Box 26, Folder 9, Hoover Institution Archives. Also see Douglas Waller, *Disciples: The World War II Missions*

of the CIA Directors Who Fought for Wild Bill Donovan (New York: Simon and Schuster, 2015), pp. 81–85.

12. Persico, *Casey*, p. 61.

13. Remarks of William J. Casey, "The Clandestine War in Europe (1942–1945)," December 5, 1974. Available in the William J. Casey Papers, Box 12, Folder 7, Hoover Institution Archives.

14. Louis Menand, "Wild Thing: Did the O.S.S. Help Win the War against Hitler?" *New Yorker*, March 14, 2011.

15. Quoted in Waller, *Disciples*, p. 85.

16. Arthur Thomas Quiller-Couch, *The Oxford Book of English Verse, 1250–1900* (Oxford: Clarendon, 1919). On Casey and the Clough poem see Persico, *Casey*, p. 62.

17. Jonathan S. Gould, "The OSS and the London 'Free Germans,'" *Studies in Intelligence*, Vol. 46, No. 1, 2002, pp. 11–29. On Casey and OSS German operations see Waller, *Disciples*, pp. 283–284, 291–311, 313–321.

18. Persico, *Casey*, p. 69.

19. Eric Pace, "William Casey, Ex-CIA Head, is Dead at 74," *New York Times*, May 7, 1987.

20. Casey, "The Hidden Struggle for Europe," p. 1.

21. Casey, "The Hidden Struggle for Europe," p. 4.

22. Casey, "The Hidden Struggle for Europe," pp. 12–13.

23. Persico, *Casey*, p. 79. Also see Casey, "The Hidden Struggle for Europe," p. 28.

24. Persico, *Casey*, p. 82.

25. National Security Act of 1947, July 26, 1947.

26. Quoted in William J. Daugherty, *Executive Secrets: Covert Action and the Presidency* (Lexington: University of Kentucky Press, 2004), p. 113. Also see George F. Kennan, "Organizing Political Warfare," April 30, 1948. Available from the History and Public Policy Program Digital Archive, Woodrow Wilson International Center for Scholars.

27. Michael Warner, *The Rise and Fall of Intelligence: An International Security History* (Washington, DC: Georgetown University Press, 2014).

28. On NSC 4-A see *FRUS 1945–1950: Emergence of the Intelligence Establishment* (Washington, DC: United States Government Printing Office, 1996), pp. 643–648; on NSC 10/2 see *FRUS 1945–1950: Emergence of the Intelligence Establishment*, pp. 713–715; on NSC 58/2 see *FRUS 1949: Eastern Europe; the*

Soviet Union, Vol. V (Washington, DC: United States Government Printing Office, 1976), pp. 42–54.

29. NSC 10/2 in *FRUS 1945-1950: Emergence of the Intelligence Establishment*, pp. 713–715.

30. William Colby and Peter Forbath, *Honorable Men: My Life in the CIA* (New York: Simon and Schuster, 1978), pp. 109, 114–120.

31. Warner, *The Rise and Fall of Intelligence*, p. 177.

32. NSC 4-A in *FRUS 1945–1950: Emergence of the Intelligence Establishment*, pp. 643–648.

33. On *Kultura* see Robert Kostrzewa, ed., *Between East and West: Writings from Kultura* (New York: Hill and Wang, 1990).

34. "Jerzy Giedroyc," *The Telegraph* (London), September 18, 2000; "Jerzy Giedroyc," *The Times* (London), September 18, 2000.

35. On the concept of "imagined community" see Benedict Anderson, *Imagined Communities: Reflections on the Origin and Spread of Nationalism* (New York: Verso, 1991).

36. Letter from Jerzy Giedroyc to Melchior Wankowicz, March 9, 1949, in Aleksandra Ziółkowska-Boehm, "Correspondence: Jerzy Giedroyc and Melchior Wankowicz," *The Sarmatian Review*, No. 3, September 1999, p. 641.

37. Letter from Giedroyc to Wankowicz, March 9, 1949, in Ziółkowska-Boehm, "Correspondence," p. 641.

38. Letter from Giedroyc to Wankowicz, July 19, 1950, in Ziółkowska-Boehm, "Correspondence," p. 644.

39. Letter from Giedroyc to Wankowicz, January 3, 1950, in Ziółkowska-Boehm, "Correspondence," p. 645.

40. Letter from Giedroyc to Wankowicz, March 8, 1950, in Ziółkowska-Boehm, "Correspondence," p. 648.

41. Letter from Giedroyc to Wankowicz, June 12, 1950, in Ziółkowska-Boehm, "Correspondence," pp. 649–650.

42. On the Office of Policy Coordination, see, for example, Warner, *The Rise and Fall of Intelligence*, pp. 141–143, 177.

43. Author interviews with multiple sources.

44. *FRUS 1945–1950: Emergence of the Intelligence Establishment*, pp. 615–745; A. Ross Johnson, *Radio Free Europe and Radio Liberty: The CIA Years and Beyond* (Stanford, CA: Stanford University Press, 2010), pp. 7–38; Michael Warner, "The CIA's Office of Policy Coordination: From NSC 10/2 to NSC 68," *Inter-*

national Journal of Intelligence and Counterintelligence, 2008, Vol. 11, No. 2, pp. 211–220; William M. Leary, ed., *The Central Intelligence Agency: History and Documents* (Tuscaloosa: University of Alabama Press, 1984); author interviews with multiple sources.

45. "Jerzy Giedroyc," *The Times* (London), September 18, 2000; author interviews with multiple sources.

46. In Fiscal Year 1977, for example, the CIA provided approximately $115,000 to *Kultura*. See *FRUS: Eastern Europe, 1977–1980*, Vol. XX (Washington, DC: United States Government Printing Office, 2015), p. 6.

47. The CIA compiled a number of press accounts of support to *Kultura*, which are available in the CIA Records Search Tool. See, for example, James Burnham, "The Case of the Mountain Climbers," *National Review*, March 10, 1970. Available at CIA-RDP80-01601R000800020001-4, CIA Records Search Tool (CREST), National Archives and Records Administration, College Park, MD. Also see Burnham, "The Case of the Mountain Climbers: II," *National Review*, March 24, 1970. Available at CIA-RDP88-01314R0001006 80013-7, CIA Records Search Tool (CREST), National Archives and Records Administration, College Park, MD.

48. Persico, *Casey*, pp. 107–108.

49. On Casey's views of the Soviet Union and Communism during World War II, see Douglas Waller, *Disciples: The World War II Missions of the CIA Directors Who Fought for Wild Bill Donovan* (New York: Simon and Schuster, 2015), p. 390; Persico, *Casey*, pp. 81–82, 91–92.

50. Persico, *Casey*, p. 123.

51. Persico, *Casey*, p. 173.

52. Persico, *Casey*, p. 174.

CHAPTER 4: COVERT ACTORS

1. *Yale Class Book 1956* (New Haven, CT: Yale University, 1956), p. 425.

2. Helen Price, "Tradition and Transition," *The Yale Herald*, October 16, 2015.

3. See, for example, Arthur S. Hulnick, *Fixing the Spy Machine: Preparing American Intelligence for the Twenty-First Century* (Westport, CT: Praeger, 2004), p. 131.

4. Richard Lee Malzahn, *Mud, Blood and Men: A Study of War Policy and Military Strategy in Britain, 1914–1918*, Draft Manuscript, p. 3. Available from the Liddell Hart Centre for Military Archives at King's College, London.

5. Malzahn, *Mud, Blood and Men*, p. 177.

6. Letter from Richard Malzahn to B. H. Liddell Hart, July 26, 1955. Available from the Liddell Hart Centre for Military Archives at King's College, London.

7. Letter from B. H. Liddell Hart to Richard Malzahn, July 16, 1959. Available from the Liddell Hart Centre for Military Archives at King's College, London.

8. *Informations-Dienst*, January 31, 1976. Available at: https://cryptome.org/dirty-work/cia-who-where.htm.

9. Benjamin Weiser, *A Secret Life: The Polish Officer, His Covert Mission, and the Price He Paid to Save His Country* (New York: PublicAffairs, 2004), p. 5.

10. Letter from Ryszard Kukliński to U.S. Embassy in Bonn, postmarked August 11, 1972. A copy of the letter is available at: www.foia.cia.gov/sites/default/files/document_conversions/47/1972-08-11.pdf.

11. The name "Walter Lang" is a pseudonym.

12. The name "Henry Morton" was his cover name.

13. Weiser, *A Secret Life*, pp. 5–13.

14. Weiser, *A Secret Life*, p. 16.

15. Central Intelligence Agency, "A Look Back ... A Cold War Hero: Colonel Ryszard Kuklinski," posted January 14, 2010. The document is available at: https://www.cia.gov/news-information/featured-story-archive/2010-featured-story-archive/colonel-ryszard-kuklinski.html.

16. Weiser, *A Secret Life*, pp. 13–14.

17. Weiser, *A Secret Life*, pp. 14–15.

18. Weiser, *A Secret Life*, p. 17

19. Weiser, *A Secret Life*, p. 19.

20. Weiser, *A Secret Life*, p. 19.

21. Thomas M. Troy, Jr., "A Secret Life," *Studies in Intelligence*, Vol. 48, No. 2, 2004. Also see Weiser, *A Secret Life*.

22. Central Intelligence Agency, "A Look Back ... A Cold War Hero."

23. Persico, *Casey*, p. 181.

CHAPTER 5: DUTCH

1. Ronald Reagan, Address Accepting the Presidential Nomination at the Republican National Convention in Detroit, July 17, 1980.

2. See the description of Reagan in Edmund Morris, *Dutch: A Memoir of Ronald Reagan* (New York: Random House, 1999), pp. 13, 174.

3. Marc Eliot, *Reagan: The Hollywood Years* (New York: Three Rivers Press, 2008), p. 48.

4. H. W. Brands, *Reagan: The Life* (New York: Doubleday, 2015), p. 41.

5. There were some reports that Reagan had been interested in Communism early in his Hollywood career, but these reports appear to be fallacious. See, for example, Morris, *Dutch*, pp. 158–159.

6. On Reagan's concerns about Communism during this period see Ronald Reagan, *An American Life: The Autobiography* (New York: Simon and Schuster, 1990), pp. 105–115.

7. Ronald Reagan, "How Do You Fight Communism?" *Fortnight*, January 22, 1951.

8. On the description of Reagan see Morris, *Dutch*, pp. 150, 174, 255.

9. Ronald Reagan, "Testimony Before the House Un-American Activities Committee," October 23, 1947.

10. On Reagan's recollections of the FBI interviews see Reagan, *An American Life*, p. 111.

11. Reagan, "How Do You Fight Communism?"

12. Anne Edwards, *Early Reagan* (New York: Taylor, 1987), p. 356.

13. Nancy Reagan, *My Turn: The Memoirs of Nancy Reagan* (New York: Random House, 1989), p. 106.

14. H. W. Brands, *Reagan: The Life* (New York: Doubleday, 2015), p. 250,

15. Central Intelligence Agency, "A Look Back . . . The National Committee for Free Europe, 1949," Published on May 29, 2007. Available from the CIA (https://www.cia.gov/news-information/featured-story-archive/2007-featured-story-archive/a-look-back.html).

16. "Wisner Update on Radio Free Europe," November 22, 1950. Available from the History and Public Policy Program Digital Archive, Woodrow Wilson International Center for Scholars.

17. "Statement of U.S. Policy Toward Eastern Europe," May 5, 1950. Available from the History and Public Policy Program Digital Archive, Woodrow Wilson International Center for Scholars.

18. Letter to Dulles from Altschul, May 20, 1955. Available from the Lehman Collection.

19. FEC Polish Guidance for 1950 and 1951. Quoted in A. Ross Johnson, *Radio Free Europe and Radio Liberty: The CIA Years and Beyond* (Stanford, CA: Stanford University Press, 2010), p. 41.

20. Quoted in Johnson, *Radio Free Europe and Radio Liberty*, p. 42.

21. Jolanta Hajdasz, *Szczekaczka czyli Rozgłośnia Polska Radia Wolna Europa* (Poznań: Media Rodzina, 2006), pp 69–72.

22. Quoted in Johnson, *Radio Free Europe and Radio Liberty*, p. 54.

23. "CIA Dissent from C. D. Jackson's Views," November 18, 1953. Available from the History and Public Policy Program Digital Archive, Woodrow Wilson International Center for Scholars.

24. Letter to C. D. Jackson from Frank Altschul, May 28, 1951. Available from the Lehman Collection.

25. "CIA-State Department Reservations about Broadcasting to the Soviet Union," September 6, 1951. Available from the History and Public Policy Program Digital Archive, Woodrow Wilson International Center for Scholars.

26. "Radio Liberty's Effectiveness Appraised," September 1, 1955; "American Committee for Liberation's Mission Redefined," July 30, 1954; "U.S. Government Policy for Radio Free Europe and Radio Liberty," July 22, 1954; "CIA Review of Radio Liberty Broadcasting," February 26, 1954. Available from the History and Public Policy Program Digital Archive, Woodrow Wilson International Center for Scholars.

27. See, for example, Neal Ascherson, "In Old Age, an Exile in Paris Has Seen His Vision Come True in the East," *Independent* (London), October 12, 1997; "Jerzy Giedroyc," *Times* (London), September 18, 2000; "Jerzy Giedroyc," *Washington Post*, September 17, 2000.

28. Markus Wolf with Anne McElvoy, *Man Without a Face: The Autobiography of Communism's Greatest Spymaster* (New York: Random House, 1997), p. 235.

29. "Polish Ministry of State Security Action Memoranda, to Regional Branches Outlining Steps to be Taken to Limit Spillover of Events in East Germany," June 19, 1953. Available from the History and Public Policy Program Digital Archive, Woodrow Wilson International Center for Scholars.

30. Arch Puddington, *Broadcasting Freedom: The Cold War Triumph of Radio Free Europe and Radio Liberty* (Lexington: University of Kentucky Press, 2000), pp. 33–35.

31. Norman Davies, *God's Playground: A History of Poland*, vol. II, Revised Edition (New York: Columbia University Press, 2005), p. 583.

32. Dana Milbank, "The New Party of Reagan," *Washington Post*, July 19, 2011.

33. Democratic Party (California), State Central Committee, *Ronald Reagan, Extremist Collaborator: An Exposé* (San Francisco: The Committee 1966).

34. David Mark, *Going Dirty: The Art of Negative Campaigning* (New York: Rowman and Littlefield, 2009), p. 55.

35. Morris, *Dutch*, p. 357.

36. Edmund G. Brown and Bill Brown, *Reagan the Political Chameleon* (New York: Praeger, 1976), p. 67.

37. James Q. Wilson, "A Guide to Reagan Country: The Political Culture of Southern California," *Commentary*, May 1, 1967.

38. Morris, *Dutch*, p. 347.

39. Ronald Reagan, "A Time for Choosing," October 27, 1964. The video and transcript of the speech are available on C-SPAN at: https://www.c-span.org/video/?153897-1/ronald-reagans-time-choosing-speech.

40. Reagan radio commentary, April 1975, in Kiron K. Skinner, Annelise Anderson, Martin Anderson, eds., *Reagan, in His Own Hand: The Writings of Ronald Reagan that Reveal His Revolutionary Vision for America* (New York: Touchstone, 2001), pp. 48–49.

41. Reagan radio commentary, June 29, 1979, in Skinner, et al., *Reagan, in His Own Hand*, p. 175.

42. Author interview with Zbigniew Brzezinski, October 2016.

43. Zbigniew Brzezinski, *Power and Principle: Memoirs of the National Security Adviser, 1977–1981* (New York: Farrar, Straus and Giroux, 1983), p. 300.

44. Author interview with Zbigniew Brzezinski, October 2016.

45. Michael Warner, *The Rise and Fall of Intelligence: An International Security History* (Washington, DC: Georgetown University Press, 2014), p. 234.

46. On the book program see Alfred A. Reisch, *Hot Books in the Cold War: The CIA-Funded Secret Western Book Distribution Program Behind the Iron Curtain* (Budapest: Central European University Press, 2013); Yale Richmond, *Cultural Exchange and the Cold War: Raising the Iron Curtain* (University Park: Pennsylvania State University Press, 2003), chapter 13; Walter L. Hixon, *Parting the Curtain: Propaganda, Culture, and the Cold War, 1945–1961* (New York: St. Martin's Press, 1997); Hugh Wilford, *The Mighty Wurlitzer, How the CIA Played America* (Cambridge, MA: Harvard University Press, 2009).

47. Reisch, *Hot Books in the Cold War*, p. 248.

48. In 1972, the CIA had *covertly* stopped funding Radio Free Europe and Radio Liberty, which were financed *overtly* by the U.S. government. Central Intelligence Agency, "CIA Ends All Involvement with Radio Free Europe and

Radio Liberty," September 19, 1972. Available from the History and Public Policy Program Digital Archive, Woodrow Wilson International Center for Scholars.

49. See, for example, "Gosteleradio Memo to CPSU Central Committee, 'Ideological Subversion on the Airwaves of Foreign Radio Stations Broadcasting in the Russian Language,'" April 14, 1967; "Polish Foreign Intelligence Report on Radio Free Europe," January 26, 1967; "Letter from Main Political Administration of the Polish Army to the Interior Minister on 'Hostile Radio Propaganda,'" February 5, 1966. Available from the History and Public Policy Program Digital Archive, Woodrow Wilson International Center for Scholars.

50. "Gosteleradio Review of Western Radio Propaganda, 'Anti-Communism Is the Main Weapon of Imperialist Radio Propaganda in the Russian Language,'" November 26, 1966. Available from the History and Public Policy Program Digital Archive, Woodrow Wilson International Center for Scholars.

51. See, for example, "KGB Report to Central Committee on Radio Liberty Policy Guidelines," December 16, 1968. Available from the History and Public Policy Program Digital Archive, Woodrow Wilson International Center for Scholars.

52. Quoted in Nigel West, *The Third Secret: The CIA, Solidarity and the KGB's Plot to Kill the Pope* (London: HarperCollins, 2000), p. 191.

53. "Polish Interior Ministry Note on Joint Meeting with PUWP CC on actions against 'Centers of Subversion,'" February 18, 1972. Available from the History and Public Policy Program Digital Archive, Woodrow Wilson International Center for Scholars.

54. Before John Paul II, the last non-Italian pope was Adrian VI, a Dutchman, who served from 1522 to 1523.

55. Timothy Garton Ash, *The Polish Revolution: Solidarity*, Third Edition (New Haven, CT: Yale University Press, 2002), p. 19.

CHAPTER 6: THE GDAŃSK AGREEMENT

1. See, for example, Nicholas G. Andrews, *Poland, 1980–81: Solidarity vs. the Party* (Washington, DC: National Defense University Press, 1985); Neal Ascherson, *The Polish August* (New York: Penguin, 1982).

2. "Poland," *National Intelligence Daily*, July 21, 1980. Available from the National Security Archive.

3. "Report by the Chairman of the Delegation from the Ministry of Internal Affairs of the People's Republic of Poland, Comrade Boguslav Staruha during Soviet Bloc Meeting on Western Radio," April 24, 1980. Available from the History and Public Policy Program Digital Archive, Woodrow Wilson International Center for Scholars.

4. Report by the Chairman of the Delegation from the Ministry of Internal Affairs of the People's Republic of Poland.

5. "Report by the Chairman of the Delegation of the Committee for State Security (KGB) of the USSR, General Colonel V. M. Chebrikov during Soviet Bloc Meeting on Western Radio," April 23, 1980. Available from the History and Public Policy Program Digital Archive, Woodrow Wilson International Center for Scholars.

6. Lech Wałęsa, *A Way of Hope* (New York: Henry Holt and Company, 1987), p. 116.

7. Matt Schudel, "Anna Walentynowicz of Poland's Solidarity Movement Dies at 80," *Washington Post*, April 14, 2010.

8. Wałęsa, *A Way of Hope*, p. 118.

9. Oliver MacDonald, ed., *The Polish August: Documents from the Beginnings of the Polish Workers' Rebellion* (San Francisco: Ztangi Press, 1981), p. 90.

10. Timothy Garton Ash, *The Polish Revolution: Solidarity*, Third Edition (New Haven, CT: Yale University Press, 2002), pp. 42.

11. Ash, *The Polish Revolution*, pp. 42–43; MacDonald, *The Polish August*, pp. 90–91.

12. Ash, *The Polish Revolution,* p. 43.

13. Ash, *The Polish Revolution*, pp. 42–43.

14. Wałęsa, *A Way of Hope*, pp. 121–122.

15. Ash, *The Polish Revolution*, p. 45–46.

16. Ash, *The Polish Revolution*, pp. 45–46.

17. I reviewed a life-size copy of the boards on display at the European Solidarity Centre in Gdańsk. The most important was Demand Number 1, in which strikers insisted that the authorities accept that the trade unions be independent.

18. MacDonald, *The Polish August,* p. 81.

19. Ash, *The Polish Revolution*, p. 48–52.

20. Lech Wałęsa, *Droga Nodziei* (Kraków, 2006), pp. 192–193. Translation courtesy of the European Solidarity Centre in Gdańsk.

21. Maciej Sandecki, "Mieczysław Jagielski: Musimy Wyrazić Zgodę," *Gazeta
Wyborcza*, 18 August 2005, p. 8. Translation courtesy of the European Solidarity Centre in Gdańsk.

22. Ash, *The Polish Revolution*, p. 68.

23. Ash, *The Polish Revolution*, p. 71.

24. Ash, *The Polish Revolution*, p. 71.

25. The Gdańsk Agreement, August 31, 1980. The text was published in Andrzej
Paczkowski and Malcolm Byrne, eds., *From Solidarity to Martial Law: The Polish Crisis of 1980–1981* (New York: Central European University Press, 2007),
pp. 70–80.

26. The monument was funded by public donations collected by the Social Committee for Constructing the Monument.

27. Tanya Talaga, "Gdansk Shipyard Sinking from Freedom to Failure," *The Star*,
January 27, 2014.

CHAPTER 7: POLISH ABYSS

1. Ronald Reagan, *An American Life: The Autobiography* (New York: Simon and
Schuster, 1990), p. 216.

2. See Jimmy Carter, The President's News Conference, December 30, 1977.
Transcript available at: http://www.presidency.ucsb.edu/ws/?pid=7075.

3. "Statement by the Honorable Ronald Reagan, Republican Candidate for
President of the United States Regarding Poland," Reagan Bush Committee,
August 22, 1980. Available in the Paula Dobriansky files, "Poland: Crisis
Management [1981–1982]," RAC Box 3, Ronald Reagan Presidential Library.

4. Memorandum for the Record, November 21, 1980, CIA Historical Collection
on Ronald Reagan.

5. "Poland: Crisis at Another Peak," *National Intelligence Daily*, October 31,
1980. Available from the National Security Archive.

6. "Polish Trends and Soviet Perceptions and Reactions," *National Intelligence
Daily*, September 20, 1980. Available from the National Security Archive.

7. "CPSU CC Politburo Decision Setting Up Suslov Commission," August 25,
1980. Released in *Cold War International History Project Bulletin*, No. 5, Spring
1995, pp. 116–117, 129–130.

8. The test of this Soviet Ministry of Defense mobilization request is presented in Mark Kramer, "In Case Military Assistance is Provided to Poland," *Cold War International History Project Bulletin*, No. 11, Winter 1998, pp. 102–109.

9. CPSU CC Politburo Commission Order to Enhance Readiness of Military Units for Possible Use in Poland, August 28, 1980. Available in Andrzej Paczkowski and Malcolm Byrne, eds., *From Solidarity to Martial Law: The Polish Crisis of 1980–1981* (New York: Central European University Press, 2007), pp. 64–65.

10. Communist Party of the Soviet Union Central Committee, "Extract from Protocol No. 213 of the Session of the CPSU CC Politburo on 3 September 1980." Available in Mark Kramer, "Soviet Deliberations During the Polish Crisis, 1980–81," Cold War International History Project Working Paper Series, Special Working Paper No. 1, pp. 35–43.

11. See, for example, Central Intelligence Agency, "Planning, Preparation, Operation and Evaluation of Warsaw Pact Exercises," Intelligence Information Report, 1981. Available from the Central Intelligence Agency at: https://www.cia.gov/library/readingroom/docs/1981-01-01.pdf.

12. "Challenge to Polish Leadership Increases," *National Intelligence Daily*, November 25, 1980. Available from the National Security Archive.

13. "Poland," Alert Memorandum, decl. December 3, 1980. DCI Turner's cover note is described in Robert M. Gates, *From the Shadows: The Ultimate Insider's Story of Five Presidents and How They Won the Cold War* (New York: Simon and Schuster, 1996), p. 166. Also see Central Intelligence Agency, "Approaching the Brink: Moscow and the Polish Crisis, November-December 1980," Intelligence Memorandum, January 1981, p. 3. Available in Executive Secretariat, NSC, "Netherlands-Poland," Box 16, Ronald Reagan Presidential Library.

14. Francis J. Meehan, "Reflections on the Polish Crisis," *Cold War International History Project Bulletin*, No. 11, Winter 1998, p. 44.

15. Lech Wałęsa, "From Romanticism to Realism: Our Struggle in the Years 1980–1982," in Andrzej Paczkowski and Malcolm Byrne, eds., *From Solidarity to Martial Law: The Polish Crisis of 1980–1981* (New York: Central European University Press, 2007), p. xvi.

16. Central Intelligence Agency, "Subject: Internal Situation within the Polish Party," February 25, 1981. Available in the Paula Dobriansky files, National Security Council Series I: Country Files, RAC Box 3, Ronald Reagan Presidential Library. Emphasis added.

17. Memorandum from Jerry Bremer to NSC Ms. Janet Colson, et al., Subject: Interagency Group on Poland, January 23, 1981. Available in Executive Secretariat, NSC, "Poland to Romania," Box 18, Ronald Reagan Presidential Library.

18. Central Intelligence Agency, "Approaching the Brink," p. 5.

19. Gates, *From the Shadows*, p. 232.

20. National Security Council Meeting Minutes, February 6, 1981. Available in Executive Secretariat, NSC, NSC 00001, Box 1, Ronald Reagan Presidential Library.

21. Memorandum from Dennis Blair to General Robert Schweitzer, "Subject: Military Responses to Soviet Intervention in Poland," March 31, 1981. Available in Paula Dobriansky files, National Security Council Series I: Country Files, RAC Box 3, Ronald Reagan Presidential Library. Also see Memorandum from Paula Dobriansky to Richard V. Allen, "Subject: Interagency Group Meeting on Poland–Military Measures," March 27, 1981. Available in Paula Dobriansky files, National Security Council Series I: Country Files, RAC Box 3, Ronald Reagan Presidential Library.

22. "Possible Unilateral or Additional Steps," National Security Council, February 15, 1981. Available in the Richard Pipes files, "CHRON 02/06/1981-02/18/1981," Box 9, Ronald Reagan Presidential Library.

23. Memorandum from William L. Stearman to Richard V. Allen, "Subject: Reflections on Unilateral Measures," April 3, 1981. Available in Paula Dobriansky files, National Security Council Series I: Country Files, RAC Box 3, Ronald Reagan Presidential Library.

24. John Lewis Gaddis, *Strategies of Containment: A Critical Appraisal of Postwar American National Security Policy* (New York: Oxford University Press, 1982), p. 86.

25. Memorandum from Richard V. Allen to the President, Subject: Status of Preparations / Contingency Planning on Poland, February 19, 2001. Available in the Richard Pipes files, "CHRON 02/19/1981-02/24/1981," Box 9, Ronald Reagan Presidential Library.

26. Author interview with Ed Meese, September 2016.

27. Central Intelligence Agency, "Poland's Prospects Over the Next Six Months," Special National Intelligence Estimate, January 30, 1981, p. 1. Available in Executive Secretariat, NSC, "Netherlands-Poland," Box 16, Ronald Reagan Presidential Library.

28. Wałęsa, "From Romanticism to Realism."

29. Central Intelligence Agency, "Poland's Prospects Over the Next Six Months," p. 8.

30. Ash, *The Polish Revolution*, p. 153.

31. Defense Intelligence Agency, "Intelligence Appraisal Poland: Martial Law and Operational Forces," March 30, 1981. Available in Executive Secretariat, NSC, Poland to Romania, Box 18, Ronald Reagan Presidential Library.

32. Ash, *The Polish Revolution*, p. 155.

33. Memorandum from Richard Pipes to Richard V. Allen, Subject: Weekly Report, March 6, 1981. Available in the Richard Pipes files, "CHRON 03/01/1981-03/10/1981," Box 9, Ronald Reagan Presidential Library.

34. Ash, *The Polish Revolution*, pp. 154–155.

35. Central Intelligence Agency, "Possible Polish Strategy During the Present Phase: Late December 1981," December 24, 1981. Available from the Central Intelligence Agency at: https://www.cia.gov/library/readingroom/docs/1981-12-24a.pdf.

36. For an overview of some of these documents see, for example, Kramer, "Soviet Deliberations During the Polish Crisis, 1980–81"; Kramer, "The Kuklinski Files and the Polish Crisis of 1980–1981: An Analysis of the Newly Released CIA Documents on Ryszard Kuklinski," Working Paper No. 59, March 2009.

37. CIA Memorandum from Max Hugel for the Secretary of State, et al., "Polish Military and Security Reactions to the Current Political Situation in Poland," June 15, 1981. Available at: https://www.wilsoncenter.org/sites/default/files/19811224a.pdf.

38. Ash, *The Polish Revolution*, p. 150.

39. Ryszard Kuklinski, "Jaruzelski's Attitude, Behavior, and Style," Paper Prepared for the Central Intelligence Agency, January 7, 1982. Available from the Central Intelligence Agency at: https://www.cia.gov/library/readingroom/docs/1983-01-01.pdf.

40. See, for example, CIA Memorandum from John Stein to the Secretary of State, et al., "Polish General Staff Evaluation of Soviet Military Presence and Activities in Poland," FIRDB-312/02264-81, July 17, 1981. Available from the Central Intelligence Agency at: https://www.cia.gov/library/readingroom/docs/1981-07-17b.pdf.

41. Ryszard Kukliński, "Jaruzelski's Attitude, Behavior, and Style."

42. Ryszard Kukliński, "The Suppression of Solidarity," in Robert Kostrzewa, ed., *Between East and West: Writings from Kultura* (New York: Hill and Wang, 1990), pp. 87–88.

43. Defense Intelligence Agency, "Intelligence Appraisal Poland."

44. Ronald Reagan, *The Reagan Diaries, Vol. I, January 1981–October 1985*, ed. Douglas Brinkley (New York: HarperCollins, 2009), p. 43.

CHAPTER 8: THE CASE FOR COVERT ACTION

1. Ronald Reagan, "Address at Commencement Exercises at the University of Notre Dame," May 17, 1981.

2. H. W. Brands, *Reagan: The Life* (New York: Doubleday, 2015), p. 250; Robert M. Gates, *From the Shadows: The Ultimate Inside Story of Five Presidents and How They Won the Cold War* (New York: Simon and Schuster, 1996), pp. 199–200, 215–216.

3. Ronald Reagan, *The Reagan Diaries, Vol. I, January 1981–October 1985*, ed. Douglas brinkley (New York: HarperCollins, 2009), p. 24.

4. Memorandum from Richard Pipes to James W. Nance, Subject: Crisis Management of Poland, March 24, 1981. Available in the Richard Pipes files, "CHRON 03/24/1981-03/25/1981," Box 9, Ronald Reagan Presidential Library.

5. Memorandum from Richard Pipes to James W. Nance, March 27, 1981. Available in the Richard Pipes files, "CHRON 03/26/1981-03/30/1981," Box 9, Ronald Reagan Presidential Library.

6. Memorandum from Richard Pipes to James W. Nance, March 27, 1981.

7. Memorandum from Richard Pipes to Richard V. Allen, Subject: Unilateral Measures, April 3, 1981. Available in the Richard Pipes files, "CHRON 04/03/1981-04/05/1981," Box 9, Ronald Reagan Presidential Library. Pipes also encouraged "upgrading" covert action in such countries as Afghanistan, Cuba, Ethiopia, and the Soviet Union in other internal memorandums. See Memorandum from Richard Pipes to Richard V. Allen, Subject: Status of Preparations / Contingency Planning on Poland, February 19, 1981. Available in the Richard Pipes files, "CHRON 02/19/1981-02/24/1981," Box 9, Ronald Reagan Presidential Library.

8. Fletcher Schoen and Christopher Lamb, *Deception, Disinformation, and Strategic Communications: How One Interagency Group Made a Major Difference,*

Strategic Perspectives 11 (Washington, DC: Institute for National Strategic Studies, National Defense University, June 2012), p. 8.

9. Letter from William J. Casey to unknown, Central Intelligence Agency, September 23, 1985. Available at CIA-RDP88B00443R001804350023-9, CIA Records Search Tool (CREST), National Archives and Records Administration, College Park, MD.

10. Fletcher Schoen and Christopher Lamb, *Deception, Disinformation, and Strategic Communications: How One Interagency Group Made a Major Difference*, Strategic Perspectives 11 (Washington, DC: Institute for National Strategic Studies, National Defense University, June 2012), p. 8.

11. See Memorandum from CIA Director of Security to Deputy Director of Central Intelligence, Subject: Newsweek Article entitled 'The Soviets' Dirty-Tricks Squad' of 23 November 1981. Available at CIA-RDP84B00890 R000700020048-9, CIA Records Search Tool (CREST), National Archives and Records Administration, College Park, MD. The memo notes that "Malzahn and three other CIA officers were issued fictional names by the HPSCI staff for inclusion in the official record."

12. "Soviet Covert Action (The Forgery Offensive)," Hearings before the Subcommittee on Oversight of the Permanent Select Committee on Intelligence, House of Representatives, February 6, 19, 1980 (Washington: U.S. Government Printing Office, 1980), p. 30. Emphasis added.

13. "Soviet Covert Action (The Forgery Offensive)."

14. See the "Interagency Intelligence Study: Soviet Active Measures" in Hearings before the Permanent Selection Committee on Intelligence, House of Representatives, July 13, 14, 1982 (Washington: U.S. Government Printing Office, 1982), p. 31.

15. Schoen and Lamb, *Deception, Disinformation, and Strategic Communications*, p. 8.

16. Bob Woodward, *Veil: The Secret Wars of the CIA, 1981–1987* (New York: Pocket Books, 1988), p. 163.

17. Gates, *From the Shadows*, pp. 202–208.

18. Douglas F. Garthoff, "Chapter III: Analyzing Soviet Politics and Foreign Policy," in Gerald K. Haines and Robert E. Legget, eds., *Watching the Bear: Essays on CIA's Analysis of the Soviet Union* (Washington: Central Intelligence Agency, 2003).

19. Gates, *From the Shadows*, pp. 203–206.

20. Reagan, *The Reagan Diaries, Vol. I*, p. 56.

21. "Poland: Protests Over Food Shortages," *National Intelligence Daily*, July 25, 1981. Available from the National Security Archive.

22. National Security Council Meeting Minutes, Subject: Further Economic Aid to Poland, September 15, 1981. Available in Executive Secretariat, NSC, [Further Economic Aid to Poland, Foreign Assistance], Box 91282, Ronald Reagan Presidential Library.

23. Central Intelligence Agency, "Implications of a Soviet Invasion of Poland," PA 81-10297, SR 81-10090, ER 81-10274, July 24, 1981. Available from the Central Intelligence Agency at: https://www.cia.gov/library/readingroom/docs/DOC_0000324317.pdf.

24. Joseph E. Persico, *Casey: From the OSS to the CIA* (New York: Viking, 1990), p. 228.

25. Persico, *Casey*, p. 218.

26. See Timothy Garton Ash, *The Polish Revolution: Solidarity*, Third Edition (New Haven, CT: Yale University Press, 2002), p. 112.

27. Solidarity, "Message to the Working People of Eastern Europe," Warsaw Radio, September 9, 1981.

28. Session of the CPSU CC Politburo, September 10, 1981. Available in Mark Kramer, "Soviet Deliberations During the Polish Crisis, 1980–81," Cold War International History Project Working Paper Series, Special Worker Paper No. 1, p. 137.

29. Ryzard Kukliński provided several key documents, including Document No. 3, Warsaw, September 15, 1981. Available in *Cold War International History Project Bulletin*, No. 11, Winter 1998, p. 55.

30. See, for example, Kramer, "Soviet Deliberations During the Polish Crisis, 1980–81."

31. Session of the CPSU CC Politburo, October 29, 1981. Available in Kramer, "Soviet Deliberations During the Polish Crisis," p. 152.

32. See, for example, Mark Kramer, "Jaruzelski, the Soviet Union, and the Imposition of Martial Law in Poland: New Light on the Mystery of December 1981," *Cold War International History Project Bulletin*, No. 11, Winter 1998, pp. 5–14.

33. See, for example, "Poland: Confronting Solidarity," *National Intelligence Daily*, September 17, 1981; and "Poland: Union Under Pressure," *National Intelligence Daily*, September 18, 1981. Available from the National Security Archive.

34. "Polish Police Battle 5,000 Protesting Arrests," *New York Times*, October 21, 1981.

35. Benjamin Weiser, *A Secret Life: The Polish Officer, His Covert Mission, and the Price He Paid to Save His Country* (New York: PublicAffairs, 2004), p. 270.

36. See Weiser, *A Secret Life*, pp. 266–291.

37. Thomas M. Troy, Jr., "A Secret Life," *Studies in Intelligence*, Vol. 48, No. 2, 2004.

38. Session of the CPSU CC Politburo, October 29, 1981. Available in Kramer, "Soviet Deliberations During the Polish Crisis," pp. 148–156.

39. "Poland: Regime's Media Campaign," *National Intelligence Daily*, December 9, 1981. Available from the National Security Archive.

40. Anoshkin, "The Anoshkin Notebook on the Polish Crisis, December 1981," pp. 25, 29.

41. Anoshkin, "The Anoshkin Notebook on the Polish Crisis," p. 28. Emphasis added.

42. "Session of the CPSU CC Politburo," October 29, 1981. Available from the History and Public Policy Program Digital Archive, Woodrow Wilson International Center for Scholars.

43. Anoshkin, "The Anoshkin Notebook on the Polish Crisis, December 1981," p. 19.

44. Ryszard Kukliński, "Jaruzelski's Attitude, Behavior, and Style," Paper Prepared for the Central Intelligence Agency, January 7, 1982. Available from the Central Intelligence Agency at: https://www.cia.gov/library/readingroom/docs/1983-01-01.pdf.

45. Wojciech Jaruzelski, 105th Landon Lecture, Kansas State University, March 11, 1996.

46. Anoshkin, "The Anoshkin Notebook on the Polish Crisis, December 1981," p. 22.

47. Session of the CPSU CC Politburo, December 10, 1981, in Kramer, "Soviet Deliberations During the Polish Crisis, 1980–1981," pp. 160–161.

48. Quoted in Kramer, "Jaruzelski, the Soviet Union, and the Imposition of Martial Law in Poland: New Light on the Mystery of December 1981," p. 10.

49. See, for example, "Telegram to Directors of Voivode Police," circa December 12, 1981. Available in Andrzej Paczkowski and Malcolm Byrne, eds., *From Solidarity to Martial Law: The Polish Crisis of 1980–1981* (New York: Central European University Press, 2007), p. 459.

50. Gregory F. Domber, *Empowering Revolution: America, Poland, and the End of the Cold War* (Chapel Hill: University of North Carolina Press, 2014), p. 41.

51. Wojciech Jaruzelski, "Commentary," *Cold War International History Project Bulletin*, No. 11, Winter 1998, p. 33.

52. Chris Niederthal, *Zawód: Fotograf* (Warsaw: Wydawnictwo Marginesy, 2011).

53. Central Intelligence Agency, "Soviet Goals and Expectations in the Global Power Arena," National Intelligence Estimate, NIE 11-4-78, July 7, 1981. Available from the National Security Archive.

54. Romuald Spasowski, *Liberation of One* (San Diego: Harcourt Brace Jovanovich, 1986).

55. Ronald Reagan, Address to the Nation About Christmas and the Situation in Poland, December 23, 1981.

56. Reagan, Address to the Nation About Christmas.

CHAPTER 9: THE BIRTH OF QRHELPFUL

1. I had an opportunity to tour the Roosevelt Room at the White House on May 9, 2015. For a description of the room see, for example, Charles Colson with Harold Ficket, *The Good Life: Seeking Purpose, Meaning, and Truth in Your Life* (Carol Stream, IL: Tyndale Publishers, 2005), pp. 12–13.

2. National Security Council Meeting Minutes, December 21, 1981. Available in Executive Secretariat, NSC, NSC 00033, Box 91283, Ronald Reagan Presidential Library.

3. National Security Council Meeting Minutes, December 21, 1981.

4. For NSC discussions on a Soviet invasion see National Security Council Meeting Minutes, Subject: Further Economic Aid to Poland, September 15, 1981. Available in Executive Secretariat, NSC, [Further Economic Aid to Poland, Foreign Assistance], Box 91282, Ronald Reagan Presidential Library. Also see Central Intelligence Agency, "Implications of a Soviet Invasion of Poland," PA 81-10297, SR 81-10090, ER 81-10274, July 24, 1981. Available from the Central Intelligence Agency at: https://www.cia.gov/library/reading room/docs/DOC_0000324317.pdf.

5. Robert M. Gates, *From the Shadows: The Ultimate Inside Story of Five Presidents and How They Won the Cold War* (New York: Simon and Schuster: 1996), pp. 194–195.

6. Gates, *From the Shadows*, p. 237.

7. Gates, *From the Shadows*, p. 233.

8. See, for example, James S. Van Wagenen, "A Review of Congressional Oversight: Critics and Defenders," Central Intelligence Agency. Available at: https://www.cia.gov/library/center-for-the-study-of-intelligence/csi-publications/csi-studies/studies/97unclass/wagenen.html. Also see Joseph E. Persico, *Casey: From the OSS to the CIA* (New York: Viking, 1990), p. 230.

9. In 1980, Congress repealed the Hughes-Ryan Amendment and replaced it with a statutory requirement that the executive branch report to two legislative committees: the Senate Select Committee on Intelligence, which was established in 1976; and the House Permanent Select Committee on Intelligence, which was established in 1977. Marshall Curtis Erwin, *Covert Action: Legislative Background and Possible Policy Questions* (Washington: Congressional Research Service, April 10, 2013), p. 1.

10. On the Afghanistan finding see, for example, William J. Daugherty, *Executive Secrets: Covert Action and the Presidency* (Lexington: University Press of Kentucky, 2004), p. 189.

11. Author interview with Richard Pipes, August 2016.

12. Author interview with Ed Meese, September 2016.

13. Memorandum from Alexander M. Haig to the President, Subject: Influencing European Attitudes on Poland, December 26, 1981. Available in the Richard Pipes files, Miscellaneous Papers, Box 3, Ronald Reagan Presidential Library.

14. Notes of Polish Ministry of Internal Affairs and Ministry of Defense Meeting on Implementation of Martial Law, January 15, 1982. See Andrzej Paczkowski and Malcolm Byrne, eds., *From Solidarity to Martial Law: The Polish Crisis of 1980–1981* (New York: Central European University Press, 2007), pp. 515–516.

15. State Department Cable, Subject: Polish Situation, January 18, 1982. Available in the Paula Dobriansky files, Poland: Church, RAC Box 3, Ronald Reagan Presidential Library.

16. Letter from the Pope to Ronald Reagan, January 4, 1982. Available in the David Gergen files, Box OA 9422, Ronald Reagan Presidential Library.

17. Manfred Schell and Werner Kalinka, *STASI and Kein Ende: Personen und Fakten* (Frankfurt and Berlin: Ullstein, 1991), p. 270.

18. Benjamin B. Fischer, "Solidarity, the CIA, and Western Technology," *International Journal of Intelligence and Counterintelligence*, 25, no. 3 (2012), p. 448.

19. Christian von Ditfurth, Gunter Bohnsack, and Herbert Brehmer, *Auftrag: Irreführung: Wie die Stasi Politik im Westen Machte* (Hamburg: Carlsen Verlag GmbH, 1993), pp. 122–125.

20. Vladimir Solovyov and Elena Klepikova, *Behind the High Kremlin Walls* (New York: Dodd, Mead & Company, Inc., 1986), pp. 94–95.

21. Markus Wolf, *Spionagechef im Geheimen Krieg: Erinnerungen* (Munich: List Verlag GmbH, 1997), p. 315.

22. Memorandum from William P. Clark to the President, Subject: Poland: One Month Under Martial Law, January 14, 1982. Available in the Richard Pipes files, "CHRON 01/08/1982-01/25/1982," Box 12, Ronald Reagan Presidential Library.

23. U.S. Department of State, "Strategy on Poland: Possible Next Steps against U.S.S.R," February 1982. Available in Executive Secretariat, NSC, NSC 00039 04 Feb 1982, Box 91083, Ronald Reagan Presidential Library.

24. Memorandum from Richard Pipes to William P. Clark, Subject: Situation in Poland, March 25, 1982. Available in the Richard Pipes files, "CHRON 03/25/1982-03/31/1982," Box 13, Ronald Reagan Presidential Library.

25. Memorandum from Richard Pipes to William P. Clark, Subject: Situation in Poland.

26. U.S. Policy Toward Eastern Europe, approximately March 1982. Available in the Richard Pipes files, "CHRON 03/01/1982-03/02/1982," Box 13, Ronald Reagan Presidential Library.

27. Memorandum from Richard Pipes to William P. Clark, Subject: Statement of U.S. Strategy Toward Soviet Union, March 5, 1982. Available in the Richard Pipes files, Box 5, Ronald Reagan Presidential Library.

28. Edmund Morris, *Dutch: A Memoir of Ronald Reagan* (New York: Random House, 1999), pp. 455, 458.

29. Morris, *Dutch*, p. 456. On the description of Clark, see pages 455–456.

30. U.S. National Security Strategy, National Security Decision Directive Number 32, May 20, 1982. Available at: http://www.reagan.utexas.edu/archives/reference/Scanned%20NSDDS/NSDD32.pdf.

31. Daugherty, *Executive Secrets*, p. 197.

32. On early discussion see, for example, Memorandum from William P. Clark to the President, Subject: Draft of NSDD on "United States Policy Toward Eastern Europe," NSC Meeting 11:15 A.M. July 21, 1982, July 20, 1982. Available in Executive Secretariat, NSC, NSC 00056, Box 91285, Ronald Reagan Presidential Library.

33. U.S. National Security Strategy, National Security Decision Directive Number 54, September 2, 1982. Available at: http://www.reagan.utexas.edu/archives/reference/Scanned%20NSDDS/NSDD54.pdf.

34. Ronald Reagan, Address to Members of the British Parliament, June 8, 1982. Available at: http://home.reaganfoundation.org/site/DocServer/Westminster_Speech_Essay_June_2012.pdf?docID=853.

35. Morris, *Dutch*, p. 461.

36. Richard Pipes, *Vixi: Memoirs of a Non-Belonger* (New Haven, CT: Yale University Press, 2003), p. 155. On other critiques of Germany and the Polish crisis, see p. 174.

37. "Minutes of 22 December NSC Meeting," December 22, 1981. Available in the Richard Pipes files, Box 3, Ronald Reagan Presidential Library.

38. The President's Concluding Remarks at the National Security Council Meeting, Friday, June 18, 1982. Available in the Richard Pipes files, Box 3, Ronald Reagan Presidential Library.

39. Roger Boyes, *The Naked President: Political Life of Lech Wałęsa* (London: Martin Secker & Warburg, 1994), pp. 106–107; Lech Wałęsa, *A Way of Hope* (New York: Henry Holt and Company, 1987), p. 215.

40. On the SB and other Polish security services, see Antoni Dudek and Andrzej Paczkowski, "Poland," in Krzysztof Persak and Lukasz Kaminski, eds., *A Handbook of the Communist Security Apparatus in East Central Europe, 1944–1989* (Warsaw: Institute of National Remembrance, 2005), pp. 221–283.

41. Piotr Gontarczyk and Sławomir Cenckiewicz, *SB a Lech Wałęsa: Przyczynek do biografii* (Warsaw: Instytut Pamięci Narodowej, 2008).

42. "Information on the Experts' Opinion on the Secret Collaborator Bolek's Files," Institute of National Remembrance, February 1, 2017; Gontarczyk and Cenckiewicz, *SB a Lech Wałęsa*; Christopher Andrew and Vasili Mitrokhin, *The Sword and the Shield: The Mitrokhin Archive and the Secret History of the KGB* (New York: Basic Books, 1999), p. 535; Boyes, *The Naked President*, pp. 307–309.

43. Mitrokhin Archives, k-20, 249. Available in the Churchill Archives at Churchill College, Cambridge, UK. For the translation see Andrew and Mitrokhin, *The Sword and the Shield*, p. 535.

44. Mitrokhin Archives, k-19, 261. Available in the Churchill Archives at Churchill College, Cambridge, UK.

45. Mitrokhin Archives, k-19, 411. Available in the Churchill Archives at Churchill College, Cambridge, UK. For the translation see Andrew and Mitrokhin, *The Sword and the Shield*, p. 535.

46. Memorandum from Richard Pipes to William P. Clark, Subject: Soviet and East European Update, April 9, 1982. Available in the Richard Pipes files,

"CHRON 04/08/1982-04/13/1982," Box 13, Ronald Reagan Presidential Library.

47. Memorandum from Richard Pipes to Bobby Inman, Subject: Events in Poland, April 27, 1982. Available in the Richard Pipes files, "CHRON 04/20/1982-04/28/1982," Box 13, Ronald Reagan Presidential Library.

48. Radio Free Europe-Radio Liberty, "Unbroken Support for Solidarity By the Polish Population: Internal Validation of RFE Poll Results," July 1982. Available in the Paula Dobriansky files, "Poland—Cables 1981–1983," RAC Box 3, Ronald Reagan Presidential Library.

49. On presidential findings see L. Britt Snider, *The Agency and the Hill: CIA's Relationship with Congress, 1946–2004* (Washington, DC: Center for the Study of Intelligence, Central Intelligence Agency, 2008), p. 274.

50. Author interviews with multiple sources.

51. Memorandum from William P. Clark to the President, Subject: Terms of Reference for NSSD on "U.S. Policy Toward the Soviet Union," August 1982. Available in the Richard Pipes files, "CHRON 08/05/1982-08/16/1982," Box 15, Ronald Reagan Presidential Library.

52. Fischer, "Solidarity, the CIA, and Western Technology," p. 434.

53. On the discussions in September see Gates, *From the Shadows*, p. 238.

54. On surrogates see, for example, Thomas L. Ahern, Jr., *Undercover Armies: CIA and Surrogate Warfare in Laos* (Washington, DC: Center for the Study of Intelligence, Central Intelligence Agency, 2006); Headquarters, Department of the Army, *Army Special Operations Forces: Unconventional Warfare*, FM 3-05.130 (Washington, DC: Headquarters, Department of the Army), p. 234.

55. Henry Kissinger, *White House Years* (Boston: Little, Brown and Company, 1979), p.601.

56. Jenner Loven, "White House Remodeling 'Situation Room,'" *Associated Press*, December 19, 2006.

57. Jim Rutenberg and David E. Sanger, "Overhaul Moves White House Data Center Into Modern Era," *New York Times*, December 19, 2006.

58. On possible measures (including psychological operations) to take against the Jaruzelski regime see Memorandum from William P. Clark to the President, Subject: Situation in Poland and Possible U.S. Countermeasures, October 19, 1982. Available in the Richard Pipes files, "CHRON 10/01/1982-10/31/1982," Box 15, Ronald Reagan Presidential Library.

59. Ronald Reagan, *The Reagan Diaries, Vol. I, January 1981–October 1985*, ed. Douglas Brinkley (New York: HarperCollins, 2009), p. 160.

60. In June 1982, Kornel Morawiecki founded Fighting Solidarity (*Solidarność Walcząca*) in Wrocław, and he supported the use of armed violence for self-defense purposes—such as in response a regime crackdown. But Fighting Solidarity was an outlier organization and, in the end, it did not resort to violence.

61. Author interview with Richard Pipes, August 2016.

62. Memorandum from Richard Pipes to William P. Clark, Subject: Possible Outlawing of Solidarity, September 23, 1982. Available in the Richard Pipes files, "CHRON 09/23/1982-09/27/1982," Box 15, Ronald Reagan Presidential Library.

63. Ronald Reagan, Radio Address to the Nation on Solidarity and United States Relations With Poland, October 9, 1982. Available at: http://www.reagan.utexas.edu/archives/speeches/1982/100982a.htm.

64. Memorandum from Michael O. Wheeler to John M. Poindexter, Subject: Attending List for the National Security Planning Group Meeting, November 3, 1982. Available in Executive Secretariat, NSC: National Security Planning Group, NSPG 0046, November 2, 1982 [Poland; Latin America], Box 91305, Ronald Reagan Presidential Library.

65. National Security Planning Group Meeting, Intelligence NSC/ICS 400325, November 4, 1982. Available in Executive Secretariat, NSC: National Security Planning Group, NSPG 0046, November 2, 1982 [Poland; Latin America], Box 91305, Ronald Reagan Presidential Library. On the president's schedule also see The Schedule of President Ronald Reagan, November 4, 1982. Office of the President: Presidential Briefing Papers, 11/04/1982, Box 23, Ronald Reagan Presidential Library.

66. Author interviews with multiple sources.

67. Peter Schweizer, *Victory: The Reagan Administration's Secret Strategy That Hastened the Collapse of the Soviet Union* (New York: Atlantic Monthly Press, 1994), p. 75.

68. Gregory F. Domber, *Empowering Revolution: America, Poland, and the End of the Cold War* (Chapel Hill: University of North Carolina, 2014), p. 110.

69. Reagan, *The Reagan Diaries, Vol. I*, p. 169.

CHAPTER 10: STRUGGLING TO SURVIVE

1. Jacek Kołtan and Ewa Konarowska, eds., *European Solidarity Centre Permanent Exhibition: Anthology* (Gdańsk: European Solidarity Centre, 2015), p. 200.

2. Basil Kerski, Konrad Knoch, Jacek Kołtan, and Paweł Golak, *European Solidarity Centre Permanent Exhibition: Catalogue* (Gdańsk: European Solidarity Centre, 2015), p. 141.

3. Kołtan and Konarowska, *European Solidarity Centre Permanent Exhibition: Anthology*, p. 200.

4. Kerski, et al., *European Solidarity Centre Permanent Exhibition: Catalogue*, pp. 141, 126.

5. Kołtan and Konarowska, *European Solidarity Centre Permanent Exhibition: Anthology*, p. 213.

6. George Sanford, *Military Rule in Poland: The Rebuilding of Communist Power, 1981–1983* (London: Croom Helm, 1986), p. 253.

7. Lech Wałęsa, *A Way of Hope* (New York: Henry Holt and Company, 1987), p. 206.

8. Wałęsa, *A Way of Hope*, p. 219.

9. Wałęsa, *A Way of Hope*, p. 224.

10. Wałęsa, *A Way of Hope*, pp. 236–237.

11. Wałęsa, *A Way of Hope*, p. 218.

12. Carl Bernstein and Marco Politi, *His Holiness: John Paul II and the Hidden History of Our Time* (New York: Doubleday, 1996), p. 348.

13. Bernstein and Politi, *His Holiness*, p. 350.

14. Wałęsa, *A Way of Hope*, p. 226.

15. Douglas J. MacEachin, *U.S. Intelligence and the Confrontation in Poland, 1980–1981* (University Park: The Pennsylvania State University Press, 2002), p. 177; Wałęsa, *A Way of Hope*, p. 226.

16. Wałęsa, *A Way of Hope*, p. 238.

17. Wałęsa, *A Way of Hope*, p. 239.

18. John Kifner, "Poles Told Wałęsa Has Been Freed," *New York Times*, November 13, 1982.

19. David Ost, *Solidarity and the Politics of Anti-Politics: Opposition and Reform in Poland since 1968* (Philadelphia: Temple University Press, 1990), p. 151.

20. Andreszj Paczkowski, *The Spring Will Be Ours: Poland and the Poles from Occupation to Freedom* (University Park: Pennsylvania State University, 2003), p. 457. Also see Agnieszka Niegowska, ed., *It All Began in Poland* (Warsaw: Institute of National Remembrance, 2009), p. 179.

21. Glenn E. Curtis, ed., "Politics and the Media," in *Poland: A Country Study* (Washington, DC: Government Printing Office, 1992).

22. Curtis, "Politics and the Media."

23. Jonathan Kwitny, *Man of the Century: The Life and Times of Pope John Paul II* (New York: Henry Holt, 1997), p. 560.

24. Benjamin B. Fischer, "Solidarity, the CIA, and Western Technology," *International Journal of Intelligence and Counterintelligence*, Vol. 25, No. 3, 2012, pp. 427–469.

25. Jan Josef Lipski, *KOR: A History of the Workers' Defense Committee in Poland, 1976–1981* (Berkeley: University of California Press, 1985), p. 181.

26. Marian Kaleta, "Powielacze na szmuglerskim szlaku. Fragmenty wspomnień emigracyjnych," at www.racjonalista.pl/kk.php/s,6111.

27. Lipski, *KOR*, p. 181.

28. Maciej Łopinski, Marcin Moskit, and Marlusz Wilk, *Konspira: Solidarity Underground* (Berkeley: University of California Press, 1990), p. 12.

29. George Vecsey, "Poland Advances Along with France," *New York Times*, July 5, 1982.

30. Courtesy of the European Solidarity Centre in Gdańsk. See their exposé on "Humour and Satire" in the European Solidarity Centre museum.

31. Wałęsa, *A Way of Hope*, p. 211.

CHAPTER II: GETTING OFF THE GROUND

1. L. Britt Snider, *The Agency and the Hill: CIA's Relationship with Congress, 1946–2004* (Washington, DC: Center for the Study of Intelligence, Central Intelligence Agency, 2008), p. 164.

2. Author interviews with multiple sources. On the types of CIA support to Solidarity, also see Peter Schweizer, *Victory: The Reagan Administration's Secret Strategy That Hastened the Collapse of the Soviet Union* (New York: Atlantic Monthly Press, 1994), pp. 75–76, 84–92. Schweizer reports that CIA money began to flow to Solidarity in March 1982 (p. 89), but CIA funding didn't begin until 1983.

3. On CIA aid to Afghanistan, see Robert M. Gates, *From the Shadows: The Ultimate Insider's Story of Five Presidents and How They Won the Cold War* (New York: Simon and Schuster, 1996), pp. 251–252.

4. On Robert Magee see Duane R. Clarridge, *A Spy for All Seasons: My Life in the CIA* (New York: Scribner, 1998), pp. 230, 265, 268.

5. On covert action during the Reagan years see William J. Daugherty, *Executive Secrets: Cover Action and the Presidency* (Lexington: University of Kentucky Press, 2004), pp. 193–211.

6. Gates, *From the Shadows*, p. 238.

7. Author interview with Zbigniew Brzezinski, October 2016. Also see Gates, *From the Shadows*, p. 238.

8. This book lists a number of cryptonyms for covert action programs (such as QRHELPFUL) and assets (such as QRGUIDE). It is somewhat unclear, at least to the author, why the CIA chose specific names and letters for each program and author—though one can guess that QRHELPFUL was designed to "help" Solidarity and QRGUIDE helped "guide" money and material to the Polish underground.

9. Peter Schweizer erroneously reported that QRHELPFUL was run out of the CIA's Frankfurt office. See Schweizer, *Victory*, p. 146. Also see Gregory F. Domber, *Empowering Revolution: America, Poland, and the End of the Cold War* (Chapel Hill: University of North Carolina, 2014), p. 110.

10. Gates, *From the Shadows*, p. 237; author interviews with multiple sources.

11. Joseph E. Persico, *Casey: From the OSS to the CIA* (New York: Viking, 1990), p. 236.

12. Author interviews with multiple sources.

13. On CIA assets see, for example, Central Intelligence Agency, INTelligence: Human Intelligence, 2010. Available at: https://www.cia.gov/news-information/featured-story-archive/2010-featured-story-archive/intelligence-human-intelligence.html. Accessed on December 23, 2015.

14. Schweizer briefly discusses some of the CIA's efforts to reach out to Polish émigrés, members of Solidarity, and others involved in smuggling goods into and out of Poland. See Schweizer, *Victory*, pp. 84–86.

15. On CIA assets see, for example, Central Intelligence Agency, INTelligence: Human Intelligence, 2010.

16. Covert action assets are foreigners recruited to help conduct covert action programs overseas. They are different from assets recruited to collect foreign intelligence.

17. Author interviews with multiple sources.

18. For an overview of CIA programs in Poland see Benjamin B. Fischer, "Solidarity, the CIA, and Western Technology," *International Journal of Intelligence and Counterintelligence*, Vol. 25, No. 3, 2012, pp. 427–469.

19. Gates, *From the Shadows*, p. 237.

20. Letter from John T. (Terry) Dolan to Michael K. Deaver, Subject: A Recommended Course of Action Regarding Poland, July 7, 1982. Available in the Paula Dobriansky files, Poland: Crisis Management [1981–1982], RAC Box 3, Ronald Reagan Presidential Library.

21. Quoted in Michael Kramer, "The Not-Quite War," *New York Magazine*, September 12, 1983, p. 42.

22. Letter from John T. (Terry) Dolan to Michael K. Deaver, Subject: A Recommended Course of Action Regarding Poland, July 7, 1982. Available in the Paula Dobriansky files, Poland: Crisis Management [1981–1982], RAC Box 3, Ronald Reagan Presidential Library. In a follow-up letter from National Security Adviser Clark to Deaver, Clark remarked that most of the suggestions "have been pursued by the Administration." Memorandum from William P. Clark to Michael Deaver, Subject: John T. Dolan's July 7 Memorandum on Poland, August 2, 1982. Available in the Paula Dobriansky files, Poland: Crisis Management [1981–1982], RAC Box 3, Ronald Reagan Presidential Library.

23. On the response to Dolan's letter see Memorandum from William P. Clark to Michael K. Deaver, Subject: John T. Dolan's July 7 Memorandum on Poland, August 2, 1982. Available in Paula Dobriansky files, National Security Council Series I: Country Files, RAC Box 3, Ronald Reagan Presidential Library.

24. Ronald Reagan, *The Reagan Diaries, Vol. I, January 1981–October 1985*, ed. Douglas Brinkley (New York: HarperCollins, 2009), p. 106.

25. Douglas Martin, "Charles Wick, 90, Information Agency Head, is Dead," *New York Times*, July 24, 2008.

26. See, for example, the video of Frank Sinatra singing the Polish folk song "Wolne Serce" in Polish at: https://www.youtube.com/watch?v=1arws R08yKo. Accessed on January 7, 2016.

27. Reagan, *The Reagan Diaries, Vol. I*, p. 110.

28. Alexander Stephan, ed., *The Americanization of Europe: Culture, Diplomacy, and Anti-Americanism after 1945* (New York: Berghahn Books, 2006), p. 227.

29. Memorandum from Richard Pipes to William P. Clark, Subject: Presidential Message for Solidarity Internees, July 21, 1982. Available in the Richard Pipes files, "CHRON 07/20/1982-07/22/1982," Box 15, Ronald Reagan Presidential Library.

30. Memorandum from Paula Dobriansky to William P. Clark, Subject: Ceremony on Friday, December 10. Available in the Paula Dobriansky files, "Poland—Cables 1981–1983," RAC Box 3, Ronald Reagan Presidential Library.

CHAPTER 12: RATLINES

1. Ronald Reagan, "Remarks at the Annual Convention of the National Association of Evangelicals in Orlando, Florida," March 8, 1983. Transcript from

the Reagan Foundation at: https://reaganlibrary.archives.gov/archives/speeches/1983/30883b.htm. Accessed on November 6, 2017.

2. Reagan, "Remarks at the Annual Convention of the National Association of Evangelicals in Orlando, Florida." Emphasis added.

3. See, for example, Arch Puddington, *Lane Kirkland: Champion of American Labor* (New York: Wiley, 2005).

4. Carl Bernstein and Marco Politi, *His Holiness: John Paul II and the Hidden History of Our Time* (New York: Doubleday, 1996); Jonathan Kwitny, *Man of the Century: The Life and Times of Pope John Paul II* (New York: Henry Holt, 1997); Tad Szulc, *John Paul II: The Biography* (New York: Scribner, 1995).

5. On humanitarian aid see, for example, Kwitny, *Man of the Century.*

6. Benjamin B. Fischer, "Solidarity, the CIA, and Western Technology," *International Journal of Intelligence and Counterintelligence* 25, no. 3 (2012), p. 443.

7. Robert M. Gates, *From the Shadows: The Ultimate Inside Story of Five Presidents and How They Won the Cold War* (New York: Simon and Schuster: 1996), p. 237.

8. On challenges with surrogates, see Thomas L. Ahern, Jr., *Undercover Armies: CIA and Surrogate Warfare in Laos* (Washington, DC: Center for the Study of Intelligence, Central Intelligence Agency, 2006).

9. Fischer, "Solidarity, the CIA, and Western Technology," p. 444.

10. Peter Schweizer, *Victory: The Reagan Administration's Secret Strategy that Hastened the Collapse of the Soviet Union* (New York: The Atlantic Monthly Press, 1994), p. 87.

11. Author interviews with multiple sources. These percentages are estimates from individuals involved in, or aware of, QRHELPFUL infiltration.

12. Małgorzata Mizerska-Wrotkowska, *Poland and Sweden in the United Europe* (Madrid: Schedas, 2015).

13. Schweizer, *Victory*, p. 146.

14. Schweizer, *Victory*, pp. 164-165; Bernstein and Politi, *His Holiness*, pp. 381–382.

15. Schweizer, *Victory*, p. 146.

16. Basil Kerski, Konrad Knoch, Jacek Kołtan, and Paweł Golak, *European Solidarity Centre Permanent Exhibition: Catalogue* (Gdańsk: European Solidarity Centre, 2015), p. 143.

17. Marian Kaleta, *Powielacze na szmuglerskim szlaku*, 2008. Available at: www.racjonalista.pl/kk.php/s,6111.

18. On Kaleta see Kaleta, *Powielacze na szmuglerskim szlaku*; Fischer, "Solidarity, the CIA, and Western Technology," pp. 444–445; Kwitny, *Man of the*

Century, p. 452; Jan Josef Lipski, *KOR: A History of the Workers' Defense Committee in Poland, 1976–1981* (Berkeley: University of California Press, 1985), p. 114; Nigel West, *The Third Secret: The CIA, Solidarity, and the KGB's Plot to Kill the Pope* (New York: HarperCollins, 2002), p. 452; Maciej Łopinski, Marcin Moskit, and Marlusz Wilk, *Konspira: Solidarity Underground* (Berkeley: University of California Press, 1990), p. 20; author interviews with multiple sources.

19. Fischer, "Solidarity, the CIA, and Western Technology," pp. 443–444.

20. On TIR see International Road Transport Union, *What Is TIR?* (Geneva: International Road Transport Union, 2011).

21. William J. Daugherty, *Executive Secrets: Covert Action and the Presidency* (Lexington: University of Kentucky Press, 2004), p. 202.

22. Schweizer, *Victory*, pp. 86–88.

23. Author interviews with multiple sources. On the Polish underground, also see Gwido Zlatkes, Paweł Sowiński, and Ann M. Frenkel, eds., *Duplicator Underground: The Independent Publishing Industry in Communist Poland, 1976–1989* (Bloomington, IN: Slavica Publishers, 2016),

24. Author interviews with multiple sources.

25. Fischer, "Solidarity, the CIA, and Western Technology," p. 443.

CHAPTER 13: THE UNDERGROUND

1. Tad Szulc, *John Paul II: The Biography* (New York: Scribner, 1995), p. 392.

2. George Sanford, *Military Rule in Poland: The Rebuilding of Communist Power, 1981–1983* (London: Croom Helm, 1986), p. 269.

3. On Polish government surveillance against Wałęsa see Lech Wałęsa, *A Way of Hope* (New York: Henry Holt and Company, 1987), pp. 255–268.

4. Lech Wałęsa, *The Struggle and the Triumph: An Autobiography* (New York: Arcade Publishing, 1991), pp. 48–49.

5. Tomas Burski and Piotr Pacewicz, *Wywiady z szefami Tygodnika Mazowsze* (Warsaw, September 15, 1988), pp. 48–50. Also see Jacek Kołtan and Ewa Konarowska, eds., *European Solidarity Centre Permanent Exhibition: Anthology* (Gdańsk: European Solidarity Centre, 2015), p. 236.

6. Burski and Pacewicz, *Wywiady z szefami Tygodnika Mazowsze*, pp. 48–50. Also see Kołtan and Konarowska, *European Solidarity Centre Permanent Exhibition: Anthology*, p. 236.

7. Jonathan Kwitny, *Man of the Century: The Life and Times of Pope John Paul II* (New York: Henry Holt, 1997), p. 432.

8. Benjamin B. Fischer, "Solidarity, the CIA, and Western Technology," *International Journal of Intelligence and Counterintelligence.* 25, no. 3 (2012), pp. 435–436; Agnieszka Niegowska, ed., *It All Began in Poland* (Warsaw: Institute of National Remembrance, 2009), p. 178.

9. Basil Kerski, Konrad Knoch, Jacek Kołtan, and Paweł Golak, *European Solidarity Centre Permanent Exhibition: Catalogue* (Gdańsk: European Solidarity Centre, 2015), p. 137.

10. Kerski et al., *European Solidarity Centre Permanent Exhibition: Catalogue*, p. 145.

11. Paweł Sowiński, " 'Printers of the Mind': The Culture of Polish Resistance, 1976–89," in Gwido Zlatkes, Paweł Sowiński, and Ann M. Frenkel, eds., *Duplicator Underground: The Independent Publishing Industry in Communist Poland, 1976–1989* (Bloomington, Indiana: Slavica Publishers, 2016), p.48.

12. Quoted in Sowiński, " 'Printers of the Mind'," p.42.

13. A special thanks to the European Solidarity Centre for allowing me to examine several types of Solidarity printers.

14. "Lewy papier, farba własnej roboty. Z Kamilą Churską, Krzysztofem Osińskim i Markiem Szymaniakiem rozmawia Sandra Fedorowicz," *Gazeta Wyborcza* [Bydgoszcz local edition], March 13, 2009, p. 8.

15. Wojciech Polak, Czas ludzi niepokornych. Niezależny Samorządny Związek Zawodowy „Solidarność" i inne ugrupowania niezależne w Toruniu i Regionie Toruńskim (13 XII 1981 – 4 VI 1989), Toruń 2003, pp. 136–137, 142.

16. Paweł Bąkowski, "Najdłuższy dzień drukarni NOWEJ," Nowy Dziennik (New York), September 9, 2007, p. 5.

17. Kołtan and Ewa, *European Solidarity Centre Permanent Exhibition: Anthology*, p. 226.

18. Carl Bernstein and Marco Politi, *His Holiness: John Paul II and the Hidden History of Our Time* (New York: Doubleday, 1996), pp. 381–382.

19. Pawlak Maciej, *Radio Solidarność w Trójmieście* (Gdańsk: Oskar, 2015).

20. Peter Schweizer, *Victory: The Reagan Administration's Secret Strategy That Hastened the Collapse of the Soviet Union* (New York: The Atlantic Monthly Press, 1994), p. 89.

21. On CIA support to Solidarity see, for example, Robert M. Gates, *From the Shadows: The Ultimate Insider's Story of Five Presidents and How They Won the Cold War* (New York: Simon and Schuster, 1996), p. 451.

22. Kwitny, *Man of the Century*, p. 439.

23. Kerski et al., *European Solidarity Centre Permanent Exhibition: Catalogue*, p. 131.

24. Idesbald Goddeeris, ed., *Solidarity with Solidarity: Western European Trade Unions and the Polish Crisis, 1980–1982* (Lanham, MD: Lexington Books, 2010); Wałęsa, *The Struggle and the Triumph*, p. 110.

25. Arch Puddington, *Lane Kirkland: Champion of American Labor* (New York: Wiley, 2005), p. 185.

26. Puddington, *Lane Kirkland*, p. 185.

CHAPTER 14: HARDBALL

1. Gregory Wolk, "To Limit, to Eradicate, or to Control? The SB and the 'Second Circulation,' 1981–89/90," in Gwido Zlatkes, Paweł Sowiński, and Ann M. Frenkel, eds., *Duplicator Underground: The Independent Publishing Industry in Communist Poland, 1976–1989* (Bloomington, IN: Slavica Publishers, 2016), p. 265.

2. "Two Fugitive Solidarity Officials Seized in Poland," *New York Times*, April 17, 1983; "Police Announce Arrests of Solidarity Activists," *UPI*, April 16, 1983.

3. "Police Announce Arrests of Solidarity Activists."

4. Letter from Brezhnev to Reagan, December 25, 1981. Available in the papers of Donald P. Regan, Manuscript Division, Box 214, Library of Congress. On the Lech Wałęsa quote see Lech Wałęsa, *The Struggle and the Triumph: An Autobiography* (New York: Arcade Publishing, 1991), p. 151.

5. KGB report no. 84/KR, January 6, 1984, in Christopher Andrew and Oleg Gordievsky, *More Instructions from the Centre: Top Secret Files on KGB Global Operations, 1975–1985* (London: Frank Cass, 1992), pp. 122, 124.

6. John Kifner, "Seizing of Polish Activists Goes on Despite Suspension of Martial Law," *New York Times*, January 10, 1983.

7. Bogdan Turek, "The Official Communist Party Newspaper Monday Attacked Former Solidarity Chief," *UPI*, December 12, 1982.

8. Kifner, "Seizing of Polish Activists Goes on Despite Suspension of Martial Law."

9. Wolk, "To Limit, to Eradicate, or to Control?" pp. 245–246.

10. Wolk, "To Limit, to Eradicate, or to Control?" pp. 242–243.

11. Peter Schweizer, *Victory: The Reagan Administration's Secret Strategy That Hastened the Collapse of the Soviet Union* (New York: The Atlantic Monthly Press, 1994), p. 91.

12. Michael Dobbs, "Ranking Soviet Makes Surprise Polish Visits," *Washington Post*, May 18, 1982.

13. John Darnton, "Warsaw Expels Two U.S. Diplomats," *New York Times*, May 11, 1982; Schweizer, *Victory*, p. 92.

14. "Warsaw Military Court Sentences Zdzislaw Najder to Death," April 29, 1982; "Letter with Opinion of Malgorzaty Mehnel-Szyc on Radio Free Europe and the Case against Zdzislaw Najder," April 11, 1983. Available from the History and Public Policy Program Digital Archive, Woodrow Wilson International Center for Scholars.

15. Memorandum from William Casey to the Assistant to the President for National Security Affairs, Subject: Poland, January 10, 1983. Available in the Paula Dobriansky files, "Poland: Memoranda 1981–1983," RAC Box 3, Ronald Reagan Presidential Library.

16. Vadimov [Kirpichenko] to London Residency, tel. no. 5101/R, January 22, 1983. See Andrew and Gordievsky, *Comrade Kryuchkov's Instructions*, p. 93.

17. Benjamin B. Fischer, "Solidarity, the CIA, and Western Technology," *International Journal of Intelligence and Counterintelligence*, Vol. 25, No. 3, 2012, p. 448.

18. Christopher Andrew and Oleg Gordievsky, *KGB: The Inside Story* (New York: HarperCollins, 1990), pp. 578–579.

19. John Kifner, "Seizing of Polish Activists Goes on Despite Suspension of Martial Law," *New York Times*, January 10, 1983.

20. Mitrokhin Archives, k-19, 321. Available in the Churchill Archives at Churchill College, Cambridge, UK.

21. Jarosław Kapsa, "In the Shadow of the Luminous Mountain: Underground Publishing in Częstochowa," in Gwido Zlatkes, Paweł Sowiński, and Ann M. Frenkel, eds., *Duplicator Underground: The Independent Publishing Industry in Communist Poland, 1976–1989* (Bloomington, IN: Slavica Publishers, 2016), p. 152.

22. Central Intelligence Agency, "Poland: Near Term Assessment," January 3, 1983. Available in the Paula Dobriansky files, "Poland: Memoranda 1981–83," RAC Box 3, Ronald Reagan Presidential Library.

23. Memorandum from William P. Clark to the President, Subject: CIA Report on Polish Internal Situation, January 11, 1983. Available in the Paula Dobriansky files, "Poland: Memoranda 1981–83," RAC Box 3, Ronald Reagan Presidential Library.

24. Central Intelligence Agency, "Poland: Near Term Assessment," January 3, 1983. Available in the Paula Dobriansky files, "Poland: Memoranda 1981–83," RAC Box 3, Ronald Reagan Presidential Library.

25. Author interviews with multiple sources. The letter from Goldwater was dated August 8, 1983.

26. On "flapper lips," see Douglas Waller, *Disciples: The World War II Missions of the CIA Directors Who Fought for Wild Bill Donovan* (New York: Simon and Schuster, 2015), p. 447.

27. Letter from Barry Goldwater and Daniel Patrick Moynihan to William J. Casey, July 19, 1983. Available at CIA-RDP85M00364R000701170003-6, CIA Records Search Tool (CREST), National Archives and Records Administration, College Park, MD.

28. Memorandum from George P. Shultz to the President, Subject: USG-Soviet Relations—Where Do We Want To Be and How Do We Get There? March 3, 1983. Available in William Clark files, U.S-Soviet Relations Papers, Box 8, Ronald Reagan Presidential Library.

29. Quoted in Schweizer, *Victory*, p. 87.

30. L. Britt Snider, *The Agency and the Hill: CIA's Relationship with Congress, 1946-2004* (Washington, DC: Center for the Study of Intelligence, Central Intelligence Agency, 2008), p. 182.

31. Bob Woodward, *Veil: The Secret Wars of the CIA, 1981-1987* (New York: Simon and Schuster, 1987), pp. 33; Joseph E. Persico, *Casey: From the OSS to the CIA* (New York: Viking, 1990), p. 1; Eric Pace, "William Casey, Ex-CIA Head, is Dead at 74," *New York Times*, May 7, 1987.

32. William J. Casey, *Where and How the War Was Fought: An Armchair Tour of the American Revolution* (New York: Morrow, 1976).

33. Woodward, *Veil*, pp. 136–137.

34. See, for example, letter from William J. Casey to the Honorable William P. Clark, March 25, 1983. Available in Executive Secretariat, NSC: Agency Files, CIA [08/16/1982-07/14/1983], Box 1 (Box 91372), Ronald Reagan Presidential Library.

35. Letter from William J. Casey to the President, December 10, 1984. Available in the William Clark files, Casey to Clark, Box 1, Ronald Reagan Presidential Library.

36. Letter from William J. Casey to the President, June 25, 1983. Available in Executive Secretariat, NSC: Agency files, CIA [08/16/1982-07/14/1983], Box 1 (Box 91372), Ronald Reagan Presidential Library.

37. Memorandum from William J. Casey to William P. Clark, Subject: Summitry, June 27, 1983. Available in Executive Secretariat, NSC: Agency files, CIA [08/16/1982-07/14/1983], Box 1 (Box 91372), Ronald Reagan Presidential Library.

38. Memorandum from William P. Clark to FBI Director William H. Webster, Subject: Soviet Involvement in the Freeze Movement, January 4, 1983. Robert Sims files, Soviet Active Measures, Box 3, Ronald Reagan Presidential Library.

39. Federal Bureau of Investigation, "Soviet Involvement in the U.S. Peace Movement," October 7, 1982. Available in the Robert Sims files, Soviet Active Measures, Box 3, Ronald Reagan Presidential Library.

40. Federal Bureau of Investigation, "Soviet Involvement in the U.S. Peace Movement."

CHAPTER 15: CRACKS IN THE FOUNDATION

1. Mitrokhin Archives, k-19, 312. Available in the Churchill Archives at Churchill College, Cambridge, UK. See also Christopher Andrew and Vasili Mitrokhin, *The Sword and the Shield: The Mitrokhin Archive and the Secret History of the KGB* (New York: Basic Books, 1999), p. 536.

2. Mitrokhin Archives, k-19, 312. Available in the Churchill Archives at Churchill College, Cambridge, UK. See also Andrew and Mitrokhin, *The Sword and the Shield*, p. 534.

3. On Kiszczak, see Antoni Dudek and Andrzej Paczkowski, "Poland," in Krzysztof Persak and Lukasz Kaminski, eds., *A Handbook of the Communist Security Apparatus in East Central Europe, 1944–1989* (Warsaw: Institute of National Remembrance, 2005), pp. 282–283.

4. John Tagliabue, "Man in the News; Tough Polish Negotiator: Czeslaw Kiszczak," *New York Times*, September 2, 1988. Also see Sam Roberts, "Gen Czeslaw Kiszczak, Poland's Last Communist Prime Minister, Dies at 90," *New York Times*, November 5, 2015.

5. Mitrokhin Archives, k-19, 261. Available in the Churchill Archives at Churchill College, Cambridge, UK.

6. Mitrokhin Archives, k-19, 642. Available in the Churchill Archives at Churchill College, Cambridge, UK. For the translation see Andrew and Mitrokhin, *The Sword and the Shield*, p. 536.

7. Mitrokhin Archives, k-19, 311. Available in the Churchill Archives at Churchill College, Cambridge, UK. For the translation see Andrew and Mitrokhin, *The Sword and the Shield*, p. 537.

8. Mitrokhin Archives, k-19, 324. Available in the Churchill Archives at Churchill College, Cambridge, UK. For the translation see Andrew and Mitrokhin, *The Sword and the Shield*, p. 537.

9. Mitrokhin Archives, k-19, 328. Available in the Churchill Archives at Churchill College, Cambridge, UK. For the translation see Andrew and Mitrokhin, *The Sword and the Shield*, p. 537.

10. Mitrokhin Archives, k-19, 337. Available in the Churchill Archives at Churchill College, Cambridge, UK. For the translation see Andrew and Mitrokhin, *The Sword and the Shield*, p. 537.

11. Mitrokhin Archives, k-19, 339. Available in the Churchill Archives at Churchill College, Cambridge, UK.

12. Mitrokhin Archives, k-19, 128. Available in the Churchill Archives at Churchill College, Cambridge, UK. For the translation see Andrew and Mitrokhin, *The Sword and the Shield*, p. 538.

13. Mitrokhin Archives, k-19, 128. Available in the Churchill Archives at Churchill College, Cambridge, UK.

14. Mitrokhin Archives, k-19, 124. Available in the Churchill Archives at Churchill College, Cambridge, UK. For the translation see Andrew and Mitrokhin, *The Sword and the Shield*, p. 538.

15. Roger Boyes, *The Naked President: Political Life of Lech Wałęsa* (London: Martin Secker &Warburg, 1994), pp. 117, 136-137; Andrew and Mitrokhin, *The Sword and the Shield*, p. 540.

16. See, for example, Philip Williams, "Regime Alleges Wałęsa Has $1 Million," *UPI*, September 27, 1983.

17. Piotr Adamowicz, Andrzej Drzycimski, and Adam Kinaszewski, *Gdańsk: According to Lech Wałęsa* (Gdańsk: Morze Możliwości, 2008), p. 78.

18. Lech Wałęsa, *A Way of Hope* (New York: Henry Holt and Company, 1987), p. 256.

19. Memorandum from William P. Clark to the President, Subject: Terms of Reference for NSSD on "U.S. Policy Toward the Soviet Union," August 16, 1982.

Available in the Richard Pipes files, "CHRON 08/05/1982-08/16/1982," Box 15, Ronald Reagan Presidential Library.

20. National Security Decision Directive Number 75, "U.S. Relations with the USSR," January 17, 1983. Available in Executive Secretariat, NSC: Records [NSDDs], NSDD 75 [U.S. Relations with the USSR], Box 91287, Ronald Reagan Presidential Library.

21. Norman Bailey, *The Strategic Plan that Won the Cold War: National Security Decision Directive 75*, Second Edition (McLean, VA: The Potomac Foundation, 1999).

22. Peter Schweizer, *Victory: The Reagan Administration's Secret Strategy That Hastened the Collapse of the Soviet Union* (New York: The Atlantic Monthly Press, 1994), p. 131.

23. Author interview with Richard Pipes, August 2016.

24. National Security Decision Directive Number 75, "U.S. Relations with the USSR."

25. National Security Decision Directive Number 75, "U.S. Relations with the USSR."

26. Memorandum from William P. Clark to the President, Subject: Messages from Imprisoned Solidarity Members, February 7, 1983. Available in the Paula Dobriansky files, "Poland: Solidarity [01/01/1983-05/31/1983]," RAC Box 4, Ronald Reagan Presidential Library.

27. Quoted in Carl Bernstein and Marco Politi, *His Holiness: John Paul II and the Hidden History of Our Time* (New York: Doubleday, 1996), p. 12.

CHAPTER 16: HOLY ALLIANCE?

1. I visited St. Bridget's Church on May 18, 2016. In the decades after Solidarity's establishment, the church added artifacts and memorials from Solidarity's rich history: bronze doors that commemorated the events of August 1980, a chapel that included a cast bronze figure of Jerzy Popieluszko, and a movie dedicated to Solidarity.

2. Michael T. Kaufman, *Mad Dreams, Saving Graces: Poland: A Nation in Conspiracy* (New York: Random House, 1989), p. 138.

3. Carl Bernstein and Marco Politi, *His Holiness: John Paul II and the Hidden History of Our Time* (New York, Doubleday, 1996), p. 12.

4. Carl Bernstein, "The Holy Alliance," *Time*, February 24, 1992.

5. Karl Marx, "Introduction" to *A Contribution to the Critique of Hegel's Philosophy of Right*, ed. Joseph O'Malley (Cambridge: Cambridge University Press, 1987), p. 171.

6. Several books and articles have discredited Bernstein and Politi's *His Holiness*. They include Tad Szulc, *John Paul II: The Biography* (New York: Scribner, 1995); Benjamin B. Fischer, "Solidarity, the CIA, and Western Technology," *International Journal of Intelligence and Counterintelligence*, 25, no. 3 (2012), pp. 427–469; Jonathan Kwitny, *Man of the Century: The Life and Times of Pope John Paul II* (New York: Henry Holt, 1997); George Weigel, *The End of the Beginning: The Victory of Freedom, the Last Years, the Legacy* (New York: Doubleday, 2010).

7. William J. Daugherty, *Executive Secrets: Covert Action and the Presidency* (Lexington: University of Kentucky Press, 2004), p. 201.

8. Letter from Ronald Reagan to His Holiness, John Paul II, May 13, 1981. Available in National Security Council, Executive Secretariat, NSC: Head of State Files, The Vatican, Box 41, Ronald Reagan Presidential Library.

9. Peter Schweizer, *Victory: The Reagan Administration's Secret Strategy That Hastened the Collapse of the Soviet Union* (New York: The Atlantic Monthly Press, 1994), p. 107.

10. Letter from Ronald Reagan to His Holiness, John Paul II, June 23, 1982. Available in National Security Council, Executive Secretariat, NSC: Head of State Files, The Vatican, Box 41, Ronald Reagan Presidential Library.

11. Message from John Paul II to Ronald Reagan, June 7, 1982. Available in National Security Council, Executive Secretariat, NSC: Head of State Files, The Vatican, Box 41, Ronald Reagan Presidential Library.

12. Ronald Reagan, *The Reagan Diaries, Vol. I, January 1981–October 1985*, ed. Douglas Brinkley (New York: HarperCollins, 2009), p. 136.

13. Letter from Ronald Reagan to His Holiness, John Paul II, June 23, 1982. Available in National Security Council, Executive Secretariat, NSC: Head of State Files, The Vatican, Box 41, Ronald Reagan Presidential Library.

14. Edmund Morris, *Dutch: A Memoir of Ronald Reagan* (New York: Random House, 1999), p. 444.

15. Schweizer, *Victory*, p. 161; Bernstein and Politi, *His Holiness*, pp. 11–12, 261–267, 269–271, 286–291.

16. Bernstein and Politi, *His Holiness*, pp. 11–12.

17. The meeting took place on July 20, 1983.

18. See, for example, Letter from Ronald Reagan to His Holiness, John Paul II, November 22, 1981. Available in National Security Council, Executive Secretariat, NSC: Head of State Files, The Vatican, Box 41, Ronald Reagan Presidential Library. Also see Letter from Ronald Reagan to His Holiness, John Paul II, April 29, 1982. Available in National Security Council, Executive Secretariat, NSC: Head of State Files, The Vatican, Box 41, Ronald Reagan Presidential Library.

19. As Reagan writes, "For the past several months we have consulted closely on the events in Poland by message, telephone and through our diplomatic representatives." Letter from Ronald Reagan to His Holiness, John Paul II, January 11, 1982. Available in National Security Council, Executive Secretariat, NSC: Head of State Files, The Vatican, Box 41, Ronald Reagan Presidential Library.

20. Letter from Ronald Reagan to His Holiness, John Paul II, December 17, 1981. Available in National Security Council, Executive Secretariat, NSC: Head of State Files, The Vatican, Box 41, Ronald Reagan Presidential Library.

21. Letter from Ronald Reagan to His Holiness, John Paul II, December 29, 1981. Available in National Security Council, Executive Secretariat, NSC: Head of State Files, The Vatican, Box 41, Ronald Reagan Presidential Library.

22. Memorandum from Dennis Blair to William P. Clark, Subject: Pope's Letter to the President, January 7, 1982. Available in National Security Council, Executive Secretariat, NSC: Head of State Files, The Vatican, Box 41, Ronald Reagan Presidential Library. Also see Letter from Ronald Reagan to His Holiness, John Paul II, February 23, 1982. Available in National Security Council, Executive Secretariat, NSC: Head of State Files, The Vatican, Box 41, Ronald Reagan Presidential Library.

23. See, for example, Memorandum from Alexander M. Haig to the President, Subject: Your Audience with Pope John Paul II, June 7, 1982. Available in National Security Council, Executive Secretariat, NSC: Trip Files, The President's Trip to Europe—Paris / Vatican / Rome / London, RAC Box 5, Ronald Reagan Presidential Library.

24. Author interviews with multiple sources.

25. Fischer, "Solidarity, the CIA, and Western Technology," p. 434; Bob Woodward, *Veil: The Secret Wars of the CIA 1981–1987* (New York: Pocket Books, 1988), p. 428.

26. Henry Tanner, "Pope Says Church is 'On Side of the Workers,'" *New York Times*, December 23, 1981.

27. Szulc, *John Paul II*, p. 377.

28. Szulc, *John Paul II*, pp. 375–377.

29. U.S. State Department Cable, Subject: Polish Catholic Church: Internal Differences? February 18, 1982. Available in Paula Dobriansky files, Poland: Church, RAC Box 3, Ronald Reagan Presidential Library.

30. U.S. Department of State, Bureau of Intelligence and Research, "Moscow's Vatican Connection and the Polish Crisis: An Appraisal," July 24, 1981. Available in Paula Dobriansky files, Poland: Church, RAC Box 3, Ronald Reagan Presidential Library.

31. See the U.S. analysis in Memorandum from Alexander M. Haig to the President, Subject: Your Audience with Pope John Paul II.

32. On the description of Glemp's office see John Darnton, "Man in the News; Poland's Quiet Prelate," *New York Times*, August 30, 1982.

33. John Darnton, "Poland's Quiet Prelate: Jozef Glemp," *New York Times*, August 30, 1982.

34. U.S. State Department Cable, Subject: Polish Situation, January 18, 1982. Available in Paula Dobriansky files, Poland: Church, RAC Box 3, Ronald Reagan Presidential Library.

35. Bernstein and Politi, *His Holiness*, p. 376

36. U.S. State Department Cable, Subject: Polish Situation.

37. Kwitny, *Man of the Century*, pp. 426–427.

38. Kwitny, *Man of the Century*, p. 427.

39. Kwitny, *Man of the Century*, p. 427.

40. Szulc, *John Paul II*, pp. 379–380.

41. Szulc, *John Paul II*, p. 381.

CHAPTER 17: AN EMOTIONAL VISIT

1. Carl Bernstein and Marco Politi, *His Holiness: John Paul II and the Hidden History of Our Time* (New York: Doubleday, 1996), p. 376.

2. Bernstein and Politi, *His Holiness*, p. 377.

3. Quoted in Bernstein and Politi, *His Holiness*, p. 377.

4. Bernstein and Politi, *His Holiness*, p. 378.

5. Tad Szulc, *John Paul II: The Biography* (New York: Scribner, 1995), p. 391.

6. Szulc, *John Paul II*, p. 389.

7. Szulc, *John Paul II*, p. 389.

8. On the pope's schedule see the Vatican, Apostolic Pilgrimage to Poland, June 16–23, 1983. Available at: https://w2.vatican.va/content/john-paul-ii/en/travels/1983/travels/documents/trav_polonia.html.

9. Szulc, *John Paul II*, p. 395.

10. Bernstein and Politi, *His Holiness*, p. 387.

11. George Sanford, *Military Rule in Poland: The Rebuilding of Communist Power, 1981–1983* (London: Croom Helm, 1986), p. 270.

12. Lech Wałęsa, *A Way of Hope* (New York: Henry Holt and Company, 1987), p. 164.

13. Wałęsa, *A Way of Hope*, p. 164.

14. Szulc, *John Paul II*, p. 392.

15. Bernstein and Politi, *His Holiness*, pp. 384–385.

16. Wałęsa, *A Way of Hope*, p. 164.

17. Bernstein and Politi, *His Holiness*, p. 385.

18. Wałęsa, *A Way of Hope*, p. 164.

19. Bernstein and Politi, *His Holiness*, p. 379.

20. Henry Kamm, "Jaruzelski Holds Surprise Meeting with the Pontiff," *New York Times*, June 23, 1983.

21. Szulc, *John Paul II*, p. 394.

22. Defense Intelligence Summary, "Outcome of Papal Visit," June 24, 1983. Available in Paula Dobriansky files, Poland: Church, RAC Box 3, Ronald Reagan Presidential Library.

23. Memorandum of the President's Meeting with Cardinal Krol, Archbishop of Philadelphia, May 11, 1983. Available in Paula Dobriansky files, Poland: Church, RAC Box 3, Ronald Reagan Presidential Library.

24. John Kifner, "Poland Says It Lifts Martial Law; Curbs Now Put in Legal Code," *New York Times*, July 22, 1983.

25. Memorandum of the President's Meeting with Cardinal Krol, Archbishop of Philadelphia, June 27, 1983. Available in Paula Dobriansky files, Poland: Church, RAC Box 3, Ronald Reagan Presidential Library.

26. Memorandum from the Apostolic Nunciature to the White House, Re: United States / Poland Relations, July 24, 1984. Available in Executive Secretariat, NSC: Country Files, Poland (07/24/1984), Box 18, Ronald Reagan Presidential Library.

27. The Vice President Visit with His Holiness Pope John Paul II, February 15, 1984. Available in National Security Council, Executive Secretariat, NSC: Head of State Files, The Vatican, Box 41, Ronald Reagan Presidential Library. On the U.S. decision to ease sanctions, also see Memorandum from Robert C. McFarlane to George P. Shultz, Subject: Poland: Response to Unofficial Emissary Schaff, February 16, 1984. Available in National Security Council, Executive Secretariat, NSC: Head of State Files, The Vatican, Box 41, Ronald Reagan Presidential Library.

28. The Vice President Visit with His Holiness Pope John Paul II.

29. See, for example, Memorandum from Robert C. McFarlane to the President, Subject: Poland: Response to Unofficial Emissary Schaff, February 16, 1984. Available in Paula Dobriansky files, Poland: Church, RAC Box 3, Ronald Reagan Presidential Library.

30. State Department Cable FRM AMEMBASSY WARSAW TO SECSTATE WASHDC, Subject: Excerpts from Wałęsa Remarks Re Sanctions, December 6, 1983. Available in Executive Secretariat, NSC: Country Files, Poland (12/06/1983-01/11/1984), Box 18, Ronald Reagan Presidential Library.

31. Letter from the Vatican, "Situation of Polish Refugees in the United States," April 30, 1984. Available in Executive Secretariat, NSC: Country Files, Poland (09/25, 1984), Box 18, Ronald Reagan Presidential Library.

32. Letter from Ronald Reagan to His Holiness, John Paul II, February 22, 1984. Available in National Security Council, Executive Secretariat, NSC: Head of State Files, The Vatican, Box 41, Ronald Reagan Presidential Library.

33. Francis X. Clines, "Reagan Lifts Some U.S. Sanctions against Poland," *New York Times*, August 4, 1984.

34. For a classified U.S. assessment of Moscow's reaction to the pope's visit, see "Contingencies for Countering Soviet Pressure Against Poland," June 1983. Available in Paula Dobriansky files, National Security Council Series I: Country Files, RAC Box 3, Ronald Reagan Presidential Library.

35. KGB, "Work on the Vatican," Vn-1, No. 2182/PR, December 19, 1984. Christopher Andrew and Oleg Gordievsky, *More Instructions from the Centre: Top Secret Files on KGB Global Operations, 1975–1985* (London: Frank Cass, 1992), p. 47.

36. KGB, "Measures to Counter the Subversive Activity of the Vatican," Attachment to No. 2182/PR, December 19, 1984. Andrew and Gordievsky, *More Instructions from the Centre*, p. 49.

37. Christopher Andrew and Vasili Mitrokhin, *The Sword and the Shield: The Mitrokhin Archive and the Secret History of the KGB* (New York: Basic Books, 1999), p. 396.

38. Szulc, *John Paul II*, p. 396.

39. Bernstein and Politi, *His Holiness*, pp. 388–389.

40. Szulc, *John Paul II*, p. 397.

41. Michael T. Kaufman, *Mad Dreams, Saving Graces: Poland: A Nation in Conspiracy* (New York: Random House, 1989), p. 141.

42. Peter Hebblethwaite, "Books: The Turbulent Priest," *Guardian*, July 25, 1986.

43. Kaufman, *Mad Dreams, Saving Graces*, p. 151.

44. On Department IV of the Ministry of Internal Affairs, see Antoni Dudek and Andrzej Paczkowski, "Poland," in Krzysztof Persak and Lukasz Kaminski, eds., *A Handbook of the Communist Security Apparatus in East Central Europe, 1944–1989* (Warsaw: Institute of National Remembrance, 2005), pp. 221–283.

45. Tina Rosenberg, *The Haunted Land: Facing Europe's Ghosts after Communism* (New York: Random House, 1995), pp. 225–226; Michael T. Kaufman, "4 Polish Officers are Put on Trial in Priest's Slaying," *New York Times*, December 28, 1984.

46. Wałęsa, *A Way of Hope*, p. 299.

47. Bradley Graham, "Slain Priest Eulogized As 'National Hero,'" *Washington Post*, November 4, 1984.

48. "Sir John Morgan," *Telegraph*, September 9, 2012.

49. "Poland: Priest Mourned as National Hero," *Tablet*, November 10, 1984.

50. "Poland: Priest Mourned as National Hero."

51. Memorandum from Colonel R. J. Affourtit, Executive Secretary, Department of Defense to Robert M. Kimmitt, Executive Secretary, National Security Council, Subject: Poland: Next Steps, December 19, 1984. Available in Paula Dobriansky files, Poland Memoranda, 1984–1985 [December 1984], RAC Box 4, Ronald Reagan Presidential Library.

52. K. M. Fierke, *Political Self-Sacrifice: Agency, Body and Emotion in International Relations* (New York: Cambridge University Press, 2013), pp. 151–152.

53. Robert M. Gates, *From the Shadows: The Ultimate Inside Story of Five Presidents and How They Won the Cold War* (New York: Simon and Schuster: 1996), p. 358; Agnieszka Niegowska, ed., *It All Began in Poland* (Warsaw: Institute of National Remembrance, 2009), p. 358.

54. Memorandum from John H. Rixse, Executive Secretary, Central Intelligence Agency to Robert M. Kimmitt, Executive Secretary, National Security Council,

Subject: CIA Comments on State Memorandum Entitled Poland Next Steps, December 14, 1984. Available in Paula Dobriansky files, Poland Memoranda, 1984–1985 [December 1984], RAC Box 4, Ronald Reagan Presidential Library.

55. "Possible KGB Involvement in Murder of Polish Priest," Central Intelligence Agency, January 10, 1985. Available at CIA-RDP87M00539R001602330007-7, CIA Records Search Tool (CREST), National Archives and Records Administration, College Park, MD.

56. National Security Council Meeting, Subject: IMF Membership for Poland, August 28, 1984. Available in Paula Dobriansky files, Poland Memoranda, 1984–1985 [August 1984], RAC Box 4, Ronald Reagan Presidential Library.

CHAPTER 18: A GLOBAL CAMPAIGN

1. Author interviews with multiple sources.

2. Author interviews with multiple sources.

3. Author interviews with multiple sources.

4. The incident at the Gare du Nord occurred in May 1983.

5. Author interviews with multiple sources.

6. Author interviews with multiple sources.

7. Robert M. Gates, *From the Shadows: The Ultimate Inside Story of Five Presidents and How They Won the Cold War* (New York: Simon and Shuster, 1996), p. 358.

8. Agnieska Niegowska, ed., *It All Began in Poland* (Warsaw: Institute of National Remembrance, 2009), p. 358; Gates, *From the Shadows*, p. 358.

9. Benjamin B. Fischer, "Solidarity, the CIA, and Western Technology," *International Journal of Intelligence and Counterintelligence*, Vol. 25, No. 3, 2012, p. 433. Also see Gates, *From the Shadows*, p. 358.

10. In a controversial move, Walter Mondale agreed to meet with Soviet Foreign Minister Andrei Gromyko during the election campaign, a decision that even Jimmy Carter's national security advisor, Zbigniew Brzezinski, condemned. As Brzezinski remarked, "It will contribute to the impression that [Mondale] is catering to the Soviets and that the Soviets are using the campaign. The prospect of American candidates rushing to the Soviets who bestow their favors is distasteful." Quoted in Charlotte Saikowski, "USSR Positions Itself in the Middle of the U.S. Election Campaign," *Christian Science Monitor*, September 18, 1984.

11. Ronald Reagan, *Public Papers of the Presidents of the United States, 1983, Book 1: January 1 to July 1, 1983* (Washington, DC: Government Printing Office, 1984), p. 440.

12. Ronald Reagan, Remarks at a White House Luncheon Marking the 40th Anniversary of the Warsaw Uprising, August 17, 1984.

13. Reagan, Remarks at a White House Luncheon.

14. Memorandum from John H. Rixse, Executive Secretary, Central Intelligence Agency to Robert M. Kimmitt, Executive Secretary, National Security Council, Subject: CIA Comments on State Memorandum Entitled Poland Next Steps, December 14, 1984. Available in Paula Dobriansky files, Poland Memoranda, 1984-1985 [December 1984], RAC Box 4, Ronald Reagan Presidential Library.

15. Memorandum from George Kolt, National Intelligence Officer for Europe, Subject: Trends in Poland, March 11, 1985. Available in Paula Dobriansky files, Poland Memoranda, 1984–1985 [April 1985], RAC Box 4, Ronald Reagan Presidential Library.

16. Memorandum from Colonel R. J. Affourtit, Executive Secretary, Department of Defense to Robert M. Kimmitt, Executive Secretary, National Security Council, Subject: Poland: Next Steps, December 19, 1984. Available in Paula Dobriansky files, Poland Memoranda, 1984–1985 [December 1984], RAC Box 4, Ronald Reagan Presidential Library.

17. Memorandum from Colonel R. J. Affourtit.

18. Michael T. Kaufman, *Mad Dreams, Saving Graces: Poland: A Nation in Conspiracy* (New York: Random House, 1989), p. 119.

19. Kaufman, *Mad Dreams, Saving Graces*, p. 129.

20. The First Reagan-Mondale Presidential Debate: Debate Transcript, Commission on Presidential Debates, October 7, 1984.

21. The Second Reagan-Mondale Presidential Debate: Debate Transcript, Commission on Presidential Debates, October 21, 1984.

22. Walter Mondale, "1984: There You Go Again . . . Again: Debating Our Destiny Transcript," Interview with Jim Lehrer, PBS NewsHour. Available at: https://web.archive.org/web/20001212070100/http://www.pbs.org/newshour/debatingourdestiny/dod/1984-broadcast.html.

23. Author interviews with multiple sources.

24. Memorandum from George Kolt.

25. Memorandum from George Kolt.

26. Bartolomiej Kaminski, *The Collapse of State Socialism: The Case of Poland* (Princeton, NJ: Princeton University Press, 2014), p. 178.

27. Central Intelligence Agency, "Poland: Economic Stagnation," July 1986, p. v. Available from the National Security Archive.

28. Memorandum from George Kolt.

29. Author interviews with multiple sources.

30. Author interviews with multiple sources.

31. Memorandum from George Kolt.

32. Edmund Morris, *Dutch: A Memoir of Ronald Reagan* (New York: Random House, 1999), p. 512.

33. Statement by the President, Office of the Press Secretary, the White House, February 5, 1985. Available in Paula Dobriansky files, Country Files: Eastern Europe (General), RAC Box 1, Ronald Reagan Presidential Library.

CHAPTER 19: THE TIDE TURNS

1. Michael T. Kaufman, *Mad Dreams, Saving Graces: Poland: A Nation in Conspiracy* (New York: Random House, 1989), p. 85.

2. Kaufman, *Mad Dreams, Saving Graces*, p. 85.

3. Author interviews with multiple sources.

4. On the Polish economy, see Robert W. Bednarzik, "Helping Poland Cope with Unemployment," *Monthly Labor Review*, United States Department of Labor, Bureau of Labor Statistics, December 1990, pp. 25–33.

5. Jane Leftwich Curry, *Poland's Journalists: Professionalism and Politics* (New York: Cambridge University Press, 1990), p. 39.

6. Danuta Grzelewska, Rafal Habielski, Andrzej Koziel, Janusz Osica, and Lidia Piwonska-Pukalo, *Prasa, Radio i telewizja w Polsce* (Warsaw: Elipsa, 2001), pp. 286–292, 314.

7. Foreign Broadcast Information Service, "Poland: New Leadership Team Shifts Focus to Economy," FB 85-10068, December 10, 1985. Available from the National Security Archive.

8. Katarzyna Pokorna-Ignatowicz, *Telewizja w systemie politycznym i medialnym PRL: Między Polityką a Widzem* (Kraków: Wydawnictwo Uniwersytetu Jagiellońskiego, 2003), p. 104.

9. Author interviews with multiple sources.

10. Robert M. Gates, *From the Shadows: The Ultimate Inside Story of Five Presidents and How They Won the Cold War* (New York: Simon and Schuster: 1996), p. 451.

11. Author interviews with multiple sources.

12. Author interviews with multiple sources.

13. Gates, *From the Shadows*, p. 451.

14. Kaufman, *Mad Dreams, Saving Graces*, p. 83.

15. Peter Schweizer, *Victory: The Reagan Administration's Secret Strategy that Hastened the Collapse of the Soviet Union* (New York: The Atlantic Monthly Press, 1994), p. 225.

16. Gates, *From the Shadows*, p. 358.

17. Kaufman, *Mad Dreams, Saving Graces*, p. 86.

18. On general KGB concerns about the United States and espionage see, for example, "Meeting Minutes of the Politburo of the CC CPSU, Regarding Persecution of Political Dissidents and Spies," September 25, 1986. Available from the History and Public Policy Program Digital Archive, Woodrow Wilson International Center for Scholars.

19. Schweizer, *Victory*, p. 223.

20. "Memorandum to Central Committee from Politburo Members Ligachev and Chebrikov on Jamming of Western Radio Stations," September 25, 1986. Available from the History and Public Policy Program Digital Archive, Woodrow Wilson International Center for Scholars.

21. Gates, *From the Shadows*, p. 450.

22. Schweizer, *Victory*, p. 257.

23. Nigel West, *The Third Secret: The CIA, Solidarity and the KGB's Plot to Kill the Pope* (London: HarperCollins, 2000), pp. 207–208.

24. Benjamin B. Fischer, "Solidarity, the CIA, and Western Technology," *International Journal of Intelligence and Counterintelligence*, Vol. 25, No. 3, 2012, p. 449; Lech Wałęsa, *The Struggle and the Triumph: An Autobiography* (New York: Arcade Publishing, 1991), p. 110.

25. Fischer, "Solidarity, the CIA, and Western Technology," p. 449; Gates, *From the Shadows*, p. 451.

26. "Polish Interior Ministry Report on Information Leaked to Radio Free Europe on Catholic Church," July 26, 1985. Available from the History and Public Policy Program Digital Archive, Woodrow Wilson International Center for Scholars.

27. Memorandum from Director, Office of European Analysis, to Director of Central Intelligence and Deputy Director of Central Intelligence, June 11, 1986. Available at CIA-RDP86T01017R000404060001-6, CIA Records Search Tool (CREST), National Archives and Records Administration, College Park, MD.

28. Jaroslaw Kapsa, "In the Shadow of the Luminous Mountain: Underground Publishing in Czestochowa," in Gwido Zlatkes, Paweł Sowiński, and Ann M. Frenkel, eds., *Duplicator Underground: The Independent Publishing Industry in Communist Poland, 1976–1989* (Bloomington, Indiana: Slavica Publishers, 2016), p. 157.

29. Bob Woodward and Michael Dobbs, "CIA Had Secret Agent on Polish General Staff," *Washington Post*, June 4, 1986. The CIA copied and saved the article in its database. Available at CIA-RDP90-00965Rr000807560040-5, CIA Records Search Tool (CREST), National Archives and Records Administration, College Park, MD.

30. Woodward and Dobbs, "CIA Had Secret Agent on Polish General Staff."

31. Memorandum from Acting Assistant National Intelligence Officer for Europe to Director of Central Intelligence, NIC-03763/86, August 12, 1986. Available at CIA-RDP87R00529R000100070037-7, CIA Records Search Tool (CREST), National Archives and Records Administration, College Park, MD.

32. Memorandum from Acting Assistant National Intelligence Officer for Europe to Director of Central Intelligence.

33. Jackson Diehl, "Defector's Account Embarrasses Warsaw," *Washington Post*, April 23, 1987. The CIA clipped this article and kept it in its files. Available at CIA-RDP90-00965R000201590001-7, CIA Records Search Tool (CREST), National Archives and Records Administration, College Park, MD.

34. Diehl, "Defector's Account Embarrasses Warsaw."

35. Edmund Morris, *Dutch: A Memoir of Ronald Reagan* (New York: Random House, 1999), p. 517.

36. Morris, *Dutch*, p. 505.

37. Ronald Reagan, *The Reagan Diaries, Vol. I, January 1981–October 1985*, ed. Douglas Brinkley (New York: HarperCollins, 2009), p. 434.

38. Gates, *From the Shadows*, pp. 327, 329.

39. Gates, *From the Shadows*, pp. 327–328.

40. Morris, *Dutch*, p. 518.

41. Morris, *Dutch*, p. 527.

42. See, for example, Memorandum from Alexander Yakovlev to Mikhail Gorbachev, "The Priority of Political Development," December 25, 1985. Available in the Electronic Briefing Book No. 168, National Security Archive.

43. Alexander Yakovlev Presentation at the Central Committee of the Communist Party of the Soviet Union Politburo Session, September 28, 1987. Available in the Electronic Briefing Book No. 168, National Security Archive.

44. Gates, *From the Shadows*, p. 327.

45. Memorandum from Director, Office of European Analysis.

46. "Polish Interior Ministry Report on Information Leaked to Radio Free Europe on Catholic Church."

47. Arch Puddington, *Lane Kirkland: Champion of American Labor* (New York: Wiley, 2005), p. 186.

48. Kaufman, *Mad Dreams, Saving Graces*, p. 165.

49. Schweizer, *Victory*, pp. 264–265.

50. See, for example, Glenn Garvin, *Everybody Had His Own Gringo: The CIA and the Contras* (Washington, DC: Brassey's, 1992); Lawrence E. Walsh, *Firewall: The Iran-Contra Conspiracy and Cover-Up* (New York: W. W. Norton, 1998); James S. Van Wagenen, "A Review of Congressional Oversight: Critics and Defenders," Central Intelligence Agency. Available at: https://www.cia.gov/library/center-for-the-study-of-intelligence/csi-publications/csi-studies/studies/97unclass/wagenen.html.

51. Author interview with Ed Meese, September 2016. Also see Morris, *Dutch*, p. 615.

52. Lou Cannon, *President Reagan: The Role of a Lifetime* (New York: Simon & Schuster, 1991), p. 738.

53. "Presidential Approval Ratings—Gallup Historical Statistics and Trends," Gallup. Accessed on May 5, 2016: www.gallup.com/poll/116677/presidential-approval-ratings-gallup-historical-statistics-trends.aspx.

54. Morris, *Dutch*, p. 590.

55. H. W. Brands, *Reagan: The Life* (New York: Doubleday, 2015), p. 250; Gates, *From the Shadows*, p. 487.

56. Joseph E. Persico, *Casey: From the OSS to the CIA* (New York: Viking, 1990), p. 306.

57. Persico, *Casey*, p. 485.

58. Gates, *From the Shadows*, p. 344.

59. Charles Krauthammer, "The Reagan Doctrine," *Time*, April 1, 1985.

60. Ronald Reagan, *An American Life: The Autobiography* (New York: Simon and Schuster, 1990), p. 552.

61. Reagan, *The Reagan Diaries, Vol. I*, p. 447.

62. Ronald Reagan, "Address from the Brandenburg Gate," June 12, 1987. Transcript available at: https://millercenter.org/the-presidency/presidential-speeches/june-12-1987-address-brandenburg-gate-berlin-wall.

CHAPTER 20: THE RETURN OF SOLIDARITY

1. John Paul II, translated by Jenny McPhee and Martha McPhee, *Crossing the Threshold of Hope* (New York: Knopf, 1994), p. 132.

2. Cezar M. Ornatowski, "Rhetoric of Pope John Paul II's Visits to Poland, 1979–1999," in Joseph R. Bailey and Joseph P. Zompetti, ed., *The Rhetoric of Pope John Paul II* (Lanham, MD: Lexington Books, 2009), p. 127.

3. "Excerpts from the Pope's Homily During Gdansk Mass," *Associated Press*, June 12, 1987.

4. John Paul II, "Mass for the Representatives of the World of Labor in Danzig," Gdańsk, June 12, 1987. Available at: https://w2.vatican.va/content/john-paul-ii/it/homilies/1987/documents/hf_jp-ii_hom_19870612_mondo-lavoro-danzica.html.

5. Carl Bernstein and Marco Politi, *His Holiness: John Paul II and the Hidden History of Our Time* (New York: Doubleday, 1996), p. 467.

6. Lech Wałęsa, *The Struggle and the Triumph: An Autobiography* (New York: Arcade Publishing, 1991), p. 112.

7. Wałęsa, *The Struggle and the Triumph*, p. 117.

8. Wałęsa, *The Struggle and the Triumph*, p. 118.

9. Piotr Adamowicz, Andrzej Drzycimski, and Adam Kinaszewski, Gdańsk: *According to Lech Wałęsa* (Gdańsk: Morze Możliwości, 2008), p. 89.

10. Jonathan Kwitny, *Man of the Century: The Life and Times of Pope John Paul II* (New York: Henry Holt, 1997), p. 567.

11. Michael T. Kaufman, "Workers and Police Clash Briefly as Pope Visits a Solidarity Center," *New York Times,* June 13, 1987.

12. Bernstein and Politi, *His Holiness*, p. 468.

13. Author interviews with multiple sources.

14. Gregory F. Domber, *Empowering Revolution: America, Poland, and the End of the Cold War* (Chapel Hill: University of North Carolina Press, 2014), p. 284.

15. Author interviews with multiple sources.

16. Robert M. Gates, *From the Shadows: The Ultimate Inside Story of Five Presidents and How They Won the Cold War* (New York: Simon and Schuster: 1996), p. 451.

17. Author interviews with multiple sources.

18. See, for example, John Raneleigh, *The Agency: The Rise and Decline of the CIA* (New York: Simon and Schuster, 1986), p. 712.

19. Eric Pace, "William Casey, Ex-CIA Head, is Dead at 74," *New York Times*, May 7, 1987.

20. Basil Kerski, Konrad Knoch, Jacek Kołton, and Paweł Gdak, *European Solidarity Centre Permanent Exhibition: Catalogue* (Gdańsk: European Solidarity Centre, 2015), p. 157.

21. Wałęsa, *The Struggle and the Triumph*, pp. 121–122.

22. Ronald Reagan, *The Reagan Diaries, Vol. II, November 1985–January 1989*, ed. Douglas Brinkley (New York: HarperCollins, 2009), p. 690.

23. For CIA reports on the National Executive Board see, for example, National Intelligence Daily, Central Intelligence Agency, November 4, 1987. Available at CIA-RDP88T01422R000100030007-8, CIA Records Search Tool (CREST), National Archives and Records Administration, College Park, MD. The report argued that Solidarity established the commission "to deal with increasing regime pressure since the amnesty last fall, as well as divisions within its top leadership."

24. Wałęsa, *The Struggle and the Triumph*, p. 123.

25. Wałęsa, *The Struggle and the Triumph*, p. 113.

26. Jim Hoagland, "'We Won't Give Up,'" *Washington Post*, November 14, 1987.

27. Jacek Kołtan and Ewa Konarowska, eds., *European Solidarity Centre Permanent Exhibition: Anthology* (Gdańsk: European Solidarity Centre, 2015), p. 250.

28. Adamowicz et al., *Gdańsk*, p. 96.

29. Adamowicz et al., *Gdańsk*, p. 96.

30. Kerski et al., *European Solidarity Centre Permanent Exhibition: Catalogue*, pp. 150–151.

CHAPTER 21: THE TRUMP CARD

1. Lech Wałęsa, *The Struggle and the Triumph: An Autobiography* (New York: Arcade Publishing, 1991), p. 153.

2. Wałęsa, *The Struggle and the Triumph*, p. 139.

3. Basil Kerski, Konrad Knoch, Jacek Kołton, and Paweł Gdak, *European Solidarity Centre Permanent Exhibition: Catalogue* (Gdańsk: European Solidarity Centre, 2015), p. 165.

4. Central Intelligence Agency, Soviet Policy Toward Eastern Europe Under Gorbachev, National Intelligence Estimate, NIE 11/12-9-88, May 1988, p. 20. Available from the National Security Archive.

5. Author interviews with multiple sources.

6. Ronald Reagan, *The Reagan Diaries, Vol. II, November 1985–January 1989*, ed. Douglas Brinkley (New York: HarperCollins, 2009), p. 881.

7. "Information Bulletin for Polish Party Leadership on Western Views of Poland," May 04, 1988. Available from the History and Public Policy Program Digital Archive, Woodrow Wilson International Center for Scholars.

8. Ronald Reagan, *An American Life: The Autobiography* (New York: Simon and Schuster, 1990), p. 703.

9. On May 10, 1988, the Central Committee of the Communist Party of the USSR issued a "closed" letter to all Communist Party members of the Soviet Union on the issue of withdrawal of troops from Afghanistan. The letter presented the Central Committee analysis of events in Afghanistan, Soviet actions, and the problems Soviet troops had faced in carrying out their mission. In particular, the letter stated that important historic and ethnic factors were overlooked when the decisions on Afghanistan were made in the Soviet Union. CC CPSU Letter on Afghanistan, May 10, 1988. Available at the National Security Archive at: nsarchive.gwu.edu/NSAEBB/NSAEBB272/ Doc%2010%201988-05-10%20CCCPSULetter%20Afghanistan.pdf.

10. Reagan, *An American Life*, p. 715.

11. The meeting was during Gorbachev's visit to Washington in December 1987, what some referred to as the Washington Summit. See Edmund Morris, *Dutch: A Memoir of Ronald Reagan* (New York: Random House, 1999), p. 630.

12. Reagan, *The Reagan Diaries, Vol. II*, p. 975.

13. Wałęsa, *The Struggle and the Triumph*, p. 109.

14. Jacek Kołtan and Ewa Konarowska, eds., *European Solidarity Centre Permanent Exhibition: Anthology* (Gdańsk: European Solidarity Centre, 2015), p. 263.

15. Kołtan and Konarowska, *European Solidarity Centre Permanent Exhibition: Anthology*, p. 263.

16. "Talking Points for DDCI," Central Intelligence Agency, August 22, 1988. Available at CIA-RDP90G01353R001500230070-8, CIA Records Search Tool (CREST), National Archives and Records Administration, College Park, MD. Also see previous CIA reports during the spring of 1988, such as "Bi-Weekly Warning Issues for the DCI," Central Intelligence Agency, May 18, 1988. Available at CIA-RDP91B00776R000400080011-8, CIA Records

Search Tool (CREST), National Archives and Records Administration, College Park, MD.

17. Kołtan and Konarowska, *European Solidarity Centre Permanent Exhibition: Anthology*, p. 249.

18. Kołtan and Konarowska, *European Solidarity Centre Permanent Exhibition: Anthology*, p. 249.

19. See, for example, Memorandum by Lech Wałęsa, "On Starting the Round Table Talks," September 4, 1989; "Report from Andrzej Stelmachowski to Lech Wałęsa," September 6, 1988; "Letter from Andrzej Stelmachowski to Lech Wałęsa," October 1, 1988. Available from the History and Public Policy Program Digital Archive, Woodrow Wilson International Center for Scholars.

20. At the September 16, 1988, meeting at Magdalenka, the government side included Czesław Kiszczak, Stanisław Ciosek, and a small group of advisors. Also present were representatives of the official pro-government unions (OPZZ) created during martial law to replaced Solidarity, as well as two representatives of the Catholic Church (Bronisław Dabrowski and Alojzy Orszulik). The Solidarity side included Lech Wałęsa, Władysław Frasyniuk, Tadeusz Mazowiecki, Alojzy Pietrzyk, Jacek Merkel, Henryk Sienkiewicz, and Andrzej Stelmachowski.

21. Memorandum from Charles E. Allen to the Director of Central Intelligence, NIC 03291-88, November 9, 1988. Available at CIA-RDP91B00776R000 400140010-2, CIA Records Search Tool (CREST), National Archives and Records Administration, College Park, MD.

CHAPTER 22: ROUND TABLE TALKS

1. Lou Cannon, *President Reagan: The Role of a Lifetime* (New York: Simon & Schuster, 1991), p. 186; Edmund Morris, *Dutch: A Memoir of Ronald Reagan* (New York: Random House, 1999), pp. 541, 543, 647–649.

2. Ronald Reagan, "Farewell Address to the Nation," January 11, 1989. Available from the Ronald Reagan Presidential Library at: https://reaganlibrary .archives.gov/archives/speeches/1989/011189i.htm.

3. National Security Council Meeting Minutes, December 21, 1981. Available in Executive Secretariat, NSC, NSC 00033, Box 91283, Ronald Reagan Presidential Library.

4. Wiktor Osiatynski interview of Wojciech Jaruzelski. See Wiktor Osiatnyski, "The Roundtable Talks in Poland," in Jon Elster, ed., *The Roundtable Talks and*

the Breakdown of Communism (Chicago: University of Chicago Press, 1996), pp. 62–63.

5. Osiatnyski, "The Roundtable Talks in Poland," pp. 24–25.

6. The declassified materials consist of circular cipher cables sent from Polish Ministry of Foreign Affairs Headquarters in Warsaw to posts abroad, such as embassies, consulates, and missions. See: http://www.msz.gov.pl/en/ministry /polish_diplomacy_archive/wybory.

7. Jacek Kołtan and Ewa Konarowska, eds., *European Solidarity Centre Permanent Exhibition: Anthology* (Gdańsk: European Solidarity Centre, 2015), pp. 260–262.

8. Lech Wałęsa, *The Struggle and the Triumph: An Autobiography* (New York: Arcade Publishing, 1991), p. 174.

9. At the January 27, 1989, meeting at Magdalenka, Solidarity members included Lech Wałęsa, Zbigniew Bujak, Władysław Fransyniuk, Bronisław Geremek, Mieczysław Gil, Lech Kaczynski, Tadeusz Mazowiecki, and Andrzej Stelmachowski. The government side included Czesław Kiszczak, Stanisław Ciosek, Andrzej Gdula, Janusz Reykowski, Jan Janowski, and Bohdan Królewski.

10. Mieczysław Rakowski comments at "Communism's Negotiated Collapse: The Polish Round Table, Ten Years Later," A Conference Held at the University of Michigan, April 7–10, 1999, p. 20. Available at https://webapps.lsa.umich .edu/ii/polishroundtable/program.html.

11. "Letter from Andrzej Stelmachowski to Jozef Glemp, Primate of Poland," October 24, 1988. Released by the History and Public Policy Program Digital Archive, Woodrow Wilson International Center for Scholars.

12. See, for example, "Letter from Andrzej Slowik to Roundtable Chair Wladyslaw Findeisen," February 12, 1989. Released by the History and Public Policy Program Digital Archive, Woodrow Wilson International Center for Scholars.

13. Wałęsa, *The Struggle and the Triumph*, p. 177.

14. Adam Michnik comments at "Communism's Negotiated Collapse: The Polish Round Table, Ten Years Later," A Conference Held at the University of Michigan, April 7–10, 1999, p. 18.

15. Michnik comments at "Communism's Negotiated Collapse."

16. Central Intelligence Agency, "Soviet Policy Toward Eastern Europe Under Gorbachev," National Intelligence Estimate, NIE 11/12-9-88, May 1988, p. 5. Available from the National Security Archive.

17. Central Intelligence Agency, "Soviet Policy Toward Eastern Europe Under Gorbachev."

18. Basil Kerski, Konrad Knoch, Jacek Kołtan, and Paweł Golak, *European Solidarity Centre Permanent Exhibition: Catalogue* (Gdańsk: European Solidarity Centre, 2015), p. 171.

19. Wałęsa, *The Struggle and the Triumph*, p. 174.

20. Wałęsa, *The Struggle and the Triumph*, p. 188.

21. Wałęsa, *The Struggle and the Triumph*, p. 181.

CHAPTER 23: FINISHING THE JOB

1. Author interviews with multiple sources.

2. Mark Kramer, "The Collapse of the East European Communism and the Repercussions within the Soviet Union (Part 2)," *Journal of Cold War Studies*, Fall 2004, Vol. 6, No. 4, p. 250.

3. Kramer, "The Collapse of the East European Communism and the Repercussions within the Soviet Union (Part 2)," p. 248.

4. Memorandum from George H. W. Bush to the Vice President, et al., National Security Directive 9, Subject: Actions to Respond to Polish Roundtable Agreement, May 8, 1989. Available from the Cold War International History Project, Woodrow Wilson International Center for Scholars.

5. Gregory F. Domber, ed., "Solidarity's Coming Victory: Big or Too Big," National Security Archive Electronic Briefing Book No. 42, April 5, 2001.

6. Cable from AMEMBASSY WARSAW to SECSTATE WASHDC, Subject: Election '89: The Year of Solidarity, April 19, 1989. Available from the National Security Archive at: http://nsarchive.gwu.edu/NSAEBB/NSAEBB42/Doc1.pdf.

7. Cable from AMEMBASSY WARSAW to SECSTATE WASHDC, Subject: Election '89: The Year of Solidarity.

8. Basil Kerski, Konrad Knoch, Jacek Kołtan, and Paweł Golak, *European Solidarity Centre Permanent Exhibition: Catalogue* (Gdańsk: European Solidarity Centre, 2015), p. 152.

9. Cable from AMEMBASSY WARSAW to SECSTATE WASHDC, Subject: Election '89: Solidarity's Coming Victory: Big or Too Big? June 2, 1989. Available from the National Security Archive at: http://nsarchive.gwu.edu/NSAEBB/NSAEBB42/Doc2.pdf.

10. Cable from AMEMBASSY WARSAW to SECSTATE WASHDC, Subject: Election '89: Solidarity's Coming Victory.

11. Approximately twenty-three candidates had to do without the famous picture with Wałęsa. Some failed to show up for the photo sessions with Wałęsa. One of the candidates, Janusz Woznica from Zamosc, was not photographed with Wałęsa, but his poster was still created using a photomontage. Lech Wałęsa, *The Struggle and the Triumph: An Autobiography* (New York: Arcade Publishing, 1991), p. 201.

12. Wałęsa, *The Struggle and the Triumph*, p. 201.

13. Kerski, et al., *European Solidarity Centre Permanent Exhibition: Catalogue*, p. 152.

14. London's Victoria and Albert Museum listed the *High Noon* poster as one of the hundred most important posters of the twentieth century.

15. Kerski et al., *European Solidarity Centre Permanent Exhibition: Catalogue*, p. 175; Thomas Sarnecki, "Solidarity Poster—High Noon 4 June 1989," Making the History of 1989, Item #699, http://chnm.gmu.edu/1989/items/show/699.

16. Wałęsa, *The Struggle and the Triumph*, p. 201.

17. Kerski et al., *European Solidarity Centre Permanent Exhibition: Catalogue*, p. 180.

18. Cable from AMEMBASSY WARSAW to SECSTATE WASHDC, Subject: Politburo Member Warns that U.S. Has Been "Dragged into the War" Over Election of Jaruzelski as President, June 16, 1989. Available from the National Security Archive.

19. Tom Blanton and Malcolm Byrne, ed., *Poland 1986–1989: The End of the System* (Washington: The National Security Archive, 1999), p. 20.

20. Cable from AMEMBASSY WARSAW to SECSTATE WASHDC, Subject: How to Elect Jaruzelski without Voting for Him, and Will He Run? June 23, 1989. Available from the National Security Archive at: http://nsarchive.gwu.edu/NSAEBB/NSAEBB42/Doc4.pdf.

21. Cable from AMEMBASSY WARSAW to SECSTATE WASHDC, Subject: How to Elect Jaruzelski without Voting for Him, and Will He Run?

22. Blanton and Byrne, *Poland 1986–1989*, p. 21; Domber, "Solidarity's Coming Victory."

23. Cable from AMEMBASSY WARSAW to SECSTATE WASHDC, Subject: Poland Looks to President Bush, June 27, 1989. Available from the National Security Archive at: http://nsarchive.gwu.edu/NSAEBB/NSAEBB42/Doc5.pdf.

24. George Bush and Brent Scowcroft, *A World Transformed* (New York: Alfred A. Knopf, 1998), p. 117.

25. Wałęsa, *The Struggle and the Triumph*, p. 212.

26. Wałęsa, *The Struggle and the Triumph*, p. 213.

27. George H. W. Bush, "Remarks at the Solidarity Workers Monument in Gdansk," July 11, 1989. Available at: https://chnm.gmu.edu/1989/archive/files/bush-solidarity-speech-89_857d27565e.pdf.

28. George H. W. Bush, "President Bush's Remarks at the Solidarity Workers Monument," Making the History of 1989, Item #36. Available at: https://chnm.gmu.edu/1989/items/show/36.

29. Wałęsa, *The Struggle and the Triumph*, p. 214.

30. Adam Michnik, "Your President, Our Prime Minister," *Gazetta Wyborcza*, July 5, 1989.

31. Domber, "Solidarity's Coming Victory."

32. Cable from AMEMBASSY WARSAW to SECSTATE WASHDC, Subject: Poland Looks to President Bush. Also see Cable from AMEMBASSY WARSAW to SECSTATE WASHDC, Subject: Peasants' Party Loosening Its Bonds with PZPR, June 16, 1989. Available from the National Security Archive.

33. See Gregory F. Domber interview with Davis, November 23, 1999, in Domber, "Solidarity's Coming Victory."

34. Cable from AMEMBASSY WARSAW to SECSTATE WASHDC, Subject: Conversation with General Kiszczak, June 16, 1989. Available from the National Security Archive at: http://nsarchive.gwu.edu/NSAEBB/NSAEBB42/Doc6.pdf.

35. Cable from AMEMBASSY WARSAW to SECSTATE WASHDC, Subject: Conversation with General Kiszczak.

36. Cable from AMEMBASSY MOSCOW to SECSTATE WASHDC, Subject: If Solidarity Takes Charge, What Will the Soviets Do? June 16, 1989. Available from the National Security Archive at: http://nsarchive.gwu.edu/NSAEBB/NSAEBB42/Doc8.pdf.

37. Cable from AMEMBASSY WARSAW to SECSTATE WASHDC, Subject: Bronislaw Geremek Explains Next Steps Toward a Solidarity Government, August 19, 1989. Available from the National Security Archive at: http://nsarchive.gwu.edu/NSAEBB/NSAEBB42/Doc9.pdf.

38. Walesa, *The Struggle and the Triumph*, p. 220.

39. Neil A. Lewis, "Clamor in the East: Gratitude and a Request," *New York Times*, November 16, 1989.

40. The first was the Marquis de Lafayette, the French nobleman who helped finance the American Revolution, who appeared in 1824. The other was Winston Churchill, who spoke after he was no longer the British prime minister.

41. One U.S. senator who wept was Barbara A. Mikulski, a Maryland Democrat whose great-grandmother came from Poland to Baltimore for an arranged marriage. "I never thought this day would come," she said afterward. "I just didn't think it was Poland's destiny to be free." Lewis, "Clamor in the East: Gratitude and a Request."

42. Wałęsa, *The Struggle and the Triumph*, p. 232.

43. Lech Wałęsa, Address to a Joint Meeting of the Congress of the United States of America, November 15, 1989. Available at: http://digitalcollections.library .cmu.edu/awweb/awarchive?type=file&item=563667.

44. Wałęsa, Address to a Joint Meeting of the Congress of the United States of America.

45. Central Intelligence Agency, "The Future of Eastern Europe," National Intelligence Estimate, NIE 12-90, April 1990, p. v. Available from the National Security Archive.

46. Author interviews with multiple sources.

47. Quotations in this paragraph are from Richard Pipes, "A Reagan Soviet Policy," Working Draft, October 1981. Available in the Richard Pipes files, Miscellaneous Papers, Box 3, Ronald Reagan Presidential Library.

CHAPTER 24: THE WHITE EAGLE

1. Transcript of speech by Lech Kaczynski, Ronald Reagan Presidential Library, Simi Valley, CA, July 17, 2007. Available at: http://www.president.pl/en/ archive/news-archive/news-2007/art,112,second-day-of-president-kaczynskis-visit-in-the-us.html.

2. U.S. National Security Strategy, National Security Decision Directive Number 32, May 20, 1982. Available at: http://www.reagan.utexas.edu/archives/ reference/Scanned%20NSDDS/NSDD32.pdf.

3. See, for example, Memorandum from William P. Clark to the President, Subject: Draft of NSDD on "United States Policy Toward Eastern Europe," NSC Meeting 11:15 A.M. July 21, 1982, July 20, 1982. Available in Executive Secretariat, NSC, NSC 00056, Box 91285, Ronald Reagan Presidential Library.

4. Ahmed Rashid, *Taliban: Militant Islam, Oil and Fundamentalism in Central Asia* (New Haven, CT: Yale University Press, 2000), p. 18; Barnett R. Rubin,

The Fragmentation of Afghanistan: State Formation and Collapse in the Interna-tional System (New Haven, CT: Yale University Press, 1995), p. 20.

5. Robert M. Gates, *From the Shadows: The Ultimate Insider's Story of Five Presi-dents and How They Won the Cold War* (New York: Simon & Schuster, 1996), pp. 251, 319–321, 348–249.

6. Mohammad Yousaf and Mark Adkin, *Afghanistan—The Bear Trap: The Defeat of a Superpower* (Havertown, PA: Casemate, 1992), pp. 78–112; Gates, *From the Shadows*, p. 349.

7. See, for example, Steve Coll, *Ghost Wars: The Secret History of the CIA, Afghanistan, and Bin Laden, from the Soviet Invasion to September 10, 2001* (New York: Penguin Press, 2004).

8. Ronald Reagan, Radio Address to the Nation on Solidarity and United States Relations With Poland, October 9, 1982. Available at: http://www.reagan.utexas .edu/archives/speeches/1982/100982a.htm.

9. See Mark Kramer's "Introduction" in Alfred A. Reisch, *Hot Books in the Cold War: The CIA-Funded Secret Western Book Distribution Program Behind the Iron Curtain* (New York: Central European University Press, 2013), p. xvi.

10. Benjamin B. Fischer, "Solidarity, the CIA, and Western Technology," *Interna-tional Journal of Intelligence and Counterintelligence*, Vol. 25, No. 3, 2012, p. 427–469.

11. Kramer, "Introduction," pp. ix–xxviii.

12. On National Endowment for Democracy data see Gregory F. Domber, *Empowering Revolution: America, Poland, and the End of the Cold War* (Chapel Hill: University of North Carolina Press, 2014), pp. 283–288.

13. Arch Puddington, *Lane Kirkland: Champion of American Labor* (New York: Wiley, 2005), p. 189.

14. The AFL-CIO raised this money through private donations, T-shirt sales, individual union donations, and shop floor collections. Domber, *Empowering Revolution*, p. 69.

15. Domber, *Empowering Revolution*, pp. 283–288.

16. There are reports that French citizen Gabriel Meretik, a journalist, provided a million dollars in the first month after martial law, though I could not inde-pendently confirm the amount. Mirosław Chojecki, "Words Against Tanks," in Gwido Zlatkes, Paweł Sowiński, and Ann M. Frenkel, eds., *Duplicator Underground: The Independent Publishing Industry in Communist Poland, 1976–1989* (Bloomington, IN: Slavica Publishers, 2016), pp. 447–448. Also see, for example, Domber, *Empowering Revolution*, pp. 267–288.

17. Jacek Kołtan and Ewa Konarowska, eds., *European Solidarity Centre Permanent Exhibition: Anthology* (Gdańsk: European Solidarity Centre, 2015), p. 236.

18. Kołtan and Konarowska, *European Solidarity Centre Permanent Exhibition: Anthology*, p. 236.

19. Domber, *Empowering Revolution*, p. 66. Also see Andrzej Paczkowski, *The Spring Will Be Ours: Poland and the Poles from Occupation to Freedom*, trans. Jane Dave (University Park: Pennsylvania State University Press, 2003), p. 455.

20. Maciej Pawlak, *Radio Solidarność w Trójmieście* (Gdańsk: Oskar, 2015).

21. Jonathan Kwitny, *Man of the Century: The Life and Times of Pope John Paul II* (New York: Henry Holt, 1997), p. 439.

22. Gregory Wolk, "To Limit, to Eradicate, or to Control? The SB and the 'Second Circulation,' 1981-89/90," in Gwido Zlatkes, Paweł Sowiński, and Ann M. Frenkel, eds., *Duplicator Underground: The Independent Publishing Industry in Communist Poland, 1976–1989* (Bloomington, IN: Slavica Publishers, 2016), pp. 237–266; Fischer, "Solidarity, the CIA, and Western Technology," p. 449.

23. Puddington, *Lane Kirkland*, p. 186.

24. Wolk, "To Limit, to Eradicate, or to Control?" pp. 238–239.

25. Wolk, "To Limit, to Eradicate, or to Control?" p. 239.

26. KGB report no. 84/KR, January 6, 1984, in Christopher Andrew and Oleg Gordievsky, *More Instructions from the Centre: Top Secret Files on KGB Global Operations, 1975–1985* (London: Frank Cass, 1992), pp. 122, 124.

27. Wolk, "To Limit, to Eradicate, or to Control?" p. 265.

28. Peter Schweizer, *Victory: The Reagan Administration's Secret Strategy that Hastened the Collapse of the Soviet Union* (New York: The Atlantic Monthly Press, 1994), p. 91.

29. Nigel West, *The Third Secret: The CIA, Solidarity and the KGB's Plot to Kill the Pope* (London: HarperCollins, 2000), pp. 195–196.

30. "KGB Annual Report for 1981 [Excerpts]," April 13, 1982. Available from the History and Public Policy Program Digital Archive, Woodrow Wilson International Center for Scholars.

31. Schweizer, *Victory*, p. 223.

EPILOGUE

1. See, for example, Wojciech Jaruzelski, *Les chaines et le refuge* [*The Chains and the Refuge*] (Paris: Lattes, 1992); Jaruzelski, *Stan wojenny dlaczego* [Why Martial Law]; (Warsaw: BGW, 1992).

2. Mark Kramer, "Jaruzelski, the Soviet Union, and the Imposition of Martial Law in Poland: New Light on the Mystery of December 1981," *Cold War International History Project Bulletin*, No. 11, Winter 1998, p. 11.

3. Wojciech Jaruzelski, "Commentary," *Cold War International History Project Bulletin*, No. 11, Winter 1998, pp. 38–39. Emphasis added.

4. Peter Finn, "Wojciech Jaruzelski, Poland's Last Communist Leader, Dies at 90," *Washington Post*, May 25, 2014.

5. Author interview with Richard Pipes, August 2016.

6. Jaruzelski, "Commentary," p. 34.

7. "Wojciech Jaruzelski, A Communist General and Military Rule of Poland, Died on May 25th, Aged 90," *Economist*, June 14, 2014.

8. "Wojciech Jaruzelski," *Economist*, May 26, 2014.

9. Quoted in Norman Davies, *God's Playground: A History of Poland*, Vol. II, Revised Edition (New York: Columbia University Press, 2005), p. 574. Also see Hugh Thomas, *Armed Truce: The Beginnings of the Cold War, 1945–46* (New York: Atheneum, 1987), p. 254.

10. The Proclamation of Martial Law by the State Council, December 13, 1981.

11. Poland enjoyed a parliamentary democracy during the Second Polish Republic, but it ended in 1926 when Marshal Józef Piłsudski orchestrated a coup d'état that overthrew the government of President Stanisław Wojciechowski and Prime Minister Wincenty Witos.

12. Jacek Kołtan and Ewa Konarowska, eds., *European Solidarity Centre Permanent Exhibition: Anthology* (Gdańsk: European Solidarity Centre, 2015), p. 256.

13. Melinda Henneberger, "Lech Wałęsa, Nobel Laureate and Former Polish President, Returns to D.C. as a Movie Star," *Washington Post*, December 5, 2013.

14. Piotr Gontarczyk and Sławomir Cenckiewicz, *SB a Lech Wałęsa: Przyczynek do biografii* (Warsaw: Instytut Pamięci Narodowej, 2008).

15. "Information on the Experts' Opinion on the Secret Collaborator Bolek's Files," Institute of National Remembrance, February 1, 2017; Joanna Berendt, "Lech Wałęsa Files Made Public Despite Forgery Claims," *New York Times*, February 22, 2016.

16. Basil Kerski, Konrad Knoch, Jacek Kołtan, and Paweł Golak, *European Solidarity Centre Permanent Exhibition: Catalogue* (Gdańsk: European Solidarity Centre, 2015), p. 245.

Index

Note: Page numbers in *italics* indicate figures.